EARTH SHATTERING

NEIL ASTLEY is editor of Bloodaxe Books. He has published several other anthologies, including *Staying Alive, Being Alive, Do Not Go Gentle, Passionfood* and (with Pamela Robertson-Pearce) *Soul Food*, as well as two eco-novels, *The End of My Tether* (Scribner), which was shortlisted for the Whitbread First Novel Award in 2002, and *The Sheep Who Changed the World* (Flambard, 2005). He lives in Northumberland.

Earth Shattering

ECOPOEMS

EDITED BY NEIL ASTLEY

BLOODAXE BOOKS

ISBN: 978 1 85224 774 4

First published 2007 by
Bloodaxe Books Ltd,
Highgreen,
Tarset,
Northumberland NE48 1RP.

www.bloodaxebooks.com
For further information about Bloodaxe titles
please visit our website or write to
the above address for a catalogue.

Bloodaxe Books Ltd acknowledges
the financial assistance of
Arts Council England, North East.

For Pamela, Noah, Luna,
Fergus, Myles, Rosie, Sofie
and other animals.

Cover design: Neil Astley & Pamela Robertson-Pearce.

Printed in Great Britain by
Bell & Bain Limited, Glasgow, Scotland.

CONTENTS

9

10

EDITORIAL NOTES

An ellipsis in square brackets […] in this anthology denotes an editorial cut to the text. An ellipsis without square brackets is part of the original text.

An arrow in square brackets followed by a number [➤ 00] refers the reader to that page in this book.

Poems whose titles appear in **bold type** in the commentary are included elsewhere in the anthology.

The original American spellings are retained in work by American poets and translators, except for *-ize* suffixes, which are modernised to *-ise*. Punctuation follows Bloodaxe's house style (single inverted commas for quotation, double for qualified expressions).

Spellings in earlier texts are modernised where this does not change the poetic effect of the poem (rhyme, assonance, etc), but original spellings are retained in dialect and other kinds of vernacular poetry.

This Bibliography at the back of the book [➤ 244-46] lists sources for references made in the introductory material and notes. Sources for poems featured in this anthology are given in the Acknowledgements [➤ 246-51].

EARTH VIEWS

James Lovelock: WHAT IS GAIA?

Most of us sense that the Earth is more than a sphere of rock with a thin layer of air, ocean and life covering the surface. We feel that we belong here as if this planet were indeed our home. Long ago the Greeks, thinking this way, gave to the Earth the name *Gaia* or, for short, *Ge*. In those days, science and theology were one and science, although less precise, had soul. […]

The new understanding has come from going forth and looking back to see the Earth from space. The vision of that splendid white-flecked blue sphere stirred us all, no matter that by now it is almost a visual cliché. It even opens the mind's eye, just as a voyage away from home enlarges the perspective of our love for those who remain there.

The first impact of those voyages was the sense of wonder given to the astronauts and to us as we shared their experience vicariously through television, but at the same time the Earth was viewed from outside by the more objective gaze of scientific instruments. These devices were quite impervious to human emotion yet they also sent back the information that let us see the Earth as a strange and beautiful anomaly. They showed our planet is made of the same elements and in much the same proportions as are Mars and Venus, but they also revealed our sibling planets to be bare and barren and as different from the Earth as a robin from a rock.

We now see that the air, the ocean and the soil are much more than a mere environment for life; they are a part of life itself. Thus the air is to life just as is the fur to a cat or the nest for a bird. Not living but something made by living things to protect against an otherwise hostile world. For life on Earth the air is our protection against the cold depths and fierce radiations of space.

There is nothing unusual in the idea of life on Earth interacting with the air, sea and rocks, but it took a view from outside to glimpse the possibility that this combination might consist of a single giant living system and one with the capacity to keep the Earth always at a state most favorable for the life upon it.

An entity comprising a whole planet and with a powerful capacity to regulate the climate needs a name to match. It was the novelist William Golding who proposed the name *Gaia*. Gladly we accepted his suggestion and Gaia is also the name of the hypothesis of science which postulates that the climate and the composition of the Earth always are close to an optimum for whatever life inhabits it.

The evidence gathered in support of Gaia is now considerable but as is often the way of science, this is less important than is its use as a kind of looking glass for seeing the world differently, and which makes us ask new questions about the nature of Earth.

If we are 'all creatures great and small', from bacteria to whales, part of Gaia, then we are all of us potentially important to her well-being. We knew in our hearts that the destruction of a whole ranges of other species was wrong but now we know why. No longer can we merely regret the passing of one of the great whales, or the blue butterfly, nor even the smallpox virus. When we eliminate one of these from Earth, we may have destroyed a part of ourselves, for we also are a part of Gaia.

There are many possibilities for comfort as there are for dismay in contemplating the consequences of our membership in this great commonwealth of living things. It may be that one role we play is as the senses and nervous system for Gaia. Through our eyes she has for the first time seen her very fair face and in our minds become aware of herself. We do indeed belong here. The earth is more than just a home, it's a living system and we are part of it.

Henri Matisse: PART OF NATURE

When we speak of Nature it is wrong to forget that we are ourselves a part of Nature. We ought to view ourselves with the same curiosity and openness with which we study a tree, the sky or a thought, because we too are linked to the entire universe.

Jonathan Bate: THE STATE OF NATURE

At the beginning of the third millennium of the Christian era, the state of nature is parlous. The litany of present and impending catastrophes is all too familiar. Carbon dioxide produced by the burning of fossil fuel is trapping the heat of the sun, causing the planet to become warmer. Glaciers and permafrost are melting, sea levels rising, rainfall patterns changing, winds growing stronger. Meanwhile, the oceans are overfished, deserts are spreading, forests shrinking, fresh water becoming scarcer. The diversity of species on the planet is diminishing. We live in a world of toxic waste, acid rain and endocrine disrupters – chemicals which interfere with the functioning of sex hormones, causing male fish and birds to change sex. The urban air carries a cocktails of pollutants: nitrogen dioxide, sulphur dioxide, benzene, carbon monoxide and more. In intensively farmed economies, the topsoil is so eroded that the growth of cereal crops is entirely dependent on artificial fertilisers. The feeding of dead poultry to living cattle has bequeathed us bovine spongiform encephalopathy ('mad cow disease'), which causes the collapse of the central nervous system and is transmissible to humans.

Jonathan Bate: *The Song of the Earth* (2000).

Al Gore: AN INCONVENIENT TRUTH

Carbon dioxide and other gases warm the surface of the planet naturally by trapping solar heat in the atmosphere. This is a good thing because it keeps our planet habitable. However, by burning fossil fuels such as coal, gas and oil and clearing forests we have dramatically increased the amount of carbon dioxide in the Earth's atmosphere and temperatures are rising.

The vast majority of scientists agree that global warming is real, it's already happening and that it is the result of our activities and not a natural occurrence. The evidence is overwhelming and undeniable.

We're already seeing changes. Glaciers are melting, plants and animals are being forced from their habitats, and the number of severe storms and droughts is increasing.

The number of Category 4 and 5 hurricanes has almost doubled in the last 30 years.

Malaria has spread to higher altitudes in places like the Colombian Andes, 7,000 feet above sea level.

The flow of ice from glaciers in Greenland has more than doubled over the past decade.

At least 279 species of plants and animals are already responding to global warming, moving closer to the poles.

If the warming continues, we can expect catastrophic consequences.

Deaths from global warming will double in just 25 years – to 300,000 people a year.

Global sea levels could rise by more than 20 feet with the loss of shelf ice in Greenland and Antarctica, devastating coastal areas worldwide.

Heat waves will be more frequent and more intense.

Droughts and wildfires will occur more often.

The Arctic Ocean could be ice-free in summer by 2050.

More than a million species worldwide could be driven to extinction by 2050.

Al Gore: *An Inconvenient Truth* (2006).

Chief Seattle: SELLING OUR LAND

How can you buy or sell the sky, the warmth of the land? The idea is strange to us.

If we do not own the freshness of the air and the sparkle of the water, how can you buy them? [...]

We know that the white man does not understand our ways. One portion of land is the same to him as the next, for he is a stranger who comes in the night and takes from the land whatever he needs. The earth is not his brother, but his enemy, and when he has conquered it, he moves on. He leaves his father's grave behind, and he does not care. He kidnaps the earth from his children, and he does not care. His father's grave, and his children's birthright are forgotten. He treats his mother, the earth, and his brother, the sky, as things to be bought, plundered, sold like sheep or bright beads. His appetite will devour the earth and leave behind only a desert. [...]

The air is precious to the red man for all things share

the same breath, the beast, the tree, the man, they all share the same breath. The white man does not seem to notice the air he breathes. Like a man dying for many days he is numb to the stench. But if we sell you our land, you must remember that the air is precious to us, that the air shares its spirit with all the life it supports. [...]

If we decide to accept, I will make one condition – the white man must treat the beasts of this land as his brothers. [...] What is man without the beasts? If all the beasts were gone, man would die from a great loneliness of the spirit. For whatever happens to the beasts, soon happens to man. All things are connected. [...]

Whatever befalls the earth befalls the sons of earth. If men spit upon the ground, they spit upon themselves.

This we know; the earth does not belong to man; man belongs to the earth. This we know. All things are connected like the blood which unites one family.

Chief Seattle (*attr.*): 1854 speech [*via Henry A. Smith & Ted Perry*]

Robert Pack: DOMINION OVER NATURE

The origin of humankind's ambivalence towards nature can be located metaphorically in the Book of Genesis. [...] The initial account is followed by God's first commandment, 'Be fruitful and multiply,' but this imperative is succeeded by a second one – 'subdue [the earth], and have dominion over the fish of the sea, and over the fowl of the air, and over every living thing that moveth upon the earth' – which will prove to be antithetical to the first.

The second commandment, to subdue and take dominion, is a projection of the human wish to possess and master and, beyond a certain limit – a limit our species confronts today – is not in harmony with a spirit of celebration and appreciation. [...]

The immemorial idea of the vastness and inexhaustibility of nature needs to be replaced with the idea of the finiteness and vulnerability of nature, for the commandment to subdue nature never assumed that nature could be subdued and replaced by human creation and human

culture on this delicate planet. If nature's evolutionary plenitude is superseded by human creation, then there will be nothing outside ourselves worthy of reverence and awe. Taking dominion over nature, finally, means that we will have nothing left but our species-centered self-idolatry to be inspired by and to worship.

Robert Pack: 'Taking Dominion over the Wilderness' (1993)

J. Scott Bryson: ECOPOETRY

Ecopoetry is a subset of nature poetry that, while adhering to certain conventions of romanticism, also advances that tradition and takes on distinctly contemporary problems and issues, thus resulting in a version of nature poetry generally marked by three primary characteristics.

The first is an emphasis on maintaining an ecocentric perspective that recognises the interdependent nature of the world; such a perspective leads to a devotion to specific places and to the land itself, along with those creatures that share it with humankind. This interconnection is part of what Black Elk called 'the sacred hoop' that pulls all things into relationship, and it can be found throughout ecopoetry. Levertov's '**Web**' [➤ 157], for example, demonstrates this interconnection [...] The 'great web' here is the one that moves through and connects all people and things, both human and inhuman. [...]

This awareness of the world as a community tends to produce the second attribute of ecopoetry: an imperative toward humility in relationships with both human and nonhuman nature. [...] ecopoets are more likely to echo Frost's reminder of how little control we actually have over the wildness of nature: "Something there is that doesn't like a wall." [...]

Related to this humility is the third attribute of ecopoetry: an intense skepticism concerning hyperrationality, a skepticism that usually leads to an indictment of an overtechnologised world and a warning concerning the very real potential for ecological catastrophe.

J. Scott Bryson: *Ecopoetry: A Critical Introduction* (2002).

INTRODUCTION

Earth Shattering is an anthology of poems addressing environmental destruction and ecological balance.

There are poems here to alert and alarm anyone willing to read or listen, whether the subject is the whole earth (global warming, climate change, extinction of species, planetary catastrophe), or landscapes, homelands and cities (polluting rivers and seas, fouling the air, felling trees and forests). Other poems illuminate the ecological balance of the rapidly vanishing natural world. The book presents an ecopicture of the whole earth in all its diversity exposing the many ways in which the very fabric of our living planet is being torn apart.

Earth Shattering includes contributions from great writers of the past as well as contemporary poets from around the world. It is the first anthology to show the full range of ecopoetry, from the wilderness poetry of ancient China to 21st-century native American poetry. It includes major voices in environmental poetry from America whose work is rarely or never featured in anthologies of contemporary nature poetry published in Britain, as well as British and Irish poets of similar importance in the ecological debate whose work is unknown to American readers.

Before the environment became a pressing issue of global importance, nature poetry was increasingly viewed as irrelevant, especially with over 80% of the UK population (and 95% of the world's population) now living in urban areas. In 1995, Wordsworth's 'Daffodils' was voted number 5 in a television poll of 'the nation's favourite poems', yet it is also the poem most likely to be cited by the less informed as demonstrating the irrelevance not just of nature poetry but of *any* poetry. The popularity of escapist and sentimental Georgian nature poetry, and the continued inclusion of such poems (by Rupert Brooke, Walter de la Mare, A.E. Housman, John Masefield and others) in schools anthologies and on radio programmes such as *Poetry Please*, fuelled the view that any poetry "about" nature was old-fashioned, old hat and only of interest to old people living in the past.

This negative image of nature poetry – even amongst dedicated poetry readers – was as much due to a lack of appreciation of how much nature poetry has changed with the times. Interest shown in the work of poets such as Ted Hughes, Seamus Heaney and Michael Longley has helped to challenge that view, but compared with America there are still relatively few highly respected poets in Britain and Ireland widely appreciated for their contribution to the environmental debate. In a recent discussion forum in *Acumen* (titled 'Nature Poetry: What is it? Do we need it? Do we write it?), Alan Brownjohn offered a short overview of changing attitudes, noting how 'in the late 20th century the modern world introduced another factor poets needed to consider: nature poetry devoted to our environmental crisis needed to be written. It seems important now to address that theme with more perception and passion than most people have so far managed.'

There are in fact numerous contemporary poets addressing the environmental crisis with perception and passion, but most are American. The fact that poets in this country know so little about American ecopoetry must have robbed them of inspiring role models. This has also helped to foster the widely held view that ecopoetry is almost by definition political, and therefore propagandist.

My hope is that *Earth Shattering* will help address these misconceptions by showing readers and writers the range of different kinds of contemporary ecopoetry being written in English on both sides of the Atlantic, as well as a sampling of poems from other parts of the world.

ECOPOETRY & ECOCRITICISM

Ecopoetry goes beyond traditional nature poetry to take on distinctly contemporary issues, recognising the interdependence of all life on earth, the wildness and otherness of nature, and the irresponsibility of our attempts to tame and plunder nature. Ecopoems dramatise the dangers and poverty of a modern world perilously cut off from nature and ruled by technology, self-interest and economic power.

The term 'ecopoetry' has only recently entered the literary critical vocabulary. Jonathan Bate coined the term 'literary ecocriticism' in *Romantic Ecology: Wordsworth and the Environmental Tradition* (1991).

'Any definition of the term *ecopoetry* should probably remain fluid at this time because scholars are only beginning to offer a thorough examination of the field,' writes J. Scott Bryson in *Ecopoetry: A Critical Introduction* (2002). However, Bryson has been able to give us what is probably the first detailed summary of the defining characteristics of ecopoetry [➤ 14]:

> These three overarching characteristics – ecocentrism, a humble appreciation of wildness, and a skepticism toward hyperrationality and its resultant overreliance on technology – represent a broad definition of the field examined here. This volume explores the way contemporary ecopoets deal with these concerns and issues. Exactly what name to give to the current manifestation of contemporary nature poetry varies from critic to critic. Most of the authors in the volume call it ecopoetry or ecological poetry; some call it environmental poetry, some simply nature poetry, and Gifford, in his essay, introduces the term *post-pastoral*.* Regardless of the terminology, each of the essays, in one way or another, deals with the present version of nature poetry that takes into account environmental and ecological lessons we have learned (or are currently learning) regarding the interaction between human and nonhuman worlds.

Bryson's collection of essays is essential reading for anyone interested in contemporary ecopoetry, although its scope (despite its title) is almost exclusively North American. All but one of its contributors are North American academics; and apart from one essay on Derek Walcott and another comparing W.B. Yeats and Robinson Jeffers, the only writers thought worthy of consideration are North American.

Ecocriticism became an accepted term in literary studies with the publication of two seminal works (on prose writing, mostly American), *The Environmental Imagination: Thoreau, Nature Writing, and the Formation of American Culture* (1995), by Lawrence Buell, and *The Ecocriticism Reader: Landmarks in Literary Ecology* (1996), edited by Cheryll Glotfelty and Harold Fromm. Laurence Coupe's *The Green Studies Reader: From Romanticism to Ecocriticism* followed in 2000.

John Elder's *Imagining the Earth: Poetry and the Vision of Nature* (1985) was greeted by Lawrence Buell as 'a pioneer work of ecocriticism' when a second edition appeared in 1996. Updated to include a new chapter on Mary Oliver, Elder's study examines a wide range of American writing from all periods, with much attention given to the work of several modern poets (A.R. Ammons, Wendell Berry, Robinson Jeffers, Denise Levertov, Gary Snyder and others). Wordsworth is a seminal poet for Elder, but like most American critics and editors, he does not appear to have read many living British and Irish poets. They are as absent from his overview of contemporary ecological poetry as most of the Americans are from recent British anthologies and critical studies.

In the supposedly holistic field of contemporary environmental studies, it is extraordinary that American critics and readers are paying so little attention to work by contemporary British and Irish writers; and that the situation on our side of the Atlantic mirrors this. Our anthologies and critical studies of contemporary nature poetry might include Wendell Berry or Gary Snyder, but poets as significant as A.R. Ammons, Joy Harjo, Denise Levertov, W.S. Merwin and Mary Oliver are rarely represented.

The first comprehensive British study of contemporary ecopoetry (in all but name) was *Green Voices: Understanding contemporary nature poetry*, published in 1995 by Terry Gifford, who then favoured the term *green poetry*:

> In our own time, "nature poetry" has become a pejorative term and it is therefore difficult to use the phrase without inverted commas in a purely descriptive way to refer to poetry that is concerned with nature, as I insist on doing in this book. I reserve the term "green poetry" for those recent nature poems which engage directly with environmental issues.

---

* The Australian poet John Kinsella [➤ 82-83] uses the term *anti-pastoral* for his own ecopoetry.

To illustrate the shift which had occurred in attitudes towards nature poetry, Gifford quotes a review by Hilary Llewellyn-Williams in the 'Special Green Issue' of *Poetry Wales* (1990) of four recent "green" anthologies:

> Poets need no longer apologise for writing about Nature. Nature poetry is more than merely descriptive: it deals with the tensions between us and our environment, our intense and often destructive relationship with it, our struggle to come to terms with the fact that we're part of the world out there and not simply observers and manipulators.

Gifford argues that a new theoretical framework is needed for the discussion of notions of nature in poetry, adding provocatively: 'If nature poetry was bad, ecological poetry must be good, presumably by avoiding somehow being nature poetry at all':

> And where does this leave green poetry? Is [Edward Thomas's] **'Bob's Lane'** [➤ 83] a nature poem or a green poem? What would it have meant if it had been included in the 'Special Green Issue' of *Poetry Wales*?
>
> Llewellyn-Williams characterises 'the new Nature poetry' as engaged with tensions of relations and responsibility, participation and power. One could argue that the best of the old writing about nature tackled just such tensions and much of this book will be examining precisely that issue. But the sense of a "new Nature poetry" is, of course, part of a wider social concern with the future of our planetary environment that has demanded a re-examination of our relationship with the natural world.

Terry Gifford's question should be answered by the selection of poems included in *Earth Shattering*.

ECOCRITICAL DEBATE

Any anthology is indebted in some degree to the work of other editors, but in the case of *Earth Shattering*, my inspiration came not from other anthologies but primarily from my own reading, spurred by books and essays by ecopoetry critics. They introduced me to the work of several important ecopoets, illuminated the poetry of many others, and also prompted me to re-read familiar writers in the light of the ecological thinking brought out and clarified in their studies. The selection of poems in *Earth Shattering* is informed by their choices and judgements in many areas, and illuminated by their comments. I am especially grateful to J. Scott Bryson and the contributors to his essay collection *Ecopoetry* for their discussions of modern American ecopoetry; to John Elder for his earlier study, *Imagining the Earth*; to Terry Gifford for balancing these with his essays on contemporary British nature poetry in *Green Voices*; but my debt is probably greatest to Jonathan Bate, for his wonderfully readable study, *The Song of the Earth* (2000) [➤ 13], whose close readings of key texts in English literature present ecology and poetry together as one body of thought and feeling. His preface shows exactly why this is such a necessary and timely book:

> This is a book about why poetry continues to matter as we enter a new millennium that will be ruled by technology. It is a book about modern Western man's alienation from nature. It is about the capacity of the writer to restore us to the earth which is our home.

As well as presenting its own overview of ecopoetry for the general reader, this book may also serve students as a companion anthology to these and other recent critical studies of environmental literature. However, I have maintained an independent line which sometimes runs counter to the views of particular critics. Terry Gifford, for example, believes that George Mackay Brown's poetry is nostalgic pastoral, and sees John Montague's evocations of the historically scarred Irish landscape as 'pastoral retreat in the face of an apparently incomprehensible present'; whereas I view the work of both poets as firmly rooted in specific historically conscious cultures and places. Jonathan Bate believes Gary Snyder's poetry is weakened by 'didacticism' and therefore cannot be called 'ecopoetry'; but I see Snyder's often rhetorical work as public poetry nourished by his deeply felt belief in 'a Zen theory of the connectedness of all things'. Bate, however, argues that the 'worthy' sentiments expressed in Snyder's **'Mother Earth: Her Whales'** [➤ 56] 'do not in any sense grow from the poetry':

The poem has been written as the expression of a set of opinions, not as an attempt to transform into language an experience of dwelling upon the earth. In this respect it is not what I would call an 'ecopoem'; it is not a thinking of the question of the nature of the *oikos*. The language itself is not being asked to do ecological work.

None of these critics pays much attention to contemporary British avant-garde poets, despite what Harriet Tarlo has called their 'complex and thought-provoking slants on locality, pastoral, land politics and ecology/environment'. Tarlo offers a helpful survey of this tantalisingly hermetic field in her *Jacket* essay 'Radical Landscapes: experiment and environment in contemporary poetry' (2007). While I wasn't persuaded to correct this imbalance in *Earth Shattering*, I have included some poets whose work bridges postmodern and mainstream, along with American contemporaries and Modernist forebears of the British avant-garde.

ECOPOETRY ANTHOLOGIES

There is little overlap between *Earth Shattering* and other anthologies of green, nature and environmental poetry. The more I read other anthologies published over the past four decades, the more convinced I became that a different kind of book was needed now, one which would bring together a range of ecopoetry reflecting more closely 21st century thinking about nature, the planet and our threatened environment. And just as my own reading had been informed by the work of various critics, I wanted my selection of poems to be framed by commentary giving the work of each poet an ecological and literary perspective; the notes are intended to offer this through a mixture of description and quotation (with sources cited in the Bibliography ➤ 244).

There were, however, three exemplary anthologies which I felt made their own particular contribution to the current ecological debate. All three are very helpful guides to the territory.

Peter Abbs's *Earth Songs: A Resurgence anthology of contemporary eco-poetry* (2002) brings together a broad selection of contemporary ecopoetry (mainly by British and Irish poets) celebrating the diversity of life on this planet, with 'poet after poet affirming, with compelling cadence, the beauty, mystery and intricacy of the natural world'. 'Defying all current literary fashions', as the blurb puts it, *Earth Songs* actually emphasises the connection many contemporary poets feel with Wordsworth (which applies as much in the States as in Britain). Writing in *Acumen*, Abbs characterises his stance thus: 'The terrible predicament we have put ourselves in requires nothing less than a dramatic re-orientation of our consciousness towards Nature. Indeed, nothing less than an inner revolution – and with it, inevitably, a reconnection with the Romantic Movement.'

Wild Reckoning (2004), edited by John Burnside and Maurice Riordan, includes an exemplary selection of work by American ecopoets within its wide historical range. This is especially appropriate for an anthology 'provoked' by Rachel Carson's *Silent Spring* (1962), the book that helped to launch the environmental movement in the States. Carson warned against the indiscriminate use of pesticides and its consequences for the environment, exposing not just the dangers of DDT but the ways in which our environment was being destroyed through the connivance of government and corporations; as Paul Brooks observed, 'she was questioning not only the indiscriminate use of poisons but the basic irresponsibility of an industrialised technological society toward the natural world'. Her legacy has been to instil a greater awareness of the centrality of ecology in all our lives over the four decades since her book appeared, a common feeling acknowledged in all the poems commissioned or selected for *Wild Reckoning*.

Alice Oswald's *The Thunder Mutters: 101 Poems for the Planet* (2005) is more idiosyncratic but no less stimulating a book. This is an anthology edited by a gardener-poet with an intuitive sense of soil and sound, dedicated to the rake, 'an age-old implement which connects the earth to our hands, and the landscape with the sky'. Oswald did not want poems which 'pronounce any one ecological message', she explains, but poems which perform ecological work by 'putting our inner worlds in contact with the outer world – a deep, slow process that used to be the remit of the rake'. Her book has 'nothing to do with the leaf-blower', the noisy machine which has supplanted the rake in gardening work. Clearly, some of the more vocal poets included in this anthology would be out of place in Alice Oswald's garden, but there are more ways than one to skin a fox.

There are common strands between *Earth Shattering* and all three of these anthologies. Drawn from different reference-points, each book presents its own map of the territory, with different routes and areas of interest highlighted. All four books should complement one another.

EARTH SHATTERING

Earth Shattering shows the progression from the descriptive or egocentric nature poetry of earlier centuries to today's ecologically aware poetry, including the work of writers whose poetry challenged widely held beliefs or assumptions regarding humanity's relationship with the natural world.

The introductory section, **Rooted in Nature**, covers earlier writers whose poetry expressed their profound sense of connection with nature, including the 'wilderness poets' of ancient China (Tu Fu and Li Po being the best-known of these), William Wordsworth, Robinson Jeffers and Rainer Maria Rilke. I didn't intend to include prose writers in this anthology of ecopoetry, but had to make Henry Thoreau one of four exceptions to this rule. Thoreau's writing and thinking has been so influential that I chose to represent his particular contribution to environmental literature with a series of extracts from *Walden*.

The second section, **Changing the Landscape**, presents another historical overview, in this case of poets writing directly about the destruction of the natural environment in the 18th and 19th centuries: Oliver Goldsmith, William Cowper, John Clare and William Barnes (with a later perspective supplied by John Montague). In selecting work from earlier centuries for this anthology, I have steered clear of poets whose nature poetry is mainly descriptive, while keeping in mind Caroline Carver's caveat that 'Good nature poetry never stops at the descriptive, but works to a level where both writer and reader feel woven into the fabric of landscape.' I also excluded nature poetry which goes against the grain of enlightened environmental thinking.

'The origin of humankind's ambivalence towards nature can be located metaphorically in the Book of Genesis,' writes Robert Pack in his essay 'Taking Dominion over the Wilderness' [➤ 14]. Pack shows how God's second commandment has been used to justify the exploitation of nature. In earlier centuries, nature poetry has expressed the ecologically unsound view that nature is man's gift from God to be subdued and mastered. Bryson shows Whitman in this light in his comparison of 'Song of a Redwood-Tree' with W.S. Merwin's treatment of the same subject in **'The Last One'** [➤ 81], 'a poem that also renders the removal of a forest but speaks out of a much different vision of the world'. Whitman's poem 'becomes a propagandistic justification for the clearing of centuries-old redwoods, who are portrayed as willingly yielding to humanity' whereas a poet 'working for an ecological perspective on the world would not be able to present the poem as Whitman has'. Whitman's speaker tells of a redwood's 'song' addressed to the other trees:

> With Nature's calm content, with tacit huge delight,
> We welcome what we have wrought for through the past,
> And leave the field for them.
> For them predicted long,
> For a superber race, they too to grandly fill their time,
> For them we abdicate, in them ourselves ye forest kings.

There were also writers whose poetry was not, in Robert Pack's phrase, 'in harmony with a spirit of celebration and appreciation' of *nature itself*. To view nature as objectifying the glory of God is a diminishing perspective out of tune with 21st century ecopoetry. Much as I admire the work of Anne Bradstreet, to take just one example, I didn't feel that her canonical nature lyric 'Contemplations' would sit easily in a modern ecopoetry anthology:

> I heard the merry grasshopper then sing.
> The black-clad cricket bear a second part;

They kept one tune and played on the same string,
Seeming to glory in their little art.
Shall creatures abject, thus their voices raise?
And in their kind, resound their Maker's praise,
Whilst I, as mute, can warble forth no higher lays?

The subsequent sections of the anthology are mostly of ecopoetry by contemporary writers. Here also there were kinds of nature poetry which didn't fit: egocentric nature poems in which nature is exploited as a metaphor for the poet's personal feelings or thoughts about something other than nature; anthropocentric nature poems in which the focus is actually more on man than nature; any nature poems in which the perspective is one-way or mirroring, as opposed to exploring relationships and connections *between* humanity and nature.

After the first two sections covering forerunners of modern ecopoetry, the later sections are thematic, each with different but related areas of concern. A writer may have poems in different sections of the book, but where I felt that a poet's whole *oeuvre* was very closely related to the concerns of one section in particular, all the poems by that writer are grouped together there.

The third section, **Killing the Wildlife**, brings together poems on that theme, including some on the extinction of species. These are followed by a series of poems on the **Unbalance of Nature** showing the effects of pollution, cutting down trees, interfering with the processes of nature, and urbanisation. **Loss and Persistence** is the title given to the fifth section: poems which celebrate the rapidly vanishing natural world, or lament what has already been lost, or even find a glimmer of hope in nature's persistence as well as in humanity's efforts to conserve, recycle and rethink.

The next section, **The Great Web**, takes its title from Denise Levertov's poem '**Web**' [➤ 157], from her metaphor of the 'great web' that 'moves through and connects all people and things, both human and inhuman' (Bryson). These poems evoke humanity's interdependence and oneness with nature, including several recalling lost or disappearing connections between the rhythms of daily life and the cycles and processes of nature.

Exploitation presents poems concerned with the destruction of both the natural world and indigenous peoples, with postcolonial and ecofeminist perspectives represented by writers such as Derek Walcott, Ernesto Cardenal, Oodgeroo and Susan Griffin. They demonstrate the impact on nature and people of colonialism, patriarchy and other insidious brands of tyranny (political, economic, technological, self-interest). This section ends with *Dispossessing America*, a series of poems mostly by contemporary Native American writers. Their work shows how indigenous people have lived for centuries in tune with the natural environment; how those connecting beliefs are still cherished by the poets and their alienated communities; and how the balance and wholeness of their lives has been devastated along with the land and wildlife of North America. All the sections of this anthology are interconnected in an appropriately ecological fashion, and the work of the Native American poets is spun from the same 'Great Web', as Bryson has shown:

> Levertov's web represents what Mohawk poet Peter Blue Cloud [➤ 182] calls 'the allness of creation', and it points toward the same lesson Joy Harjo offers in her famous poem '**Remember**' [➤ 176], which concludes with its speaker imploring her audience to 'Remember you are all people and all people are you. / Remember you are this universe and this universe is you.'

The poems in the **Force of Nature** section show the effects of global warming and climate change, forming a prelude to the final section, **Natural Disasters**, whose poems challenge the accuracy of that expression. After covering both man-made environmental disasters (nuclear accidents) and so-called "acts of God" (hurricanes and cyclones, earthquakes, drought, floods and tsunami), *Earth Shattering* ends with planetary catastrophe and Eco-Armageddon.

As the world's politicians and corporations orchestrate our headlong rush towards Eco-Armageddon, poetry may seem like a hopeless gesture. But *Earth Shattering* shows that the power of poetry is in the detail, in the force of each individual poem, in every poem's effect on every reader. And anyone whose resolve is stirred will strengthen the collective call for change.

1. ROOTED IN NATURE

THE WILDERNESS POETRY OF ANCIENT CHINA

This introductory section covers earlier writers whose poetry expressed their profound sense of connection with nature. With its wisdom rooted in ancient Taoist and Ch'an (Zen) thought, China's wilderness or "rivers-and-mountains" poetry has influenced many modern writers, from Ezra Pound to Gary Snyder. These ancient poems articulate the experience of living as an organic part of the natural world and its processes.

David Hinton: 'Originating in the early 5th Century C.E. and stretching across two millennia, China's tradition of rivers-and-mountains *(shan-shui)* poetry represents the earliest and most extensive literary engagement with wilderness in human history. Fundamentally different from writing that employs the "natural world" as the stage or materials for human concerns, this poetry articulates a profound and spiritual sense of belonging to a wilderness of truly awesome dimensions. This is not wilderness in the superficial sense of "nature" or "landscape", terms the Western cultural lens has generally applied to this most fundamental aspect of Chinese poetry. "Nature" calls up a false dichotomy between human and nature, and "landscape" suggests a picturesque realm seen from a spectator's distance – but the Chinese wilderness is nothing less than a dynamic cosmology in which humans participate in the most fundamental way. The poetry of this wilderness cosmology feels utterly contemporary, and in an age of global ecological disruption and mass extinction, this engagement with wilderness makes it more urgently and universally important by the day.' (*Mountain Home: The Wilderness Poetry of Ancient China*, 2002.)

This selection includes translations of poems by seven key wilderness poets. All quotations in the author notes after the poems are from David Hinton's book.

T'AO CH'IEN
Home Again Among Fields and Gardens
translated from the Chinese by David Hinton

Nothing like all the others, even as a child,
rooted in such love for hills and mountains,

I stumbled into their net of dust, that one
departure a blunder lasting thirteen years.

But a tethered bird longs for its old forest,
and a pond fish its deep waters – so now,

my southern outlands cleared, I nurture
simplicity among these fields and gardens,

home again. I've got nearly two acres here,
and four or five rooms in this thatch hut,

elms and willows shading the eaves in back,
and in front, peach and plum spread wide.

Villages lost across mist-and-haze distances.
kitchen smoke drifting wide-open country,

dogs bark deep among back roads out here,
and roosters crow from mulberry treetops.

No confusion within these gates, no dust,
my empty home harbors idleness to spare.

Back again: after so long caged in that trap,
I've returned to occurrence coming of itself.

■ **T'ao Ch'ien** (365-427) essentially initiated the Chinese poetic tradition. '**Home Again Among Fields and Gardens**' tells the story of this "first poet" giving up the empty pursuit of professional ambition and returning home to the more spiritually fulfilling life of a recluse in the mountains. 'T'ao's return to his farm became a legendary ideal that virtually all later poets and intellectuals revered [...] neither escapism nor sentimental pastoralism: it is a poem about returning to a life in which the perpetual unfolding of [Taoist master] Lao Tzu's organic cosmology is the very texture of daily experience. The vision of *tzu-jan* recognises earth to be a boundless generative organism, and this vision gives rise to a very different experience of the world. Rather than the metaphysics of time and space, it knows the world as an all-eoncompassing present, a constant burgeoning forth that includes everything we think of as past and future.'

WANG WEI

In Reply to Su, Who Visited My Wheel-Rim River Hermitage When I Wasn't There to Welcome Him

translated from the Chinese by David Hinton

I live humbly near the canyon's mouth
where stately trees ring village ruins.

When you came on twisted rocky paths,
who welcomed you at my mountain gate?

Fishing boats frozen into icy shallows,
hunting fires out across cold headlands,

and in all this quiet beyond white clouds,
wild gibbons heard among distant bells.

■ **Wang Wei** (701-61) was revered as both poet and painter, traditionally spoken of as the first to paint the inner spirit of landscape. 'Wang Wei's poetry is especially celebrated for the way he could make himself disappear into a landscape, and so dwell as belonging utterly to China's wilderness cosmology.'

LI PO

Reverence-Pavilion Mountain, Sitting Alone

translated from the Chinese by David Hinton

The birds have vanished into deep skies.
A last cloud drifts away, all idleness.

Inexhaustible, this mountain and I
gaze at each other, it alone remaining.

LI PO

Gazing at the Thatch-Hut Mountain Waterfall

translated from the Chinese by David Hinton

1

Climbing west toward Incense-Burner Peak,
I look south and see a falls of water, a cascade

hanging there, three thousand feet high,
then seething dozens of miles down canyons.

Sudden as lightning breaking into flight,
its white rainbow of mystery appears. Afraid

at first the celestial Star River is falling,
splitting and dissolving into cloud heavens,

I look up into force churning in strength,
all power, the very workings of Change-Maker.

It keeps ocean winds blowing ceaselessly,
shines a mountain moon back into empty space,

empty space it tumbles and sprays through,
rinsing green cliffs clean on both sides,

sending pearls in flight scattering into mist
and whitewater seething down towering rock.

Here, after wandering among these renowned
mountains, the heart grows rich with idleness.

Why talk of cleansing elixirs of immortality?
Here, the world's dust rinsed from my face,

I'll stay close to what I've always loved,
content to leave that peopled world forever.

2

Sunlight on Incense-Burner kindles violet smoke.
Watching the distant falls hanging there, river

headwaters plummeting three thousand feet in flight,
I see the Star River falling through nine heavens.

■ **Li Po** (701-62) achieved fame by his death as well as in life: according to legend, he fell into a river when drunk and drowned trying to embrace the moon. 'He is called "the Banished Immortal", an exiled spirit moving through the world with an unearthly ease and freedom from attachment. But at the same time he belongs to earth in the most profound way [...] He is primarily engaged by the natural world in its wild, rather than domestic, forms.'

TU FU
Spring Prospect
translated from the Chinese by Burton Watson

The nation shattered, mountains and rivers remain;
City in spring, grass and trees burgeoning.
Feeling the times, blossoms draw tears;
Hating separation, birds alarm the heart.
Beacon fires three months in succession,
A letter from home worth ten thousand in gold.
White hairs, fewer for the scratching,
Soon too few to hold a hairpin up.

TU FU
Dawn Landscape
translated from the Chinese by David Hinton

The last watch has sounded in K'uei-chou.
Color spreading above Solar-Terrace Mountain,

a cold sun clears high peaks. Clouds linger,
blotting out canyons below tangled ridges,

and deep Yangtze banks keep sails hidden.
Beneath clear skies: clatter of falling leaves.

And these deer at my bramble gate: so close
here, we touch our own kind in each other.

■ **Tu Fu** (712-70) was China's greatest poet. He became a recluse and wanderer in his 40s after a catastrophic civil war devastated the country. 'Tu achieved a panoramic view of the human drama: he saw it as part of China's vast landscape of natural process, a vision distilled in one of the most famous lines in Chinese poetry: "The nation falls into ruins; rivers and mountains continue." [...] Poised between black despair and exquisite beauty, his was a geologic perspective, a vision of the human cast against the elemental sweep of the universe.'

HAN SHAN (COLD MOUNTAIN)
I've lived out tens of thousands of years
translated from the Chinese by David Hinton

I've lived out tens of thousands of years
on Cold Mountain. Given to the seasons,

I vanished among forests and cascades,
gazed into things so utterly themselves.

No one ventures up into all these cliffs
hidden forever in white mist and cloud.

It's just me, thin grass my sleeping mat
and azure heaven my comforting quilt:

happily pillowed on stone, I'm given to
heaven and earth changing on and on.

■ **Cold Mountain** or **Han Shan** (*c.* 7th-9th centuries) 'exists more as legend than historical fact [...] he lived alone on Cold Mountain, a summit in the Heaven-Terrace Mountains of southeast China, taking it as his namesake, and eventually his very identity [...] he roamed the mountains alone, a wild

Ch'an sage writing poems on rocks and trees. These poems were collected by the local government prefect who, recognising Cold Mountain's genius, assembled them into a collection that has been preserved. [...] According to the legend, Cold Mountain the poet was last seen when, slipping into a crevice that closed behind him, he vanished utterly into the mountain.'

CHIA TAO

Evening Landscape, Clearing Snow

translated from the Chinese by David Hinton

Walking-stick in hand, I watch snow clear,
Ten thousand clouds and streams banked up,

woodcutters return to their simple homes,
and soon a cold sun sets among risky peaks.

A wildfire burns among ridgeline grasses.
Scraps of mist rise, born of rock and pine.

On the road back to a mountain monastery,
I hear it struck: that bell of evening skies!

■ **Chia Tao** (779-843) was a Ch'an monk living in mountain monasteries before he became an impoverished poet in the capital of Ch'ang-an and a leading member of the mid-T'ang experimental movement. '**Evening Landscape, Clearing Snow**' is about the experience of attending to the movements of a primal cosmology oriented around the earth's mysterious generative force. David Hinton unravels its background in *Mountain Home*, concluding: 'So the poem locates us in the midst of this spiritual ecology of being and nonbeing; then, as mist is born in the third-to-last line (the Chinese believed clouds originated like this in the mountains), the poem moves toward the center of this cosmology, that perpetual moment in which the ten thousand things are generated out of nonbeing. And finally, hearing the sudden call of a bell emerging from the empty silence, ground of both landscape and consciousness, we come to a kind of sudden enlightenment in which we find ourselves there at the very origin of things, in the pregnant emptiness at the heart of this Cosmos.'

SU TUNG-P'O

6th Moon, 27th Sun: Sipping Wine at Lake-View Tower

translated from the Chinese by David Hinton

1

Black clouds, soaring ink, nearly blot out these
    mountains.
White raindrops, skipping pearls, skitter wildly into
    the boat,

then wind comes across furling earth, scatters them
    away,
and below Lake-View Tower, lakewater suddenly turns
    to sky.

2

Setting animals loose – fish and turtles – I'm an exile
    out here,
but no one owns waterlilies everywhere blooming,
    blooming.

This lake pillows mountains, starts them glancing up
    and down,
and my breezy boat wanders free, drifts with an aimless
    moon.

■ **Su Tung-p'o** or **Su Shih** (1037-1101) was the Sung Dynasty's greatest poet. Often out of favour, he spent most of his life in the provinces, including many years of hardship in exile, and came to know China's rivers and mountains with 'an intimacy so deep that Su took his literary name, Tung-p'o ("East Slope"), from the site where he lived for some years as a subsistence farmer'. His selfless poetics extended the interiorisation of wilderness: 'Rather than consciousness giving shape to the world it encounters, Su's poems enact consciousness wandering like water, the operant metaphor for Tao, taking shape according to what it encounters [...] this weaving of consciousness into the fabric of wilderness allowed Su a detachment and emotional balance, even lightheartedness, that has endured as part of the Chinese cultural legend.'

HENRY THOREAU
from **Walden**

The phenomena of the year take place every day in a pond on a small scale. Every morning, generally speaking, the shallow water is being warmed more rapidly than the deep, though it may not be made so warm after all, and every evening it is being cooled more rapidly until the morning. The day is an epitome of the year. The night is the winter, the morning and evening are the spring and fall, and the noon is the summer. The cracking and booming of the ice indicate a change of temperature. One pleasant morning after a cold night, February 24th, 1850, having gone to Flints' Pond to spend the day, I noticed with surprise, that when I struck the ice with the head of my axe, it resounded like a gong for many rods around, or as if I had struck on a tight drum-head. The pond began to boom about an hour after sunrise, when it felt the influence of the sun's rays slanted upon it from over the hills; it stretched itself and yawned like a waking man with a gradually increasing tumult, which was kept up three or four hours. It took a short siesta at noon, and boomed once more toward night, as the sun was withdrawing his influence. In the right stage of the weather a pond fires its evening gun with great regularity. But in the middle of the day, being full of cracks, and the air also being less elastic, it had completely lost its resonance, and probably fishes and muskrats could not then have been stunned by a blow on it. The fishermen say that the 'thundering of the pond' scares the fishes and prevents their biting. The pond does not thunder every evening, and I cannot tell surely when to expect its thundering; but though I may perceive no difference in the weather, it does. Who would have suspected so large and cold and thick-skinned a thing to be so sensitive? Yet it has its law to which it thunders obedience when it should as surely as the buds expand in the spring. The earth is all alive and covered with papillae. The largest pond is as sensitive to atmospheric changes as the globule of mercury in its tube.

One attraction in coming to the woods to live was that I should have leisure and opportunity to see the spring come in. The ice in the pond at length begins to be honeycombed, and I can set my heel in it as I walk. Fogs and rains and warmer suns are gradually melting the snow; the days have grown sensibly longer; and I see how I shall get through the winter without adding to my woodpile, for large fires are no longer necessary. I am on the alert for the first signs of spring, to hear the chance note of some arriving bird, or the striped squirrel's chirp, for his stores must be now nearly exhausted, or see the woodchuck venture out of his winter quarters. On the 13th of March, after I had heard the blue-bird, song-sparrow, and red-wing, the ice was still nearly a foot thick. As the weather grew warmer it was not sensibly worn away by the water, nor broken up and floated off as in rivers, but, though it was completely melted for half a rod in width about the shore, the middle was merely honeycombed and saturated with water, so that you could put your foot through it when six inches thick; but by the next day evening, perhaps, after a warm rain followed by fog, it would have wholly disappeared, all gone off with the fog, spirited away. One year I went across the middle five days before it disappeared entirely. [...]

Few phenomena gave me more delight than to observe the forms which thawing sand and clay assume in flowing down the sides of a deep cut on the railroad through which I passed on my way to the village, a phenomenon not very common on so large a scale, though the number of freshly exposed banks of the right material must have been greatly multiplied since railroads were invented. The material was sand of every degree of fineness and of various rich colors, commonly mixed with a little clay. When the frost comes out in the spring, and even in a thawing day in the winter, the sand begins to flow down the slopes like lava, sometimes bursting out through the snow and overflowing it where no sand was to be seen before. Innumerable little streams overlap and interlace one with another, exhibiting a sort of hybrid product, which obeys half way the law of currents, and half way that of vegetation. As it flows it takes the forms of sappy leaves or vines, making heaps of pulpy sprays a foot or more in depth, and resembling, as you look down on them, the laciniated, lobed, and imbricated thalluses of some lichens; or you are reminded of coral, of leopard's paws or birds' feet, of brains or lungs or bowels, and excrements of all kinds. It is a truly *grotesque* vegetation, whose forms and color we see imitated in bronze, a sort of architectural foliage more ancient and typical than acanthus, chiccory, ivy, vine, or any vegetable leaves; destined perhaps, under some circumstances, to become a puzzle to future geologists. The whole cut impressed me as if it were a cave with its stalactites laid open to the light. The various shades of the sand are singularly rich and agreeable, embracing the different iron colors, brown, gray, yellowish, and reddish. When the flowing mass reaches the drain at the foot of the bank it spreads out flatter into *strands*, the separate streams losing their semicylindrical form and gradually becoming more flat and broad, running together as they are more moist, till they form an almost flat *sand*, still variously and beautifully shaded, but in which you call trace the original forms of vegetation; till at length, in the water itself, they are converted into banks, like those formed off the mouths of rivers, and the forms of vegetation are lost in the ripple marks on the bottom.

The whole bank, which is from twenty to forty feet high, is sometimes overlaid with a mass of this kind of foliage, or sandy rupture, for a quarter of a mile on one or both sides, the produce of one spring day. What makes this sand foliage remarkable is its springing into existence thus suddenly. When I see on the one side the inert bank, – for the sun acts on one side first, – and on the other this luxuriant foliage, the creation of an hour, I am affected as if in a peculiar sense I stood in the laboratory of the Artist who made the world and me, – had come to where he was still at work, sporting on this bank, and with excess of energy strewing his fresh designs about. I feel as if I were nearer to the vitals of the globe, for this sandy overflow is something such a foliaceous mass as the vitals of the animal body. You find thus in the very sands an anticipation of the veg-

etable leaf. No wonder that the earth expresses itself outwardly in leaves, it so labors with the idea inwardly. The atoms have already learned this law, and are pregnant by it. The overhanging leaf sees here its prototype. *Internally*, whether in the globe or animal body, it is a moist thick *lobe*, a word especially applicable to the liver and lungs and the *leaves* of fat (λειβω, *labor*, *lapsus*, to flow or slip downward, a lapsing; λοβος, *globus*, lobe, globe; also lap, flap, and many other words); *externally* a dry thin *leaf*, even as the *f* and *v* are a pressed and dried *b*. The radicals of lobe are *lb*, the soft mass of the *b* (single-lobed, or B, double-lobed), with the liquid *l* behind it pressing it forward. In globe, *glb*, the guttural *g* adds to the meaning the capacity of the throat. The feathers and wings of birds are still drier and thinner leaves. Thus, also, you pass from the lumpish grub in the earth to the airy and fluttering butterfly. The very globe continually transcends and translates itself, and becomes winged in its orbit. Even ice begins with delicate crystal leaves, as if it had flowed into moulds which the fronds of waterplants have impressed on the watery mirror. The whole tree itself is but one leaf, and rivers are still vaster leaves whose pulp is intervening earth, and towns and cities are the ova of insects in their axils.

When the sun withdraws the sand ceases to flow, but in the morning the streams will start once more and branch and branch again into a myriad of others. You here see perchance how blood-vessels are formed. If you look closely you observe that first there pushes forward from the thawing mass a stream of softened sand with a drop-like point, like the ball of the finger, feeling its way slowly and blindly downward, until at last with more heat and moisture, as the sun gets higher, the most fluid portion, in its effort to obey the law to which the most inert also yields, separates from the latter and forms for itself a meandering channel or artery within that, in which is seen a little silvery stream glancing like lightning from one stage of pulpy leaves or branches to another, and ever and anon swallowed up in the sand. It is wonderful how rapidly yet perfectly the sand organises itself as it flows, using the best material its mass affords to form the sharp edges of its channel. Such are the sources of rivers. In the silicious matter which the water deposits is perhaps the bony system, and in the still finer soil and organic matter the fleshy fibre or cellular tissue. What is man but a mass of thawing clay? The ball of the human finger is but a drop congealed. The fingers and toes flow to their extent from the thawing mass of the body. Who knows what the human body would expand and flow out to under a more genial heaven? Is not the hand a spreading *palm* leaf with its lobes and veins? The ear may be regarded, fancifully, as a lichen, *umbilicaria*, on the side of the head, with its lobe or drop. The lip – *labium*, from *labor* (?) – laps or lapses from the sides of the cavernous mouth. The nose is a manifest congealed drop or stalactite. The chin is a still larger drop, the confluent dripping of the face. The cheeks are a slide from the brows into the valley of the face, opposed and diffused by the cheek bones. Each rounded lobe of the vegetable leaf, too, is a thick and now loitering drop, larger or smaller; the lobes are the fingers of the leaf; and as many lobes as it has, in so many directions it tends to flow, and more heat or other genial influences would have caused it to flow yet farther.

Thus it seemed that this one hillside illustrated the principle of all the operations of Nature. The Maker of this earth but patented a leaf. What Champollion will decipher this hieroglyphic for us, that we may turn over a new leaf at last? This phenomenon is more exhilarating to me than the luxuriance and fertility of vineyards. True, it is somewhat excrementitious in its character, and there is no end to the heaps of liver, lights, and bowels, as if the globe were turned wrong side outward; but this suggests at least that Nature has some bowels, and there again is mother of humanity. This is the frost coming out of the ground; this is Spring. It precedes the green and flowery spring, as mythology precedes regular poetry. I know of nothing more purgative of winter fumes and indigestions. It convinces me that Earth is still in her swaddling-clothes, and stretches forth baby fingers on every side. Fresh curls spring from the baldest brow. There is

nothing inorganic. These foliaceous heaps lie along the bank like the slag of a furnace, showing that Nature is "in full blast" within. The earth is not a mere fragment of dead history, stratum upon stratum like the leaves of a book, to be studied by geologists and antiquaries chiefly, but living poetry like the leaves of a tree, which precede flowers and fruit – not a fossil earth, but a living earth; compared with whose great central life all animal and vegetable life is merely parasitic. Its throes will heave our exuviae from their graves. You may melt your metals and cast them into the most beautiful moulds you can; they will never excite me like the forms which this molten earth flows out into. And not only it, but the institutions upon it are plastic like clay in the hands of the potter. [...]

Our village life would stagnate if it were not for the unexplored forests and meadows which surround it. We need the tonic of wildness, – to wade sometimes in marshes where the bittern and the meadow-hen lurk, and hear the booming of the snipe; to smell the whispering sedge where only some wilder and more solitary fowl builds her nest, and the mink crawls with its belly close to the ground. At the same time that we are earnest to explore and learn all things, we require that all things be mysterious and unexplorable, that land and sea be infinitely wild, unsurveyed and unfathomed by us because unfathomable. We can never have enough of Nature. We must be refreshed by the sight of inexhaustible vigor, vast and titanic features, the sea-coast with its wrecks, the wilderness with its living and its decaying trees, the thunder-cloud, and the rain which lasts three weeks and produces freshets. We need to witness our own limits transgressed, and some life pasturing freely where we never wander. We are cheered when we observe the vulture feeding on the carrion which disgusts and disheartens us, and deriving health and strength from the repast. There was a dead horse in the hollow by the path to my house, which compelled me sometimes to go out of my way, especially in the night when the air was heavy, but the assurance it gave me of the strong appetite and inviolable health of Nature was my compensation for this. I love to see that

Nature is so rife with life that myriads can be afforded to be sacrificed and suffered to prey on one another; that tender organisations can be so serenely squashed out of existence like pulp, – tadpoles which herons gobble up, and tortoises and toads run over in the road; and that sometimes it has rained flesh and blood! With the liability to accident, we must see how little account is to be made of it. The impression made on a wise man is that of universal innocence. Poison is not poisonous after all, nor are any wounds fatal. Compassion is a very untenable ground. It must be expeditious. Its pleadings will not bear to be stereotyped.

Early in May, the oaks, hickories, maples, and other trees, just putting out amidst the pine woods around the pond, imparted a brightness like sunshine to the landscape, especially in cloudy days, as if the sun were breaking through mists and shining faintly on the hillsides here and there. On the third or fourth of May I saw a loon in the pond, and during the first week of the month I heard the whip-poor-will, the brown thrasher, the veery, the wood pewee, the chewink, and other birds. I had heard the wood thrush long before. The phoebe had already come once more and looked in at my door and window, to see if my house was cavern-like enough for her, sustaining herself on humming winds with clinched talons, as if she held by the air, while she surveyed the premises. The sulphur-like pollen of the pitch pine soon covered the pond and the stones and rotten wood along the shore, so that you could have collected a barrelful. This is the "sulphur showers" we hear of. Even in Calidas' drama of Sacontala, we read of 'rills dyed yellow with the golden dust of the lotus'. And so the seasons went rolling on into summer, as one rambles into higher and higher grass.

Thus was my first year's life in the woods completed; and the second year was similar to it. I finally left Walden September 6th, 1847.

■ **Henry David Thoreau** (1817-62) was a highly influential American essayist and practical philosopher who lived the doctrines of Transcendentalism. In 1845 he built a cabin in the woods at Walden Pond, just outside Concord, Massachusetts, on land belonging to his friend, the writer Ralph Waldo Emerson, and lived there for two years, keeping a journal which provided the source material for the 18 essays of **Walden**, one of the seminal books in American environmental literature.

The above extracts from *Walden* are from the penultimate chapter, 'Spring', the emotional apex of the book, coinciding with that time of year when the Earth renews itself. In his extended description of the melting sandbank, Thoreau acknowledges that supposedly natural phenomena are affected by human manipulation of the land. And the same laws that create the flows of sand are responsible for the physical appearance of humans. Nature is alive and is still capable of creation.

Thoreau characterises the Earth in textual terms which set a puzzle, asking 'What Champillion will decipher this hieroglyphic for us, that we may turn over a new leaf at last?', a reference to Jean-François Champollion, who deciphered the Egyptian hieroglyphs, and in 1822 translated parts of the Rosetta Stone. He wants someone to understand the design of Nature as well.

'In Wildness is the preservation of the World,' wrote Thoreau in his essay 'Walking' (1862), but he says much more on the subject in *Walden*. His idea of Nature includes both death and violence, as well as an acceptance that Nature ignores compassion.

'Thoreau, in *Walden*, insists that not only human beings, animals, trees, and ponds exist in an ecological complex, but that cultural artifacts such as texts and railroad cuts also participate in our perception of ecological relationships and are, therefore, overlooked parts of any particular ecology. Our relationships with not only the human but also the nonhuman world – and the expression of those relationships in language – are interlocked.' (Cornelius Browne)

WILLIAM WORDSWORTH

Lines Composed a Few Miles above Tintern Abbey, on Revisiting the Banks of the Wye during a Tour. July 13, 1798

Five years have past; five summers, with the length
Of five long winters! and again I hear
These waters, rolling from their mountain-springs
With a soft inland murmur. – Once again
Do I behold these steep and lofty cliffs,
That on a wild secluded scene impress
Thoughts of more deep seclusion; and connect
The landscape with the quiet of the sky.
The day is come when I again repose
Here, under this dark sycamore, and view
These plots of cottage-ground, these orchard-tufts,
Which at this season, with their unripe fruits,
Are clad in one green hue, and lose themselves
’Mid groves and copses. Once again I see
These hedge-rows, hardly hedge-rows, little lines
Of sportive wood run wild: these pastoral farms,
Green to the very door; and wreaths of smoke
Sent up, in silence, from among the trees!
With some uncertain notice, as might seem
Of vagrant dwellers in the houseless woods,
Or of some Hermit’s cave, where by his fire
The Hermit sits alone.
                              These beauteous forms,
Through a long absence, have not been to me
As is a landscape to a blind man’s eye:
But oft, in lonely rooms, and ’mid the din
Of towns and cities, I have owed to them,
In hours of weariness, sensations sweet,
Felt in the blood, and felt along the heart;
And passing even into my purer mind,
With tranquil restoration: – feelings too
Of unremembered pleasure: such, perhaps,
As have no slight or trivial influence
On that best portion of a good man’s life,
His little, nameless, unremembered, acts
Of kindness and of love. Nor less, I trust,

To them I may have owed another gift,
Of aspect more sublime; that blessed mood,
In which the burthen of the mystery,
In which the heavy and the weary weight
Of all this unintelligible world,
Is lightened: – that serene and blessed mood,
In which the affections gently lead us on, –
Until, the breath of this corporeal frame
And even the motion of our human blood
Almost suspended, we are laid asleep
In body, and become a living soul:
While with an eye made quiet by the power
Of harmony, and the deep power of joy,
We see into the life of things.
                              If this
Be but a vain belief, yet, oh! how oft –
In darkness and amid the many shapes
Of joyless daylight; when the fretful stir
Unprofitable, and the fever of the world,
Have hung upon the beatings of my heart –
How oft, in spirit, have I turned to thee,
O sylvan Wye! thou wanderer thro’ the woods,
How often has my spirit turned to thee!
    And now, with gleams of half-extinguished thought,
With many recognitions dim and faint,
And somewhat of a sad perplexity,
The picture of the mind revives again:
While here I stand, not only with the sense
Of present pleasure, but with pleasing thoughts
That in this moment there is life and food
For future years. And so I dare to hope,
Though changed, no doubt, from what I was when first
I came among these hills; when like a roe
I bounded o’er the mountains, by the sides
Of the deep rivers, and the lonely streams,
Wherever nature led: more like a man
Flying from something that he dreads, than one
Who sought the thing he loved. For nature then
(The coarser pleasures of my boyish days,
And their glad animal movements all gone by)
To me was all in all. – I cannot paint
What then I was. The sounding cataract

Haunted me like a passion: the tall rock,
The mountain, and the deep and gloomy wood,
Their colours and their forms, were then to me
An appetite; a feeling and a love,
That had no need of a remoter charm,
By thought supplied, nor any interest
Unborrowed from the eye. – That time is past,
And all its aching joys are now no more,
And all its dizzy raptures. Not for this
Faint I, nor mourn nor murmur; other gifts
Have followed; for such loss, I would believe,
Abundant recompence. For I have learned
To look on nature, not as in the hour
Of thoughtless youth; but hearing oftentimes
The still, sad music of humanity,
Nor harsh nor grating, though of ample power
To chasten and subdue. And I have felt
A presence that disturbs me with the joy
Of elevated thoughts; a sense sublime
Of something far more deeply interfused,
Whose dwelling is the light of setting suns,
And the round ocean and the living air,
And the blue sky, and in the mind of man;
A motion and a spirit, that impels
All thinking things, all objects of all thought,
And rolls through all things. Therefore am I still
A lover of the meadows and the woods,
And mountains; and of all that we behold
From this green earth; of all the mighty world
Of eye, and ear, – both what they half create,
And what perceive; well pleased to recognise
In nature and the language of the sense
The anchor of my purest thoughts, the nurse,
The guide, the guardian of my heart, and soul
Of all my moral being.
                              Nor perchance,
If I were not thus taught, should I the more
Suffer my genial spirits to decay:
For thou art with me here upon the banks
Of this fair river; thou my dearest Friend,
My dear, dear Friend; and in thy voice I catch
The language of my former heart, and read

My former pleasures in the shooting lights
Of thy wild eyes. Oh! yet a little while
May I behold in thee what I was once,
My dear, dear Sister! and this prayer I make,
Knowing that Nature never did betray
The heart that loved her; 'tis her privilege,
Through all the years of this our life, to lead
From joy to joy: for she can so inform
The mind that is within us, so impress
With quietness and beauty, and so feed
With lofty thoughts, that neither evil tongues,
Rash judgments, nor the sneers of selfish men,
Nor greetings where no kindness is, nor all
The dreary intercourse of daily life,
Shall e'er prevail against us, or disturb
Our cheerful faith, that all which we behold
Is full of blessings. Therefore let the moon
Shine on thee in thy solitary walk;
And let the misty mountain-winds be free
To blow against thee: and, in after years,
When these wild ecstasies shall be matured
Into a sober pleasure; when thy mind
Shall be a mansion for all lovely forms,
Thy memory be as a dwelling-place
For all sweet sounds and harmonies; oh! then,
If solitude, or fear, or pain, or grief,
Should be thy portion, with what healing thoughts
Of tender joy wilt thou remember me,
And these my exhortations! Nor, perchance –
If I should be where I no more can hear
Thy voice, nor catch from thy wild eyes these gleams
Of past existence – wilt thou then forget
That on the banks of this delightful stream
We stood together; and that I, so long
A worshipper of Nature, hither came
Unwearied in that service: rather say
With warmer love – oh! with far deeper zeal
Of holier love. Nor wilt thou then forget,
That after many wanderings, many years
Of absence, these steep woods and lofty cliffs,
And this green pastoral landscape, were to me
More dear, both for themselves and for thy sake!

■ **William Wordsworth** (1770-1850) launched the English Romantic movement with Samuel Taylor Coleridge with their joint publication of *Lyrical Ballads* in 1798. Born in Cockermouth, he spent most of his life in England's Lake District, whose landscape deeply affected his imagination, making him feel profoundly connected with the forces of nature and inspiring much of his poetry. Wordsworth's most productive years were at Dove Cottage (1799-1808), celebrated in his poem 'Home at Grasmere' and chronicled by his sister Dorothy in her *Grasmere Journals*, which include many evocative descriptions of nature. He often used her journal as a starting-point for poems, including 'I wandered lonely as a Cloud' (1804), whose description of daffodils was inspired by her account of a walk they had taken two years earlier.

Pamela Woof (2002) tells how 'from his earliest infancy, he heard the murmuring of the River Derwent as it flowed past the garden of his childhood home. Later, he recorded his gratitude for this, and described how, as a child, its "steady cadence" had given him "A knowledge, a dim earnest, of the calm / Which Nature breathes among the hills and groves" [*Prelude*, 1805 ➤ 31]. Somewhere within him Wordsworth kept that child, knew that possibility of stillness, and he strove to express it in his poetry. [...] Stillness and an openness to receive were the basic slate of Wordsworth's being. Dorothy records a day spent on the fells above Rydal [...] and tells of how she and Coleridge "left William sitting on the stones feasting with silence" [*Grasmere Journal*, 23 April 1802]. As Wordsworth grew up, a more dramatic relationship with Nature came to co-exist with this passivity.'

Nature, in all its forms, was important to Wordsworth, but he rarely uses simple descriptions. Instead he concentrates on the ways in which he responds and relates to the world, using poetry both to look at the relationship between nature and human life and to explore the belief that nature can have an impact on our emotional and spiritual lives. This selection draws on three works central to understanding Wordsworth's sense of connectness with nature, 'Tintern Abbey', 'Home at Grasmere' and his great autobiographical poem, *The Prelude*.

Jonathan Bate's essential study *The Song of the Earth* (2000) includes a fascinating discussion of **'Tintern Abbey'** in which he shows how Wordsworth's "ecopoetic" differs fundamentally from the objectifying aesthetic of earlier 18th century proponents of the "picturesque" like William Gilpin: 'The reader's first impression is that "thoughts of a more deep seclusion" are being pressed on Wordsworth's mind – but what Wordsworth in fact states is that the thoughts are impressed on the

scene itself. Nature is made capable of feeling. The "I" is written out, or rather absorbed into the scene. Religious retreat means seclusion from worldliness and submission of the self to the divine will; Wordsworthian "deep seclusion" means dissolution of the self from perceiving eye into ecologically connected organism. [...] The key word – emphasised through Wordsworth's favourite metrical trick of suspension at the line-ending – is "connect". Where the picturesque looks, the ecopoetic connects. [...]

'In the central section of the poem, Wordsworth turns to the psychological work which nature can do for alienated urban man. The crucial move here is the idea of quieting the eye, giving up on the picturesque quest for mastery over a landscape, and submitting instead to an inner vision which enables one to "see into the life of things". The memory of the Wye valley teaches the poet that all "things", even apparently dead matter such as earth and rock, have a life, an animating spirit. We may call this pantheism: "I, so long / A worshipper of Nature". Or we may call it a recognition of what in our time the ecologist James Lovelock has called the Gaia hypothesis [➤ 12], the idea that the whole earth is a single vast, living, breathing ecosystem. [...] Wordsworth's distinctive version of the Gaia principle refuses to carve the world into object and subject; the same force animates both consciousness ("the mind of man") and "all things". Is a river or a plant an object of thought or is it itself a thinking thing? Wordsworth says it is both and that the distinction between subject and object is a murderous dissection.'

The extract printed here from **'Home at Grasmere'** is from a passage published as the 'Prospectus' to *The Excursion* (1814), which Wordsworth originally conceived as the second part of a massive poetic work (including *The Prelude*) to be called *The Recluse or views of Nature, Man, and Society*. In *Green Voices: Understanding contemporary nature poetry* (1995), Terry Gifford shows how Wordsworth is a key figure for today's ecopoets, citing 'the remarkable climax of "Home at Grasmere" [where] Wordsworth struggles to express the biological basis of his metaphysic. The human mind ought to be able to comprehend its connection with nature because it is formed by nature to fit the natural world.'

Wordsworth revised and expanded **The Prelude** several times. He wrote the first version while in Germany in 1799, the so-called 'two-part *Prelude*' which contains almost all the major parts of the later versions. By 1805 he had expanded it into 13 books, and the excerpts chosen here are from that version. *The Prelude* was not actually published and given its title until 1850, after Wordsworth's death, but that 14-book version includes cuts and changes which reflect the conservativism of his later years, his acceptance of orthodox, Anglican Christianity and a renunciation of his early radicalism.

The excerpts which follow are from the first two books of *The Prelude*. Later in the poem, he writes: 'There are in our existence spots of time, / Which with distinct pre-eminence retain / A renovating Virtue, whence [...] our minds / Are nourished and invisibly repaired' (XI, 258-78). 'Spots of time' for Wordsworth are past experiences through which he can trace his own development, as a man and as a poet, and which continue to resonate with new meanings many years after the events themselves, many arising out of moments of activity (ice-skating in the extract here), or in response to a particular feeling (guilt after stealing the rowing boat) or a time of emotional intensity, such as the death of his father. The boat-stealing passage shows how Wordsworth projects his own feelings onto a landscape. His feeling of 'troubled pleasure' on stealing the boat is given substance by the looming mountains, which eventually become 'the trouble of my dreams'. When he recalls ice-skating on frozen Esthwaite Water at night, the centre of the experience is the way in which the people and the landscape are all involved. Another 'spot of time' recalled is of another schoolboy adventure, when the young William and friends hired horses and raced them along the sands near Furness Abbey. The 'internal breezes, sobbings of the place' are contrasted with the living energy of the horse riders. 'The wonder of the universe and a sense of timelessness: perceptions like these cut into the boisterous activities of the schoolboy,' writes Pamela Woof. 'The eternal was glimpsed. Wordsworth knew that Nature had let him "drink" a "visionary power". It reminds us that he is perhaps our greatest poet of transcendence, that through Nature he could apprehend the spiritual beyond the immediacy of the material.'

WILLIAM WORDSWORTH
from Home at Grasmere

On man, on Nature, and on human life,
Thinking in solitude, from time to time
I feel sweet passions traversing my soul
Like music; unto these, where'er I may,
I would give utterance in numerous verse.
Of truth, of grandeur, beauty, love, and hope –
Hope for this earth and hope beyond the grave –
Of virtue and of intellectual power,
Of blessed consolations in distress,
Of joy in widest commonalty spread,
Of the individual mind that keeps its own
Inviolate retirement, and consists
With being limitless, the one great life,
I sing; fit audience let me find, though few!
[...]
           The darkest pit
Of the profoundest hell, chaos, night,
Nor aught of blinder vacancy scooped out
By help of dreams, can breed such fear and awe
As fall upon us often when we look
Into our minds, into the mind of man,
My haunt, and the main region of my song.
Beauty, whose living home is the green earth,
Surpassing the most fair ideal forms
The craft of delicate spirits hath composed
From earth's materials, waits upon my steps,
Pitches her tents before me where I move,
An hourly neighbour. Paradise and groves
Elysian, fortunate islands, fields like those of old
In the deep ocean – wherefore should they be
A history, or but a dream, when minds
Once wedded to this outward frame of things
In love, find these the growth of common day?
I, long before the blessèd hour arrives,
Would sing in solitude the spousal verse
Of this great consummation, would proclaim –
Speaking of nothing more than what we are –
How exquisitely the individual mind
(And the progressive powers perhaps no less
Of the whole species) to the external world
Is fitted; and how exquisitely too –
Theme this but little heard of among men –
The external world is fitted to the mind;
And the creation (by no lower name
Can it be called) which they with blended might
Accomplish: this is my great argument.

WILLIAM WORDSWORTH
from **The Prelude** (1805)

from BOOK I *(271-501)*

                    Was it for this
That one, the fairest of all rivers, loved
To blend his murmurs with my nurse's song,
And from his alder shades and rocky falls,
And from his fords and shallows, sent a voice
That flowed along my dreams? For this, didst thou,
O Derwent! travelling over the green plains
Near my 'sweet birthplace', didst thou, beauteous stream,
Make ceaseless music through the night and day
Which with its steady cadence, tempering
Our human waywardness, composed my thoughts
To more than infant softness, giving me,
Among the fretful dwellings of mankind,
A knowledge, a dim earnest, of the calm
Which Nature breathes among the hills and groves.
When, having left his mountains, to the towers
Of Cockermouth that beauteous river came,
Behind my father's house he passed, close by,
Along the margin of our terrace walk.
He was a playmate whom we dearly loved.
Oh! many a time have I, a five years' child,
A naked boy, in one delightful rill,
A little mill-race severed from his stream,
Made one long bathing of a summer's day,
Basked in the sun, and plunged, and basked again
Alternate all a summer's day, or coursed
Over the sandy fields, leaping through groves
Of yellow grunsel, or when crag and hill,
The woods, and distant Skiddaw's lofty height,
Were bronzed with a deep radiance, stood alone
Beneath the sky, as if I had been born
On Indian plains, and from my mother's hut
Had run abroad in wantonness, to sport,
A naked savage, in the thunder shower.

   Fair seed-time had my soul, and I grew up
Fostered alike by beauty and by fear;

Much favoured in my birthplace, and no less
In that beloved vale to which, erelong,
I was transplanted. Well I call to mind
('Twas at an early age, ere I had seen
Nine summers) when upon the mountain slope
The frost and breath of frosty wind had snapped
The last autumnal crocus, 'twas my joy
To wander half the night among the cliffs
And the smooth hollows, where the woodcocks ran
Along the open turf. In thought and wish
That time, my shoulder all with springes hung,
I was a fell destroyer. On the heights
Scudding away from snare to snare, I plied
My anxious visitation, hurrying on,
Still hurrying, hurrying onward; moon and stars
Were shining o'er my head; I was alone,
And seemed to be a trouble to the peace
That was among them. Sometimes it befell
In these night-wanderings, that a strong desire
O'erpowered my better reason, and the bird
Which was the captive of another's toils
Became my prey; and, when the deed was done
I heard among the solitary hills
Low breathings coming after me, and sounds
Of undistinguishable motion, steps
Almost as silent as the turf they trod.
Nor less in springtime when on southern banks
The shining sun had from his knot of leaves
Decoyed the primrose flower, and when the vales
And woods were warm, was I a plunderer then
In the high places, on the lonesome peaks
Where'er, among the mountains and the winds,
The mother bird had built her lodge. Though mean
My object, and inglorious, yet the end
Was not ignoble. Oh! when I have hung
Above the raven's nest, by knots of grass
And half-inch fissures in the slippery rock
But ill sustained, and almost, as it seemed,
Suspended by the blast which blew amain,
Shouldering the naked crag; Oh! at that time,
While on the perilous ridge I hung alone,
With what strange utterance did the loud dry wind

Blow through my ears! the sky seemed not a sky
Of earth, and with what motion moved the clouds!

The mind of Man is framed even like the breath
And harmony of music. There is a dark
Invisible workmanship that reconciles
Discordant elements, and makes them move
In one society. Ah me! that all
The terrors, all the early miseries
Regrets, vexations, lassitudes, that all
The thoughts and feelings which have been infused
Into my mind, should ever have made up
The calm existence that is mine when I
Am worthy of myself! Praise to the end!
Thanks likewise for the means! But I believe
That Nature, oftentimes, when she would frame
A favoured being, from his earliest dawn
Of infancy doth open out the clouds,
As at the touch of lightning, seeking him
With gentlest visitation; not the less,
Though haply aiming at the self-same end,
Does it delight her sometimes to employ
Severer interventions, ministry
More palpable, and so she dealt with me.

One evening (surely I was led by her)
I went alone into a shepherd's boat,
A skiff that to a willow tree was tied
Within a rocky cave, its usual home.
'Twas by the shores of Patterdale, a vale
Wherein I was a stranger, thither come
A school-boy traveller, at the holidays.
Forth rambled from the village inn alone,
No sooner had I sight of this small skiff,
Discovered thus by unexpected chance,
Than I unloosed her tether and embarked.
The moon was up, the lake was shining clear
Among the hoary mountains; from the shore
I pushed, and struck the oars and struck again
In cadence, and my little boat moved on
Even like a man who walks with stately step
Though bent on speed. It was an act of stealth

And troubled pleasure; not without the voice
Of mountain-echoes did my boat move on,
Leaving behind her still on either side
Small circles glittering idly in the moon,
Until they melted all into one track
Of sparkling light. A rocky steep uprose
Above the cavern of the willow tree
And now, as suited one who proudly rowed
With his best skill, I fixed a steady view
Upon the top of that same craggy ridge,
The bound of the horizon, for behind
Was nothing but the stars and the grey sky.
She was an elfin pinnace; lustily
I dipped my oars into the silent lake,
And, as I rose upon the stroke, my boat
Went heaving through the water, like a swan;
When from behind that craggy steep, till then
The bound of the horizon, a huge cliff,
As if with voluntary power instinct,
Upreared its head. I struck, and struck again,
And, growing still in stature, the huge cliff
Rose up between me and the stars, and still,
With measured motion, like a living thing,
Strode after me. With trembling hands I turned,
And through the silent water stole my way
Back to the cavern of the willow tree.
There, in her mooring-place, I left my bark,
And, through the meadows homeward went, with grave
And serious thoughts; and after I had seen
That spectacle, for many days, my brain
Worked with a dim and undetermined sense
Of unknown modes of being; in my thoughts
There was a darkness, call it solitude,
Or blank desertion, no familiar shapes
Of hourly objects, images of trees,
Of sea or sky, no colours of green fields;
By huge and mighty forms that do not live
Like living men moved slowly through my mind.
By day and were the trouble of my dreams.

Wisdom and Spirit of the universe!
Thou Soul that art the Eternity of Thought!

That giv'st to forms and images a breath
And everlasting motion! not in vain,
By day or star-light thus from my first dawn
Of childhood didst Thou intertwine for me
The passions that build up our human soul,
Not with the mean and vulgar works of Man,
But with high objects, with enduring things,
With life and nature, purifying thus
The elements of feeling and of thought,
And sanctifying, by such discipline,
Both pain and fear, until we recognise
A grandeur in the beatings of the heart.

Nor was this fellowship vouchsafed to me
With stinted kindness. In November days,
When vapours, rolling down the valleys, made
A lonely scene more lonesome; among woods
At noon, and 'mid the calm of summer nights,
When, by the margin of the trembling lake,
Beneath the gloomy hills I homeward went
In solitude, such intercourse was mine;
'Twas mine among the fields both day and night,
And by the waters all the summer long.

And in the frosty season, when the sun
Was set, and visible for many a mile
The cottage windows through the twilight blazed,
I heeded not the summons: – happy time
It was, indeed, for all of us; to me
It was a time of rapture: clear and loud
The village clock tolled six; I wheeled about,
Proud and exulting, like an untired horse,
That cares not for its home. – All shod with steel,
We hissed along the polished ice, in games
Confederate, imitative of the chase
And woodland pleasures, the resounding horn,
The pack loud bellowing, and the hunted hare.
So through the darkness and the cold we flew,
And not a voice was idle; with the din,
Meanwhile, the precipices rang aloud,
The leafless trees, and every icy crag
Tinkled like iron, while the distant hills

Into the tumult sent an alien sound
Of melancholy, not unnoticed, while the stars,
Eastward, were sparkling clear, and in the west
The orange sky of evening died away.

Not seldom from the uproar I retired
Into a silent bay, or sportively
Glanced sideway, leaving the tumultuous throng,
To cut across the image of a star
That gleamed upon the ice: and oftentimes
When we had given our bodies to the wind,
And all the shadowy banks, on either side,
Came sweeping through the darkness, spinning still
The rapid line of motion; then at once
Have I, reclining back upon my heels,
Stopped short, yet still the solitary cliffs
Wheeled by me, even as if the earth had rolled
With visible motion her diurnal round;
Behind me did they stretch in solemn train
Feebler and feebler, and I stood and watched
Till all was tranquil as a dreamless sleep.

Ye Presences of Nature, in the sky
Or on the earth! Ye Visions of the hills!
And Souls of lonely places! can I think
A vulgar hope was yours when Ye employed
Such ministry, when Ye through many a year
Haunting me thus among my boyish sports,
On caves and trees, upon the woods and hills,
Impressed upon all forms the characters
Of danger or desire, and thus did make
The surface of the universal earth
With triumph, and delight, and hope, and fear,
Work like a sea?

from **BOOK II** *(99-144)*
Nor is my aim neglected, if I tell
How twice in the long length of those half-years
We from our funds, perhaps, with bolder hand
Drew largely, anxious for one day, at least,
To feel the motion of the galloping steed;

And with the good old inn-keeper, in truth,
On such occasion sometimes we employed
Sly subterfuge; for the intended bound
Of the day's journey was too distant far
For any cautious man, a structure famed
Beyond its neighbourhood, the antique walls
Of that large abbey which within the vale
Of nightshade, to St Mary's honour built,
Stands yet, a mouldering pile, with fractured arch,
Belfry, and images, and living trees,
A holy scene! along the smooth green turf
Our horses grazed: to more than inland peace
Left by the sea wind passing overhead
(Though wind of roughest temper) trees and towers
May in that valley oftentimes be seen,
Both silent and both motionless alike;
Such is the shelter that is there, and such
The safeguard for repose and quietness.

    Our steeds remounted, and the summons given,
With whip and spur we by the chauntry flew
In uncouth race, and left the cross-legged knight,
And the stone-abbot, and that single wren
Which one day sang so sweetly in the nave
Of the old church, that, though from recent showers
The earth was comfortless, and, touched by faint
Internal breezes, sobbings of the place,
And respirations, from the roofless walls
The shuddering ivy dripped large drops, yet still,
So sweetly 'mid the gloom the invisible bird
Sang to itself, that there I could have made
My dwelling-place, and lived for ever there
To hear such music. Through the walls we flew
And down the valley, and a circuit made
In wantonness of heart, through rough and smooth
We scampered homeward. Oh! ye rocks and streams,
And that still Spirit of the evening air!
Even in this joyous time I sometimes felt
Your presence, when with slackened step we breathed
Along the sides of the steep hills, or when
Lighted by gleams of moonlight from the sea,
We beat with thundering hoofs the level sand.

ROBINSON JEFFERS
The Coast-Road

A horseman high alone as an eagle on the spur of the mountain
    over Mirmas Canyon draws rein, looks down
At the bridge-builders, men, trucks, and power-shovels, the
    teeming end of the new coast-road at the mountain's
    base.
He sees the loops of the road go northward, headland beyond
    headland, into gray mist over Fraser's Point,
He shakes his fist and makes the gesture of wringing a
    chicken's neck, scowls and rides higher.

            I too
Believe that the life of men who ride horses, herders of cattle
    on the mountain pasture, plowers of remote
Rock-narrowed farms in poverty and freedom, is a good life.
    At the far end of those loops of road
Is what will come and destroy it, a rich and vulgar and
    bewildered civilisation dying at the core,
A world that is feverishly preparing new wars, peculiarly
    vicious ones, and heavier tyrannies, a strangely
Missionary world, road-builder, wind-rider, educator, printer
    and picture-maker and broadcaster,
So eager, like an old drunken whore, pathetically eager to
    impose the seduction of her fled charms
On all that through ignorance or isolation might have escaped
    them. I hope the weathered horseman up yonder
Will die before he knows what this eager world will do to
    his children. More tough-minded men
Can repulse an old whore, or cynically accept her drunken
    kindnesses for what they are worth,
But the innocent and credulous are soon corrupted.

                 Where is our
    consolation? Beautiful beyond belief
The heights glimmer in the sliding cloud, the great bronze
    gorge cut sides of the mountain tower up invincibly,
Not the least hurt by this ribbon of road carved on their
    sea-foot.

ROBINSON JEFFERS
Life from the Lifeless

Spirits and illusions have died,
The naked mind lives
In the beauty of inanimate things.

Flowers wither, grass fades, trees wilt,
The forest is burnt;
The rock is not burnt.

The deer starve, the winter birds
Die on their twigs and lie
In the blue dawns in the snow.

Men suffer want and become
Curiously ignoble; as prosperity
Made them curiously vile.

But look how noble the world is,
The lonely-flowing waters, the secret-
Keeping stones, the flowing sky.

ROBINSON JEFFERS
from De Rerum Virtute

I

Here is the skull of a man: a man's thoughts and emotions
Have moved under the thin bone vault like clouds
Under the blue one: love and desire and pain,
Thunderclouds of wrath and white gales of fear
Have hung inside here: and sometimes the curious
    desire of knowing
Values and purpose and the causes of things
Has coasted like a little observer air-plane over the images
That filled this mind: it never discovered much,
And now all's empty, a bone bubble, a blown-out eggshell.

II

That's what it's like: for the egg too has a mind,
Doing what our able chemists will never do,
Building the body of a hatchling, choosing among the
    proteins:
These for the young wing-muscles, these for the great
Crystalline eyes, these for the flighty nerves and brain:
Choosing and forming: a limited but superhuman
    intelligence,
Prophetic of the future and aware of the past:
The hawk's egg will make a hawk, and the serpent's
A gliding serpent: but each with a little difference
From its ancestors – and slowly, if it works, the race
Forms a new race: that also is a part of the plan
Within the egg. I believe the first living cell
Had echoes of the future in it, and felt
Direction and the great animals, the deep green forest
And whale's-track sea; I believe this globed earth
Not all by chance and fortune brings forth her broods,
But feels and chooses. And the Galaxy, the firewheel
On which we are pinned, the whirlwind of stars in
    which our sun is one dust-grain, one electron,
    this giant atom of the universe
Is not blind force, but fulfils its life and intends its
    courses. 'All things are full of God.
Winter and summer, day and night, war and peace are
    God.'
[...]

V

One light is left us: the beauty of things, not men;
The immense beauty of the world, not the human world.
Look – and without imagination, desire nor dream –
    directly
At the mountains and sea. Are they not beautiful?
These plunging promontories and flame-shaped peaks
Stopping the sombre stupendous glory, the storm-fed
    ocean? Look at the Lobos Rocks off the shore,
With foam flying at their flanks, and the long sea-lions
Couching on them. Look at the gulls on the cliff-wind,
And the soaring hawk under the cloud-stream –

But in the sage-brush desert, all one sun-stricken
Color of dust, or in the reeking tropical rain-forest,
Or in the intolerant north and high thrones of ice – is the
    earth not beautiful?
Nor the great skies over the earth?
The beauty of things means virtue and value in them.
It is in the beholder's eye, not the world? Certainly.
It is the human mind's translation of the transhuman
Intrinsic glory. It means that the world is sound,
Whatever the sick microbe does. But he too is part of it.

ROBINSON JEFFERS
Carmel Point

The extraordinary patience of things!
This beautiful place defaced with a crop of suburban
    houses –
How beautiful when we first beheld it,
Unbroken field of poppy and lupin walled with clean cliffs;
No intrusion but two or three horses pasturing,
Or a few milch cows rubbing their flanks on the outcrop
    rock-heads –
Now the spoiler has come: does it care?
Not faintly. It has all time. It knows the people are a tide
That swells and in time will ebb, and all
Their works dissolve. Meanwhile the image of the pristine
    beauty
Lives in the very grain of the granite,
Safe as the endless ocean that climbs our cliff. – As for us:
We must uncenter our minds from ourselves;
We must unhumanise our views a little, and become
    confident
As the rock and ocean that we were made from.

■ **Robinson Jeffers** (1887-1962) was born in Pittsburgh, Pennsylvania. His family moved to California in 1903, where he studied medicine, forestry and literature. In 1914 he visited Carmel on the Big Sur coast in central California, and knew that it was his 'inevitable place'.

Inspired by Thoor Ballylee, W.B. Yeats's tower in Ireland (which he later visited three times without ever meeting Yeats), Jeffers worked with a stonemason to build his own house and adjacent tower on the edge of the Pacific using granite boulders collected from the beach below. Jeffers's Tor House in Carmel is now a national historic monument.

In her essay 'Landscape and Self in Yeats and Jeffers', Deborah Fleming argues that both poets 'were able to realise their artistic aims by locating their work in specific landscapes through which they could in part establish their poetic identities. [...] Although it was Jeffers's purpose to describe landscape apart from the human to emphasise his belief in separation of the land itself from the anthropomorphic vision of it, there can be no doubt that the Big Sur coast and its human as well as geologic history empowered Jeffers not only to create but to sustain his poetic vision. [...] For Jeffers, the earth is greater and more beautiful than all human tragedy. Thus, whereas Yeats turned to landscape to create a new literary tradition for Ireland, Jeffers celebrated the earth primarily.'

Jeffers's poetry and aesthetic have divided critical opinion:

X.J. Kennedy/Dana Gioia: 'Jeffers's poetry reflects his closeness to nature that made up his daily life. His philosophy of "inhumanism" refused to put mankind above the rest of nature; he demanded that humanity see itself as part of the vast interdependent reality of nature – a message that made his poetry esteemed by environmentalists.'

Michael Schmidt: 'Jeffers has staunch partisans who present him as a prototypical ecopoet. Certainly the politics that follow from his vision accentuate some of the human risks of Green ideology. [...] The natural world of Ted Hughes is not far from Jeffers [...] he is one of the reactionary, anti-Modernist poles of American poetry.'

David Morris: 'In an age of global warming and looming environmental catastrophe, Jeffers's vision is more relevant and important than ever.'

John Elder: 'Robinson Jeffers is one of the most important precursors of contemporary nature poetry, especially in his radical critique of Western civilisation. [...] The human capacity for subduing nature seemed to Jeffers, as to many who have lived along his beautiful coast, to have a frightening momentum. He came to view humanity in the collective as antagonistic to the wild beauty which he loved. In his poetry, as in the wilderness ethic which he so influenced, Jeffers thus called for a protective separation between man and nature, rather than striving like Wordsworth for a balance.'

RAINER MARIA RILKE
The Eighth Duino Elegy
translated from the German by Stephen Mitchell

With all its eyes the natural world looks out
into the Open. Only *our* eyes are turned
backward, and surround plant, animal, child
like traps, as they emerge into their freedom.
We know what is really out there only from
the animal's gaze; for we take the very young
child and force it around, so that it sees
objects – not the Open, which is so
deep in animals' faces. Free from death.
We, only, can see death; the free animal
has its decline in back of it, forever,
and God in front, and when it moves, it moves
already in eternity, like a fountain.

    Never, not for a single day, do *we* have
before us that pure space into which flowers
endlessly open. Always there is World
and never Nowhere without the No: that pure
unseparated element which one breathes
without desire and endlessly *knows*. A child
may wander there for hours, through the timeless
stillness, may get lost in it and be
shaken back. Or someone, dies and *is* it.
For, nearing death, one doesn't see death; but stares
beyond, perhaps with an animal's vast gaze.
Lovers, if the beloved were not there
blocking the view, are close to it, and marvel…
As if by some mistake, it opens for them
behind each other… But neither can move past
the other, and it changes back to World.

Forever turned toward objects, we see in them
the mere reflection of the realm of freedom,
which we have dimmed. Or when some animal
mutely, serenely, looks us through and through.
That is what fate means: to be opposite,
to be opposite and nothing else, forever.
If the animal moving toward us so securely

in a different direction had our kind of
consciousness –, it would wrench us around and drag us
along its path. But it feels its life as boundless,
unfathomable, and without regard
to its own condition: pure, like its outward gaze.
And where we see the future, it sees all time
and itself within all time, forever healed.

Yet in the alert, warm animal there lies
the pain and burden of an enormous sadness.
For it too feels the presence of what often
overwhelms us: a memory, as if
the element we keep pressing toward was once
more intimate, more true, and our communion
infinitely tender. Here all is distance;
there it was breath. After that first home,
the second seems ambiguous and drafty.
    Oh bliss of the *tiny* creature which remains
forever inside the womb that was its shelter;
joy of the gnat which, still *within*, leaps up
even at its marriage: for everything is womb.
And look at the half-assurance of the bird,
which knows both inner and outer, from its source,
as if it were the soul of an Etruscan,
flown out of a dead man received inside a space,
but with his reclining image as the lid.

And how bewildered is any womb-born creature
that has to fly. As if terrified and fleeing
from itself, it zigzags through the air, the way
a crack runs through a teacup. So the bat
quivers across the porcelain of evening.

And we: spectators, always, everywhere,
turned toward the world of objects, never outward.
It fills us. We arrange it. It breaks down.
We rearrange it, then break down ourselves.
Who has twisted us around like this, so that
no matter what we do, we are in the posture
of someone going away? Just as, upon
the farthest hill, which shows him his whole valley
one last time, he turns, stops, lingers –,
so we live here, forever taking leave.

DON PATERSON

from Orpheus: A Version of Rilke's
Die Sonette an Orpheus

Taste

Gooseberry, banana, pear
and apple, all the ripenesses...
Read it in the child's face:
the life-and-death the tongue hears

as she eats... This comes from far away.
What is happening to your mouth?
Where there were words, discovery
flows, all shocked out of the pith –

What we call *apple*... Do you dare
give it a name? This sweet-sharp fire
rising in the taste, to grow

clarified, awake, twin-sensed,
of the sun and earth, the here and the now –
the sensual joy, the whole Immense!

The Dead

Our business is with fruit and leaf and bloom.
Though they speak with more than just the season's
    tongue –
the colours that they blaze from the dark loam
all have something of the jealous tang

of the dead about them. What do we know of their part
in this, those secret brothers of the harrow,
invigorators of the soil – oiling the dirt
so liberally with their essence, their black marrow?

But here's the question: are the flower and fruit
held out to us in love, or merely thrust
up at us, their masters, like a fist?

Or are *they* the lords, asleep amongst the roots,
granting to us in their great largesse
this hybrid thing – part brute force, part mute kiss?

Dog

My dumb friend... You are so alone
because of us, each word and sign
we use to make this world our own –
the fraction that we should decline.

But can we point towards a scent?
You know the powers that threaten us.
You bark out when the dead are present;
you shrink back from the spell and curse.

These broken views we must pretend
form the whole and not the part.
Helping you will be difficult

and never plant me in your heart –
I'd grow too fast. But I'd guide his hand,
saying: *Here. This is Esau in his pelt.*

Cycles

Today, if you listen, you can hear the rough breath
of the early harrows, the human rhythm sing
in the deep ingathered stillness of the earth,
the strong Earth rising in its early Spring...

The word is old, but never seems outdated
and every year arrives like something new,
though it has come so often. Always anticipated,
though not once did you catch it. It caught you.

Even the old leaves of the wintered oak
seem, in this late light, some future hue.
The winds exchange a word in their own tongue.

The leafless trees are black, and yet the horse-dung
heaped up in the fields, a richer black.
Each hour grows younger as it passes through.

Being

Silent comrade of the distances,
know that space dilates with your own breath;
ring out, as a bell into the Earth
from the dark rafters of its own high place –

then watch what feeds on you grow strong again.
Learn the transformations through and through:
what in your life has most tormented you?
If the water's sour, turn it into wine.

Our senses cannot fathom this night, so
be the meaning of their strange encounter;
at their crossing, be the radiant centre.

And should the world itself forget your name
say this to the still earth: *I flow.*
Say this to the quick stream: *I am.*

■ The poetry of **Rainer Maria Rilke** (1875-1926) addresses questions of how to live and relate to the world in a voice simultaneously prophetic and intensely personal. Most of his major work was written in German, including the *Duino Elegies* and *Sonnets to Orpheus*. Born in Prague, he lived in France from 1902 and then Switzerland from 1919 until his death.

The **Duino Elegies** take their name from the Duino Castle on the Adriatic Sea, where he spent the winter of 1911-12 and wrote the first two Elegies; the Third and most of the Sixth came a year later, and the Fourth in 1915. Then, after years of excruciating patience, the other Elegies, including the Eighth, came to him in a few days in February 1922 at the freezing cold Château de Muzot in the Rhône valley near Sierre in Switzerland. In that same extraordinary month Rilke wrote all 55 of the *Sonnets to Orpheus*. The Duino Elegies were Rilke's response to the transience of all earthly things: 'Affirmation of *life-AND-death* turns out to be one in the Elegies. [...] It is our task to imprint this temporary perishable earth into ourselves so deeply, so painfully and passionately, that its essence can rise again, "invisibly", inside us. We are the bees of the invisible. We wildly collect the honey of the visible, to store it in the great golden hive of the invisible. The Elegies show us at this work, the work of continual conversion of the beloved and tangible world into the invisible vibrations and agitation of our own nature [...] Elegies and Sonnets support each other constantly –, and I consider it an infinite grace that, with the same breath, I was permitted to fill both these sails: the little rust-coloured sail of the Sonnets and the Elegies' gigantic white canvas.' (Letter to Witold Hulewicz, 13 November 1925)

Jonathan Bate offers this gloss on the letter: 'With this ambition Rilke remains in the mainstream of Romanticism. The language of unification and transformation, the yoking of earth and consciousness, the divinisation of the imminent world as against a withdrawal to a transcendent realm: these are all the moves which Wordsworth made in '**Tintern Abbey**'. [➢ 29] [...] But as in a Romantic meditation on mortality such as Keats's '**To Autumn**' [➢ 151], the purpose is not to elevate "naive" modes of being over thoughtful ones but rather to seek to reconcile the two. [...] For Rilke, precisely because nature is so vulnerable as we are, because the earth shares our provisionality, we must be attuned to nature, we must not "run down and degrade" all that is here and now. The things of the earth must be our "familiars", as they were for our ancestors.

Rilke's **Sonnets to Orpheus** draw on the myth of Orpheus, who could tame wild beasts with his music. Failing to bring his bride Eurydice back from the underworld, he was killed and dismembered by the Maenads, with his singing head and still-sounding lyre surviving in some versions of the legend.

The Sonnets sound 'a terrible warning', says Don Paterson: 'Any animal which develops, as a by-product of its blind evolution, an inwardly-reflected self-image [...] might also have reached a fatal evolutionary impasse. It becomes lost in its dream, being essentially the infinite extension of its technological instinct, which we have seen grow from flinthead to cityscape. That is to say: everywhere we look, we see the world purely in the highly restricted synecdoche of its human *use*. [...] We are then in danger of blithely or accidentally destroying our *real* element and habitat, with which we no longer feel any physical continuity. [...] No one could mistake the timeliness of Rilke's call to confront our own nature, to address our own endangered species [...] How in heaven's name are we to live, now the soul we have bred into ourselves no longer has a heaven to ascend to? The word *Earth* is the Sonnets' heartbeat, and is offered as an answer in itself.'

Don Paterson (*b.* 1963) is a Scottish poet, musician and editor whose sharply contemporary work skilfully blends traditional and postmodern styles. As well as *Orpheus* (2006), his books include *Nil Nil* (1993), *God's Gift to Women* (1997), *The Eyes: a version of Antonio Machado* (1999), *Landing Light* (2003) and *The Book of Shadows* (2004).

2. CHANGING THE LANDSCAPE

Changes in agriculture in modern times have resulted in the wholesale destruction of habitats, and the consequent loss or extinction of many species. In the 18th century, the Enclosure Movement caused radical changes not just in the landscape but to ordinary people's lives, both witnessed by **John Clare**.

Enclosure meant consolidating scattered pieces of land formerly held in strips by villagers into separate farms each owned by one farmer, who could then divide his land into fields enclosed by fences, hedges or ditches. Aristocratic landowners wanting to adopt new farming technology and systems of crop rotation used an Act of Parliament to force the agrarian poor off the old "village commons", which then became "enclosed" as private property. Common rights had included not just the right of grazing cattle or sheep, but also the grazing of geese (as in the second poem by **William Barnes**), foraging for pigs, gleaning, berrying and fuel gathering. Many people who had previously lived off the land were now forced into the towns and cities, where they became the working class of the Industrial Revolution; others sought passage to a new life in the New World. Rural depopulation resulted in whole villages being deserted. Industrialisation and urban living eroded people's connectedness with nature and the seasonal cycles. The rich language of daily life was impoverished by these changes; regional dialects went into gradual decline.

■ **Oliver Goldsmith** (?1730-74), playwright, poet, novelist and essayist, is best-known for his novel *The Vicar of Wakefield* (1766) and his play *She Stoops to Conquer* (1773). The son of a clergyman, he grew up in an Anglo-Irish Protestant household, spending much of his childhood in Lissoy, Co. Westmeath. His poem **The Deserted Village** (1770) is a lament for the loss of a whole way of life. Auburn has been associated with Lissoy, but the picture of Auburn is a composite one, drawn from his experience of both Ireland and England.

Terry Gifford (1995): 'Oliver Goldsmith wrote *The Deserted Village* in order to engage with the pressures of his own particular place and time. Enclosure of the commons and the consequent depopulation of the villages was taking place in England as well as Ireland in the mid-18th century. [...] There is a new callousness behind the new commercial approach to agriculture [...] the supplanting of village values by the culture of exploitation.'

OLIVER GOLDSMITH
from The Deserted Village

Sweet smiling village, loveliest of the lawn,
Thy sports are fled, and all thy charms withdrawn;
Amidst thy bowers the tyrant's hand is seen,
And desolation saddens all thy green:
One only master grasps the whole domain,
And half a tillage stints thy smiling plain;
No more thy glassy brook reflects the day,
But choked with sedges, works its weedy way.
Along thy glades, a solitary guest,
The hollow sounding bittern guards its nest;
Amidst thy desert walks the lapwing flies,
And tires their echoes with unvaried cries.
Sunk are thy bowers in shapeless ruin all,
And the long grass o'ertops the mouldering wall,
And trembling, shrinking from the spoiler's hand,
Far, far away thy children leave the land.

Ill fares the land, to hastening ills a prey,
Where wealth accumulates, and men decay;
Princes and lords may flourish, or may fade;
A breath can make them, as a breath has made.
But a bold peasantry, their country's pride,
When once destroyed, can never be supplied.

A time there was, ere England's griefs began,
When every rood of ground maintained its man;
For him light labour spread her wholesome store,
Just gave what life required, but gave no more.
His best companions, innocence and health;
And his best riches, ignorance of wealth.

But times are altered; trade's unfeeling train
Usurp the land and dispossess the swain;
Along the lawn, where scattered hamlets rose,
Unwieldy wealth, and cumbrous pomp repose,
And every want to opulence allied,
And every pang that folly pays to pride.
These gentle hours that plenty bade to bloom,
Those calm desires that asked but little room,

Those healthful sports that graced the peaceful scene,
Lived in each look, and brightened all the green;
These far departing seek a kinder shore,
And rural mirth and manners are no more.

Sweet Auburn! parent of the blissful hour,
Thy glades forlorn confess the tyrant's power.
Here as I take my solitary rounds,
Amidst thy tangling walks, and ruined grounds,
And, many a year elapsed, return to view
Where once the cottage stood, the hawthorn grew,
Here, as with doubtful, pensive steps I range,
Trace every scene, and wonder at the change,
Remembrance wakes with all her busy train,
Swells at my breast, and turns the past to pain. [...]

Ye friends to truth, ye statesmen who survey
The rich man's joys increase, the poor's decay,
'Tis yours to judge, how wide the limits stand
Between a splendid and an happy land.
Proud swells the tide with loads of freighted ore,
And shouting Folly hails them from her shore;
Hoards, even beyond the miser's wish abound,
And rich men flock from all the world around.
Yet count our gains. This wealth is but a name
That leaves our useful products still the same.
Not so the loss. The man of wealth and pride,
Takes up a space that many poor supplied;
Space for his lake, his park's extended bounds,
Space for his horses, equipage, and hounds;
The robe that wraps his limbs in silken sloth,
Has robbed the neighbouring fields of half their growth;
His seat, where solitary sports are seen,
Indignant spurns the cottage from the green;
Around the world each needful product flies,
For all the luxuries the world supplies.
While thus the land adorned for pleasure all
In barren splendour feebly waits the fall. [...]

Thus fares the land, by luxury betrayed,
In nature's simplest charms at first arrayed,
But verging to decline, its splendours rise,
Its vistas strike, its palaces surprise;

While scourged by famine from the smiling land,
The mournful peasant leads his humble band;
And while he sinks without one arm to save,
The country blooms – a garden, and a grave.

Where then, ah, where shall poverty reside,
To scape the pressure of contiguous pride;
If to some common's fenceless limits strayed,
He drives his flock to pick the scanty blade,
Those fenceless fields the sons of wealth divide,
Even the bare-worn common is denied. [...]

Oh luxury! Thou curst by heaven's decree,
How ill exchanged are things like these for thee!
How do thy potions with insidious joy,
Diffuse their pleasures only to destroy!
Kingdoms by thee, to sickly greatness grown,
Boast of a florid vigour not their own.
At every draught more large and large they grow,
A bloated mass of rank unwieldy woe;
Till sapped their strength, and every part unsound,
Down, down they sink, and spread a ruin round.

Even now the devastation is begun,
And half the business of destruction done;
Even now, methinks, as pondering here I stand,
I see the rural virtues leave the land. [...]

WILLIAM COWPER
The Poplar-Field

The poplars are felled, farewell to the shade
And the whispering sound of the cool colonnade,
The winds play no longer and sing in the leaves,
Nor Ouse on his bosom their image receives.

Twelve years have elapsed since I last took a view
Of my favourite field, and the bank where they grew,
And now in the grass behold they are laid,
And the tree is my seat that once lent me a shade.

The blackbird has fled to another retreat
Where the hazels afford him a screen from the heat,
And the scene where his melody charmed me before,
Resounds with his sweet-flowing ditty no more.

My fugitive years are all hasting away,
And I must e're long lie as lowly as they,
With a turf on my breast and a stone on my head,
E're another such grove shall arise in its stead.

'Tis a sight to engage me, if anything can
To muse on the perishing pleasures of Man;
Though his life be a dream, his enjoyments, I see,
Have a Being less durable even than he.

■ **William Cowper** (1731-1800) was an English poet (pronounced *Cooper*) who spent much of his life trying to cope with recurrent bouts of depression, helped by a wide circle of friends who cared for his welfare, including Mary Unwin, the widow of a clergyman friend. In 1767 they settled at Olney in Buckinghamshire, where he wrote '**The Poplar-Field**' (in 1784) and his long poem *The Task* (1785), before moving to nearby Weston Underwood in 1786. After Mary's death in 1794, he became a physical and mental invalid, writing 'The Castaway' shortly before his death. Cowper addressed simple human and rural themes in his poetry, his sympathetic feeling for nature presaging the Romanticism of the next century.

In *The Song of the Earth*, Jonathan Bate describes how Jane Austen and William Cowper were both sceptical of the "improving" activities of the new landowners. In *The Task* – Austen's favourite poem – Cowper attacks 'Capability' Brown for 'altering houses and landscapes that had for generations been integrated with their local environment', while in *Mansfield Park* (1814) Fanny Price quotes Cowper on hearing 'that an avenue of trees must come down in the name of Mr Rushworth's improvement of his estate, a result of his faddish obsession with the landscape designs of Humphrey Repton'. The line she quotes – 'Ye fallen avenues, once more I mourn your fate unmerited' – is from a passage in Cowper's poem 'concerning Sir John Throckmorton's enclosure and improvement of his estate at Weston Underwood [...] "The Poplar-Field", one of Cowper's best-known lyrics [...] was a further lament occasioned by the gentleman improver's changes to his local environment.'

JOHN CLARE
The Moors

Far spread the moory ground, a level scene
Bespread with rush and one eternal green
That never felt the rage of blundering plough
Though centuries wreathed spring's blossoms on its brow,
Still meeting plains that stretched them far away
In unchecked shadows of green, brown and grey.
Unbounded freedom ruled the wandering scene
Nor fence of ownership crept in between
To hide the prospect of the following eye –
Its only bondage was the circling sky.
One mighty flat undwarfed by bush and tree
Spread its faint shadow of immensity
And lost itself, which seemed to eke its bounds,
In the blue mist the horizon's edge surrounds.
Now this sweet vision of my boyish hours,
Free as spring clouds and wild as summer flowers,
Is faded all – a hope that blossomed free,
And hath been once, no more shall ever be.
Enclosure came and trampled on the grave
Of labour's rights and left the poor a slave,
And memory's pride, ere want to wealth did bow,
Is both the shadow and the substance now.
The sheep and cows were free to range as then
Where change might prompt, nor felt the bonds of men:
Cows went and came with evening, morn and night
To the wild pasture as their common right,
And sheep unfolded with the rising sun
Heard the swains shout and felt their freedom won,
Tracked the red fallow field and heath and plain,
Then met the brook and drank and roamed again –
The brook that dribbled on as clear as glass
Beneath the roots they hid among the grass –
While the glad shepherd traced their tracks along,
Free as the lark and happy as her song.
But now all's fled and flats of many a dye
That seemed to lengthen with the following eye,
Moors losing from the sight, far, smooth and blea,
Where swopt the plover in its pleasure free,

Are vanished now with commons wild and gay
As poets' visions of life's early day.
Mulberry bushes where the boy would run
To fill his hands with fruit are grubbed and done,
And hedgerow briars – flower-lovers overjoyed
Came and got flower pots – these are all destroyed,
And sky-bound moors in mangled garbs are left
Like mighty giants of their limbs bereft.
Fence now meets fence in owners' little bounds
Of field and meadow, large as garden grounds,
In little parcels little minds to please
With men and flocks imprisoned, ill at ease.
Each little path that led its pleasant way
As sweet as morning leading night astray,
Where little flowers bloomed round, a varied host,
That Travel felt delighted to be lost
Nor grudged the steps that he had ta'en as vain
When right roads traced his journey's end again;
Nay on a broken tree he'd sit awhile
To see the moors and fields and meadows smile,
Sometimes with cowslips smothered – then all white
With daisies – then the summers splendid sight
Of corn fields crimson o'er, the "headache" bloomed
Like splendid armies for the battle plumed;
He gazed upon them with wild fancy's eye
As fallen landscapes from an evening sky.
These paths are stopped – the rude philistine's thrall
Is laid upon them and destroyed them all.
Each little tyrant with his little sign
Shows where man claims, earth glows no more divine.
On paths to freedom and to childhood dear
A board sticks up to notice 'no road here'
And on the tree with ivy overhung
The hated sign by vulgar taste is hung
As though the very birds should learn to know
When they go there they must no further go.
Thus, with the poor, scared freedom bade goodbye
And much they feel it in the smothered sigh,
And birds and trees and flowers without a name
All sighed when lawless law's enclosure came,
And dreams of plunder in such rebel schemes
Have found too truly that they were but dreams.

JOHN CLARE
Round Oak and Eastwell

In my own native field two fountains run
All desolate and naked to the sun;
The fell destroyer's hand hath reft their side
Of every tree that hid and beautified
Their shallow waters in delightful clumps,
That sunburnt now o'er pebbles skips and jumps.
One where stone quarries in its hills are broke
Still keeps its ancient pastoral name, Round Oak.
Although one little solitary tree
Is all that's left of its old pedigree;
The other, more deformed, creeps down the dell,
Scarcely the shade of what was once Eastwell,
While the elm-groves that groaned beneath no tax
Have paid their tribute to the lawless axe,
And the old rooks that waited other springs
Have fled to stranger scenes on startled wings.
The place all lonely and all naked lies,
And Eastwell spring in change's symphonies
Boils up its sound unnoticed and alone,
To all its former happiness unknown,
Its glory gone, its Sunday pastimes o'er,
The haunts of shepherds and of maids no more.
The passer-by unheeding tramples on
Nor heeds the spring, nor trees nor bushes gone,
While the stray poet's memory haunts the spot
Like a friend's features time hath nigh forgot.

■ **John Clare** (1793-1864) was born in Northamptonshire, where he worked as an agricultural labourer. Celebrated during the 1820s by literary London as "the peasant poet", he published four books of poetry between 1820 and 1835. Clare felt alienated by a series of losses: of his first love, of his native village of Helpston after moving three miles away, of a childhood landscape changed after landowners enclosed the common lands after a local enclosure Act was passed in 1809. He suffered from severe depression, and in 1837 was certified insane and spent most of the rest of his life in asylums, where he continued to write. His work was neglected for over a century, and Clare has only recently received full recognition as one of the great English poets of the Romantic period. Many of his poems bear witness to how the English countryside was carved up in the early part of the 19th century, and to the effects of this on the wildlife, land and people, as he writes in **'The Moors'**: 'Enclosure came and trampled on the grave / Of labour's rights and left the poor a slave.'

Clare's reputation has suffered from the modern perception that nature poetry is irrelevant to people living in today's predominantly urban society, a fallacy reinforced by literary theorists who argued – as Jonathan Bate has written – 'that the bond with nature is forged in a retreat from social commitment, that it is a symptom of middle-class escapism'. Bate refutes this in *The Song of the Earth*: 'For Clare, the most authentically "working-class" of all major English poets, social relations and environmental relations were not set in opposition to each other in this way. He viewed "the rights of man" and the "rights of nature" as co-extensive and co-dependent.'

In 'The Moors', writes Bate, 'enclosure is imagined as an impediment to dwelling in the world. The "littleness" is not that of miniature, but of the mean and grasping mind that encloses for the sake of economic gain. The birds are presented as victims of such minds every bit as much as the poor. The sign of the property-owner blocks the road to the freedom of the common land and in so doing also changes the configuration of the poet's mental space, severing the memory's way back to childhood. The two Rousseauesque states of nature – childhood and a relationship to the land that is anterior to the proprietorial – are simultaneously foreclosed.' [Other poem ➤ 136]

WILLIAM BARNES
The Leäne

They do zay that a travellen chap
  Have a-put in the newspeäper now,
That the bit o' green ground on the knap
  Should be all a-took in vor the plough.
He do fancy 'tis easy to show
  That we can be but stunpolls at best,
Vor to leäve a green spot where a flower can grow,
  Or a voot-weary walker mid rest.
'Tis hedge-grubben, Thomas, an' ledge-grubben,
    Never a-done
While a sov'ren mwore's to be won.

The road, he do zay, is so wide
  As 'tis wanted vor travellers' wheels,
As if all that did travel did ride
  An' did never get galls on their heels.
He would leäve sich a thin strip o' groun',
  That, if a man's veet in his shoes
Wer a-burnen an' zore, why he coulden zit down
  But the wheels would run over his tooes.
Vor 'tis meäke money, Thomas, an' teäke money,
    What's zwold an' bought
Is all that is worthy o' thought.

Years agoo the leäne-zides did bear grass,
  Vor to pull wi' the geeses' red bills,
That did hiss at the vo'k that did pass,
  Or the bwoys that pick'd up their white quills.
But shortly, if vower or vive
  Ov our goslens do creep vrom the agg,
They must mwope in the gearden, mwore dead than alive,
  In a coop, or a-tied by the lag.
Vor to catch at land, Thomas, an' snatch at land,
    Now is the plan;
Meäke money wherever you can.

The childern wull soon have noo pleäce
  Vor to play in, an' if they do grow,
They wull have a thin musheroom feäce,
  Wi' their bodies so sumple as dough.
But a man is a-meäde ov a child,
  An' his limbs do grow worksome by plaÿ;
An' if the young child's little body's a-spweil'd,
  Why, the man's wull the sooner decaÿ.
But wealth is wo'th now mwore than health is wo'th;
    Let it all goo,
If't 'ull bring but a sov'ren or two.

Vor to breed the young fox or the heäre,
  We can gi'e up whole eäcres o' ground,
But the greens be a-grudg'd, vor to rear
  Our young childern up healthy an' sound;
Why, there woon't be a-left the next age
  A green spot where their veet can goo free;
An' the goocoo wull soon be committed to cage

Vor a trespass in zomebody's tree.
Vor 'tis locken up, Thomas, an' blocken up,
        Stranger or brother,
Men mussen come nigh woone another.

Woone day I went in at a geäte,
  Wi' my child, where an echo did sound,
An' the owner came up, an' did reäte
  Me as if I would car off his ground.
But his vield an' the grass wer a-let,
  An' the damage that he could a-took
Wer at mwost that the while I did open the geäte
  I did rub roun' the eye on the hook.
But 'tis drevèn out, Thomas, an' heven out.
        Trample noo grounds,
Unless you be after the hounds.

Ah! the Squier a' Culver-dell Hall
  Wer as diff'rent as light is vrom dark,
Wi' zome vo'k that, as evenen did vail,
  Had a-broke drough long grass in his park;
Vor he went, wi' a smile, vor to meet
  Wi' the trespassers while they did pass,
An' he zaid, 'I do fear you'll catch cwold in your veet,
  You've a-walk'd drough so much o' my grass.'
His mild words, Thomas, cut em like swords, Thomas,
        Newly a-whet,
An' went vurder wi' them than a dreat.

WILLIAM BARNES
Eclogue: The Common A-Took In
Thomas an' John

THOMAS
  Good morn t'ye, John. How b'ye? how b'ye?
  Zoo you be gwaïn to market, I do zee.
  Why, you be quite a-lwoaded wi' your geese.

JOHN
  Ees, Thomas, ees.
  Why, I'm a-getten rid ov ev'ry goose
  An' goslen I've a-got: an' what is woose,
  I fear that I must zell my little cow.

THOMAS
  How zoo, then, John? Why, what's the matter now?
  What, can't ye get along? B'ye run a-ground?
  An' can't paÿ twenty shillens vor a pound?
  What, can't ye put a lwoaf on shelf?

JOHN
                Ees, now;
  But I do fear I shan't 'ithout my cow.
  No; they do meän to teäke the moor in, I do hear,
  An' 'twill be soon begun upon;
  Zoo I must zell my bit o' stock to-year,
  Because they woon't have any groun' to run upon.

THOMAS
  Why, what d'ye tell o'? I be very zorry
  To hear what they be gwaïn about;
  But yet I s'pose there'll be a 'lotment vor ye,
  When they do come to mark it out.

JOHN
  No; not vor me, I fear. An' if there should,
  Why 'twoulden be so handy as 'tis now;
  Vor 'tis the common that do do me good,
  The run vor my vew geese, or vor my cow.

THOMAS
  Ees, that's the job; why 'tis a handy thing
  To have a bit o' common, I do know,
  To put a little cow upon in Spring,
  The while woone's bit ov orcha'd grass do grow.

JOHN
  Aye, that's the thing, you zee. Now I do mow
  My bit o' grass, an' meäke a little rick;
  An' in the zummer, while do grow,
  My cow do run in common vor to pick
  A bleäde or two o' grass, if she can vind em,
  Vor tother cattle don't leäve much behind em.
  Zoo in the evenen, we do put a lock
  O' nice fresh grass avore the wicket;
  An' she do come at vive or zix o'clock,
  As constant as the zun, to pick it.
  An' then, bezides the cow, why we do let
  Our geese run out among the emmet hills;
  An' then when we do pluck em, we do get

Vor zeäle zome veathers an' zome quills;
An' in the winter we do fat em well,
An' car em to the market vor to zell
To gentlevo'ks, vor we don't oft avvword
To put a goose a-top ov ouer bwoard;
But we do get our feäst, – vor we be eäble
To clap the giblets up a-top o' teäble.

THOMAS

An' I don't know o' many better things,
Than geese's heads and gizzards, lags an' wings.

JOHN

An' then, when I ha' nothen else to do,
Why I can teake my hook an' gloves, an' goo
To cut a lot o' vuzz and briars
Vor heten ovens, or vor lighten viers.
An' when the childern be too young to eärn
A penny, they can g'out in zunny weather,
An' run about, an' get together
A bag o' cow-dung vor to burn.

THOMAS

'Tis handy to live near a common;
But I've a-zeed, an' I've a-zaid,
That if a poor man got a bit o'bread,
They'll try to teäke it vrom en.
But I wer twold back tother day,
That they be got into a way
O' letten bits o' groun out to the poor.

JOHN

Well, I do hope 'tis true, I'm sure;
An' I do hope that they will do it here,
Or I must goo to workhouse, I do fear.

GLOSSARY: *avvword*: afford; *car*: to carry; *drough*: through; *emmet*: ant; *geäte*: gate; *goo*: go; *goocoo*: cuckoo; *gwaïn*: going; *knap*: hillock; *lag*: leg; *leäne*: lane; *stunpolls*: blockheads; *sumple*: supple; *veet*: feet; *vo'k*: folk; *vor*: for; *vuzz*: furze; *zoo*: so.

■ **William Barnes** (1801-86) grew up in the Vale of Blackmore in Dorset. A self-taught linguist and scholar, he worked as a schoolmaster for 40 years, and was then priest of a parish near Dorchester for the last 24 years of his life. His neighbour Thomas Hardy knew him as 'an aged clergyman,

quaintly attired in caped cloak, knee-breeches, and buckled shoes, with a leather satchel slung over his shoulders, and a stout staff in his hand', who went on his rounds accompanied by a little grey dog. Hopkins called him 'a perfect artist. It is as if Dorset life and Dorset landscape had taken flesh and blood in this man.' His poetry is set in a rural Dorset threatened by enclosure, the background to the two poems printed here.

Barnes wrote his best work in Dorset dialect: 'I cannot help it. It is my mother tongue, and is to my mind the only true speech of the life that I draw.' (Preface to *Poems of Rural Life, in the Dorset Dialect, Third Collection*, 1862)

Robert Nye: 'Barnes, philologist as well a poet, was in search of a shape within English which could contain as much as the Doric within Greek. It appears, indeed, that he took the *Idyllia* of Theocritus quite consciously as an example. [...] Barnes looked for it through the rhythms he associated with the language of his childhood, and the tangy speech of Blackmore Vale. [...] His deepest thoughts and feelings came to him at one with the first speech sounds he had heard, as a boy in the parish of Sturminster Newton at the start of the 19th century.'

C.H. Sisson on **'The Common A-Took In'**: 'It is the very inflection of ordinary speech, and where else would you look for that in the verse written in England in 1833? It is not in the odd line or two that Barnes has caught it; all the eclogues in his first volume of Dorset poems have it throughout, combined with an utter sureness in the handling of metre.'

Kim Taplin: 'Barnes's English countryside is beautiful, but he also knows how it works. He recognises that it is largely a planted, a maintained beauty, not a timeless, magical place, nor yet a wilderness. In the economy he portrays, trees are for use as well as beauty. The proper management of woodland, including such skills as coppicing, form an integral part of it. [...] Trees could be dangerous, and trees could be crops; but Barnes was appalled by the idea that financial profit should be the sole motive in man's dealings with nature. He wrote against enclosures and encroachment on common land. In his poem "Picken o' Scroff" he deplores the fact that children are no longer allowed to gather brushwood after coppicing, and his protest is against the erosion of one more traditional right of the poor. But characteristically it is also the spiritual value of the beauty of the scene that he laments on their behalf. [...] In his poem "Pity" [...] we are recalled to proper humanity by the reminder that we are "As branches of a livèn tree" and that: "Whatever you've a done to mine / Is all a-done to me." This fact he took to encompass the whole of nature.'

JOHN MONTAGUE
Driving South
(*Epilogue to* The Rough Field)

Driving South, we pass through Cavan,
lakeside orchards in first bloom,
hawthorn with a surplice whiteness,
binding the small holdings of Monaghan.

A changing rural pattern means clack
of tractor for horse, sentinel shape
of silo, hum of milking machine:
the same from Ulster to the Ukraine.

Only a sentimentalist would wish
to see such degradation again:
heavy tasks from spring to harvest;
the sack-cloth pilgrimages under rain

to repair the slabbery gaps of winter
with the labourer hibernating
in his cottage for half the year
to greet the indignity of the Hiring Fair.

Fewer hands, bigger markets, larger farms.
Yet something mourns. The iron-ribbed
lamp flitting through the yard at dark,
the hissing froth, and fodder-scented warmth

of a wood-stalled byre, or leather thong
of flail curling in a barn, were part
of a world where action had been wrung
through painstaking years to ritual.

Acknowledged when the priest blessed
the green-tipped corn, or Protestant
lugged thick turnip, swollen marrow
to robe the kirk for Thanksgiving.

Palmer's softly lit Vale of Shoreham
commemorates it, or Chagall's lovers
floating above a childhood village
remote but friendly as Goldsmith's Auburn –

Our finally lost dream of man at home
in a rural setting! A giant hand,
as we pass by, reaches down
to grasp the fields we gazed upon.

Harsh landscape that haunts me,
well and stone, in the bleak moors of dream
with all my circling a failure to return
to what is already going
                                        going
                                                GONE

■ **John Montague** (*b.* 1929) is an Irish poet, short story writer and memoirist. Born in Brooklyn of Irish parents, he was sent at the age of four to live with his aunts on his grandfather's farm at Garvaghey on the edge of the Clogher Valley in Co. Tyrone. He lived in America and France during the 1950s and 60s before settling in Cork in 1974.

Montague's poems chart boyhood, schooldays, love and relationships. Family and personal history and Ireland's history are prominent themes in his work, notably in his cycle of poems, *The Rough Field* (1972), whose title is an English translation of the Irish *garbh achaidh* or Garvaghey. '**Driving South**' is the epilogue to that sequence, which represents his home place as a microcosm of the Northern Irish "Troubles": their historical origins in oppression and bigotry, and their contemporary horror. While his territory may be local, Montague's themes are universal, and his influences are a cosmopolitan mixture of American, English and European writers as well as the whole Irish literary and oral tradition. He has translated several French poets, including Francis Ponge, Claude Esteban and Guillevic [➤ 143-44].

'Palmer's softly lit Vale of Shoreham': valley near Sevenoaks in Kent, from which the English painter and engraver Samuel Palmer (1806-81), a member of Blake's circle, drew his pastoral idealisation of seasonal village life.

'Goldsmith's Auburn': ➤ *The Deserted Village*, 42.

[Other poems ➤ 50, 87, 114]

3. KILLING THE WILDLIFE

JOHN MONTAGUE
The Last Monster

First, the dodo disappeared,
Leaving a legend of a simpleton's head,
Grotesque nut-cracker nose:
But a rum, a rare old one,
With feathers like old clothes.

The great Auk struck out for St Kilda's,
Settled with shaggy Highlanders,
Skin divers and such:
Learned the language of oblivion,
Finally lost touch.

Gone also, as Goldsmith noted,
The bird of Nazareth and lesser tatou,
Beasts of strange pattern and birds past belief:
Even to number their names, like witchcraft,
Affords sensual relief.

Golden-pawed snowman of Everest,
Wildcat of the Grampians,
Bower-bird of Peru:
Stay hidden wherever you are,
The final inventory is after you!

Somewhere on the ultimate scarp
The last monster will watch
With hooded eyes,
While tiny men trek importantly towards him,
Bristling with strange supplies.

WILLIAM MATTHEWS
Names

Ten kinds of wolf are gone and twelve of rat
and not a single insect species.
Three sorts of skink are history and two
of minnow, two of pupfish, ten of owl.
Seventeen kinds of rail are out of here
and five of finch. It comforts us to think
the dinosaurs bought their farms all at once,
but they died at a rate of one species
per thousand years. Life in a faster lane
erased the speckled dace, the thicktail chub,
two kinds of thrush and six of wren, the heath
hen and Ash Meadows killfish. There are four
kinds of sucker not born any minute
any more. The Christmas Island musk shrew
is defunct. Some places molt and peel so fast
it's a wonder they have any name:
the Chatham Island bellbird flew the coop
as did the Chatham Island fernbird, the
Lord Howe Island fantail and the Lord Howe
Island blackbird. The Utah Lake sculpin,
Arizona jaguar and Puerto
Rican caviomorph, the Vegas Valley
leopard frog and New Caledonian lorikeet?
They've hit the road for which there is no name
a mouth surrounds so well as it did theirs.
The sea mink's crossed the bar and the great auk's
ground time here was brief. Four forms the macaw
took are cancelled checks. Sad Adam fills his lungs
with haunted air, and so does angry Eve:
they meant no name they made up for farewell.
They were just a couple starting out,
a place they could afford, a few laughs,
no champagne but a bottle of rosé.
In fact Adam and Eve are not their names.

■ John Montague ➢ 49.

■ William Matthews ➢ 122.

JAMES DICKEY
For the Last Wolverine

They will soon be down

To one, but he still will be
For a little while   still will be stopping

The flakes in the air with a look,
Surrounding himself with the silence
Of whitening snarls. Let him eat
The last red meal of the condemned

To extinction, tearing the guts

From an elk. Yet that is not enough
For me. I would have him eat

The heart, and, from it, have an idea
Stream into his gnawing head
That he no longer has a thing
To lose, and so can walk

Out into the open, in the full

Pale of the sub-Arctic sun
Where a single spruce tree is dying

Higher and higher. Let him climb it
With all his meanness and strength.
Lord, we have come to the end
Of this kind of vision of heaven,

As the sky breaks open

Its fans around him and shimmers
And into its northern gates he rises

Snarling   complete   in the joy of a weasel
With an elk's horned heart in his stomach
Looking straight into the eternal
Blue, where he hauls his kind. I would have it all

My way: at the top of that tree I place

The New World's last eagle
Hunched in mangy feathers   giving

Up on the theory of flight.
Dear God of the wildness of poetry, let them mate
To the death in the rotten branches,
Let the tree sway and burst into flame

And mingle them, crackling with feathers,

In crownfire. Let something come
Of it   something gigantic   legendary

Rise beyond reason over hills
Of ice   SCREAMING   that it cannot die,
That it has come back, this time
On wings, and will spare no earthly thing:

That it will hover, made purely of northern

Lights, at dusk   and fall
On men building roads: will perch

On the moose's horn like a falcon
Riding into battle   into holy war against
Screaming railroad crews: will pull
Whole traplines like fibers from the snow

In the long-jawed night of fur trappers.

But, small, filthy, unwinged,
You will soon be crouching

Alone, with maybe some dim racial notion
Of being the last, but none of how much
Your unnoticed going will mean:

How much the timid poem needs

The mindless explosion of your rage,

The glutton's internal fire   the elk's
Heart in the belly, sprouting wings,

The pact of the 'blind swallowing
Thing', with himself, to eat

The world, and not to be driven off it
Until it is gone, even if it takes

Forever. I take you as you are

And make of you what I will,
Skunk-bear, carcajou, bloodthirsty

Non-survivor.
           Lord, let me die   but not die
Out.

■ **James Dickey** (1923-97) was an American poet and novelist best-known for his novel *Deliverance* (1970), which was made into a film (for which he wrote the screenplay). A football player and champion hurdler in his youth, he served as a fighter-bomber pilot during the Second World War, logging more than 50 combat flights; rejoined the Air Force in the Korean War; and later worked as an advertising copywriter. He taught at the University of South Carolina from 1969 to 1997, and died four days after giving his last class. His poetry often features pilots, football players and backwoodsmen, with themes including nature, metaphysics, history and religion.

MARGARET ATWOOD
Elegy for the Giant Tortoises

Let others pray for the passenger pigeon
the dodo, the whooping crane, the eskimo:
everyone must specialise

I will confine myself to a meditation
upon the giant tortoises
withering finally on a remote island.

I concentrate in subway stations,
in parks, I can't quite see them,
they move to the peripheries of my eyes

but on the last day they will be there;
already the event
like a wave travelling shapes vision;

on the road where I stand they will materialise,
plodding past me in a straggling line
awkward without water

their small heads pondering
from side to side, their useless armour
sadder than tanks and history,

in their closed gaze ocean and sunlight paralysed,
lumbering up the steps, under the archways
toward the square glass altars

where the brittle gods are kept,
the relics of what we have destroyed,
our holy and obsolete symbols.

■ **Margaret Atwood** (*b.* 1939) is Canada's leading poet and novelist. Her fiction and poetry, 'at once comic and grim, often deal with alienation and the destructiveness of human relationships' (Kennedy & Gioia), but she has always concerned herself with nature, notably in her novel *Surfacing* (1972), in which a woman rediscovers herself in the wilderness, and in all her poetry collections. Her father was an entomologist, and brought home samples for his nature-loving daughter; she later studied chemistry, biology and zoology, and told one interviewer that 'if I hadn't been a writer I'd have gone on with that' (*Conversations*, 1990).

Richard Hunt: 'Atwood is far from anthropocentric in much of her nature poetry [...] she is often highly attentive to environmental issues [...] from the exploitation of resources and animal rights in the earliest work to environmental degradation and species extinction in more recent poems.'
[Other poems ➤ 70, 162]

■ **Fleur Adcock** (*b.* 1934) emigrated from New Zealand to Britain in 1963, having spent parts of a wartime childhood in rural England. She writes about men and women, childhood, identity, roots and rootlessness, memory and loss, animals and dreams, as well as our interactions with nature and place. Her poised, ironic poems are remarkable for their wry wit, conversational tone and psychological insight, unmasking the deceptions of love or unravelling family lives.
[Other poem ➤ 198]

■ **David Constantine** ➤ 237.

FLEUR ADCOCK
The Last Moa

Somewhere in the bush, the last moa
is not still lingering in some hidden valley.
She is not stretching her swanlike neck
(but longer, more massive than any swan's)
for a high cluster of miro berries,
or grubbing up fern roots with her beak.

Alice McKenzie didn't see her
among the sandhills at Martin's Bay
in 1880 – a large blue bird
as tall as herself, which turned and chased her.
Moas were taller than seven-year-old
pioneer children; moas weren't blue.

Twenty or thirty distinct species –
all of them, even the small bush moa,
taller than Alice – and none of their bones
carbon-dated to less than five centuries.
The sad, affronted mummified head
in the museum is as old as a Pharoah.

Not the last moa, that; but neither
was Alice's harshly grunting pursuer.
Possibly Alice met a takahe,
the extinct bird that rose from extinction
in 1948, near Te Anau.
No late reprieve, though, for the moa.

Her thigh-bones, longer than a giraffe's,
are lying steeped in a swamp, or smashed
in a midden, with her unstrung vertebrae.
Our predecessors hunted and ate her,
gobbled her up: as we'd have done
in their place; as we're gobbling the world.

DAVID CONSTANTINE
Endangered Species

No wonder we love the whales. Do they not carry
Our warm blood below and we remember
Falling asleep in a feeling element
And our voices beating a musical way

To a larger kindred, around the world? Mostly
We wake too quickly, the sleep runs off our heads
And we are employed at once in the usual
Coveting and schemes. I was luckier today

And remembered leaving a house in the Dales
Like home for a night, the four under one roof,
I left them sleeping without a moon or stars
And followed my dreaming self along a road.

Daylight augmented in a fine rain.
I had the sensation of dawning on my face.
But for the animals (and they had gathered
The dark standing in fields and now appeared

Replete) the night dissolved, but in the light,
A grey-eyed light, under the draining hills
Some pools of woodland remained and in them owls
And beside my sleepwalking, along the borders

Owls accompanied me, they were echoing
From wood to wood, into the hesitant day
I carried the owls in their surviving wells
Of night-time. The fittest are a fatal breed.

They'd do without sleep if they possibly could
And meter it for the rest of us. I like
Humans who harbour the dark in their open
Eyes all day. They seem more kin, more kind. They are

The ones not listening while the ruling voices
Further impair our hearing. They are away
With the owls, they ride the dreaming hooting hills
Down, down, into an infinite pacific.

W.S. MERWIN
For a Coming Extinction

Gray whale
Now that we are sending you to The End
That great god
Tell him
That we who follow you invented forgiveness
And forgive nothing

I write as though you could understand
And I could say it
One must always pretend something
Among the dying
When you have left the seas nodding on their stalks
Empty of you
Tell him that we were made
On another day

The bewilderment will diminish like an echo
Winding along your inner mountains
Unheard by us
And find its way out
Leaving behind it the future
Dead
And ours

When you will not see again
The whale calves trying the light
Consider what you will find in the black garden
And its court
The sea cows the Great Auks the gorillas
The irreplaceable hosts ranged countless
And foreordaining as stars
Our sacrifices

Join your word to theirs
Tell him
That it is we who are important

■ W.S. Merwin ➤ 78.

W.S. MERWIN
The Shore

How can anyone know that a whale
two hundred years ago could hear another
whale at the opposite end of the earth
or tell how long the eyes
of a whale have faced both halves of the world
and have found light far down in old company

with the sounds of hollow iron charging
clanging through the oceans and with the circuitries
and the harpoons of humans
and the poisoning of the seas
a whale can hear no father through the present
than a jet can fly in a few minutes

in days of their hearing the great Blues gathered like clouds
the sunlight under the sea's surfaces sank
into their backs as into the water around them
through which they flew invisible from above
except as flashes of movement
and they could hear each other's voices wherever they went

once it is on its own a Blue can wander
the whole world beholding both sides of the water
raising in each ocean the songs of the Blues
that it learned from distances it can no longer hear
it can fly all its life without ever meeting another Blue
this is what we are doing this is the way we sing oh Blue Blue

TED HUGHES
Little Whale Song
(for Charles Causley)

What do they think of themselves
With their global brains –
The tide-power voltage illumination
Of those brains? Their X-ray all-dimension

Grasp of this world's structures, their brains budded
Clone replicas of the electron world
Lit and re-imagining the world,
Perfectly tuned receivers and perceivers,

Each one a whole tremulous world
Feeling through the world? What
Do they make of each other?

'We are beautiful. We stir

Our self-colour in the pot of colours
Which is the world. At each
Tail-stroke we deepen
Our being into the world's lit substance,

And our joy into the world's
Spinning bliss, and our peace
Into the world's floating, plumed peace.'

Their body-tons, echo-chambered,

Amplify the whisper
Of currents and airs, of sea-peoples
And planetary manoeuvres,
Of seasons, of shores, and of their own

Moon-lifted incantation, as they dance
Through the original Earth-drama
In which they perform, as from the beginning,
The Royal House.
                    The loftiest, spermiest

Passions, the most exquisite pleasures,
The noblest characters, the most god-like
Oceanic presence and poise –

The most terrible fall.

■ Ted Hughes ➤ 66.

MARK DOTY
Visitation

When I heard he had entered the harbor,
and circled the wharf for days,
I expected the worst: shallow water,

confusion, some accident to bring
the young humpback to grief.
Don't they depend on a compass

lodged in the salt-flooded folds
of the brain, some delicate
musical mechanism to navigate

their true course? How many ways,
in our century's late iron hours,
might we have led him to disaster?

That, in those days, was how
I'd come to see the world:
dark upon dark, any sense

of spirit an embattled flame
sparked against wind-driven rain
till pain snuffed it out. I thought,

This is what experience gives us,
and I moved carefully through my life
while I waited… Enough,

it wasn't that way at all. The whale
– exuberant, proud maybe, playful,
like the early music of Beethoven –

cruised the footings for smelts
clustered near the pylons
in mercury flocks. He

(do I have the gender right?)
would negotiate the rusty hulls
of the Portuguese fishing boats

– Holy Infant, Little Marie –
with what could only be read
as pleasure, coming close

then diving, trailing on the surface
big spreading circles
until he'd breach, thrilling us

with the release of pressured breath,
and the bulk of his sleek young head
– a wet black leather sofa

already barnacled with ghostly lice –
and his elegant and unlikely mouth,
and the marvelous afterthought of the flukes,

and the way his broad flippers
resembled a pair of clownish gloves
or puppet hands, looming greenish white

beneath the bay's clouded sheen.
When he had consumed his pleasure
of the shimmering swarm, his pleasure, perhaps,

in his own admired performance,
he swam out the harbor mouth,
into the Atlantic. And though grief

has seemed to me itself a dim,
salt suspension in which I've moved,
blind thing, day by day,

through the wreckage, barely aware
of what I stumbled toward, even I
couldn't help but look

at the way this immense figure
graces the dark medium,
and shines so: heaviness

which is no burden to itself.
What did you think, that joy
was some slight thing?

■ **Mark Doty** (*b.* 1953) is an American writer noted for the compassion, relish and wild muscularity of his highly personal poetry. Central to Doty's work are animals and his concern for the need to cope nobly and gracefully with what is beyond our control. Exploring our preoccupation with the past and the future, he encourages us to live more in the present. His poetry universalises themes of loss, mortality and renewal, and expresses a remarkable empathy for all human and animal life. He has published seven collections, including *My Alexandria* (1993) and *Atlantis* (1995), which deal poignantly with the failing health and ultimate death of his partner from AIDS and with his almost crippling grief – also the subject of his prose memoir *Heaven's Coast* (1996). His other books include the memoirs *Firebird* (1999) and *Dog Years* (2007), and *Fire to Fire: New and Selected Poems* (2008). [Other poem ➤ 126]

■ **Gary Snyder** ➤ 103.

GARY SNYDER
Mother Earth: Her Whales

An owl winks in the shadows
A lizard lifts on tiptoe, breathing hard
Young male sparrow stretches up his neck,
          big head, watching –

The grasses are working in the sun. Turn it green.
Turn it sweet. That we may eat.
Grow our meat.

Brazil says 'sovereign use of Natural Resources'
Thirty thousand kinds of unknown plants.
The living actual people of the jungle
          sold and tortured –
And a robot in a suit who peddles a delusion called 'Brazil'
          can speak for *them*?

          The whales turn and glisten, plunge
               and sound and rise again,
          Hanging over subtly darkening deeps
          Flowing like breathing planets
               in the sparkling whorls of
                    living light –

And Japan quibbles for words on
      what kinds of whales they can kill?
A once-great Buddhist nation
      dribbles methyl mercury
      like gonorrhea
         in the sea.

Père David's Deer, the Elaphure,
Lived in the tule marshes of the Yellow River
Two thousand years ago – and lost its home to rice –
The forests of Lo-yang were logged and all the silt &
Sand flowed down, and gone, by 1200 AD –

Wild Geese hatched out in Siberia
      head south over basins of the Chiang, the Ho,
      what we call 'China'
On flyways they have used a million years.
Ah China, where are the tigers, the wild boars,
      the monkeys,
        like the snows of yesteryear
Gone in a mist, a flash, and the dry hard ground
Is parking space for fifty thousand trucks.
IS man most precious of all things?
– then let us love him, and his brothers, all those
Fading living beings –

North America, Turtle Island, taken by invaders
      who wage war around the world.
May ants, may abalone, otters, wolves and elk
Rise! and pull away their giving
      from the robot nations.

Solidarity. The People.
Standing Tree People!
Flying Bird People!
Swimming Sea People!
Four-legged, two-legged, people!

How can the head-heavy power-hungry politic scientist
Government   two-world   Capitalist-Imperialist
Third-world   Communist   paper-shuffling male
      non-farmer   jet-set   bureaucrats
Speak for the green of the leaf? Speak for the soil?

(Ah Margaret Mead…do you sometimes dream of Samoa?)

The robots argue how to parcel out our Mother Earth
To last a little longer
      like vultures flapping
Belching, gurgling,
      near a dying Doe.

'In yonder field a slain knight lies –
We'll fly to him and eat his eyes
      with a down
    derry derry derry down down.'

    An Owl winks in the shadow
    A lizard lifts on tiptoe
      breathing hard
    The whales turn and glisten
      plunge and
    Sound, and rise again
    Flowing like breathing planets

    In the sparkling whorls

    Of living light.

HEATHCOTE WILLIAMS
from Whale Nation

When whales breed
They breed with ecological consideration:
They breed in precise relation to the amount of food in
    the sea.

After a season foraging under the Arctic ice-floes,
Through which the Narwhal has made breathing holes
With its unicorn horn, for the use of all species,
The baleen whales leave their pinnacled ice-palaces,
And find their way south, to mate.
With glowing tracks behind them in the water, large as
    ships',
The Humpacks use the rotational forces of the planet,

The azimuth of the sun,
The taste and temperature of the tides,
The contours of the sea-bed:
Canyons, plains, vaults;
The mountainous summits of the mid-Atlantic ridge,
    twice the width of the Andes,
Which stretches for ten thousand miles, from Iceland
    to Patagonia;
Guided by hydrothermal vents in the earth's crust,
The topography of coral reefs,
The position of the moon, and its tidal pull;
Navigating with a lodestone disk made of polarised
    magnetite,
A compass in the brain,
Sensitive to the geomagnetic flow of force-fields
Under phosphorescent seas,
They find their way to the mating grounds.

On arriving at their liquid seraglio,
Sealed off from the outside world by riptides,
Success in courtship is determined by whoever sings
    the most absorbing song.
And whoever makes the wildest movements with their
    body;
Knifing through foam
Spinning and wave-riding,
Spy-hopping, lob-tailing,
Breaching and tail-slapping;
Turning upside-down
And thwacking their bat-like flukes against the surface
With sharp, echoing cracks;
Throwing themselves into odd, alluring shapes;
Sinuously whirling and flickering through the sea
They glide past each other,
Swishing contemplatively,
Testing congenial feelings,
Judging the suppleness of motion,
Judging sensation, with gentle discrimination.

Mutual attraction is an elaborate, thoughtful process:
In whales the male member is erected voluntarily,
Unsheathed from within deep abdominal folds,

Erected, and then collapsed and concealed again, by an
    act of will –
Unlike in man,
Where it has an unseasonal disconnected life of its own.
…And the Blue Whale's penis is nine feet long,
Which may require additional self-control.

The two whales draw closer,
Fanning each other,
Then stroking each other with their pectoral fins.
Giant pink genital lips roll back underneath the water.

They join forces. Embrace.
Mating face to face, like man.

Stirring their huge tail-flukes,
Their heads emerge slowly above the water.
They clutch each other, their long flippers around each
    other,
The accordion pleats of their grooved bellies interleave,
They move their flukes backwards and forwards beneath
    them,
Their bodies are pressed closer and closer,
As they drive themselves upwards,
Rising out of the sea,
Out of the shimmering green shadows below,
Into the exhilarating glare of the sky.
With a last movement,
Powerfully churning their flukes in unison, fifty feet below,
They propel themselves upwards,
Gallons of water sluicing down their sides,
They both jump clear,
Held together, in mid-air, for their massive climax.

The sea moves,
And any earthly thing nearby is swamped.

They dive.
Curving their bodies, they dive a mile down.
Dropping their heart-beat,
Collapsing their lungs.
Folding in their ribs along atriculated joints, to counter-
    act the bends,

Happily slipping through the pressure of five hundred
     atmospheres,
A quarter of a million tons of dense water at the sea-bed
Exerted on their bodies.

Half an hour later, an hour later,
They emerge,
Triumphantly blowing like blast furnaces.
Three thousand times the contents of the human lung
Is expelled in two seconds through their air-pipes,
In a great sigh of steam.

Plumes of warm mist, twenty feet high,
Jet from their blow-holes; exuberant exclamation marks
     punctuating the sky.
Their spouting exhalations are audible for half a mile,
Sounding like distant thunder,
And looking like puffs of chimney smoke
From an underwater town.

They inhale.
As the air enters the endless corridors of their bodies,
It gives off the sound of a reverberating bell.

■ **Heathcote Williams** (*b.* 1941) is an English poet, playwright,
actor and songwriter best-known for his book-length ecopoems:
Autogeddon (1985/1991), *Whale Nation* (1988), *Falling for a
Dolphin* (1988) and *Sacred Elephant* (1989). These have been
published as illustrated books including photographs and
documentary material as well as being adapted for television,
stage, and recordings on cassette and CD (the work read by
Williams and two actors, with classical music).

   Ted Hughes called *Whale Nation* 'overwhelming…brilliant,
cunning, dramatic and wonderfully moving, a steady accum-
ulation of grandeur and dreadfulness – and never any sense
of exploring the subject for poetic or literary effects, just a
measured unfolding of real things from the heart of the subject.'

■ Helen Dunmore ➢ 82.

Dolphins whistling

Yes, we believed that the oceans were endless
surging with whales, serpents and mermaids,
demon-haunted and full of sweet voices
to lure us over the edge of the world,

we were conquerors, pirates, explorers, vagabonds
war-makers, sea-rovers, we ploughed
the wave's furrow, made maps
that led others to the sea's harvest

and sometimes we believed we heard dolphins whistling,
through the wine-dark waters we heard dolphins
     whistling.

We were restless and the oceans were endless,
rich in cod and silver-scaled herring
so thick with pilchard we dipped in our buckets
and threw the waste on the fields to rot,

we were mariners, fishers of Iceland, Newfoundlanders
fortune-makers, sea-rovers, we ploughed
the wave's furrow and earned our harvest
hungrily trawling the broad waters,

and sometimes we believed we heard dolphins whistling,
through blue-green depths we heard dolphins whistling.

The catch was good and the oceans were endless
so we fed them with run-off and chemical rivers
pair-fished them, scoured the sea-bed for pearls
and searched the deep where the sperm-whale plays,

we were ambergris merchants, fish farmers, cod-bank
     strippers
coral-crushers, reef-poisoners, we ploughed
the sea's furrow and seized our harvest
although we had to go far to find it

for the fish grew small and the whales were strangers,
coral was grey and cod-banks empty,

59

algae bloomed and the pilchards vanished
while the huer's lookout was sold for a chalet,

and the dolphins called their names to one another
through the dark spaces of the water
as mothers call their children at nightfall
and grow fearful for an answer.

We were conquerors, pirates, explorers, vagabonds
war-makers, sea-rovers, we ploughed
the wave's furrow, drew maps
to leads others to the sea's harvest,

and we believed that the oceans were endless
and we believed we could hear the dolphins whistling.

■ **Edward Thomas** (1878-1917) was an English poet of
Welsh descent usually thought of as a First World War poet,
but who wrote nothing directly about the trenches; also seen
as a "nature poet", his symbolic reach and generic range
expose the limits of that category too. Thomas wrote a life-
time's poetry in two years. Already a dedicated prose writer
and influential critic, he became a poet only in December
1914, at the age of 36. ('**The Combe**' is dated 30 December
1914.) In April 1917 he was killed at Arras. A central figure
in modern poetry, he is among the half-dozen poets who
remade English poetry in the early 20th century.

Edna Longley: 'He grew up in London, but developed a
passion for nature. Hating the economic forces that had
destroyed agricultural communities and expanded cities,
Thomas absorbed, as his poetry shows, the literary and folk
traditions of the English countryside. [...] His thinking about
England was conditioned by social change, war and his eco-
logical sense of habitats and history.'
[Other poems ➤ 83]

■ **Michael Longley** (*b.* 1939) is an Irish poet of English par-
entage who has spent most of his life in Belfast and at his
second home at Carrigskeewan on the coast of Co. Mayo. A
dedicated naturalist, he studied Classics at Trinity College
Dublin, and worked for the Arts Council of Northern Ireland
from 1970 to 1991. Longley's poetry is formally inventive and
precisely observed, spanning and blending love poetry, war
poetry, nature poetry, elegies, satires, verse epistles, art and
the art of poetry. He has extended the capacity of the lyric
to absorb dark matter: the Great War, the Holocaust, the
Northern Irish 'Troubles'; and his translations from classical
poets speak to contemporary issues.

Interviewed by Jody AllenRandolph, Longley said: 'The
most urgent political problems are ecological: how we share
the planet with the plants and the other animals. My nature
writing is my most political. In my Mayo poems I am not
trying to escape from political violence. I want the light from
Carrigskeewaun to irradiate the northern darkness. Describing
the world in a meticulous way is a consecration and a stay
against damaging dogmatism.'
[Other poems ➤ 121, 124, 127]

■ **Colin Simms** (*b.* 1939) is a poet and naturalist who lives
in a remote cottage near Alston in the Pennines, and has
travelled and lived throughout the northern hemisphere,
wherever the martens, otters, birds of prey and other enthu-
siams have drawn him. He is not an orthodox conservationist,
but insists of the privacy, "isness", for wildlife which modern
trends deny. He has published thousands of natural-history
letters, articles, reports and scientific papers, as well as 1500
poems in small press publications, many of these recently
collected in *Otters and Martens* (2004) and *The American Poems*
(2005). [Other poems ➤ 82, 228]

EDWARD THOMAS
The Combe

The Combe was ever dark, ancient and dark.
Its mouth is stopped with bramble, thorn, and briar;
And no one scrambles over the sliding chalk
By beech and yew and perishing juniper
Down the half precipices of its sides, with roots
And rabbit holes for steps. The sun of Winter,
The moon of Summer, and all the singing birds
Except the missel-thrush that loves juniper,
Are quite shut out. But far more ancient and dark
The Combe looks since they killed the badger there,
Dug him out and gave him to the hounds,
That most ancient Briton of English beasts.

MICHAEL LONGLEY
Badger

(for Raymond Piper)

I

Pushing the wedge of his body
Between cromlech and stone circle,
He excavates down mine shafts
And back into the depths of the hill.

His path straight and narrow
And not like the fox's zigzags,
The arc of the hare who leaves
A silhouette on the sky line.

Night's silence around his shoulders,
His face lit by the moon, he
Manages the earth with his paws,
Returns underground to die.

II

An intestine taking in
patches of dog's-mercury,
brambles, the bluebell wood;
a heel revolving acorns;
a head with a price on it
brushing cuckoo-spit, goose-grass;
a name that parishes borrow.

III

For the digger, the earth-dog
It is a difficult delivery
Once the tongs take hold,

Vulnerable his pig's snout
That lifted cow-pats for beetles,
Hedgehogs for the soft meat,

His limbs dragging after them
So many stones turned over,
The trees they tilted.

COLIN SIMMS
Three Years in Glen Garry

Three years' accounts from gamekeepers' records, an estate
kept for seasonal deer-stalking, all manner of Game preservation.
The statistics are false only in that the categories are derived
from dialect, gaelic names for fauna; they are not stories contrived...
Three hundred and seventy-one rough-legged buzzards (both Buteos?)
Two hundred and seventy-five 'Kitehawks'; which might, ought,
to have included unknown amounts of various 'shitehawks'.
Two hundred and forty-six martens, precious today our marten
One hundred and ninety-eight wild cats, a hundred and six polecats
– the one much reduced but recovering, the other yet to come back from
     the feral.
Ninety-eight peregrine falcons, six even of the Arctic gyr-falcons
seventy-eight merlins, no kestrels? (further, seven 'orange-legged' falcons)
sixty-three harriers, probably mainly hen-harriers. Ditto goshawks.
Thirty-five 'horned' owls (the 'eared' species of owls, *incertae sedis*)
twenty-seven 'white-tailed' eagles (some the young, fifteen golden eagles)
eighteen ospreys, eleven hobbies; which might be average say for today.
The Clearances were not only of the people, but of most of the other
     indigenes
at their climax; their dynamic climax, proliferating genes
culminating food-chains, being the noblest, most beautiful, most evolved.
A country that was ours to inherit, and theirs, gone under oxters' sweep.
'Garry, stretch thy bare limbs in sleep; it gars me sair to see ye weep.'

COLIN SIMMS
'Apart from a hundred peacocks': a menu...

Four thousand pigeons – some of them no doubt bred
in dovecotes. Three thousand wild duck – about split
half and half mallard and the smaller teal!
Two thousand geese – wild greylag from Humberhead
and some domestic. Over a thousand 'egrit'
(soon to be extinct in the North) and quail.
Four hundred swans encouraged to nest, and fed
four hundred herons also 'bred up for it'
four hundred plovers, lapwings trapped wholesale.

Four hundred woodcock, got 'at springs' it was said,
as many partridges and of ruff, godwit
two hundred or two hundred dozen; numbers fail...
Over two hundred bitterns, only, it was said,
a hundred curlew; we can't be sure of it
or any of it...before those marshes were drained...

1466 enthronement feast of the Archbishop of York
source: Leland *Collectorem* and W.B. Yapp:
Birds in Medieval Mss (London, 1981)

■ **Sylvia Plath** (1932-63) was an American poet and fiction writer whose work achieved world renown only after her death. Plath wrote with a force and pain rarely matched in modern poetry, and yet only *The Colossus* (1960) and her searing autobiographical novel *The Bell Jar* (1963) were published in her life-time. Drawing on the circumstances and experiences of her own life, she transmuted personal suffering into agonised poetry of universal power, telling her story through narratives drawn from classical myth, nature and history. Her poetry is both angry and gleeful, technically exact and daringly open, covering areas rarely considered appropriate for poetry, let alone writing by women, before the 1960s. The full range of her work only became evident in 1981 with the publication of her *Collected Poems*.

Plath studied at Smith College, Massachusetts, and won a Fulbright scholarship to Newnham College, Cambridge, where in 1956 she met and married Ted Hughes [➤ 66]. Their daughter Frieda was born in 1960, and their son Nicholas in January 1962. ('**Pheasant**' dates from April of that year.) They separated in October 1962, Plath remaining at their house in Devon; and then, in just two months, she wrote the 40 poems of rage, despair, love and vengeance that have chiefly been responsible for her immense posthumous fame, published after her death as *Ariel* (1965). In December, she moved with the children to a flat in London, just as the country was gripped by one of the worst winters of the century. In February 1963, suffering from clinical depression, she committed suicide.

■ **David Wagoner** (*b.*1926) is an American poet and novelist known for his compassionate observation of both the natural and the human worlds. In a style by turns direct and intricate, he distils essential emotions from people's encounters with each other, with nature and with themselves. His many books include *Traveling Light: Collected and New Poems* (1999). His 1978 collection *Who Shall Be the Sun?* is a book of poems based on the folklore, legends and myths of indigenous peoples of the Northwest Coast and Plateau regions.   [Other poems ➤ 72]

[Other poems ➤ 72]

SYLVIA PLATH

Pheasant

You said you would kill it this morning.
Do not kill it. It startles me still,
The jut of that odd, dark head, pacing

Through the uncut grass on the elm's hill.
It is something to own a pheasant,
Or just to be visited at all.

I am not mystical: it isn't
As if I thought it had a spirit.
It is simply in its element.

That gives it a kingliness, a right.
The print of its big foot last winter,
The tail-track, on the snow in our court –

The wonder of it, in that pallor,
Through crosshatch of sparrow and starling.
Is it its rareness, then? It is rare.

But a dozen would be worth having,
A hundred, on that hill – green and red,
Crossing and recrossing: a fine thing!

It is such a good shape, so vivid.
It's a little cornucopia.
It unclaps, brown as a leaf, and loud,

Settles in the elm, and is easy.
It was sunning in the narcissi.
I trespass stupidly. Let be, let be.

ANDREW MOTION
Sparrow

No longer
country clubber,
barn bouncer,
hedgerow flasher,
bran dipper,
puddle bather,
dust bowler,
stubble scrounger,
dew nibbler
creeper sleeper,
dung dobbler.
No longer
city slicker,
curb crawler,
gutter weaver,
brick clinger,
dotty mobster,
sill scruffer,
traffic dodger,
drain dogger,
putty pecker,
car bomber.
No longer
daily greeter
scratch singer
piebald shitter,
bib bobber
cocky bugger
boss brawler,
gossip spinner,
crowd pleaser,
heaven filler,
wing dancer.
No longer.

DAVID WAGONER
The Author of *American Ornithology* Sketches a Bird, Now Extinct
Alexander Wilson, Wilmington, NC, 1809

When he walked through town, the wing-shot bird he'd hidden
Inside his coat began to cry like a baby,
High and plaintive and loud as the calls he'd heard
While hunting it in the woods, and goodwives stared
And scurried indoors to guard their own from harm.

And the innkeeper and the goodmen in the tavern
Asked him whether his child was sick, then laughed,
Slapped knees, and laughed as he unswaddled his prize,
His pride and burden: an ivory-billed woodpecker
As big as a crow, still wailing and squealing.

Upstairs, when he let it go in his workroom,
It fell silent at last. He told at dinner
How devoted masters of birds drawn from the life
Must gather their flocks around them with a rifle
And make them live forever inside books.

Later, he found his bedspread covered with plaster
And the bird clinging beside a hole in the wall
Clear through to already splintered weatherboards
And the sky beyond. While he tied one of its legs
To a table leg, it started wailing again

And went on wailing as if toward cypress groves
While the artist drew and tinted on fine vellum
Its red cockade, gray claws, and sepia eyes
From which a white wedge flowed to the lame wing
Like light flying and ended there in blackness.

He drew and studied for days, eating and dreaming
Fitfully through the dancing and loud drumming
Of an ivory bill that refused pecans and beetles,
Chestnuts and sweet-sour fruit of magnolias,
Riddling his table, slashing his fingers, wailing.

He watched it die, he said, with great regret.

TONY HARRISON
from Art & Extinction

When I hear of the destruction of a species I feel as if all the works of some great writer had perished.

THEODORE ROOSEVELT, 1899

1 *The Birds of America*

[i] JOHN JAMES AUDUBON (1785-1851)

The struggle to preserve once spoken words
from already too well-stuffed taxonomies
is a bit like Audubon's when painting birds,
whose method an admirer said was this:
Kill 'em, wire 'em, paint 'em, kill a fresh 'un!

The plumage even of the brightest faded.
The artist had to shoot in quick succession
till all the feathers were correctly shaded.

Birds don't pose for pictures when alive!
Audubon's idea of restraint,
doing the Pelican, was 25
dead specimens a day for *one* in paint.

By using them do we save words or not?

As much as Audubon's art could save a,
say, godwit, or a grackle, which he shot
and then saw 'multiplied by Havell's graver'.

TONY HARRISON
Fire & Ice
The dusky, extinct 16 June 1987, Florida

A sprinkler simulates the rain.
A man in Lysolled wellies brings
live larvae to it, crickets, grain,
and the dusky, near extinction, sings.

The dusky in its quarantine 's
the very last there'll ever be.
In a Georgia lab its frozen genes
stay fledged with numb non-entity.

It's mocked up well its habitat.
The meal-supply's well-meaning.
Though there's no mate to warble at
the dusky goes on preening.

So let's be glad that it dropped dead
in that life-affirming mood.
The keeper found its little head
still buried in its food.

The Saxon saw man's spirit fly
like a bird though glowing firelight,
a warmth between two blanks of sky,
a briefly broken night.

Ours could be a dusky clone,
the freezered phoenix of our fate,
that flies, preens, even sings, alone
singed by the sparks from its charred mate.

■ **Tony Harrison** (*b.* 1937) is Britain's leading film and theatre poet. Fired by tension between his working-class upbringing and a university education in Classics, he writes metrical verse drawing on English speech rhythms. Like Brecht, he is both a major social poet and an innovative dramatist. His *Plays* (5 vols, 1999-2004), *Collected Poems* (2007) and *Collected Film Poetry* (2007) show particular concerns dominating all his poetry: class, society and culture; language and eloquence; art and poetry; family, sex, war and the environment.

■ **Andrew Motion** (*b.* 1952) is an English poet, critic, editor, biographer and novelist who became Britain's Poet Laureate in 1999. His poetry combines narrative and lyricism, although some of his concerns are distinctly postmodern. Many of his poems question whether any meaning can be gleaned from life's random events. His main literary influences include Wordsworth, Hardy, Edward Thomas and Larkin, and he has written biographies of both Larkin (1993) and Keats (2000).

4. UNBALANCE OF NATURE

These poems are concerned with the effects of pollution;
with forests and tree-felling; interfering with the processes
of nature; and with urbanisation and alienation from nature
in cities.

POLLUTION

TED HUGHES
If

If the sky is infected
The river has to drink it

If earth has a disease which could be fatal
The river has to drink it

If you have infected the sky and the earth
Caught its disease off you – you are the virus

If the sea drinks the river
And the earth drinks the sea

It is one quenching and one termination

If your blood is trying to clean itself
In the filter of your corrupted flesh
And the sores run – that is the rivers

The five rivers of Paradise

Where will you get a pure drink now?

Already – the drop has returned to the cup

Already you are your ditch, and there you drink

TED HUGHES
from 1984 on 'The Tarka Trail'

I

The River is suddenly green – dense bottle green.
Hard in the sun, dark as spinach.
Drought pools bleach their craters.
The river's floor is a fleece –
Tresses of some vile stuff
That disintegrates to a slime as you touch it
Leaving your fingers fouled with a stink of diesel.

The river's glutted – a boom of plenty for algae.
A festering olla podrida, poured slowly.
Surfactants, ammonia, phosphates – the whole banquet
Flushed in by sporadic thunderbursts
But never a flood enough to scour a sewer,
Never enough to resurrect a river.

A bottleful is like sap, a rich urine,
With minuscule flying saucers whizzing in it.
Down near the estuary – this goes into the mains.
But nothing can help the patient. In the August afternoon
The golden picnic sunrays, leaning dustily
Through the conifers, gaze down
At a ditch-carcase, a puddled horror –
Bile draining from rags, the hulk of ribs.

Charlie found a stranded mussel. He brought it
Up the fishing ladder.
The lips gaped. We peered in, and pried wider,
Parted her pearly gates to get a peek
At her curtained uvula: Queen of the River
Still in her silken chamber, or was it – ?
A yawn of putrid phlegm.

Then the stench hit us. He yelled
And flailed it from his fingers as if it had burnt him
Into a blaze of willowherb
'God! The river's dead! Oh God!
Even the mussels are finished!'

The tale of a dying river
Does not end where you stand with the visitors
At a sickbed, feeling the usual
Nothing more than mangled helplessness.
You cannot leave this hospital because
Peter, the good corn farmer, with his three plus
Tons of quality grain to the acre (behind him
The Min. of Ag. and Fish.'s hard guarantee
Which is the hired assurance of hired science)
Heaps the poisons into you too.

His upriver neighbour – just as overwhelmed –
Wades through slurry and silage. Where his dad
Milked a herd of twenty, he milks ninety –
Oozing effluent 'equal to the untreated
Sewage of a city the size of Gloucester'.

But Peter, our clean corn farmer, nature protector,
Striding between lush hedgebanks he lets go bush
To gladden the spider, past his carefully nursed
Neglected nettles (a crèche for the butterflies),
The birdwatcher, binoculars thumping his sternum,
Has measured his medicines towards that maximum yield
Into your dish for years. Yes, and smiled
Up towards the colluding sun. And returned
Over his corn (which now, near ripe, seems burned
Oak-dark with some fungus) thirteen times
Between the drill and the reaper.

Three hundredweight of 20–10–10 to the acre,
A hundredweight and a half straight Nitram.
Pesticides, herbicides, fungicides, the grand slam –
Each time twenty gallons to the acre
Into your dish, with top-ups. And slug-pellets
A bonus, with the rest, into your cup
(Via the lifeless ditch – meaning your tap).
Now you are as loaded with the data
That cultivate his hopes, in this brief gamble
As this river is –
                    as he is too,
He can't escape either, nor can his lively young wife,
Who laughs if you ask them why they do what they do

(Her voice ventriloqual, her shoulders jerking on their
    strings)
'But the children have to be educated.'

■ **Ted Hughes** (1930-98) was one of the major English poets of the last 50 years as well as a popular writer of poetry and fiction for children. He grew up in Yorkshire, whose wind-blasted moorland landscapes, wildlife and abandoned industrial sites were primary influences on his work, and lived on a farm in Devon from 1970. His poetic imagination is marked by un-flinching observation of the natural world and of the shaping, often damaging, presence of man, as well as by the mythical beliefs expounded in his critical works *Shakespeare and the Goddess of Complete Being* (1992) and *Winter Pollen* (1994). Animals appear frequently in his poems as deity, metaphor, persona and icon, most notably the protagonist of *Crow* (1970).

Edna Longley: 'All his poetic models were Romantic: Yeats's mysticism, Graves's White Goddess, Dylan Thomas. And Hughes's own rejection of narrow nonconformism made him receptive to Lawrence's insistence, in his animal poems, on sensory and unconscious life. A Romantic view of monarchy as symbolising "an essential centre" in a community lay behind his acceptance of the Poet Laureateship in 1984. [...] Hughes implies that the human animal should be less contained by logic, society and religion. "The Otter" (which recalls Edward Thomas's 'The Combe') [≻ 60] obliquely mourns human self-estrangement and "the old shape" of England. For Hughes, writing poetry parallels the way in which a Native American shaman communes with spirit-animals on behalf of his people. His relationship with his wife Sylvia Plath [≻ 62], who committed suicide in 1963, led him to take this mystical or Freudian perspective possibly too far.'

Jonathan Bate has described how Ted Hughes's poetry 'graphically presents a nature that is, in Tennyson's phrase, "red in tooth and claw". Yet whilst relishing the violence of nature's own processes, Hughes in his later years became increasingly angry about the violence wrought by man upon nature. He cared deeply about the pollution of the country-side and the decimation of Britain's wildlife population.'

Hughes wrote that it was imperative to salvage 'all nature from the pressures and oversights of our runaway populations, and from the monstrous anti-Nature that we have created, the now nearly-autonomous Technosphere'. In 1970, in a review of Max Nicholson's *The Environmental Revolution*, one of the earliest books to enumerate the full extent of our ecological crisis, he castigated modern capitalism for its exploitative attitude to the earth: 'While the mice in the field are listening to the Universe, and moving in the body of nature, where every living cell is sacred to every other, and all are inter-dependent, the Developer is peering at the field through a visor, and behind him stands the whole army of madmen's ideas, and shareholders, impatient to cash in the world.'

[Other poems ➤ 54-55, 200, 203]

■ **Alden Nowlan** (1933-83) is Canada's most popular modern poet, widely celebrated for his heart-warming, plain-speaking poems. Born in the Nova Scotia backwoods, he left school at 12 and worked in a sawmill before becoming a local newspaper reporter. His early poems bear witness to the harshness and hypocrisy of lives brutalised by poverty and ignorance in a remote Canadian backwater. But as Nowlan finds love and lifelong friendship, so his work achieves authority and lasting warmth. His poems present universal portrayals of human life: teasingly ironic, wryly humorous, sympathetic, quizzical and morally astute.

ALDEN NOWLAN
St John River

The colour of a bayonet this river
that glitters blue and solid on the page
in tourist folders, yet some thirty towns
use it as a latrine, the sewerage
seeping back to their wells, and farmers maddened
by debt or queer religions winter down
under the ice, the river bottom strewn
with heaps of decomposing bark torn loose
from pulpwood driven south, its acid juice
killing the salmon. August, when the stink
of the corrupted water floats like gas
along these streets, what most astonishes
is that the pictures haven't lied, the real
river is beautiful, as blue as steel.

■ **Brendan Kennelly** (*b.* 1936) is an Irish poet, critic and dramatist who taught at Trinity College Dublin for over 30 years. He grew up in the village of Ballylongford in Co. Kerry, and most of his work is concerned with the people, landscapes, wildlife and history of Ireland, and with language, religion and politics. Best-known for three controversial poetry books, *Cromwell* (1983), *The Book of Judas* (1991) and *Poetry My Arse* (1995), he is a much loved public figure in Ireland, and a popular guest on television programmes. 'His poems shine with the wisdom of somebody who has thought deeply about the paradoxical strangeness and familiarity and wonder of life' (Sister Stanislaus Kennedy).

BRENDAN KENNELLY
Milk

I

Three men
On a morning in early summer
Tipped a lorryload of poisoned whey
Into the Line river.

The water opened
And gulped it down.

It was a white poison.
The river swelled with the
Evil milk,
A snowy vein of death
Piercing the land's body.

All through the land
Seeped the scum in a murderous rut,
Through fields and
Meadows waiting to be cut,
Past villages and townlands
Into the sea.

II

Everything died in the milky river.
Brown trout, eels, fluke, young salmon
Perished, every one.

White bellies to the light
Fish floated down the river
Corpses jostling in the tide.

In the summer morning
Poison entered the sun,
Riddled the light
On land and sea,
Possessed the invisible stars
Turned to dust in the air
Dropped like a gentle malignant shiver of snow
Into the hearts of three men
Standing on a bank
Of the Line river.

III

Men working in the fields
Saw white bellies of fish.
Pain jabbed the hearts of some.
They waded in as far as they could go
Collected the bodies in bags
Returned to the banks
Spread the fish in the fields –
Row after glittering row.

Strange to see
Fishbodies
In the rivery grass,
Men bending over them
Incomprehension in their eyes.

Looking back at the river
They saw countless trout
Try to leap from the water
As if wanting to be alone,
Preferring to die
In an alien element
Than in their poisoned own.

A few fish reached the grass, gravel, stones
The air pressing on every side.
They stirred, leaped, flickered in the sun
And died.

IV

Milk of peace, milk of human kindness, sign of the fish –
The fields were strewn with dead metaphors.
Language had fought a pitched battle and lost
And now the choicest of its soldiers
Lay corpsed in the sun,
Their hearts yanked out and flung at random on the grass.
What grass would grow from these abandoned hearts
Would be sour as the words of a man
Whose days were black pits
Of disappointment.
Light that might have been a light of love
Circled like a bird of prey
Above the fields
Where nothing could be done or said
To halt the carrion light
From ravaging the dead.

V

The men who poisoned the river
Seemed hardly to know what was done.
Would they know what they did
If they poisoned the sun?
When they dumped death into the water
What did they do or say?
They turned their backs on a job well-done
And walked away.

VI

Later,
People walking through or near the fields
Were forced to drink the stench.
Implacable as cancer
It pierced their clothes and skin
Lived there
White and vile as leprosy.

The whiter, the viler.

It seemed to many women and men
That God's air
Would never be clean again.

VII

In time
Fishbodies would be clay and grass,
Pain in the men's eyes
Lessen
But the river will never
Recover
Its own creatures rotting in light.

The river
And the land it flows for
Will not forget
The summer of poisoned white.

BRENDAN KENNELLY
The Hope of Wings

The girl forces the gull's beak open with
A spoon and starts to scrape the oil away.
Rampant the sky's colours, legend and myth
Sustain the attention of those beset by
Traditional hungers, but now I foresee
A bird-emptied sky, the world's shores
Hilled with crippled things, the thick, black
Smothering oil murdering the hope of wings.
And this girl – she can't be into her teens –
Would, if her working now is a guide,
Spend all her years remaking these stunned birds
Littering the sea, dead flops among stones.
She'd give a white-winged creature to the sky
Before black tides drown mere human words.

FRED REED
On the Beach

Stop up aheight! Aye, scream for aall yo're worth,
But divvn't light on man-infested orth!
Aw! Aa'll be cumen t' the beach ne mair

T' blub sick pity on the stinkin' air.
Amang this junk, french lettors, tyres 'n' tords,
The sewer-vent hes lured these hideous bords,
An' heor crude oil, a black deeth thick 'n' clingin',
Hes put a horror's end t' their free wingin'.
Aw hell! Ne fiends that wiv lost sowls contend
Could hev contrived se pitiless an end!
An' look! You blood-hued monstor wetter-borne
Amang the murk noo blorts its doom-waatch horn
An' spews its sworlin' reek. That horn's deeth-caall
Is not jist for the bords, but us inaall!

■ **Fred Reed** (1900-85) was Northumberland's best-known dialect poet of the 20th century, and drew on the 'pitmatic' variety of Northumbrian dialect particular to his native pit-town of Ashington. He went down the pit at 14, and in 1928 'escaped and became a clerk and educational lecturer'. In *Cumen and Gannin* (1977), he wrote: 'The dialect I have found to be highly expressive and of maximum desired impact, and dialect verse to be the music of rhythmical vocal sound, when the mind is suffused with feeling and it finds adequate expression.' [Note on dialect verse of William Barnes ➤ 48.]

■ **Anne Stevenson** ➤ 71.

ANNE STEVENSON
The Fish Are All Sick

The fish are all sick, the great whales dead,
The villages stranded in stone on the coast,
Ornamental, like pearls on the fringe of a coat.
Sea men who knew what the ocean did,
Turned their low houses away from the surf.
But new men, who come to be rural and safe,
Add big glass views and begonia beds.

Water keeps to itself.
White lip after lip
Curls to a close on the littered beach.
Something is sicker and blacker than fish.
And closing its grip, and closing its grip.

SEAMUS HEANEY
Augury

The fish faced into the current,
Its mouth agape,
Its whole head opened like a valve.
You said 'It's diseased.'

A pale crusted sore
Turned like a coin
And wound to the bottom,
Unsettling silt off a weed.

We hang charmed
On the trembling catwalk:
What can fend us now
Can soothe the hurt eye

Of the sun,
Unpoison great lakes,
Turn back
The rat on the road.

MARGARET ATWOOD
Frogless

The sore trees cast their leaves
too early. Each twig pinching
shut like a jabbed clam.
Soon there will be a hot gauze of snow
searing the roots.

Booze in the spring runoff,
pure antifreeze;
the stream worms drunk and burning.
Tadpoles wrecked in the puddles.

Here comes an eel with a dead eye
grown from its cheek.
Would you cook it?
You would if.

The people eat sick fish
because there are no others.
Then they get born wrong.

This is not sport, sir.
This is not good weather.
This is not blue and green.

This is home.
Travel anywhere in a year, five years,
and you'll end up here.

WILLIAM HEYEN
The Host

In the dying pond,
under an oilspilled rainbow where
cement clumped, cans rusted, and slick tires
glinted their whitewall irises,
at the edge where liquid congealed,
a lump of mud shifted.
I knew what it was,
and knelt to poke it with a wire
from the saddest mattress in the world.

Maybe a month out of its rubbery egg,
the young snapper hid,
or tried to, drew back its head,
but algae-scum outlined its oval shell,
its ridged chine diminished
toward its tail,
and I lifted the turtle
into the air, its jaws open,
its crooked neck unfolding upward.

70

It twisted, could not reach me.
I found out its soft, small undershell where,
already, a leech lodged
beneath its left hindleg, sucking
some of whatever blood
its host could filter from the pond, its host.
They would grow together, if the snapper lived.
Its yellow eyes insisted it would.
I gave it back to the oil sludge

where it was bom, and watched it
bury itself, in time, and disappear....
I'd like to leave it living there,
but churned slime above it blurs, burns,
bursts into black glare, every atom
of chemical water, rust residue, human vomit
shining in deathlight. The snapper's
bleached shell ascends the 21st century,
empty, beyond illusion.

DENISE LEVERTOV
The Stricken Children

The Wishing Well was a spring
bubbling clear and soundless into a shallow pool
less than three feet across, a hood of rocks
protecting it, smallest of grottoes, from falling leaves,
the pebbles of past wishes peacefully underwater, old
    desires
forgotten or fulfilled. No one threw money in, one had
    to search
for the right small stone.

This was the place from which
year after year in childhood I demanded my departure,
my journeying forth into the world of magical
cities, mountains, otherness – the place which gave
what I asked, and more; to which
still wandering, I returned this year, as if

to gaze once more at the face
of an ancient grandmother.
And I found the well
filled to the shallow brim
with debris of a culture's sickness –
with bottles, tins, paper, plastic –
the soiled bandages
of its aching unconsciousness.

Does the clogged spring still moisten
the underlayer of waste?
Was it children threw in the rubbish?

Children who don't dream, or dismiss
their own desires and
toss them down, discarded packaging?
I move away, walking fast, the impetus
of so many journeys pushes me on,
but where are the stricken children of this time, this
    place,
to travel to, in Time if not in Place,
the grandmother wellspring choked, and themselves not
    aware
of all they are doing-without?

■ **Anne Stevenson** (*b.* 1933) is an American and British poet, born in Cambridge of American parents, who grew up in the States but has lived in Britain for most of her adult life. Rooted in close observation of the world and acute psychological insight, her poems continually question how we see and think about the world. They are incisive as well as entertaining, marrying critical rigour with personal feeling, and a sharp wit with an original brand of serious humour.

■ **Seamus Heaney** ➤ 213.

■ **Margaret Atwood** ➤ 52.

■ **William Heyen** ➤ 171.

■ **Denise Levertov** ➤ 157.

DAVID WAGONER
Waiting in a Rain Forest

The rain does not fall here: it stands in the air around you
Always, drifting from time to time like breath
And gathering on the leaflike
Pale shield lichen as clearly as the intricate channels
Along the bloodwort gleaming like moths' eyes,
Out of the maidenhair
And the running pine and the soft small towers of club
    moss
Where you must rest now under a green sky
In a land without flowers
Where the wind has fixed its roots and the motionless
    weather
Leaves you with nothing to do but watch the unbroken
Promises of the earth
And know whatever lies down, like you or a fallen
    nurse-log,
Will taste the deepest longing of young hemlocks
And learn without fear or favor
This gentlest of undertakings: moss mending your ways
While many spring from one to a wild garden
Flourishing in silence.

DAVID WAGONER
Lost

Stand still. The trees ahead and bushes beside you
Are not lost. Wherever you are is called Here,
And you must treat it as a powerful stranger,
Must ask permission to know it and be known.
The forest breathes. Listen. It answers,
I have made this place around you.
If you leave it, you may come back again, saying Here.
No two trees are the same to Raven.

No two branches are the same to Wren.
If what a tree or a bush does is lost on you,
You are surely lost. Stand still. The forest knows
Where you are. You must let it find you.

SUSAN STEWART
The Forest

You should lie down now and remember the forest,
for it is disappearing –
no, the truth is it is gone now
and so what details you can bring back
might have a kind of life.

Not the one you had hoped for, but a life
– you should lie down now and remember the forest –
nonetheless, you might call it 'in the forest',
no the truth is, it is gone now,
starting somewhere near the beginning, that edge,

Or instead the first layer, the place you remember
(not the one you had hoped for, but a life)
as if it were firm, underfoot, for that place is a sea,
nonetheless, you might call it 'in the forest',
which we can never drift above, we were there or we
    were not,

No surface, skimming. And blank in life, too,
or instead the first layer, the place you remember,
as layers fold in time, black humus there,
as if it were firm, underfoot, for that place is a sea,
like a light left hand descending, always on the same keys.

The flecked birds of the forest sing behind and before
no surface, skimming. And blank in life, too,
sing without a music where there cannot be an order,
as layers fold in time, black humus there,
where wide swatches of light slice between gray trunks,

Where the air has a texture of drying moss,
the flecked birds of the forest sing behind and before:
a musk from the mushrooms and scalloped molds.
They sing without a music where there cannot be an order,
though high in the dry leaves something does fall,

Nothing comes down to us here.
Where the air has a texture of drying moss,
(in that place where I was raised) the forest was tangled,
a musk from the mushrooms and scalloped molds,
tangled with brambles, soft-starred and moving, ferns

And the marred twines of cinquefoil, false strawberry, sumac –
nothing comes down to us here,
stained. A low branch swinging above a brook
in that place where I was raised, the forest was tangled,
and a cave just the width of shoulder-blades.

You can understand what I am doing when I think of the
        entry –
and the marred twines of cinquefoil, false strawberry, sumac –
as a kind of limit. Sometimes I imagine us walking there
(…pokeberry, stained. A low branch swinging above a brook)
in a place that is something like a forest.

But perhaps the other kind, where the ground is covered
(you can understand what I am doing when I think of the entry)
by pliant green needles, there below the piney fronds,
a kind of limit. Sometimes I imagine us walking there.
And quickening below lie the sharp brown blades,

The disfiguring blackness, then the bulbed phosphorescence
        of the roots.
But perhaps the other kind, where the ground is covered,
so strangely alike and yet singular, too, below
the pliant green needles, the piney fronds.
Once we were lost in the forest, *so strangely alike and yet
        singular, too*,
but the truth is, it is, lost to us now.

■ **Susan Stewart** (*b*. 1952) is an American poet and critic who teaches the history of poetry, aesthetics and the philosophy of literature at Princeton University. 'The Forest' is the title-poem of her third collection, *The Forest* (1995). Robert Pogue (author of *Forests: The Shadows of Civilisation*) wrote: 'In this book a forest of memories gives way to a memory of forests through the most astonishing and adamantine lyrics of recollection – recollection of a collective species-past which continues to haunt and which the poet names through her own personal ghosts. Just when I thought I knew what a forest is, what place it occupies in our cultural imagination, I read these poems. Now I am not sure any more. The shadows have returned. Such is the power of this poetry.'

■ **David Wagoner** ➤ 62.

GERARD MANLEY HOPKINS
Binsey Poplars
felled 1879

My aspens dear, whose airy cages quelled,
Quelled or quenched in leaves the leaping sun,
All felled, felled, are all felled;
    Of a fresh and following folded rank
        Not spared, not one
        That dandled a sandalled
    Shadow that swam or sank
On meadow and river and wind-wandering weed-
            winding bank.

O if we but knew what we do
        When we delve or hew –
    Hack and rack the growing green!
        Since country is so tender
    To touch, her being só slender,
    That, like this sleek and seeing ball
    But a prick will make no eye at all,
    Where we, even where we mean

To mend her we end her,
When we hew or delve:
After-comers cannot guess the beauty been.
Ten or twelve, only ten or twelve
Strokes of havoc únselve
The sweet especial scene,
Rural scene, a rural scene,
Sweet especial rural scene.

GERARD MANLEY HOPKINS
God's Grandeur

The world is charged with the grandeur of God.
It will flame out, like shining from shook foil;
It gathers to a greatness, like the ooze of oil
Crushed. Why do men then now not reck his rod?
Generations have trod, have trod, have trod;
And all is seared with trade; bleared, smeared with toil;
And wears man's smudge and shares man's smell: the soil
Is bare now, nor can foot feel, being shod.

And for all this, nature is never spent;
There lives the dearest freshness deep down things;
And though the last lights off the black West went
Oh, morning, at the brown brink eastward, springs –
Because the Holy Ghost over the bent
World broods with warm breast and with ah! bright wings.

GERARD MANLEY HOPKINS
Inversnaid

This darksome burn, horseback brown,
His rollrock highroad roaring down,
In coop and in comb the fleece of his foam
Flutes and low to the lake falls home.

A windpuff-bonnet of fáwn-fróth
Turns and twindles over the broth
Of a pool so pitchblack, féll-frówning,
It rounds and rounds Despair to drowning.

Degged with dew, dappled with dew
Are the groins of the braes that the brook treads
   through,
Wiry heathpacks, flitches of fern,
And the beadbonny ash that sits over the burn.

What would the world be, once bereft
Of wet and of wildness? Let them be left,
O let them be left, wildness and wet;
Long live the weeds and the wilderness yet.

■ **Gerard Manley Hopkins** (1844-89) was a major poet of the Victorian period. An English Jesuit priest, he was virtually unknown as a writer in his lifetime. His highly original poetry – notable for its musicality and innovative "sprung rhythm" – was not published until 1918, many years after his death. 'His poems, letters, and journals reflect his whole-hearted involvement in all aspects of his life – his sense of vocation (sometimes conflicting) as priest and poet, his love of beauty in nature and man, his technical interest in prosody, and his search for a unifying sacramental view of creation' (Margaret Drabble).

Kim Taplin: 'Like Barnes, Hopkins saw the divine hand everywhere in nature. But whereas Barnes saw a dispensation, a tidy, planned and orderly world, Hopkins saw God as an artist whose world was full of beauty and idiosyncrasy and wild inventiveness. [...] Hopkins found "deep / Poetry" only in what connected him to heaven, and although all created nature did this, it was by means of trees in particular that his spirit was lifted [...] He conveys a profound understanding of the sense we have of the common bond between humankind and the rest of creation, and this was what led him to be able to think and write ecologically before the concept was common property. For there is much more to '**Binsey Poplars**' than a conservative spirit lamenting change to a personally loved landscape – though such feelings have a kind of value that has no place within the so-called economy that prevails. And how else can we view the last verse of '**Inversnaid**' but as a prophetic vision? It fears and foretells the ruthless, stupidly self-depriving way in which our species is destroying not only the habitats of other species but some of the growing ground of its own soul.'

CHARLOTTE MEW
The Trees are Down

– and he cried with a loud voice:
Hurt not the earth, neither the sea, nor the trees –
REVELATION

They are cutting down the great plane trees at the end of the gardens.
For days there has been the grate of the saw, the swish of the branches as they fall,
The crash of trunks, the rustle of trodden leaves,
With the 'Whoops' and the 'Whoas', the loud common talk, the loud common laughs of the men, above it all.

I remember one evening of a long past Spring
Turning in at a gate, getting out of a cart, and finding a large dead rat in the mud of the drive.
I remember thinking: alive or dead, a rat was a god-forsaken thing,
But at least, in May, that even a rat should be alive.

The week's work here is as good as done. There is just one bough
   On the roped bole, in the fine grey rain,
      Green and high
      And lonely against the sky.
       (Down now! –)
      And but for that,
      If an old dead rat
Did once, for a moment, unmake the Spring, I might never have thought of him again.

It is not for a moment the Spring is unmade today;
These were great trees, it was in them from root to stem:
When the men with the 'Whoops' and the 'Whoas' have carted the whole of the whispering loveliness away
Half the Spring, for me, will have gone with them.

It is going now, and my heart has been struck with the hearts of the planes;
Half my life it has beat with these, in the sun, in the rains,
      In the March wind, the May breeze,
In the great gales that came over to them across the roofs from the great seas.
      There was only a quiet rain when they were dying;
      They must have heard the sparrows flying,
And the small creeping creatures in the earth when they were lying –
      But I, all day, I heard an angel crying:
        'Hurt not the trees.'

CHARLOTTE MEW
Domus Caedet Arboretum

Ever since the great planes were murdered at the end of the gardens
The city, to me, at night has the look of a Spirit brooding crime;
As if the dark houses watching the trees from dark windows
        Were simply biding their time.

THOMAS HARDY
Throwing a Tree
New Forest

The two executioners stalk along over the knolls,
Bearing two axes with heavy heads shining and wide,
And a long limp two-handled saw toothed for cutting great boles,
And so they approach the proud tree that bears the death-mark on its side.

Jackets doffed they swing axes and chop away just above ground,
And the chips fly about and lie white on the moss and fallen leaves;
Till a broad deep gash in the bark is hewn all the way round,
And one of them tries to hook upward a rope, which at last he achieves.

The saw then begins, till the top of the tall giant shivers:
The shivers are seen to grow greater each cut than before:
They edge out the saw, tug the rope; but the tree only quivers,
And kneeling; and sawing again, they step back to try pulling once more.

Then, lastly, the living mast sways, further sways: with a shout
Job and Ike rush aside. Reached the end of its long staying powers;
The tree crashes downward: it shakes all its neighbours throughout,
And two hundred years' steady growth has been ended in less than two hours.

■ **Thomas Hardy** (1840-1928) was an English poet, novelist and short story writer. Much of his poetry and prose depicts people struggling against their passions and circumstances. He gave up fiction after the hostile reception given to *Jude the Obscure* (1895), but had written poetry from an early age, finally publishing his first collection in 1898.

Edna Longley: 'Thomas Hardy anticipates every crossroads of modern poetry in the British Isles. He stands between folk-traditions and literature; region and metropolis; Christianity and the post-Darwinian crisis of faith; Victorian and modern consciousness; prose-fiction and poetry; "things [that] go onward the same" and modern war.'

Dan Jacobson: 'For Hardy, nature is never inert – neither in itself as a theatre of continual change; nor as the terrain, begrudging and generous in turn, from which we and all other animals have to glean a living; nor in the ever renewed power it has to evoke a response in those who regard it. In fact, a paradox that the verse presses upon us – and here we come upon one of its philosophic dimensions – is that even when it is at its harshest, bleakest, its apparently most remote and indifferent, nature is understood as having these aspects only because we ourselves are compelled to see it as such. Thus, almost in spite of ourselves, we remain a part of it, and it remains a part of us.'

Jonathan Bate: 'He values a world – for him vanishing, for us long vanished – in which people *live in rhythm with nature*.'

[Other poem ➤ 119]

■ **Charlotte Mew** (1869-1928) was an English poet whose work spans the transition from Victorian poetry into modernism. 'Her poems are sensual, melancholic, and subjective, reflecting a lonely and eccentric life. [...] Her themes are death, ephemerality, love (usually lost or hopeless), God (also lost or uncompassionate), and the overriding tone is elegiac.' (Claire Harman)

In 'Men and Trees' (1913), Charlotte Mew argued that civilisation had replaced the old gods and devils by the worship of self; civilisation was shocked by the blood sacrifices of the old religions, but it had its own blood sacrifices in the commercial exploitation of the rubber trees of the equatorial forests and the destruction of the barbarian cultures of their inhabitants. 'The great tropical forests are being gradually penetrated; they are not yet ours,' she wrote, in an essay which shows her familiarity with all aspects of tree lore and mythology (Frazer's *Golden Bough* and elsewhere); praising 'the living tree, aloof, splendid', she mourns the daily victims 'of butchery, the axe and the rope and the saw': 'The London trees are all the prisoners of men, some unreasonably mutilated like the lopped crowd in Greenwich Park, while, now and then, there is a wholesale massacre such as that of the seven hundred in Kensington Gardens, which took place, no one knows why, some thirty years ago, against which even the executioners protested and perhaps the homeless rooks as vainly. In my own wooded neighbourhood one after another falls; progress pulls down the old spacious shabby houses and puts up flats for the half-world; a popular draper rears a proud monument to success; the green vanishes: even tomorrow one may miss the familiar plane of yesterday, and the birds go with the trees.'

W.S. MERWIN
Witness

I want to tell what the forests
were like

I will have to speak
in a forgotten language

W.S. MERWIN
Place

On the last day of the world
I would want to plant a tree

what for
not for the fruit

the tree that bears the fruit
is not the one that was planted

I want the tree that stands
in the earth for the first time

with the sun already
going down

and the water
touching its roots

in the earth full of the dead
and the clouds passing

one by one
over its leaves

W.S. MERWIN
To the Insects

Elders

we have been here so short a time
and we pretend that we have invented memory

we have forgotten what it is like to be you
who do not remember us

we remember imagining that what survived us
would be like us

and would remember the world as it appears to us
but it will be your eyes that will fill with light

we kill you again and again
and we turn into you

eating the forests
eating the earth and the water

and dying of them
departing from ourselves

leaving you the morning
in its antiquity

■ **W.S. Merwin** (*b.* 1927) is arguably the most influential American poet of the last half-century, known especially for continually renewing his poetry, for his intimate feeling for nature and language, and for several classic translations. His poetry has moved beyond the traditional verse of his early years to revolutionary open forms that engage a vast array of influences and possibilities. His recent poetry is perhaps his most personal, arising from his deeply held beliefs. Merwin is not only profoundly anti-imperialist, pacifist and environmentalist, but also possessed by an intimate feeling for landscape and language and the ways in which land and language interflow. He lives on the Pacific island of Maui, where he tends to his writing and to his garden of rare and endangered palm trees. Long been viewed in the States as an essential voice in modern American literature, his poetry was unavailable in Britain for over 35 years until the publication of his UK *Selected Poems* in 2007.

J. Scott Bryson: 'Like most ecopoets, Merwin attempts to depict the world as a community founded on reciprocity between human and non-human nature. [...] Merwin's poetry laments the "placelessness" of modern society, whose members often seem completely unaware of the bonds between themselves and the rest of the world. [...] Some of Merwin's best-known poems deal with the disappearance of species that result from this lack of place-awareness. [...] And as he points out in **'The Asians Dying'** [➤ 166], the exploitation and destruction of parts of the nonhuman world offer serious consequences for the human world as well.'

W.S. Merwin: 'The natural world is inseparable from us, and our attitude toward it, our use of it, is political action. If you pick up any part of it you pick up the whole thing. Sometimes I feel more immediately concerned with what's happening to the elements, the sea, the animals, the language, than I do with any particular society. I don't make a distinction in terms of importance. The poisoning of the soil, the imminence of nuclear disaster, are the same thing. You shut your eyes and you open them and you're staring at the same thing though the form of it may look different. [...]

'I feel close to [Robinson Jeffers's] feelings about our human self-importance, which I think is one of the things strangling us, our own bloated species-ego. The assumption that human beings are different in kind and in importance from other species is something I've had difficulty accepting for 25 years or so. I think our importance is not separable from the rest of life. If we say we are the only kind of life that's of any importance, we automatically destroy our own importance. Our real importance is our capacity for responsibility for every form of life, the recognition that we are a part of the entire universe. We're not the only valuable thing that's ever appeared in the universe.' (Interview with Daniel Bourne)

[Other poems ➤ 54, 81, 124, 152, 166]

WILLIAM BLAKE
The Sick Rose

O rose, thou art sick:
The invisible worm
That flies in the night,
In the howling storm,

Has found out thy bed
Of crimson joy:
And his dark secret love
Does thy life destroy.

ANONYMOUS
The Robin and the Redbreast

The robin and the redbreast,
  The robin and the wren,
If you take them out of their nest,
  Ye'll never thrive again.

The robin and the redbreast,
  The martin and the swallow;
If you touch one of their eggs,
  Ill luck is sure to follow.

■ **William Blake** (1757-1827) is much celebrated now as a great English poet and artist, but his work was little-known in his lifetime. Blake was an apocalyptic visionary and a fiercely independent thinker – both profound and naïve – who resisted the narrow orthodoxies of his age. **'The Sick Rose'** is from his *Songs of Innocence and of Experience* (1794), which contrasts pastoral innocence and childhood with adult corruption and repression.

JOHN KEATS
Song

I had a dove and the sweet dove died;
  And I have thought it died of grieving:
O, what could it grieve for? Its feet were tied,
  With a silken thread of my own hand's weaving;
Sweet little red feet! why should you die –
Why should you leave me, sweet dove! why?
You lived alone on the forest-tree,
Why, pretty thing! could you not live with me?
I kissed you oft and gave you white peas;
Why not live sweetly, as in the green trees?

RAINER MARIA RILKE
The Panther
In the Jardin des Plantes, Paris
translated from the German by Stephen Mitchell

His vision, from the constantly passing bars,
has grown so weary that it cannot hold
anything else. It seems to him there are
a thousand bars; and behind the bars, no world.

As he paces in cramped circles, over and over,
the movement of his powerful soft strides
is like a ritual dance around a center
in which a mighty will stands paralysed.

Only at times, the curtain of the pupils
lifts, quietly –. An image enters in,
rushes down through the tensed, arrested muscle,
plunges into the heart and is gone.

■ **John Keats** ➤ 152.

■ **Rainer Maria Rilke** ➤ 41.

WISŁAWA SZYMBORSKA
In praise of feeling bad about yourself
translated from the Polish by Stanisław Barańczak & Clare Cavanagh

The buzzard never says it is to blame,
The panther wouldn't know what scruples mean.
When the piranha strikes, it feels no shame.
If snakes had hands, they'd claim their hands were clean.

A jackal doesn't understand remorse.
Lions and lice don't waver in their course.
Why should they, when they know they're right?

Though hearts of killer whales may weigh a ton,
in every other way they're light.

On this third planet of the sun
among the signs of bestiality
a clear conscience is Number One.

■ **Wisława Szymborska** (*b.* 1923) is Poland's foremost living poet. She won the Nobel Prize in Literature in 1996 'for poetry that with ironic precision allows the historical and biological context to come to light in fragments of human reality'. Her short poems are concerned with large existential issues, exploring the human condition with sceptical wit and ironic understatement.

■ **Edwin Brock** (1927-97) was an English poet known especially for two poems, '**Song of the Battery Hen**' and 'Five Ways to Kill a Man'. After two years in the Royal Navy, he became a policeman and later combined working as an advertising copywriter with editing *Ambit* magazine. Influenced by American confessional poets, Brock wrote chiefly about family relationships and childhood memories.

■ **W.S. Merwin** ➤ 78.

EDWIN BROCK
Song of the Battery Hen

We can't grumble about accommodation:
we have a new concrete floor that's
always dry, four walls that are
painted white, and a sheet-iron roof
the rain drums on. A fan blows warm air
beneath our feet to disperse the smell
of chicken-shit and, on dull days,
fluorescent lighting sees us.

You can tell me: if you come by
the north door, I am in the twelfth pen
on the left-hand side of the third row
from the floor; and in that pen
I am usually the middle one of three.
But, even without directions, you'd
discover me. I have the same orange-
red comb, yellow beak and auburn
feathers, but as the door opens and you
hear above the electric fan a kind of
one-word wail, I am the one
who sounds loudest in my head.

Listen. Outside this house there's an
orchard with small moss-green apple
trees; beyond that, two fields of
cabbages; then, on the far side of
the road, a broiler house. Listen:
one cockerel grows out of there, as
tall and proud as the first hour of sun.
Sometimes I stop calling with the others
to listen, and wonder if he hears me.

The next time you come here, look for me.
Notice the way I sound inside my head.
God made us all quite differently,
and blessed us with this expensive home.

W.S. MERWIN
The Last One

Well they made up their minds to be everywhere because
     why not.
Everywhere was theirs because they thought so.
They with two leaves they whom the birds despise.
In the middle of stones they made up their minds.
They started to cut.

Well they cut everything because why not.
Everything was theirs because they thought so.
It fell into its shadows and they took both away.
Some to have some for burning.

Well cutting everything they came to the water.
They came to the end of the day there was one left standing.
They would cut it tomorrow they went away.
The night gathered in the last branches.
The shadow of the night gathered in the shadow on the
     water.
The night and the shadow put on the same head.
And it said Now.

Well in the morning they cut the last one.
Like the others the last one fell into its shadow.
It fell into its shadow on the water.
They took it away its shadow stayed on the water.

Well they shrugged they started trying to get the shadow
     away.
They cut right to the ground the shadow stayed whole.
They laid boards on it the shadow came out on top.
They shone lights on it the shadow got blacker and clearer.
They exploded the water the shadow rocked.
They built a huge fire on the roots.
They sent up black smoke between the shadow and the sun.
The new shadow flowed without changing the old one.
They shrugged they went away to get stones.

They came back the shadow was growing.
They started setting up stones it was growing.
They looked the other way it went on growing.

They decided they would make a stone out of it.
They took stones to the water they poured them into
     the shadow.
They poured them in they poured them in the stones
     vanished.
The shadow was not filled it went on growing.
That was one day.

The next day was just the same it went on growing.
They did all the same things it was just the same.
They decided to take its water from under it.
They took away water they took it away the water
     went down.
The shadow stayed where it was before.
It went on growing it grew onto the land.
They started to scrape the shadow with machines.
When it touched the machines it stayed on them.
They started to beat the shadow with sticks.
Where it touched the sticks it stayed on them.
They started to beat the shadow with hands.
Where it touched the hands it stayed on them.
That was another day.

Well the next day started about the same it went on
     growing.
They pushed lights into the shadow.
Where the shadow got onto them they went out.
They began to stomp on the edge it got their feet.
And when it got their feet they fell down.
It got into eyes the eyes went blind.

The ones that fell down it grew over and they vanished.
The ones that went blind and walked into it vanished.
The ones that could see and stood still
It swallowed their shadows.
Then it swallowed them too and they vanished.
Well the others ran.

The ones that were left went away to live if it would
     let them.
They went as far as they could.
The lucky ones with their shadows.

HELEN DUNMORE
Ploughing the roughlands

It's not the four-wheeled drive crawler
spitting up dew and herbs,

not Dalapon followed by dressings
of dense phosphates,

nor ryegrass greening behind wire as behind glass,

not labourers wading in moonsuits
through mud gelded by paraquat –

but now, the sun-yellow, sky-blue
vehicles mount the pale chalk,

the sky bowls on the white hoops
and white breast of the roughland,

the farmer with Dutch eyes
guides forward the quick plough.

Now, flush after flush of Italian ryegrass
furs up the roughland

with its attentive, bright,
levelled-off growth –

pale monoculture
sweating off rivers of filth

fenced by the primary
colours of crawler and silo.

■ **Helen Dunmore** (*b.* 1952) is an English poet, novelist, short story writer and children's writer who won the first Orange Prize for fiction in 1996. Her many collections include *The Raw Garden* (1988), which questions our sense of the "natural", relating changes wrought in the landscape through centuries of human intervention to the state of change made possible by advances in genetic engineering. In *Bestiary* (1997), she enters the animal world, exploring our relationships with animals and confronting our own animal nature. The poems of *Glad of These Times* (2007) capture the fleetingness of life, its sweetness and intensity, the short time we have on earth and the pleasures of the earth, with death as the frame which sharpens everything and gives it shape.

[Other poems ➤ 59, 207]

■ **Colin Simms** ➤ 60.

COLIN SIMMS
'Now that the rivers…'

Now that the rivers are bringing down some loam
of husbandman's love off these enlarged winter fields
not merely silt, which would quicken water meadows,
they've cleared the willows to speed the water's flow.
Ings, otters' homes, all else of alder-carr goes
a balance of centuries to the balance-sheet yields.

Floods will increase, and still they gripp
uplands, deep-plough for the new forests, let rip
earth-movers to straighten courses in places
they curse as stagnant, and drain out the bogs
had held the rain in, sphagnum, let it go slowly.
Nature reasserts with storms and man's span
is merely money washed out with dead moles and voles
more for the crows. Lost less slowly; frogs and otters'
        graces.

Vale of York floods 1968
(for C.M.R. and M.E.B.)

■ **John Kinsella** (*b.* 1963) is a prolific Australian poet, critic, editor and publisher. His father managed a farm in the northern wheatlands of Western Australia, a landscape that dominates his 'anti-pastoral' poems, which highlight aspects of the far-from-idyllic modern rural world, such as salinity, pesticides, road kill, soil erosion and the dispossession of indigenous peoples. In his anthology *Landbridge* (1999), he writes: 'I'm particularly interested in the "radical pastoral" – in blending the so-called pastoral tradition with the linguistically innovative

[...] My work may be symptomatic of late modernism (even post-modernism) in its exploration of the processes of its own creation and investigation of language as a thing-in-itself, but its concerns are primarily ethical and moral in nature.'

■ Edward Thomas ➤ 60. 'Women He Liked' has been given the title 'Bob's Lane' by some editors.

JOHN KINSELLA

Why They Stripped the Last Trees from the Banks of the Creek

They stripped the last trees
from the banks of this creek
twenty years ago. The old man
couldn't stand the thought
of bare paddocks with a creek
covered by trees slap bang
in the middle of them.
A kind of guilt I guess.
Anyway, he was old
and we humoured him –
chains, rabbit rippers,
chainsaws. We cleared
those banks until the water
ran a stale sort of red.
Until salt crept into
the surrounding soaks.
Furious he was – the salt
left lines on the bath,
the soap wouldn't lather.

EDWARD THOMAS

Women He Liked

Women he liked, did shovel-bearded Bob,
Old Farmer Hayward of the Heath, but he
Loved horses. He himself was like a cob,
And leather-coloured. Also he loved a tree.

For the life in them he loved most living things,
But a tree chiefly. All along the lane
He planted elms where now the stormcock sings
That travellers hear from the slow-climbing train.

Till then the track had never had a name
For all its thicket and the nightingales
That should have earned it. No one was to blame.
To name a thing beloved man sometimes fails.

Many years since, Bob Hayward died, and now
None passes there because the mist and the rain
Out of the elms have turned the lane to slough
And gloom, the name alone survives, Bob's Lane.

EDWARD THOMAS

First Known When Lost

I never had noticed it until
'Twas gone, – the narrow copse
Where now the woodman lops
The last of the willows with his bill.

It was not more than a hedge overgrown.
One meadow's breadth away
I passed it day by day.
Now the soil is bare as a bone,

And black betwixt two meadows green,
Though fresh-cut faggot ends
Of hazel make some amends
With a gleam as if flowers they had been.

Strange it could have hidden so near!
And now I see as I look
That the small winding brook,
A tributary's tributary, rises there.

JOHN HEATH-STUBBS
The Green Man's Last Will and Testament

In a ragged spinney (scheduled
For prompt development as a bijou housing estate)
I saw the green daemon of England's wood
As he wrote his testament. The grey goose
Had given him one of her quills for a pen;
The robin's breast was a crimson seal;
The long yellow centipede held a candle.

He seemed like a hollow oak-trunk, smothered with ivy:
At his feet or roots clustered the witnesses,
Like hectic toadstools, or pallid as broom-rape:
Wood-elves – goodfellows, hobs and lobs,
Black Anis, the child-devouring hag,
From her cave in the Dane Hills, saucer-eyed
Phantom dogs, Black Shuck and Barghest, with the cruel
    nymphs
Of the northern streams, Peg Powler of the Tees
And Jenny Greenteeth of the Ribble,
Sisters of Bellisama, the very fair one.

'I am sick, I must die,' he said. 'Poisoned like Lord
    Randal
From hedges and ditches. My ditches run with pollution,
My hedgerows are gone, and the hedgerow singers.
The rooks, disconsolate, have lost their rookery:
The elms are all dead of the Dutch pox.
No longer the nightjar churns in the twilit glade,
Nor the owl, like a white phantom, silent-feathered
Glides to the barn. The red-beaked chough,
Enclosing Arthur's soul, is seen no more
Wheeling and calling over the Cornish cliffs.
Old Tod has vacated his deep-dug earth;
He has gone to rummage in the city dustbins.
Tiggy is squashed flat on the M1.

'My delicate deer are culled, and on offshore islands
My sleek silkies, where puffin and guillemot
Smother and drown in oil and tar.
The mechanical reaper has guillotined

Ortygometra, though she was no traitor,
Crouching over her cradle – no longer resounds
Crek-crek, crek-crek, among the wheatfields,
Where the scarlet cockle is missing and the blue
    cornflower.
My orchids and wild hyacinths are raped and torn,
My lenten lilies and my fritillaries.
Less frequent now the debate
Of cuckoo and nightingale – and where is the cuckoo's
    maid,
The snake-necked bird sacred to Venus,
Her mysteries and the amber twirling wheel?
In no brightness of air dance now the butterflies –
Their hairy mallyshags are slaughtered among the nettles.
The innocent bats are evicted from the belfries,
The death-watch remains, and masticates history.

'I'll leave to the people of England
All that remains:
Rags and patches – a few old tales
And bawdy jokes, snatches of song and galumphing
    dance-steps.
Above all my obstinacy – obstinacy of flintstones
That breed in the soil, and pertinacity
Of unlovely weeds – chickweed and groundsel,
Plantain, shepherd's purse and Jack-by-the-hedge.
Let them keep it as they wander in the inhuman towns.

'And the little children, imprisoned in ogrish towers,
    enchanted
By a one-eyed troll in front of a joyless fire –
I would have them remember the old games and the old
    dances:
Sir Roger is dead, Sir Roger is dead,
She raised him up under the apple tree;
Poor Mary is a-weeping, weeping like Ariadne,
Weeping for her husband on a bright summer's day.'

■ **John Heath-Stubbs** (1918-2006) was a renowned English poet, critic and translator, who drew on classical and British mythology in much of his work, including his long Arthurian poem *Artorius* (1973) and **'The Green Man's Last Will and**

Testament'. At Oxford his close circle included Drummond Allison and Sidney Keyes, both killed later in the War, but he was out of step with the younger 'Movement' group including Kingsley Amis and Philip Larkin, and his resolutely individual and technically versatile poetry always ran counter to current fashions, although critics tried to describe him first as a Romantic, then as a Classicist. Although afflicted by blindness from the 1960s, and completely without sight from 1978, he continued to write into his 80s.

Neil Powell: 'Perhaps his immunity from fashion was partly informed by his lifelong immersion in history and classical mythologies. In his poems an encounter with Shakespeare, or Li Po or Plato is as natural and immediate as his description of a stone-chat or death-watch beetle. This is not to suggest Heath-Stubbs' work is archaic, far from it; his distinctive achievement was to forge a modern pastoral out of unlikely sources, a style which can encompass Yeatsian symbolism and dry irony.

■ The penultimate chapter of my eco-novel *The End of My Tether: a myth of England* (2002) begins in rhythmical prose, echoing the description of Gawain's arrival at the Green Chapel in the alliterative 14th-century Middle English poem *Gawain and the Green Knight*. In this extract, the book's villains – all dead by this time – are unaware that this is the place where they will be called to account for their murder of the English countryside and its wildlife. My Green Knight's lament is modelled on the incantations attributed to the 10th-century Irish poet Amergin Glúngel in *Lebor Gabála*, the pseudo-historical 'Book of Invasions' (with a sideways nod to Gray's *Elegy*). All the species he names were either threatened or had disappeared in many parts of England at the time of writing.

NEIL ASTLEY
The Green Knight's Lament
FROM *The End of My Tether*

Even in the dark cavernous barrow, his green skin shone; he moved towards them purposefully, a great stooping figure, grassy hair spilling in a silky fan from his shoulders, his beard a tumbling nest of leaves. Stilling their instinct to back away, the green axe held out like Excalibur, all powerful.

– Welcome, he said. You know the pact we pledged. We made our covenant, I bared my neck like Barleycorn to take your blade. Now take off your headgear, bow your heads that I may give you answer with my axe.

– There must be some mistake, stammered Oliver de Foie.

– It's Kernan you want, surely? said Hockle. He struck off your head off, he took what was yours.

– No mistake, he responded. Kernan is a part of me, and I of him. My head was his head, he took it and I took it back, a twelvemonth gone, a year ago today. But you men took what was not yours, you killed my country; what you've done has cost the earth, my plants and people, my birds and beasts who were not yours to take. No general good was served, no one's interests but your own.

– Where are we? asked Maw. Who are you, in God's name?

– I am the Green Knight and the Green Man, Cernunnos and Kernan. I am foxglove and fleabane, cat's-ear and cowslip, hogweed and cow parsnip. I am hare-bell and hare's-foot clover, stork's bill and bird's-foot-trefoil. I am dove-foot crane's-bill and mouse-ear chickweed. I am bee orchid and dog-violet, dog-rose and dog's mercury. I am toad and toadflax.

He moved towards them.

– I am the linnet and bullfinch, the whistling lapwing. I am the spotted flycatcher, the song thrush and tree sparrow. I am the barn owl and the grey partridge. All these you killed.

I am the cornflower, the corn buttercup,
corncockle, corn gromwell, cornsalad,
corn parsley and lamb's succory.
I am fumitory and pheasant's eye,
shepherd's needle and thorow-wax.
I am the pink bindweed in the cornfield,
the bright red poppy, yellow corn crowsfoot,
broad-leaved spurge and red hemp-nettle.
I am the purple knapweed in the meadow,
bryony in the hedgerow, I am finch and warbler
darting among the dog roses.

I am weed knotgrass in the wheatfield
with six pink flower-spikes, food
for the red-yellow leaf beetle, no more.
I am the larvae of the leaf beetle, food
for farmland bird chicks, no more.
I am the weevil and rove beetle,
the larvae of moths and sawflies, food
for songbirds, not now, all killed,
bindweed, beetles, birds, all gone.

I am seed of weeds. I am seed-eating birds.
I am corn bunting, cirl bunting, yellowhammer.
I am the insects. I am the insect-eaters.
I am the hovering lark and fieldfare.
I am the vole, the shrew and the fieldmouse.
I am the owl and the kestrel.
I am marshes and wetland, all drained,
moorland and water meadows, all gone.

I am the cowslip on the chalk down,
the dropwort, the devil's-bit scabious,
dwarf sedge, burnt orchid and toadflax.
I am the clustered bellflower.
I am the chalk hill butterfly
feeding on the horseshoe vetch.
I am the marbled white, the chequered skipper,
adonis blue, pearl-bordered fritillary.
I am hay-rattle yellow in the hayfield,
the black knapweed, the wild daffodil.
I am the cowslip and the meadow buttercup,
the adder's tongue fern, the green-winged orchid.

I am the silent field of ryegrass too,
the silage field of ryegrass, no grass
but ryegrass, no plant permitted
but ryegrass, nothing but ryegrass.
No ploughman treads this empty space
where all the air a solemn stillness holds,
no beetle wheels his droning flight,
no drowsy tinklings lull the distant folds.

Where are the owls and insects?
Where are the finches and cornflowers,
mice and moths, beetles and butterflies?
Where are the people, the farmers
who lived off the land, who gave us our food,
people and plants, birds and beasts all one?
All gone, all gone, all driven from the land.

And why, you men of greed?
Your cash crops killed us off,
your fertilisers forced us out,
you poisoned with pesticides,
you looted the land, and why?
You pulled up the hedgerows,
made big farms bigger, rich men richer,
small farms fail, money out of misery.
You turned our land into badlands
where nothing grows but money.
When money fails, nothing left,
nothing left to grow. You took it all.
There's nothing, nothing, nothing left.

JOHN MONTAGUE
Demolition Ireland

Observe the giant machines trundle over
this craggy land, crushing old contours,
trampling down the nearly naked earth.
Dragon rocks dragged into the open,
dislodged from their primeval dream.
Riverbanks, so slowly, lushly formed,
haunt of the otter and waterhen,
bulldozed into a stern, straight line;
dark trout pools dredged clean
so that doomed cattle may drink any time.
Once mysteries coiled in the tansled clefts
of weed and whin, land left to itself...
But see, the rushes rise again, by stealth,
tireless warriors, on the earth's behalf.

JOHN MONTAGUE
from Hymn to the New Omagh Road

As the bulldozer bites into the tree-ringed hillfort
Its grapnel jaws lift the mouse, the flower,
With equal attention, and the plaited twigs
And clay of the bird's nest, shaken by the traffic,
Fall from a crevice under the bridge
Into the slow-flowing mud-choked stream
Below the quarry, where the mountain trout
Turns up its pale belly to die.

Balance Sheet

LOSS

Item: The shearing away of an old barn
criss-cross of beams where pigeons moan
high small window where the swallow built
white-washed dry-stone walls.

Item: The suppression of stone-lined paths
old potato-boiler full of crocuses
overhanging lilac or laburnum
sweet pea climbing the fence.

Item: The filling-in of chance streams
uncovered wells, all unchannelled sources
of water that might weaken foundations
bubbling over the macadam.

Item: The disappearance of all signs
of wild life, wren's or robin's nest,
a rabbit nibbling a coltsfoot leaf,
a stray squirrel or water rat.

Item: The uprooting of wayside hedges
with their accomplices, devil's bit and pee the bed,
prim rose and dog rose, an unlawful
assembly of thistles.

Item: The removal of all hillocks
and humps, superstition-styled fairy forts
and long barrows, now legally to be regarded
as obstacles masking a driver's view.

GAIN

Item: 10 men from the district being for a period of
time fully employed, their 10 wives could buy
groceries and clothes to send 30 children content
to school for a few months, and raise local mer-
chants' hearts by paying their bills.

Item: A man driving from Belfast to Londonderry can
arrive a quarter of an hour earlier, a lorry load of
goods ditto, thus making Ulster more competitive
in the international market.

Item: A local travelling from the prefabricated suburbs
of bypassed villages can manage an average of 50
rather than 40 M.P.H. on his way to see relatives
in Omagh hospital or lunatic asylum.

Item: The dead of Garvaghey Graveyard (including my
grandfather) can have an unobstructed view –
the trees having been sheared away for a carpark
– of the living passing at great speed, sometimes
quick enough to come straight in:

> *Let it be clear*
> *That I do not grudge my grandfather*
> *This long delayed pleasure!*
> *I like the idea of him*
> *Rising from the rotting boards of the coffin*
> *With his JP's white beard*
> *And penalising drivers*
> *For travelling faster*
> *Than jaunting cars*

■ **John Montague** ➤ 49.

■ **Max Garland** (*b.* 1950) is an American poet who has pub-
lished two collections, *The Postal Confessions* (1995) and *Hunger
Wide as Heaven* (2006). Born and brought up in Kentucky, he
lives and teaches in Eau Claire, Wisconsin. 'For grassroots
American melancholy, Max Garland is the pure tobacco: free
of poetic fashions, the wind in the linden his muse, surprised
by the light that has traveled so far to find his transparent self
on the dark glass of a hotel window, "a man still / in the midst
of transmission", through which our transient world can be
seen.' (Eleanor Wilner)

MAX GARLAND
You Miss It

It's less lonely than it used to be,
what with the forests stripped down
to the minimum now, and the white lines
painted on the Oakwood Mall lot

and the cars parked like brothers,
in order of their arrival,
the sheen of the Lord upon them,
however, the last as blessed
with brightness as the first.

It's less lonely without the animals
broadcasting their strange sense
of themselves, as if being were enough,
if you sang it incessantly
from a high enough branch,
or possibly barked it into the night.

It's less lonely without the barking,
or the baying, or the night itself,
the small eyes clicking off and on
from the brambles, the lit green eyes,
the yellow. Though you miss it,
the loneliness, the size of it mostly,

the way you rose up to meet it
in fear, and were enlarged,
somehow, by the rising
and your own fumbling for sounds,
sequences, syllables

to cast yourself like a spell
into the midst of something
you neither made, nor imagined,
nor could keep from imagining.

PHILIP LARKIN
Going, Going

I thought it would last my time –
The sense that, beyond the town,
There would always be fields and farms,
Where the village louts could climb
Such trees as were not cut down;
I knew there'd be false alarms

In the papers about old streets
And split-level shopping, but some
Have always been left so far;
And when the old part retreats
As the bleak high-risers come
We can always escape in the car.

Things are tougher than we are, just
As earth will always respond
However we mess it about;
Chuck filth in the sea, if you must:
The tides will be clean beyond.
– But what do I feel now? Doubt?

Or age, simply? The crowd
Is young in the M1 café;
Their kids are screaming for more –
More houses, more parking allowed,
More caravan sites, more pay.
On the Business Page, a score

Of spectacled grins approve
Some takeover bid that entails
Five per cent profit (and ten
Per cent more in the estuaries): move
Your works to the unspoilt dales
(Grey area grants)! And when

You try to get near the sea
In summer…

               It seems, just now,
To be happening so very fast;
Despite all the land left free
For the first time I feel somehow
That it isn't going to last,

That before I snuff it, the whole
Boiling will be bricked in
Except for the tourist parts –
First slum of Europe: a role
It won't be so hard to win,
With a cast of crooks and tarts.

And that will be England gone,
The shadows, the meadows, the lanes,
The guildhalls, the carved choirs.
There'll be books; it will linger on
In galleries; but all that remains
For us will be concrete and tyres.

Most things are never meant.
This won't be, most likely: but greeds
And garbage are too thick-strewn
To be swept up now, or invent
Excuses that make them all needs.
I just think it will happen, soon.

■ In *The Song of the Earth*, Jonathan Bate writes: 'Meadow is grassland mown for hay, which serves as winter feed for cattle. It is the supreme example of culture working together with nature: the grass grows naturally (it is not sown in the manner of arable crops), but it needs to be maintained artificially (if not mown, it would revert to wildwood). Larkin wrote **'Going, Going'**, a poem commissioned by the Department of the Environment, in 1972. He was prescient about the loss of England's flower-rich hay meadows: since the Second World War no less than ninety-seven per cent of their acreage has gone. England no longer offers many 'sweet views' [Jane Austen, *Emma*] of the chequered fields that are characteristic of mixed farmland. Instead, most of the country is now covered by vast unbroken tracts of intensive cereal crop and a monoculture of artificially fertilised perennial ryegrass. As for winter feed, the consequence of replacing hay with a compound including ground-down animal carcasses has been BSE, or "mad cow disease".'

   [Philip Larkin: note with 'The Trees' ➤ 122]

JOHN BETJEMAN
Harvest Hymn

We spray the fields and scatter
   The poison on the ground
So that no wicked wild flowers
   Upon our farm be found.
We like whatever helps us
   To line our purse with pence;
The twenty-four-hour broiler-house
   And neat electric fence.

All concrete sheds around us
  And Jaguars in the yard,
The telly lounge and deep-freeze
  Are ours from working hard.

We fire the fields for harvest,
  The hedges swell the flame,
The oak trees and the cottages
  From which our fathers came.
We give no compensation,
  The earth is ours today,
And if we lose on arable,
  Then bungalows will pay.

All concrete sheds...etc

JOHN BETJEMAN
Inexpensive Progress

Encase your legs in nylons,
Bestride your hills with pylons
  O age without a soul;
Away with gentle willows
And all the elmy billows
  That through your valleys roll.

Let's say goodbye to hedges
And roads with grassy edges
  And winding country lanes;
Let all things travel faster
Where motorcar is master
  Till only Speed remains.

Destroy the ancient inn-signs
But strew the roads with tin signs
  'Keep Left', 'M4', 'Keep Out!'
Command, instruction, warning,
Repetitive adorning
  The rockeried roundabout;

For every raw obscenity
Must have its small 'amenity',
  Its patch of shaven green,
And hoardings look a wonder
In banks of floribunda
  With floodlights in between.

Leave no old village standing
Which could provide a landing
  For aeroplanes to roar,
But spare such cheap defacements
As huts with shattered casements
  Unlived-in since the war.

Let no provincial High Street
Which might be your or my street
  Look as it used to do,
But let the chain stores place here
Their miles of black glass fascia
  And traffic thunder through.

And if there is some scenery,
Some unpretentious greenery,
  Surviving anywhere,
It does not need protecting
For soon we'll be erecting
  A Power Station there.

When all our roads are lighted
By concrete monsters sited
  Like gallows overhead,
Bathed in the yellow vomit
Each monster belches from it,
  We'll know that we are dead.

■ **Sir John Betjeman** (1906-84) was an English poet, writer, broadcaster and campaigner for architectural conservation who was Poet Laureate from 1972 to 1984. He made many radio and television appearances, most notably in *Metro-land* (1973), a documentary on the London suburbs bordering the Metropolitan line. His comic gifts and sharp-witted "light verse" as well as his eccentric Englishness have contributed to his enduring appeal. Jocelyn Brooke described him as 'as a writer who uses the medium of light verse for a serious purpose: not merely as a vehicle for satire or social commentary, but as a means of expressing a peculiar and specialised form of aesthetic emotion, in which nostalgia and humour are about equally blended'. Betjeman viewed architecture as the visible manifestation of both society's spiritual life and its political and economic structure, attacking speculators and bureaucrats for their rapacity and lack of imagination.

In his preface to *First and Last Loves* (1952), he writes: 'We accept the collapse of the fabrics of our old churches, the thieving of lead and objects from them, the commandeering and butchery of our scenery by the services, the despoiling of landscaped parks and the abandonment to a fate worse than the workhouse of our country houses, because we are convinced we must save money.'

CYNTHIA GOMEZ
San José: a poem

There's a land with a heart of silicon
A land of computer chips and movie theaters
A hole in a valley sprawling out of control
A land of quinceañeras and taquierias and Our Lady of
    Sorrows Church
Swarmed over with dirty buses, coughing exhaust,
    teeming with brown skins
Pimpled with painted storefronts in stripmalls scream-
    ing foreign tongues
Stomped by shiny boots and shiny suits on their way
    to the glittering Silicon City
Where chips that aren't made for eating feed colonies
    of engineers in neat condos

Highways grow like a gash here, crisscrossing the earth
Through track homes and golf courses to projects and
    crack houses
And then to creeping cold playgrounds run with bright-
    clothed children
To pink music-piped malls full of baseball caps and
    baggy pants

And then to college where screaming yellow Spartan
    boys cheer on a losing team,
And to where crowds of teeming teal Shark fans swarm
    into a tinfoil arena

This land is piled with cinder-block gray hotels, new
    schools, malls
To cover the ashes of the yellow peril, burned long ago
And still the brown fists marched in protest thirty years
    past
This land wants espresso to flow in its veins, not blood,
Wants to be made of foccacia dough instead of earth
And its news station broadcasts smile on shiny new
    downtown,
Not to where armies of brown faces and hard-working
    hands march dead sidewalks on cold mornings
Before being whisked away backwards in faceless
    trucks to do day work
Or where small Saigon hands cut hair and jabber in
    Vietnamese

Dreams float like bumping balloons here, out of little
    brown and black and yellow heads
Over miles of little ticky-tacky boxes,
Over the glittering lights and polished porticoes of
    Willow Glen,
Over the leaf-clogged creek and over the garbage dumps,
To where they settle, heavy, weighed down by smog,
To rot, preserved in cement and chrome
As a proud sign proclaims a new San José.

ESTHER IVEREM
Earth Screaming

I *Omega*

This still mountain night is not still.
It rings loud and shaking like maracas.
Night bugs – locusts, cicadas – are screaming.

There has been no water here.
Falls trickle pitifully down rocks.
Even at night, on this cool, Pennsylvania mountain,
it is too hot.
With the upper atmospheres disappearing,
    stars so close,
      the unknown so near, coming so direct,
      settling on my head to crush my body,
      my foolish species.

Night bugs sound electric
clicking a morse code about omega.
An ancient rain chant rises from the trees.

You must come here.
Come out of the city's human hum,
to really hear
the earth screaming.

II *Alpha*

With untrained eyes over a thousand sweaty backs,
men picking the earth like cats to build the Erie Canal,
    Benjamin Wright saw malaria kill
in the Montezuma Swamp. Dewy tree after tree fall,
moist root upturned.
Silent warnings for the mingling of waters.

No Niagara Falls could stop progress,
No deadly beauty, no deafening, gleaming barrier,
whose every drop says, 'Do Not Enter'.

Now what slithering alien creatures,
future, fill the Great Lakes?
These watery, fat fingers
pointing to the heart
of America.

Fat sea snakes
with round mouths
on the sides
of their faces.

Tiny living swords
spit out by bleeding
baby fishes.

Tiny mussels blanket
the lakes' floors
sucking up oxygen.
Sending up bubbles.

A rattle heard
only by
the frightened.

III *Meanwhile*

This bumpy hill of Queens Boulevard is man-made tar.
Subways boom overhead, a rust-streaked overpass
shakes with rage, machinery, boredom, impermanence.
Oh, our treeless earth.

We are in a cave of metal.
We, rivers of cars, puffing exhaust
like a fat cigar man.

Trapped, ashamed, sad for our ugliness,
for ourselves, for living inside these metal bowels,
we look timidly across the road's faded yellow line
and don't meet eyes.

Sparrows nesting in wires and railings
beneath the subway tracks
in between the roar and rattle of the trains
They squeal! They have gone crazy!

How miserable we are
waiting in two columns
to cross this creaky outer roadway
overlooking the Hudson River
sealed in by concrete.

DENISE LEVERTOV
Those Who Want Out

In their homes, much glass and steel. Their cars
are fast – walking's for children, except in rooms.
When they take longer trips, they think with contempt
of the jet's archaic slowness. Monastic
in dedication to work, they apply honed skills,
impatient of less than perfection. They sleep by day
when the bustle of lives might disturb their research,
and labor beneath fluorescent light in controlled
     environments
fitting their needs, as the dialects
in which they converse, with each other or with
the machines (which are not called machines)
are controlled and fitting. The air they breathe
is conditioned. Coffee and coke keep them alert.
But no one can say they don't dream,
that they have no vision. Their vision
consumes them, they think all the time
of the city in space, they long for the permanent colony,
not just a lab up there, the whole works,
malls, raquet courts, hot tubs, state-of-the-art
ski machines, entertainment… Imagine it, they think,
way out there, outside of 'nature', unhampered,
a place contrived by man, supreme
triumph of reason. They know it will happen.
They do not love the earth.

■ **Denise Levertov** ➤ 157.

■ **Esther Iverem** (*b.* 1960) is an American journalist, author
and poet; born in New York City, she now lives in Washington,
DC. Her reviews regularly appear on SeeingBlack.com, a web-
site she founded in 2001 'for the dissemination of reviews,
news and commentary from a Black perspective'. She is a
former staff writer for *The Washington Post*, *New York News-
day*, and *The New York Times*, and is a contributing critic for
BET.com and Pacifica Radio. She has published two poetry
collections, *The Time: Portrait of a Journey Home* (1994) and
Living in Babylon (2005).

■ Sweden's **Tomas Tranströmer** (*b.* 1931) is Scandinavia's
best-known and most influential contemporary poet, and
worked as a psychologist for 30 years. He has been called a
'buzzard poet' (by Lasse Söderberg) because his haunting,
visionary poetry shows the world from a height, in a mystic
dimension, but brings every detail of the natural world into
sharp focus. Since his childhood he has spent long summers
on the island of Runmarö in the Stockholm archipelago,
evoking that landscape in his early work, which draws on the
aesthetic tradition of Swedish nature poetry. His later poetry
is more personal, open and relaxed, often reflecting his broad
interests: travel, music, painting, archaeology and natural
sciences. Robin Fulton's authoritative English translations of
his work are published in Tranströmer's *New Collected Poems*
(1997) in Britain, the American edition of which is titled *The
Great Enigma* (2006).

TOMAS TRANSTRÖMER
Schubertiana
translated from the Swedish by Robin Fulton

1

In the evening darkness in a place outside New York,
    an outlook point where one single glance will
    encompass the homes of eight million people.
The giant city over there is a long shimmering drift, a
    spiral galaxy seen from the side.
Within the galaxy coffee-cups are pushed across the
    counter, the shop-windows beg from passers-by,
    a flurry of shoes that leave no prints.
The climbing fire escapes, the lift doors that glide shut,
    behind doors with police locks a perpetual seethe
    of voices.
Slouched bodies doze in subway coaches, the hurtling
    catacombs.
I know too – without statistics – that right now Schubert
    is being played in some room over there and that for
    someone the notes are more real than all the rest.

2

The endless expanses of the human brain are crumpled
to the size of a fist.
In April the swallow returns to last year's nest under
the guttering of this very barn in this very parish.
She flies from Transvaal, passes the equator, flies for six
weeks over two continents, makes for precisely this
vanishing dot in the land-mass.
And the man who catches the signals from a whole life
in a few ordinary chords for five strings,
who makes a river flow through the eye of a needle,
is a stout young gentleman from Vienna known to his
friends as 'The Mushroom', who slept with his
glasses on
and stood at his writing desk punctually of a morning.
And then the wonderful centipedes of his manuscript
were set in motion.

3

The string quintet is playing. I walk home through warm
forests with the ground springy under me,
curl up like an embryo, fall asleep, roll weightless into the
future, suddenly feel that the plants have thoughts.

4

So much we have to trust, simply to live through our
daily day without sinking through the earth!
Trust the piled snow clinging to the mountain slope
above the village.
Trust the promises of silence and the smile of under-
standing, trust that the accident telegram isn't for
us and that the sudden axe-blow from within won't
come.
Trust the axles that carry us on the highway in the
middle of the three hundred times life-size bee-
swarm of steel.
But none of that is really worth our confidence.
The five strings say we can trust something else. And
they keep us company part of the way there.
As when the time-switch clicks off in the stairwell and
the fingers – trustingly – follow the blind handrail
that finds its way in the darkness.

5

We squeeze together at the piano and play with four
hands in F minor, two coachmen on the same
coach, it looks a little ridiculous.
The hands seem to be moving resonant weights to and
fro, as if we were tampering with the counterweights
in an effort to disturb the great scale arm's terrible balance:
joy and suffering weighing exactly the same.
Annie said, 'This music is so heroic,' and she's right.
But those whose eyes enviously follow men of action, who
secretly despise themselves for not being murderers,
don't recognise themselves here,
and the many who buy and sell people and believe that
everyone can be bought, don't recognise themselves
here.
Not their music. The long melody that remains itself in
all its transformations, sometimes glittering and
pliant, sometimes rugged and strong, snail-track
and steel wire.
The perpetual humming that follows us – now –
up
the depths.

■ **Chase Twichell** (*b.* 1950) is an American poet, editor and publisher; she is founder-editor of Ausable Press. She spent parts of her childhood in the Adirondack Mountains south of Montreal, where her family had lived for generations, and where she now lives and works. Her six books of poems map very different but related territories, including the human destruction of the natural world in *The Ghost of Eden* (1995), from which the three poems here are selected. Elegy, lament-ation and foreboding weave through this book-length sequence with the strength and clarity of apocalyptic utterance; through memories, observations and insights, the poems present the stark evidence of our fall from grace.

She is a practising Buddhist, and her poetry reflects her spiritual practice within the ancient tradition of Basho and Dogen and the contemporary company of Gary Snyder and W.S. Merwin. Her other collections include *Perdido* (1992), *The Snow Watcher* (1999) and *Dog Language* (2006).

CHASE TWICHELL
City Animals

Just before the tunnel, the train
lurches through a landscape
snatched from a dream. Flame blurts

from high up on the skeletal refinery,
all pipes and tanks. Then a tail of smoke.

The winter twilight looks like fire, too,

smeared above the bleached grasses
of the marsh, and in the shards of water

where an egret the color of newspaper
holds perfectly still, like a small angel

come to study what's wrong with the world.

In the blond reeds, a cat picks her way
from tire to oil drum,

hunting in the petrochemical stink.

Row of nipples, row of sharp ribs.
No fish in the iridescence.
Maybe a sick pigeon, or a mouse.

Across the Hudson,
Manhattan's black geometry begins to spark

as the smut of evening rises in the streets.

Somewhere in it,
a woman in fur with a plastic bag in her hand
follows a dachshund in a purple sweater,

letting him sniff a small square of dirt
studded with cigarette butts.
And in the park a scarred Dobermann

drags on his choke chain toward another fight,

but his master yanks him back.
It's like the Buddhist vision of the beasts
in their temporary afterlife, each creature

locked in its own cell of misery,
the horse pulling always uphill
with its terrible load, the whip

flicking bits of skin from its back,
the cornered bear woofing with fear,

the fox's mouth red from the leg in the trap.

Animal islands, without comfort between them.
Which shall inherit the earth?

Not the interlocking kittens frozen in the trash.

Not the dog yapping itself to death
on the twentieth floor. And not the egret,
fishing in the feculent marsh

for the condom and the drowned gun.

No, the earth belongs to the spirits
that haunt the air above the sewer grates,

the dark plumes trailing the highway's
diesel moan, the multitudes
pouring from the smokestacks of the citadel

into the gaseous ocean overhead.

Where will the angel rest itself?
What map will guide it home?

CHASE TWICHELL
The Devil I Don't Know

It seems to be the purpose of mourning

to change the mourner, to tip over,
in the end, the urn that holds the grief.

When a loved person dies,
elegy formalises that work.

But what if it's the holy thing itself,
the thing beseeched with prayer,
that's the deceased? What good is elegy then?

I was pushing my cart through the sharp
fluorescence of the supermarket,

lost in this question. People pawed
through the shrink-wrapped meats

which look like body parts to me
since I stopped eating them,

things that should have been buried,

and I thought, to what should I pray?
I'd always prayed to the ineffable
in its body the earth,

to the sacred violence of storms,
huge tracts of seaweeds rocked in the dark,

the icy crystals of the stars above the snow,
the mystery untameable and pure.

So what should I pray to now
in the hour of my abandonment?

Should I stand in my shining cart and shout
that the age of darkness is upon us?

Or turn inward to the old disciplines
and wander like a disembodied soul
through the wreckage, honoring my vows,

faithful to the end? A pilgrim
grown bright and clean as a flame,

eating only the gifts of the plants
and trees, what fattens among leaves
or swells in the soil underfoot.

Pure offerings. That means

no to fellow creatures bloated with steroids,

no to the heavy metals that shine
in the mackerel like tarnished silver,

no to the black-veined shrimp
in their see-through shells.

No to the embalming liquids
injected with needles,

no to the little chops packaged in rows
like a litter of stillborn puppies,

no to the chickens' sputum-colored
globules of fat, no to the devil I know.

The circular blade started up in the deli,

pink sheets of ham drooping into the plastic
glove of the man behind the counter.

What am I, an empty vessel waiting
for some new holy thing to come pour itself
into me? Where is the new divine?

I want to feed myself
into the machines of grief

and come out changed, transformed,
a new soul with a new consciousness.

I want a new inscrutable to worship,

to turn to in times of uncertainty and fear.
But there's only
the soft hiss of the lobster tank,

and the one surviving lobster, just sold,
waving its pegged claws from the scale.

A small swordfish gleams behind the glass.
Dear higher power, dear corpse of the world,

gutted, garnished, laid out on ice.

CHASE TWICHELL
The Rule of the North Star

I should be ashamed to love
the first hard frost the way I do,

the way it glitters
over the surface of everything,

erasing whatever's human.

But I'm not. So I stand for a minute
in the crystalline grass
with an armload of frozen firewood,

letting a little of the ruthlessness
enter my bones, breathing
white sparrows into the air.

Oh, I know where the logic leads.
If the lights of the town

spoil the dark... If the trucks
downshifting on the Cascade hill
infect the wind...

If humanity's the enemy, the enemy is me.

But there's something in me, an arrow
that points toward wilderness,

toward the mountain that governs
such loves, its ledges high enough
to have caught last night's

faint halo of snow.
Wherever I am, in all weathers,
I look up, and it's there,

it always has been, rising even
above the charred towers of cities,
under the north star which glints down

onto its sharp summit,
and onto each withered grass blade,

each rattling pod, each burned-out-car,
each smaller star of broken glass.

The mountain which has no name
burns in the distance

with a beautiful, radical plainness,

ledges bright with snowmelt.
It's the shrine,

the afterimage of the moment in which
I first imagined the world's death,

and knew at the same stroke
that though it would survive in some form,

it would not survive in this form.

The firewood aches in my arms.
Its smoke will cross over,

touching both the ash in the fireplace
and the lace of the mirage.

The north star
comes out earlier each evening.

It shines down onto the cloudy
or snowy or clear-skied world,

the wars, the droughts, the famines,

the ethnic cleansings,
just as it shone on the plagues,

the witch trials, the forced marches,
the purges, the great extinctions.

It will still be the sharpest spark
in the heavens long after my death,

your death, the next death of language –

a spark that will preside over the world
we leave behind, where acres of bones

catch the starlight, and a gray wind
scribbles in the drifts of ash.

■ **A.R. Ammons** (1926-2001) was one of America's most innovative and environmentally-tuned poets. The son of a tobacco farmer, he grew up in North Carolina, and taught at Cornell University for more than three decades. His formal invention and restless curiosity about every aspect of nature and of the mind are embodied in poetry remarkable for its extraordinary mixture of 'wisdom, pathos, humor, moral longing, and intimations of immortality' (David Lehman).

Interviewed by William Warsh in 1996, Ammons said: 'I love the land and the terrible dependency on the weather and the rain and the wind. [...] That's where I got my closeness and attention to the soil, weeds, plants, insects and trees.'

Gyorgyi Voros: 'Although much ecocritical analysis in recent decades has focused on the Western attitude of domination toward physical nature, the model of conquest and exploitation describes only one (albeit prevailing) stance toward nature. Carolyn Merchant has shown that this version itself arose when "a mechanistic world view in which nature was reconstructed as dead and passive" replaced an earlier conceit of an "organic cosmos with a living female earth at its center." [...] One alternative construction that has held sway since the Book of Job, and with which the poet A.R. Ammons has spent a career grappling, is nature as unattainable Other, unanswerable to human need or desire, with whom the human exists in a state of awe, fear, or, as is most often the case in Ammons, erotic longing. Ammons frames questions of how to live with, and within, the vast inhuman Otherness of nature in two recurring tropes: mirror and echoing voice.'

In *A Continuous Harmony*, Wendell Berry speaks to values underlying the qualities of simplicity and transparency in his own poetry in a comment on Ammons's religious vision, which refuses 'the presumptions of the closed forms of a humanistic art. Form, he believes, is in all things, but the forms comprehended in nature or achieved in art are necessarily partial forms, fragments, inferior to the form of the whole creation, which can neither be comprehended nor imagined.'

John Elder devotes a whole chapter of *Imagining the Earth* to 'the vision of A.R. Ammons, for whom the mental sphere expands to comprehend the swirls of body and earth. Ammons's poetry is a lyric of self-awareness, but, like Wordsworth, he is also taking a long walk through the world.' A key poem is **'Identity'** [➤ 158], which 'reveals, more precisely than any of Ammons's other poems, the way in which nature supplies the mind's terrain [...] the spider web, with its own formal circularity and balance, shows especially clearly the place of human meaning in the world and of the natural world in poetry.'

A.R. AMMONS
Gravelly Run

I don't know somehow it seems sufficient
to see and hear whatever coming and going is,
losing the self to the victory
    of stones and trees,
of bending sandpit lakes, crescent
round groves of dwarf pine:

for it is not so much to know the self
as to know it as it is known
    by galaxy and cedar cone,
as if birth had never found it
and death could never end it:

the swamp's slow water comes
down Gravelly Run fanning the long
    stone-held algal
hair and narrowing roils between
the shoulders of the highway bridge:

holly grows on the banks in the woods there,
and the cedars' gothic-clustered
    spires could make
green religion in winter bones:

so I look and reflect, but the air's glass
jail seals each thing in its entity:

no use to make any philosophies here:
    I see no
god in the holly, hear no song from
the snowbroken weeds: Hegel is not the winter
yellow in the pines: the sunlight has never
heard of trees: surrendered self among
    unwelcoming forms: stranger,
hoist your burdens, get on down the road.

A.R. AMMONS
The City Limits

When you consider the radiance, that it does not withhold
itself but pours its abundance without selection into every
nook and cranny not overhung or hidden; when you consider

that birds' bones make no awful noise against the light but
lie low in the light as in a high testimony; when you consider
the radiance, that it will look into the guiltiest

swervings of the weaving heart and bear itself upon them,
not flinching into disguise or darkening; when you consider
the abundance of such resource as illuminates the glow-blue

bodies and gold-skeined wings of flies swarming the dumped
guts of a natural slaughter or the coil of shit and in no
way winces from its storms of generosity; when you consider

that air or vacuum, snow or shale, squid or wolf, rose or lichen,
each is accepted into as much light as it will take, then
the heart moves roomier, the man stands and looks about, the

leaf does not increase itself above the grass, and the dark
work of the deepest cells is of a tune with May bushes
and fear lit by the breadth of such calmly turns to praise.

A.R. AMMONS
Corsons Inlet

I went for a walk over the dunes again this morning
to the sea,
then turned right along
    the surf
                rounded a naked headland
                and returned

    along the inlet shore:

it was muggy sunny, the wind from the sea steady and high,
crisp in the running sand,
          some breakthroughs of sun
     but after a bit

continuous overcast:

the walk liberating, I was released from forms,
from the perpendiculars,
          straight lines, blocks, boxes, binds
of thought
into the hues, shadings, rises, flowing bends and blends
          of sight:

                    I allow myself eddies of meaning:
yield to a direction of significance
running
like a stream through the geography of my work:
     you can find
in my sayings
                    swerves of action
               like the inlet's cutting edge:
          there are dunes of motion,
organisations of grass, white sandy paths of remembrance
in the overall wandering of mirroring mind:

but Overall is beyond me: is the sum of these events
I cannot draw, the ledger I cannot keep, the accounting
beyond the account:

in nature there are few sharp lines: there are areas of
primrose
          more or less dispersed;
disorderly orders of bayberry; between the rows
of dunes,
irregular swamps of reeds,
though not reeds alone, but grass, bayberry, yarrow, all…
predominantly reeds:

I have reached no conclusions, have erected no boundaries,
shutting out and shutting in, separating inside
          from outside: I have
          drawn no lines:
          as

manifold events of sand
change the dune's shape that will not be the same shape
tomorrow,

so I am willing to go along, to accept
the becoming
thought, to stake off no beginnings or ends, establish
               no walls:

by transitions the land falls from grassy dunes to creek
to undercreek: but there are no lines, though
          change in that transition is clear
          as any sharpness: but "sharpness" spread out,
allowed to occur over a wider range
than mental lines can keep:

the moon was full last night: today, low tide was low:
black shoals of mussels exposed to the risk
of air
and, earlier, of sun,
waved in and out with the waterline, waterline inexact,
caught always in the event of change:
          a young mottled gull stood free on the shoals
          and ate
to vomiting: another gull, squawking possession, cracked a crab,
picked out the entrails, swallowed the soft-shelled legs, a ruddy
turnstone running in to snatch leftover bits:

risk is full: every living thing in
siege: the demand is life, to keep life: the small
white blacklegged egret, how beautiful, quietly stalks and spears
               the shallows, darts to shore
                    to stab – what? I couldn't
          see against the black mudflats – a frightened
          fiddler crab?

          the news to my left over the dunes and
reeds and bayberry clumps was
          fall: thousands of tree swallows
          gathering for flight:
          an order held
          in constant change: a congregation

rich with entropy: nevertheless, separable, noticeable
      as one event,
             not chaos: preparations for
flight from winter,
cheet, cheet, cheet, cheet, wings rifling the green clumps,
beaks
at the bayberries
    a perception full of wind, flight, curve,
    sound:
    the possibility of rule as the sum of rulelessness:
the "field" of action
with moving, incalculable center:

in the smaller view, order tight with shape:
blue tiny flowers on a leafless weed: carapace of crab:
snail shell:
        pulsations of order
        in the bellies of minnows: orders swallowed,
broken down, transferred through membranes
to strengthen larger orders: but in the large view, no
lines or changeless shapes: the working in and out, together
        and against, of millions of events: this,
                so that I make
                no form of
                formlessness:

orders as summaries, as outcomes of actions override
or in some way result, not predictably (seeing me gain
the top of a dune,
the swallows
could take flight – some other fields of bayberry
        could enter fall
        berryless) and there is serenity:

        no arranged terror: no forcing of image, plan,
or thought:
no propaganda, no humbling of reality to precept:

terror pervades but is not arranged, all possibilities
of escape open: no route shut, except in
    the sudden loss of all routes:

I see narrow orders, limited tightness, but will
not run to that easy victory:
    still around the looser, wider forces work:
    I will try
    to fasten into order enlarging grasps of disorder, widening
scope, but enjoying the freedom that
Scope eludes my grasp, that there is no finality of vision,
that I have perceived nothing completely,
    that tomorrow a new walk is a new walk.

G.F. DUTTON

the high flats at Craigston

    the high flats at Craigston stand
    rawboned in a raw land,
    washed by thunderstorm and sun
    and cloud shadows rolling on

    from the bare hills behind, each one
    out-staring the wind;
    that every night
    cling together and tremble with light.

■ G.F. Dutton ➤ 209.

5. LOSS AND PERSISTENCE

These poems celebrate the rapidly vanishing natural world, or lament what has already been lost. Some find a glimmer of hope in efforts to conserve, recycle or rethink.

GARY SNYDER

Front Lines

The edge of the cancer
Swells against the hill – we feel
        a foul breeze –
And it sinks back down.
The deer winter here
A chainsaw growls in the gorge.

Ten wet days and the log trucks stop,
The trees breathe.
Sunday the 4-wheel jeep of the
Realty Company brings in
Landseekers, lookers, they say
To the land,
Spread your legs.

The jets crack sound overhead, it's OK here;
Every pulse of the rot at the heart
In the sick fat veins of Amerika
Pushes the edge up closer –

A bulldozer grinding and slobbering
Sideslipping and belching on top of
The skinned-up bodies of still-live bushes
In the pay of a man
From town.

Behind is a forest that goes to the Arctic
And a desert that still belongs to the Piute
And here we must draw
Our line.

GARY SNYDER

For All

Ah to be alive
    on a mid-September morn
    fording a stream
    barefoot, pants rolled up,
    holding boots, pack on,
    sunshine, ice in the shallows,
    northern rockies.

Rustle and shimmer of icy creek waters
stones turn underfoot, small and hard as toes
    cold nose dripping
    singing inside
    creek music, heart music,
    smell of sun on gravel.

    I pledge allegiance

I pledge allegiance to the soil
    of Turtle Island,
and to the beings who thereon dwell
    one ecosystem
    in diversity
    under the sun
With joyful interpenetration for all.

GARY SNYDER

For the Children

The rising hills, the slopes,
of statistics
lie before us,
the steep climb
of everything, going up,
up, as we all
go down.

In the next century
or the one beyond that,
they say,
are valleys, pastures,
we can meet there in peace
if we make it.

To climb these coming crests
one word to you, to
you and your children:

stay together
learn the flowers
go light

GARY SNYDER
By Frazier Creek Falls

Standing up on lifted, folded rock
looking out and down –

The creek falls to a far valley.
hills beyond that
facing, half-forested, dry
– clear sky
strong wind in the
stiff glittering needle clusters
of the pine – their brown
round trunk bodies
straight, still;
rustling trembling limbs and twigs

listen.

This living flowing land
is all there is, forever

We *are* it
it sings through us –

We could live on this Earth
without clothes or tools!

■ Gary Snyder (*b.* 1930) is an American poet, essayist and environmental activist who has been described as the 'Laureate of Deep Ecology'. A key figure in both the Beat Generation and the Black Mountain Poets, Snyder has pursued a radical vision which integrates Zen Buddhism, Native American practices, ecological thinking and wilderness values, seeking a cultural wholeness that is also respectful of the larger balance of life on the earth. Deep ecology grants intrinsic value to all life, shallow ecology sees only utilitarian value, as Snyder noted in his journal (20 August 1953) while working as a mountain lookout at Sourdough Mountain: 'Forest equals crop / Scenery equals recreation / Public equals money. : : The shopkeeper's view of nature.' [Other poem ➢ 56]

Robert Hass has called Snyder 'a major poet and ethical voice in the best honored traditions of the American Thoreau and the Japanese haiku-master Dogen. His work [...] heartens us to the challenges and promises of restoration to a natural place from which many of us now feel ourselves estranged.'

Terry Gifford (2002): 'Fundamental to Gary Snyder's Buddhism is a position of humility that emerges from a contemplation of the huge complexity behind the simplicity of the natural world we inhabit with other species, forms, and energies.'

Snyder studied ethnography at Reed College and at Indiana University, and John Elder has described how Snyder draws on anthropological perspectives in his work, 'asserting that the cycles of human life only achieve health and wholeness in a community which also includes the earth's nonhuman processes and entities. [...] Modern science has illuminated nature's creative cycles in ways that make the organic metaphor of culture even more helpful. Genetic information is retained and exchanged with a precision worthy of comparison with human memory, both with that of the individual and that – which we call culture – of the species.'

In his essay 'The Wilderness', Snyder writes: 'If we can tentatively accommodate the possibility that nature has a degree of authenticity and intelligence that requires that we look at it more sensitively, we can move on to the next step. "Intelligence" is not really the right word. The ecologist Eugene Odum suggests the term "biomass" [...] stored information in the cells and in the genes.'

Most of his poems are selected from *Turtle Island* (1974), 'the old/new name for the continent, based on many creation myths of the people who have been living here for millennia, and reapplied by some of them to "North America" in recent years. Also, an idea found world-wide, of the earth, or cosmos even, sustained by a great turtle or serpent-of-eternity.'

DAVID CRAIG
Against Looting

Leave the mahogany where it is!
Leave the mahogany trees in Borneo
Where the orangs embrace them gently.

Leave the geodes where they are!
Great egg-wombs toothed with crystal,
Leave them in the Brazilian darkness.

Leave the edelweiss where it is!
Its foliage woven of frost,
Leave it to root on the bergs of the Dolomites.

Leave the ambergris where it is!
Leave it, oily and fragrant,
In the gut of the sperm whale.

Leave the harp seals where they are!
Leave them to breed
In their nurseries on the floes.

Leave the scorpions where they are!
Leave them to sting in the mating battle
Under the rocks of Atlas.

Leave the white-lipped amethyst where it is!
Glistening arachnid sculptured in quartz,
Leave it to lurk in Mexico's granite caves.

Leave the urchins where they are!
Slow sunbursts spined with rays,
Leave them to graze on the skerries.

Leave the eggs of the osprey where they are!
Leave them to hatch
High on a resinous bower in the pines of Garten.

Leave the tortoises where they are!
Leave them to warm their shells in Lombardy.

Leave the orcas to wrestle with the squids,
                    leave them:
Leave the snail-gatherers of Papua
Grooming each other beside their waterfalls,
                    leave them, leave them:

Leave them in memory of the slaves
Stowed like carcases in the holds,
In memory of the elephants chained and swaying
In concrete hangars, in memory of the gorilla
Counting the links of his chain
Over and over and over, and leave them
For the sake of the children
That they may never laugh at a prisoner
Or try to buy a life with a coin.

■ **David Craig** (*b.* 1932) is an Aberdeen-born writer whose many books include three novels, five books of travel and oral history, and four collections of poetry, including *Against Looting* (1987) and *The Fourth Quarter* (2005). He has worked in schools, adult education and universities in Scotland, Sri Lanka and England, taught Creative Writing at the University of Lancaster from 1969 to 1992, and lives in Cumbria. Terry Gifford says that David Craig's **'Against Looting'** is 'probably the most didactic green poem' to have been published in the period covered by his study *Green Voices: understanding contemporary nature poetry* (1995): 'It expresses the political concerns of the green movement with a directness that is none the less powerfully poetic.'

■ **Peter Reading** (*b.* 1946) is an English poet notorious for his angry, gruesomely ironic, hilarious and heartbreaking portrayal of contemporary Britain through 25 books of poetry. After mapping national decline over 30 years, he reinvented himself in his later work. The bitter social critic turned into a millennial prophet of doom, directing his venom and sorrow at the destruction of the world's wildlife and environment, notably in *Faunal* (2002) and *-273.15* (2005). But this was no change of heart: Reading has been a dedicated naturalist and birder since childhood. **-273.15** [absolute zero] is a book-length poem, a lament, a tirade, a disaster warning, and an anthropologist's catalogue of our final expedition addressed to an earlier survivor of global catastrophe, Noah of the Flood.

[Other poems ➤ 111, 163, 238].

PETER READING
from **-273.15**

(After the heatwaves: Heat Death, Entropy,
Absolute Zero...)

Noye, Noye,
Could you handle,
Atop t'others,
337 species of *Pheidole*
New to Science
And recently charted
By Edward O. Wilson?

*

'Chuck 'em aboard;
Chuck 'em aboard me bucko mate
An' let's heave aweigh.'

*

and didya read how a survey of all them Brit birds and
butterflies shows there's some sorta population decline?,
[Yes, in a series of censuses that combed about every
square yard of England, Scotland and Wales over forty
years, more than 20,000 volunteers managed to count
each bird, native plant and butterfly they could find. They
reported that the populations of all the species surveyed
were in sharp decline – many extirpated completely.]
and didya read how two surveys of 1,200 sumthin plants
showed a decrease of 28%? [Yes, frail planet undergoing
its sixth great extinction – Cambrian, Devonian, Permian,
Triassic, Cretaceous, Holocene   ]

*

Ahoy! Noye! *Oimoi!*
32% of world's amphibian species,
Brink of extinction.
And what of the fissipeds,
Having toes that are separated
From one another, as dogs, cats, bears,

And similar carnivores?
What of the fissirostrals?
Of the Elegant Trogons?
The Meerkats?

UK numbers of summer-visiting *Cuculus canorus*
Down 50% in 30 years –
Scientists at the Rothamstead Research Centre
Say that seven or eight species
Of moth caterpillars, important in the bird's diet,
Are in serious decline:
Caterpillars of the Tiger Moth,
The Magpie Moth,
The Lackey Moth,
The Figure-of-eight Moth
(The larvae over-winter,
And this recent warm, wet
January and February weather
Favours fungal pathogens
Which kill them)...

*

'F'c's'le, standing-room only.
Y'all look lively *Now!*'

[...]

thus we know that Global Warming, rather than causing
gradual, centuries-spanning change, will push the cli-
mate to tip-point, fast. The ocean/atmosphere system
controlling their frail planet's climate will change things
radically – maybe in less than a decade. [The struggle
naught availeth.] And consider the geopolitical implica-
tions. And consider the urgency of underwhelmed soc-
ieties, the haves and have nots. And consider the 4% of
the Arctic ice cap melted per decade since about 1970,
the decline of the North Atlantic's salinity reduced over
the past forty years, the possible effect of this on the
Great Atlantic Current, the cooling of much of Europe
and the U.S. if the flow ceased, the droughts, the dust-
bowls and the ashes... [You, at the back, should've sat
up and fuckingwell paid attention   ]

Sir, Sir, will eu emploie
Cockes, kytes, croes,
Rookes, ravens, divers hoopoes,
Cuckoes, curlues, kakapos,
Ich one in his kinde?

*

'Ham, Ham, it's muckle late:

Nothing can ever be done,
Things are intractably thus,
Those having precognition suffer
Heat Death beforehand.'

*

Noye, Noye,
I see Mi people in deede and thoughte
Are sette full fowle in synne.
Bestes and fugols with thee thu may take,
He and shee, mate to mate;
Nathless, hit be Mi lykinge
Eall lif for to destroye –
Destroyed eall thes weorold shall be,
E'en eower shippe, gentil Noye,
Eower cargo's rich biodiversitye,
Each cell sincan.

[…]

and didya read how them corporates own all the water?,
sure gonna trigger big global shit in a few years,
[Nights, the cops' 'copters are beaming the NO-GOs;
days, the CCTV yellow/blue/white vans
circuit the zones most likely to get hit.]

and didya read how them albatrosses in the Antarctic
is gettin extinct through gettin all snagged in them
two-mile fish-lines?,
[These are the days of the auspices' headlines;
days to consider the vast ineluctable,
vast ineluctable.]

For it is My Likinge
Mankinde for to anoye.

*

Sir, here are Lions, Leopards,
Birches, Hawthorns, Rosebay Willowherbs,
Horses, Oxen, Peccaries,
Shrews, Voles, various species of Ants,
Goats and Sheep,
A duo of *Alligator mississippiensis*,
A couple of Nine-banded Armadillos,
Two *Lycosa tarentula*,
Don't forget the Pygmy Nuthatches,
(Too late for the Ivory-billed Woodpeckers,
But chuck in a pair of Pileateds),
Coyotes, Chamois, Chimps,
Woodlice, Carp, Morons,
Budgies, Yosemite Bears,
Rats, Pipistrelles, Sprats, Brats,
Yeasts, Yobs, Silver-back Gorillas,
And here are Doves, Ducks, Drakes, Redshanks,
Kyrie eleison, diverse Bacteria,
Don't forget the Slime Moulds…

*

Clang, clang, clang: All aboard for Ararat.

*

Oi!, never omit the Natterjack Toads, the Palmate Newts,
The Slow Worms, the Gnats, the Gnus, the Tape-Worms, the

[…]

and didya read how we fished them sand eels
    out of existence?,
sure gonna fuck them kittiwakes good, plus
    fulmars and puffins,
no goddam plankton, ya know?, for them mother
    sand eels to feed on,
due to that global shit, ya know?, heatwave
    followed by deepfreeze?,

Past midnight, and my umpteenth Zinfandel.
I type the Science Spotlight for tomorrow's
edition of the *Global Sentinel*:
    The earth is losing species at a rate
    comparable with the mass extinctions of
    the Cambrian, Devonian, Permian,
    Triassic and Cretaceous. The Golden Toad
    lived on a mountain ridge in Costa Rica,
    and has not been seen there for 15 years.
    The Hawaiian Thrush was extirpated by
    destruction of its forest habitat,
    pathogens brought by introduced mosquitoes,
    and competition from non-native species.
    The Hawaiian Crow is also now extinct.
    Pantanodon madagascariensis
    (a fish from Malagasy) disappeared
    when swamps it lived in were converted to
    fields to grow rice. A 'new' Brazilian
    amphibian has not been sighted since
    it was discovered 80 years ago.
    What's happening now is more than can be seen
    anywhere in the fossil record. These
    annihilations, taking place for reasons
    of climate change and new disease emergence,
    are indications of climacteric things
    which will affect us and our fraily balanced
    productive economic systems, *soon*.
In my same column thirty-eight years back:
    The earth is threatened by its own pollution...
    Western Industrial Man is facing, *now*,
    not just a challenge but a climacteric...
(Those in the front seats should have paid attention.)

For I will consider our shippe's cat.
For having performed the rolly-polly and curly-paw,
For entertainment she tackles the tenfold cogitations.
For first she frets over rainforest depletions.
For secondly she condemns our otiose CO_2 emissions
For these fuck up her atmosphericals.
For thirdly she bids a peremptory adieu to biodiversicals.
For fourthly she regrets that 8 Burmese Pythons,

4 Emus, an Anaconda and 12 Colombian Red-tail Boas
Have been left back at the zoo awaiting *Diluvium*.
For fifthly she grieves the accelerating pace
Of melting Antarctic glaciers
(Smokestack and tailpipe gas)
For these drain the West Antarctic Ice Sheet –
Region containing enough ice
To raise sea levels 20 feet
(Tough luck, Bangladesh, New Orleans).
For sixthly she calculates the numbers
Of *Cuculus canorus* visiting UK
Down 50% in 30 years.
For seventhly she flinches
From the cathode-ray tube's dire tidings.
For eighthly she strenuously denies deities.
For ninthly their accipitrine unleashing scares her shitless.
For tenthly she apprehends devenustation.

[...]

and didya read how that
Everest snow-line's
five miles above where it
was fifty years back?,
and didya read how them
climate extremes is
happenin faster and
faster and faster?,
and didya read how that
Everest snow-melt
(climatic change again,
see what I mean like?)
fills all them lakes in the
Himalayas?, –
when them lakes *burst*, better
look out *then* mate!,
and didya read how (and
this sounds crazy)
this Global Warming'll
cause a Great Ice Age?,
and didya and did

PABLO NERUDA
Oh Earth, Wait For Me
translated from the Spanish by Alastair Reid

Return me, oh sun,
to my wild destiny,
rain of the ancient wood,
bring me back the aroma and the swords
that fall from the sky,
the solitary peace of pasture and rock,
the damp at the river-margins,
the smell of the larch tree,
the wind alive like a heart
beating in the crowded restlessness
of the towering araucaria.

Earth, give me back your pure gifts,
the towers of silence which rose
from the solemnity of their roots.
I want to go back to being what I have not been,
and learn to go back from such deeps
that amongst all natural things
I could live or not live; it does not matter
to be one stone more, the dark stone,
the pure stone which the river bears away.

DENISE LEVERTOV
Come into Animal Presence

Come into animal presence.
No man is so guileless as
the serpent. The lonely white
rabbit on the roof is a star
twitching its ears at the rain.
The llama intricately
folding its hind legs to be seated
not disdains but mildly
disregards human approval.

What joy when the insouciant
armadillo glances at us and doesn't
quicken his trotting
across the track into the palm brush.

What is this joy? That no animal
falters, but knows what it must do?
That the snake has no blemish,
that the rabbit inspects his strange surroundings
in white star-silence? The llama
rests in dignity, the armadillo
has some intention to pursue in the palm-forest.
Those who were sacred have remained so,
holiness does not dissolve, it is a presence
of bronze, only the sight that saw it
faltered and turned from it.
An old joy returns in holy presence.

PHILIP LEVINE
Animals Are Passing from Our Lives

It's wonderful how I jog
on four honed-down ivory toes
my massive buttocks slipping
like oiled parts with each light step.

I'm to market. I can smell
the sour, grooved block, I can smell
the blade that opens the hole
and the pudgy white fingers

that shake out the intestines
like a hankie. In my dreams
the snouts drool on the marble,
suffering children, suffering flies,

suffering the consumers
who won't meet their steady eyes
for fear they could see. The boy
who drives me along believes

that any moment I'll fall
on my side and drum my toes
like a typewriter or squeal
and shit like a new housewife

discovering television,
or that I'll turn like a beast
cleverly to hook his teeth
with my teeth. No. Not this pig.

PAAL-HELGE HAUGEN
(He comes into view)
FROM *Brother Pig*
translated from the Norwegian by Roger Greenwald

On history's surface
in the great battle tapestries, he turns up
almost invisible in the background
in the dust clouds from long forgotten
destruction, in the tumult of murder
or offered up on an oil-slick canvas
of gluttony, drained of blood and at table
to be digested

Half-choked squeals through white noise
the static of old radio programs
the pig's signal through the goading speeches
Or on careless sepia photographs
trembling in the low underbrush
as boots march by
on their way to becoming shadows flickering
across the mired fields and artillery zones

Or almost visible against white underground
walls in laboratories, beeping screens and precision
when new methods are being developed
Someone bends over him now
and slides the hypodermic into the swollen vein
presses the plunger, observes

And finally, all by himself
the light almost gone
along the shifting pathways
in the cortex, a light
in the whirlwind, a fragile lamp that goes out

and behind the retina, fragments of a second
last snap: the lights enormous negative image:
concentrated, inevitable darkness

■ **Pablo Neruda** ➤ 142.

■ **Denise Levertov** ➤ 157.

■ **Philip Levine** (*b.* 1928) is an American poet of Russian-Jewish immigrant stock viewed by many as the authentic voice of America's urban poor. Born and raised in Detroit, he spent his early years doing a succession of heavy labouring jobs. Much of his poetry addresses the joys and sufferings of industrial life, with radiant feeling as well as painful irony. Always a poet of memory and invention, Levine has continually written poems which search for universal truths. His plain-speaking poetry is a testament to the durability of love, the strength of the human spirit and the persistence of life in the face of death. His books include 16 collections of poetry, two books of essays and his recent UK selection, *Stranger to Nothing: Selected Poems* (2006).

■ **Paal-Helge Haugen** (*b.* 1945) is a Norwegian poet and librettist. Born in the valley of Setesdal in southern Norway, he now lives in Nodeland, near the south coast. '(He comes into view)' is the first section of a seven-part poem, 'Brother Pig', from his 1985 collection *Wintering with the Light*. Taking as his motif the light that outlasts winter, Haugen explores survivals, moving among personal, historical, artistic and political dimensions. He is concerned not only with the remnants of value we inherit or seek out, but with what we can make of them and how we can maintain the meanings we discover. Known for the spare, honed style of his poetry, Haugen reveals the poetic potential of even the smallest creatures and things.

ALLISON FUNK
The Whooping Cranes

Perhaps it began with a disturbance
hardly worth mentioning,
or something larger, some hurt we need to name,

having felt endangered
as – shy, secretive –
the whooping cranes have been.

Farmers, hunters, high power-lines.

Of the hundreds once: a few dozen cranes.
And those remaining have forgotten their way

so that – who would believe? – to save them
a man dresses up in a crane costume,
his head, face, the rest swaddled in white cotton.

Not unlike us, the way writers pretend,

the biologist starting in the bulrushes
with the olive-buff eggs he'll protect,

later helping the chicks find minnows and snails,
frogs and larvas to grow on,
this man who has not begotten them,

but father-like leads the fledglings around the refuge,
their plumage whitening
against the black muck of the marsh

before they follow him into the sky

to ride the wing of the ultra-light aircraft
he pilots, glide behind.

And while they're aloft
the man who looks like he's towing the flock
confuses himself with the cranes –
as they do themselves with him –

their cries in his throat,
his costume, down-soft,
nothing his own but blue eyes showing.

Under a spell as he flies,
he remembers the story
of the seven ravens he loved as a child –

how anger, one burst from their father,
turned the sons into birds.

Lifting off in an early mist he wonders
if he'd want in the end
the gift their sister brings to the glass mountain,

unsure if freedom lies in becoming human.

How well he knows
it's only the beginning of a long migration –

a thousand miles
starting from Wisconsin's wetlands, stopping
for high winds and hail, then on in formation
over ponds, swales and grasslands, the ridges of Appalachia

to where, if they arrive, the flock will winter over
in the southern haven of a salt marsh
and, come spring, fly back without him, wild.

PETER READING
Endangered

Down on the Gulf Coast of Texas, in the Aransas wetland,
    Johnston and I were observing a posse of Whooping Cranes
(*Grus americana*), Titanium White in crisp focus
    through the Bausch & Lomb, red facial skin, black primaries,
    and a Goddam wingspan of eighty-seven inches.
When they took flight, the trumpets sounded over the marshes,
kerloo kerleeloo, kerloo kerleeloo, kerloo kerleeloo,
and we knew, we knew we would die without seeing the species
        again.

KATHLEEN JAMIE
Frogs

But for her green
palpitating throat, they lay
inert as a stone, the male
fastened like a package
to her back. They became,

as you looked, almost
beautiful, her back
mottled to leafy brown,
his marked with two stripes,
pale as over-wintered grass.

When he bucked, once,
neither so much as blinked;
their oval, gold-lined eyes
held to some bog-dull
imperative. The car

that would smear them
into one – belly
to belly, tongue thrust
utterly into soft brain –
approached and pressed on

Oh how we press on –
the car and passengers, the slow
creatures of this earth,
the woman by the verge
with her hands cupped.

DORIANNE LAUX
The Orgasms of Organisms

Above the lawn the wild beetles mate
and mate, skew their tough wings
and join. They light in our hair,
on our arms, fall twirling and twinning

into our laps. And below us, in the grass,
the bugs are seeking each other out,
antennae lifted and trembling, tiny legs
scuttling, then the infinitesimal
ah's of their meeting, the awkward joy
of their turnings around. O end to end
they meet again and swoon as only bugs can.
This is why, sometimes, the grass feels electric
under our feet, each blade quivering, and why
the air comes undone over our heads
and washes down around our ears like rain.
But it has to be spring, and you have to be
in love – acutely, painfully, achingly in love –
to hear the black-robed choir of their sighs.

■ **Allison Funk** ➢ 222.

■ **Peter Reading** ➢ 104.

■ **Kathleen Jamie** (*b.*1962) is a Scottish writer whose early work was fed by her experiences of life in the wilder parts of Pakistan and Tibet. Her subsequent poetry addresses Scottish and gender issues, including national and personal identity in *The Queen of Sheba* (1994) and motherhood in *Jizzen* (1999). Her interest in nature emerges fully in *The Tree House* (2004), where she asks how human beings can live in a balance with the natural world. Her lyrical poetry is intelligent and subtle, her language inventive and keenly tuned to her subject-matter.

■ **Dorianne Laux** (*b.*1952) is an American poet of Irish, French and Algonquin Indian heritage. Her poetry is noted for its emotional honesty, immediacy and passion. Her books include *Awake* (1990), *What We Carry* (1994), *Smoke* (2000) and *Facts About the Moon* (2005); she co-edited *The Poet's Companion: A Guide to the Pleasures of Writing Poetry* (1997) with Kim Addonizio.
  Tony Hoagland: 'Laux is a believer in desire, and she takes her stance as a hero of the ordinary, with both feet firmly planted in the luminous material world. Her poems are those of a grown American woman, one who looks clearly, passionately, and affectionately at rites of passage, motherhood, the life of work, sisterhood, and especially sexual love, in a celebratory fashion. What we carry, she says, is the ashes of the dead under the station wagon seat, our losses and defeats, and the obligation to continue the human project.' (*Gettysburg Review*)

STANLEY KUNITZ
The Snakes of September

All summer I heard them
rustling in the shrubbery,
outracing me from tier
to tier in my garden,
a whisper among the viburnums,
a signal flashed from the hedgerow,
a shadow pulsing
in the barberry thicket.
Now that the nights are chill
and the annuals spent,
I should have thought them gone,
in a torpor of blood
slipped to the nether world
before the sickle frost.
Not so. In the deceptive balm
of noon, as if defiant of the curse
that spoiled another garden,
these two appear on show
through a narrow slit
in the dense green brocade
of a north-country spruce,
dangling head-down, entwined
in a brazen love-knot.
I put out my hand and stroke
the fine, dry grit of their skins.
After all,
we are partners in this land,
co-signers of a covenant,
At my touch the wild
braid of creation
trembles.

■ **Stanley Kunitz** (1905-2006) was a highly influential American poet, editor, translator and teacher committed to fostering community amongst artists. His poetry is autobiographical but also fiercely visionary. Drawing on Jungian symbolism, he engaged with personal tragedy and public conscience to produce a resilient poetry of testing wisdom. His last work,

published on his 100th birthday, was *The Wild Braid: A Poet Reflects on a Century in the Garden* (2005), a gathering of poems and photographs from the garden he created over 40 years at his summer home in Provincetown, Cape Cod, interwoven with Kunitz's reflections on poetry, nature, life, death and the creative process. Like Derek Jarman's garden patch at Dungeness, Kunitz's seaside garden is both real and metaphorical, leading him to 'an appreciation of the natural universe, and to a meditation on the connection between the self and the natural universe'. In one of his conversations with Genine Lentine, Kunitz says: 'The universe is a continuous web. Touch it at any point and the whole web quivers.' In another, he describes how a spruce in the garden represented for him 'the rising of the sun, since it always caught the morning light':

'And, as it was host to a whole family of garden snakes, it became the source of the poem **'The Snakes of September'**. As each summer approached its end, they got bolder and bolder, dangling from the top of the spruce to the bottom, snugly entwined, as they sought the warmth of the sun. I saw them as the "wild braid of creation".

'The snakes had learned they were in no danger, and allowed me to stroke them. What gave me particular satisfaction was that they had become so accustomed to my stroking, they seemed to quiver in a kind of ecstasy.

'As the days grew cooler, and the snakes become more lethargic, I felt they were actually waiting for me to appear, that it had become part of their ritual of survival. I imagined over the years that this awareness was bred into the family, that they had passed on the news. They usually stopped appearing in mid-October, just before my time of departure.

'In the poem, I refer to the snakes as being "co-signers of a covenant". There's something very important to me about having a kind of relationship, with plants and animals, that can be transacted wholly without language. The warmth of one's body is a form of communication. The stroke of one's hand is a means of communication. In the garden those forms are heightened. I have a tendency when I'm walking in the garden to brush the flowers as I go by, anticipating the fragrant eloquence of their response. I get a sense of reciprocity that is very comforting, consoling.

'There are forms of communication that have to do not only with the body, but with the spirit itself, a permeation of one's being. I strongly identify with Henry James when he wrote, in answer to a letter asking him what compelled him to write, "The port from which I set out was, I think, that of the essential loneliness of my life..." One of the great satisfactions of the human spirit is to feel that one's family extends across the borders of the species and belongs to everything that lives. I feel I'm not only sharing the planet, but also sharing my life, as one does with a domestic animal. Certainly this is one of the great joys of living in this garden.'

D.H. LAWRENCE

Snake

A snake came to my water-trough
On a hot, hot day, and I in pyjamas for the heat,
To drink there.

In the deep, strange-scented shade of the great dark
     carob tree
I came down the steps with my pitcher
And must wait, must stand and wait, for there he was
     at the trough before me.

He reached down from a fissure in the earth-wall in
     the gloom
And trailed his yellow-brown slackness soft-bellied
     down, over the edge of the stone trough
And rested his throat upon the stone bottom,
And where the water had dripped from the tap, in a
     small clearness,
He sipped with his straight mouth,
Softly drank through his straight gums, into his slack
     long body,
Silently.

Someone was before me at my water-trough,
And I, like a second comer, waiting.

He lifted his head from his drinking, as cattle do,
And looked at me vaguely, as drinking cattle do,
And flickered his two-forked tongue from his lips, and
     mused a moment,
And stooped and drank a little more,
Being earth-brown, earth-golden from the burning
     bowels of the earth
On the day of Sicilian July, with Etna smoking.

The voice of my education said to me
He must be killed,
For in Sicily the black, black snakes are innocent, the
     gold are venomous.

And voices in me said, If you were a man
You would take a stick and break him now, and finish
     him off.

But must I confess how I liked him,
How glad I was he had come like a guest in quiet, to
     drink at my water-trough
And depart peaceful, pacified, and thankless,
Into the burning bowels of this earth?

Was it cowardice, that I dared not kill him?
Was it perversity, that I longed to talk to him?
Was it humility, to feel so honoured?
I felt so honoured.

And yet those voices:
If you were not afraid, you would kill him!

And truly I was afraid, I was most afraid,
But even so, honoured still more
That he should seek my hospitality
From out the dark door of the secret earth.

He drank enough
And lifted his head, dreamily, as one who has drunken,
And flickered his tongue like a forked night on the air,
     so black,
Seeming to lick his lips,
And looked around like a god, unseeing, into the air,
And slowly turned his head,
And slowly, very slowly, as if thrice adream,
Proceeded to draw his slow length curving round
And climb again the broken bank of my wall-face.

And as he put his head into that dreadful hole,
And as he slowly drew up, snake-easing his shoulders,
     and entered farther,
A sort of horror, a sort of protest against his withdrawing
     into that horrid black hole,

Deliberately going into the blackness, and slowly
    drawing himself after,
Overcame me now his back was turned.

I looked round, I put down my pitcher,
I picked up a clumsy log
And threw it at the water-trough with a clatter.

I think it did not hit him,
But suddenly that part of him that was left behind
    convulsed in undignified haste,
Writhed like lightning, and was gone
Into the black hole, the earth-lipped fissure in the
    wall-front.
At which, in the intense still noon, I stared with
    fascination.

And immediately I regretted it.
I thought how paltry, how vulgar, what a mean act!
I despised myself and the voices of my accursed human
    education.

And I thought of the albatross,
And I wished he would come back, my snake.

For he seemed to me again like a king,
Like a king in exile, uncrowned in the underworld,
Now due to be crowned again.

And so, I missed my chance with one of the lords
Of life.
And I have something to expiate;
A pettiness.

■ **D.H. Lawrence** (1885-1930) was one of the major English writers of the 20th century, a controversial novelist as well as a visionary poet who saw his verse as 'direct utterance from the instant, whole man'. '**Snake**' appeared in *Birds, Beasts and Flowers* (1923), a collection including some of his finest reflections on the flux of life and the "otherness" of the non-human world. Lawrence affirms the grandeur and mystery of nature through his complete truthfulness to experience in these poems. His snake is both an ordinary 'earth-brown, earth-golden' Sicilian snake, probably a venomous asp viper, but at the same time also a mythical, godlike lord of the underworld, an embodiment of all those dark mysterious forces of nature which humans fear and neglect. W.H. Auden called *Birds, Beasts and Flowers* 'the peak of Lawrence's achievement as a poet': 'Like the Romantics [his] starting-point in these poems is a personal encounter between himself and some animal or flower, but, unlike the Romantics, he never confuses the feelings they arouse in him with what he sees and hears and knows about them. The lucidity of his language matches the intensity of his vision; he can make the reader see what he is saying as very few writers can.'

JOHN MONTAGUE

The Trout

Flat on the bank I parted
Rushes to ease my hands
In the water without a ripple
And tilt them slowly downstream
To where he lay, tendril-light,
In his fluid sensual dream.

Bodiless lord of creation,
I hung briefly above him
Savouring my own absence,
Senses expanding in the slow
Motion, the photographic calm
That grows before action.

As the curve of my hands
Swung under his body
He surged, with visible pleasure.
I was so preternaturally close
I could count every stipple
But still cast no shadow, until

The two palms crossed in a cage
Under the lightly pulsing gills.
Then (entering my own enlarged
Shape, which rode on the water)
I gripped. To this day I can
Taste his terror on my hands.

RICHARD HUGO
Trout

Quick and yet he moves like silt.
I envy dreams that see his curving
silver in the weeds. When stiff as snags
he blends with certain stones.
When evening pulls the ceiling tight
across his back he leaps for bugs.

I wedged hard water to validate his skin –
call it chrome, say red is on
his side like apples in a fog, gold
gills. Swirls always looked one way
until he carved the water into any
kinds of current with his nerve-edged nose.

And I have stared at steelhead teeth
to know him, savage in his sea-run growth,
to drug his facts, catalog his fins
with wings and arms, to bleach the black
back of the first I saw and frame the cries
that sent him snaking to oblivions of cress.

■ **Richard Hugo** (1923-82) was an American poet from Seattle whose work celebrated marginalised people and places. Surviving an unhappy childhood, he flew 35 combat missions as a bombardier during the war. He later attended Theodore Roethke's poetry classes, and worked as a technical writer for Boeing from 1951 to 1963. After publishing his first collection at the age of 37, he taught at the University of Montana for nearly 18 years. His poems often celebrate the abandoned towns, landscapes and people of the Pacific Northwest, particularly the Duwamish River where he learned to fish. 'The more austere or remote or forsaken the land or the person, the more certain was Hugo to reach out with love and understanding. His poems have already made legends of places on the map that before his coming were lost in empty space.' (William Stafford)

■ **John Montague** ➤ 49.

ANDREW HUDGINS
The Persistence of Nature in Our Lives

You find them in the darker woods
occasionally – those swollen lumps
of fungus, twisted, moist, and yellow –
but when they show up on the lawn
it's like they've tracked me home. In spring
the persistence of nature in our lives
rises from below, drifts from above.
The pollen settles on my skin
and waits for me to bloom, trying
to work green magic on my flesh.
They're indiscriminate, these firs.
They'll mate with anything. A great
green-yellow cloud of pollen sifts
across the house. The waste of it
leaves nothing out – not even men.
The pollen doesn't care I'm not
a tree. The golden storm descends.
Wind lifts it from the branches, lofts
it in descending arches of need
and search, a grainy yellow haze
that settles over everything
as if it's all the same. I love
the utter waste of pollen, a scum
of it on every pond and puddle.
It rides the ripples and, when they dry,
remains, a line of yellow dust
zigzagging in the shape of waves.
One night, perhaps a little drunk,
I stretched out on the porch, watching
the Milky Way. At dawn I woke
to find a man-shape on the hard
wood floor, outlined in pollen – a sharp
spread-eagle figure drawn there like
the body at a murder scene.
Except for that spot, the whole damn house
glittered, green-gold. I wandered out
across the lawn, my bare feet damp
with dew, the wet ground soft, forgiving,

beneath my step. I understood
I am, as much as anyone,
the golden beast who staggers home,
in June, beneath the yearning trees.

■ **Andrew Hudgins** (*b.* 1951) is an American poet and critic
who grew up in a Southern Baptist military family, living in
various parts of America as well as England and France, but
despite this apparent rootlessness derives much of the material
for his often darkly humorous narrative poetry from the
images, idioms and folkways of the Deep South. Mark Strand
has praised his poetry for its 'intelligence, vitality, and grace.
And there is a beautiful oddness about it. Dark moments
seem charged with an eerie luminosity and the most humdrum
events assume a startling lyric intensity. A deep resonant humor
is everywhere, and everywhere amazing.'

■ **Seamus Heaney** ➤ 213.

SEAMUS HEANEY
from **Squarings**

XLII

Heather and kesh and turf stacks reappear
Summer by summer still, grasshoppers and all,
The same yet rarer: fields of the nearly blessed

Where gaunt ones in their shirtsleeves stooped and dug
Or stood alone at dusk surveying bog-banks –
Apparitions now, yet active still

And territorial, still sure of their ground,
Still interested, not knowing how far
The country of the shades has been pushed back,

How long the lark has stopped outside these fields
And only seems unstoppable to them
Caught like a far hill in a freak of sunshine.

ALICE OSWALD
Birdsong for Two Voices

A spiral ascending the morning,
climbing by means of a song into the sun,
to be sung reciprocally by two birds at intervals
in the same tree but not quite in time.

A song that assembles the earth
out of nine notes and silence.
out of the unformed gloom before dawn
where every tree is a problem to be solved by birdsong.

Crex Crex Corcorovado,
letting the pieces fall where they may,
every dawn divides into the distinct
misgiving between alternate voices

sung repeatedly by two birds at intervals
out of nine notes and silence,
while the sun, with its fingers to the earth,
as the sun proceeds so it gathers instruments:

it gathers the yard with its echoes and scaffolding sounds,
it gathers the swerving away sound of the road,
it gathers the river shivering in a wet field,
it gathers the three small bones in the dark of the eardrum;

it gathers the big bass silence of clouds
and the mind whispering in its shell
and all trees, with their ears to the air,
seeking a steady state and singing it over till it settles.

ALICE OSWALD
Song of a Stone

there was a woman from the north
picked a stone up from the earth.
when the stone began to dream
it was a flower folded in

when the flower began to fruit
it was a circle full of light,
when the light began to break
it was a flood across a plain

when the plain began to stretch
the length scattered from the width
and when the width began to climb
it was a lark above a cliff

the lark singing for its life
was the muscle of a heart,
the heart flickering away
was an offthrow of the sea

and when the sea began to dance
it was the labyrinth of a conscience,
when the conscience pricked the heart
it was a man lost in thought

like milk that sours in the light,
like vapour twisting in the heat,
the thought was fugitive – a flare of gold –
it was an iris in a field

and when the man began to murmur
it was a question with no answer,
when the question changed its form
it was the same point driven home

it was a problem, a lamentation:
'What the buggery's going on?
This existence is an outrage!
Give me an arguer to shout with!'

and when the arguer appeared
it was an angel of the Lord,
and when the angel touched his chest,
it was his heartbeat being pushed

and when his heart began to break
it was the jarring of an earthquake
when the earth began to groan
they laid him in it six by one

dark bigger than his head,
pain swifter than his blood,
as good as gone, what could he do?
as deep as stone, what could he know?

■ **Alice Oswald** (*b.* 1966) is an English poet who trained as a classicist and worked as a gardener for several years. Her books include *The Thing in the Gap-Stone Stile* (1996); *Dart* (2002), a long work combining poetry and prose which tells the story of the River Dart in Devon; *Woods etc.* (2005), a series of lyrics and ballads about the natural order and the individual life within; and the anthology *The Thunder Mutters: 101 Poems for the Planet* (2005) [➤ 18].

Jules Smith: 'She is perhaps a nature mystic, attempting to express the intangible and spiritual, in ways oddly beautiful and visionary. Her poetry takes place in the open, and usually on water – the sea, rivers, estuaries, or in gardens soaked by "soft malevolent" English rain. It is full of romantic imagery, energised by free-flowing rhythms, songs and ballads, and the oddities of speech.'

The two poems here are from *Woods etc.*, which 'records the orchestrations of nature free from the organisation of human narrative […] voicing her sometimes perilous immersion in the natural world. Her language is intimately attentive to that perilousness, as well as to the perils of ecological stress. For Oswald, the human presence is component rather than dominant. While she asserts and renews the traditions of the English nature poem, Alice Oswald's is a contemporary experience…' (Geoffrey Faber Memorial Prize citation by judges Neil Corcoran, Lavinia Greenlaw and Ciaran Carson)

■ **Philippe Jaccottet** (*b.* 1925) is a leading French poet and translator, born in Switzerland, whose work is rooted in the Drôme region of south-east France, which gives it a rich sense of place. Meditative, immediate and sensuous, his poetry is largely grounded in landscape and the visual world, pursuing an anxious and persistent questioning of natural signs, meticulously conveyed in a syntax of great inventiveness. His work is animated by a fascination with the visible world from which he translates visual objects into verbal images and ultimately into figures of language.

Derek Mahon: 'He is a secular mystic. "The natural object is always the adequate symbol," said Pound; and Jaccottet's symbols are the elemental, pre-Socratic ones: tree, flower, sun, moon, road, hill, wind, water, bird, house, lamp. […] Jaccottet's poems take place, characteristically, in the absence of most other noise; but in the tentative birdsong, running water and rustling leaves of his landscape one hears an enchantment, what used to be called the music of the spheres: "If they speak above us / in the starry trees of their April".'

PHILIPPE JACCOTTET
'Each flower is a little night'
translated from the French by Derek Mahon

Each flower is a little night
pretending to draw near

But where its scent rises
I cannot hope to enter
which is why it bothers me
so much and why I sit so long
before this closed door

Each colour, each incarnation
begins where the eyes stop

This world is merely the tip
of an unseen conflagration

PHILIPPE JACCOTTET
The Voice
translated from the French by Derek Mahon

What is it that sings when the other voices are silent?
Whose is that pure, deaf voice, that sibilant song?
Is it down the road on a snow-covered lawn
or close at hand, unaware of an audience?
This is the mysterious first bird of dawn.
Do you hear the voice increase in volume
and, as a March wind quickens a creaking tree,
sing mildly to us without fear,
content in the fact of death? Do you hear?
What does it sing in the grey dawn? Nobody knows;
but the voice is audible only to those
whose hearts seek neither possession nor victory.

ROBERT HAYDEN
The Night-Blooming Cereus

And so for nights
we waited, hoping to see
the heavy bud
        break into flower.

On its neck-like tube
hooking down from the edge
of the leaf-branch
        nearly to the floor,

the bud packed
tight with its miracle swayed
stiffly on breaths
        of air, moved

as though impelled
by stirrings within itself.
It repelled as much
        as it fascinated me

sometimes – snake,
eyeless bird head,
beak that would gape
        with grotesque life-squawk.

But you, my dear,
conceded less to the bizarre
than to the imminence
        of bloom. Yet we agreed

we ought
to celebrate the blossom,
paint ourselves, dance
        in honor of

archaic mysteries
when it appeared. Meanwhile
we waited, aware
        of rigorous design.

Backsters's
polygraph, I thought,
would have shown
    (as clearly as it had

    a philodendron's
fear) tribal sentience
in the cactus, focused
    energy of will.

    That belling of
tropic perfume – that
signalling
    not meant for us;

    the darkness
cloyed with summoning
fragrance. We dropped
    trivial tasks

    and marvelling
beheld at last the achieved
flower. Its moonlight
    petals were

    still unfold-
ing, the spike fringe of the outer
perianth recessing
    as we watched.

    Lunar presence,
foredoomed, already dying,
it charged the room
    with plangency

    older than human
cries, ancient as prayers
invoking Osiris, Krishna,
    Tezcátlipóca.

    We spoke
in whispers when
we spoke
    at all...

THOMAS HARDY

An August Midnight

I

A shaded lamp and a waving blind,
And the beat of a clock from a distant floor:
On this scene enter – winged, horned, and spined –
A longlegs, a moth, and a dumbledore;
While 'mid my page there idly stands
A sleepy fly, that rubs its hands....

II

Thus meet we five, in this still place,
At this point of time, at this point in space.
– My guests besmear my new-penned line,
Or bang at the lamp and fall supine.
'God's humblest, they!' I muse. Yet why?
They know Earth-secrets that know not I.

■ **Robert Hayden** (1913-80) was a African American poet, essayist and educator, and the first black American Consultant in Poetry to the Library of Congress (later called the Poet Laureate). Hayden was influenced by a wide range of modern writers, from Yeats and Auden (whom he studied with at the University of Michigan) to the poets of the Harlem Renaissance, and is known especially for his much anthologised poem 'Those Winter Sundays', inspired by a traumatic childhood. Much of Hayden's poetry is concerned with the social and political plight of African Americans, black history, slavery and racism, as well as drawing on his Bahá'í faith.

X.J. Kennedy & Dana Gioia: 'Hayden occupied a difficult and ambiguous position in American poetry. Marginalised by the literary mainstream at the start of his career as a "Negro poet", he was considered not black enough by more militant writers and theorists in the 1960s. Such issues of literary identity had an upsetting parallel, the full extent of which he would only belatedly discover, in his personal life. Throughout decades of neglect and scorn, he clung steadfastly to his artistic and human values, producing a body of work whose artistry and emotional richness placed him at or very near the front rank of an especially talented generation of American poets.

■ **Thomas Hardy** ➤ 76.

■ **Giacomo Leopardi** (1798-1837) was the greatest lyric poet in the Italian tradition as well as a scholar and philosopher. A precocious, congenitally deformed child of noble but apparently insensitive parents, he devoted his childhood and youth to his studies in the family palace's 12,000-volume library, mastering many languages and subjects; but suffering from nervous disorders, his eyesight weakened and he became a hunchback. So frail and unattractive a man could never be loved by a woman, he felt; it would require great courage 'to love a virtuous man whose only beauty is his soul'.

Leopardi's poetry is noted for its philosophical toughness and bittersweet lyricism informed by unflinching realism in the face of unavoidable human loss. Much of his work is concerned with mutability, landscape and love, and portrays a world where humanity is subjected to a hopeless state of boredom and despair by forces of nature wholly indifferent to its plight. His poetry asserts his belief that joy is nothing but the momentary subsidence of pain and that only in death can a man find lasting happiness, yet despite this pessimistic outlook there are many shining images in his poetry which show him in a completely different light, as the enraptured admirer of nature's beauty and believer in the power of imagination.

■ **Michael Longley** ➤ 60.

GIACOMO LEOPARDI
The Solitary Thrush
translated from the Italian by Eamon Grennan

    Perched on top of that old tower,
    You sing as long as daylight lasts,
    The sweet sound of you winding
    Round and round the valley.
    Spring shimmers
    In the air, comes with a green rush
    Through the open fields, is a sight
    To soften any heart. You can hear
    Sheep bleating, bellowing cattle,
    While the other birds swoop and wheel
    Cheerily round the wide blue sky,
    Having the time of their lives together.
    Like an outsider, lost in thought,
    You are looking on at it all:

Neither companions nor wild nights
Fire your heart; games like these
Mean nothing to you. You sing,
And in singing spend the best
Part of your life and the passing year.

Ah, how these habits of mine
Are just like yours! Whatever the reason,
I haven't time for the light heart and laughter
Belonging to youth, nor any time
For you, youth's own companion, love,
Which later brings many a bitter sigh.
In truth I'm a fugitive from it all
And, still young, I all but live
The life of a hermit, a stranger even
In the place I was born.
This day already dwindling into dusk
Is a feast in these parts. You can hear
The bells ring round a clear sky
And a far-off thunder of guns
Booming and booming from farm to farm.

All dressed up in their Sunday best,
The young who live around here
Leave their houses and stroll the roads,
Looking and looked at, joy in their hearts.
Alone in this remote corner,
I walk out all by myself,
Putting off pleasure, postponing play:
And gazing about at the radiant air
I'm struck by how the sinking sun
After a day as perfect as this one
Melts among the distant hills,
And seems to say
That blessed youth itself is fading.

Solitary little singer, when you
Reach the evening of those days
Which the stars have numbered for you,
You'll not grieve, surely,
For the life you've led, since even
The slightest twist of your will

Is nature's way. But to me,
If I fail to escape
Loathsome old age –
When these eyes will mean nothing
To any other heart, the world be nothing
But a blank to them,
Each day more desolate, every day
Darker than the one before – what then
Will this longing for solitude
Seem like to me? What then
Will these years, or even I myself,
Seem to have been? Alas,
I'll be sick with regret, and over and over,
But inconsolable, looking back.

MICHAEL LONGLEY
Leopardi's Song Thrush

Have they eaten all the thrushes here in Italy?
In the resonant Valle del Serchio I have heard
Thunder claps, church bells, the melancholy banter
Of gods and party-goers, echoes from mountaintops
And Alessandro's hillside bar, but not one thrush.

Rather than the missel thrush, the stormcock fluting
Through bad weather on its diet of mistletoe,
I mourn five or six sky-coloured eggs, anvil stones
For tenderising snails, repetitious phrases,
Leopardi's thrush, the song thrush in particular.

My lamentation a batsqueak from the balcony,
I stick some thorns onto the poet's beloved broom
And call it gorse (or whin or furze), a prickly
Sanctuary for the song thrush among yellow flowers,
Its underwing flashing yellow as it disappears.

WILLIAM MATTHEWS
Civilisation and Its Discontents

*Integration in, or adaptation to, a human community appears
as a scarcely avoidable condition which must be fullfilled
before [our] aim of happiness can be achieved. If it could be
done without that condition, it would perhaps be preferable.*
        FREUD

How much of the great poetry
of solitude in the woods is one
long cadenza on the sadness

of civilisation, and how much
thought on beaches, between drowsing
and sleep, along the borders,

between one place and another,
as if such poise were home to us?
On the far side of these woods, stew,

gelatinous from cracked lamb shanks,
is being ladled into bowls, and
a family scuffs its chairs close

to an inherited table.
Maybe there's wine, maybe not. We don't
know because our thoughts are with

the great sad soul in the woods again.
We suppose that even now
some poignant speck of litter

borne by the river of psychic murmur
has been grafted by the brooding soul
to a beloved piece of music,

and that from the general plaint
a shape is about to be made, though
maybe not: we can't see into

the soul the way we can into
that cottage where now they're done with food
until next meal. Here's what I think:

the soul in the woods is not alone.
All he came there to leave behind
is in him, like a garrison

in a conquered city. When he goes
back to it, and goes gratefully
because it's nearly time for dinner,

he will be entering himself,
though when he faced the woods,
from the road, that's what he thought then, too.

■ **William Matthews** (1942-97) was an American poet and
essayist who was born in Cincinnati and grew up on the edge
of town or in the country in Ohio, where his father worked for
the Soil Conservation Service. Influenced by writers ranging
from Horace, Freud and Auden to Merwin and James Wright,
his poetry is distinctively individual and characterised by 'good
sense, wit, an insatiable curiosity, an affable authorial presence,
and a slightly shambling quest for wisdom [...] small and
querulous reckonings with contemporary culture, a culture
whose complexity offers a staggeringly large number of new
opportunities, both funny and unsettling, to express human
folly' (David Wojahn). [Other poem ➤ 50].

■ **Philip Larkin** (1922-85) was an influential and popular
English poet, the leading figure in the 'Movement' group
whose plain-speaking, descriptive poetry using traditional
forms was the dominant poetic mode in British poetry of the
1950s and early 60s. His main themes are love, marriage,
freedom, destiny, loss, ageing and death. Influenced by Yeats,
Eliot, Auden and Hardy, Larkin was a late Romantic lyric
poet who evolved a persona suited to his pessimistic postwar
outlook on life: dry, sceptical, modest and unshowy, thinking
aloud in an apparently commensensical fashion, yet also hon-
est, emotional and capable of rich surprises of thought and
imagery. Also a novelist and jazz critic, he worked in Hull in
the university librarian for the last 30 years of his life.

[Other poem and further note ➤ 89]

PHILIP LARKIN
The Trees

The trees are coming into leaf
Like something almost being said;
The recent buds relax and spread,
Their greenness is a kind of grief.

Is it that they are born again
And we grow old? No, they die too.
Their yearly trick of looking new
Is written down in rings of grain.

Yet still the unresting castles thresh
In fullgrown thickness every May.
Last year is dead, they seem to say,
Begin afresh, afresh, afresh.

6. THE GREAT WEB

This section takes its title from Denise Levertov's poem **'Web'** [➤ 157], from her metaphor of the 'great web' that 'moves through and connects all people and things, both human and inhuman' (J. Scott Bryson). These poems evoke humanity's interdependence and oneness with nature, including several recalling lost or disappearing connections between the rhythms of daily life and the cycles and processes of nature.

■ **Robert Adamson** (*b.* 1943) is an Australian poet, editor, publisher, fishing writer and wildlife artist who has been nourished for much of his life by the Hawkesbury River north of Sydney. His grandfather worked the Hawkesbury as a fisherman, and Adamson now fishes the same river for food and inspiration (as in **'Meshing bends in the light'**). His poetry praises nature – red in tooth and claw – and celebrates existence as a mythological quest. He shares his river life with photographer Juno Gemes, and published a series of Hawkesbury poems with her pictures in The *Language of Oysters* (1997). His other books include *Reading the River: Selected Poems* (2004) and *Inside Out: An Autobiography* (2004).

In his article 'The King Mulloway', Adamson writes: 'I grew up fishing on the Hawkesbury River and during those early years it seeped in, beyond the reach of conscious memory. Once it's in your blood it enters your life and you are governed by the tides, the fauna and flora, the mangroves and mudflats. Memory is an active part of fishing, not simply the recording of facts but the deeper upper reaches of the subconscious river, the places where we once had to fish to survive. Fishing sustains the soul because it was once one of the most natural things a human being could do, that is why you can enter that state of grace, that lightness of being, while fishing. It is to do with the field of being, you can project yourself back to the original lores, rites and rituals.' (*Fishing World*, August 1997) [Other poem ➤ 127]

ROBERT ADAMSON
Meshing bends in the light

Just under the surface
mullet roll in the current;
their pale bellies catch
the sunken light, the skin
of the river erupts
above purling. The sky
hangs over the boat a wall
of shuddering light
smudging the wings
of a whistling-kite,
mudflats glow
in the developing chemicals,
black crabs hold their
claws up into the light
of the enlarger, yabbies
ping in the drain. A westerly
howls through the
darkroom. The tide
is always working
at the base of the brain.
The turning moon is
up-ended, setting on the silver
gelatin page: a hook
stopped spinning in space.
Owls shuffle their silent wings
and dissolve in the fixer.
Shape words over what you see.
The river flows from your
eyes into the sink, bulrushes
hum with mosquitoes
that speckle the print.
The last riverboat mail-run
scatters letters across
the surface, the ink
runs into the brackish tide.

GALWAY KINNELL
Daybreak

On the tidal mud, just before sunset,
dozens of starfishes
were creeping. It was
as though the mud were a sky
and enormous, imperfect stars
moved across it as slowly
as the actual stars cross heaven.
All at once they stopped,
and, as if they had simply
increased their receptivity
to gravity, they sank down
into the mud, faded down
into it and lay still, and by the time
pink of sunset broke across them
they were as invisible
as the true stars at daybreak.

W.S. MERWIN
Shore Birds

While I think of them they are growing rare
after the distances they have followed
all the way to the end for the first time
tracing a memory they did not have
until they set out to remember it
at an hour when all at once it was late
and newly silent and the white had turned
white around them then they rose in their choir
on a single note each of them alone
between the pull of the moon and the hummed
undertone of the earth below them
the glass curtains kept falling around them
as they flew in search of their place before
they were anywhere and storms winnowed them
they flew among the places with towers

and passed the tower lights where some vanished
with their long legs for wading in shadow
others were caught and stayed in the countries of
the nets and in the lands of the limetwigs
some fastened and after the countries of
guns at first light fewer of them than I
remember would be here to recognise
the light of late summer when they found it
playing with darkness along the wet sand

MICHAEL LONGLEY
Echoes

I

I am describing to you on the phone
Stonechats backlit by an October sunset,
A pair that seems to be flirting in the cold.
I am looking out of the bedroom window.
They fluster along the fuchsia hedge and perch
On bare twigs the wind has stripped for them.

II

As beautiful as bog asphodel in flower
Is bog asphodel in seed. Or nearly.
An echo. Rusty-orange October tones.
This late there are gentians and centaury
And a bumble bee on a thistle head
Suspended, neither feeding nor dying.

III

Forty-two whoopers call, then the echoes
As though there are more swans over the ridge.

■ **Galway Kinnell** ➤ 161.

■ **W.S. Merwin** ➤ 78.

■ **Michael Longley** ➤ 60.

DERMOT HEALY
A Ball of Starlings

As evening falls
over the bulrushes

parties of starlings
arrive in flurries

to join the other shape-makers
at the alt. The swarm blows

high, dives out of sight
in a beautiful aside,

till there's scarce a trace
of a bird –

then a set of arched wings appears,
then another,

hundreds turn
as one,

and suddenly over the lough
a whispering ball of starlings

rises into
the blue night

like a shoal of sardines
gambolling underwater

and, changing shape,
the birds

rise in the vast dark
like hayseed

till the puff-ball
explodes

and the birds
suddenly flip

again into nothingness:
and when the roost reappears out of the deep

in a great teeming net
of birdsong

the din grows intense
as they build

these last perfect
arcs, these ghostly

gall-bows,
before making

one final sweep
that ends

in a ticking globe
above the reeds;

then, chattering, the starlings spill
across the black fields.

■ **Dermot Healy** (*b.* 1947) is an Irish novelist, playwright and poet. Born in Co. Westmeath, he lives in Ballyconnell, Co. Sligo on the west coast of Ireland, where much of his work is set. His poems are notable for their compassion, acute insight and observation, and for the way in which he presents dramas of the daily world lit by moments of transcendence. Healy's many books include three collections of poetry, *The Ballyconnel Colours* (1995), *What the Hammer* (1998) and *The Reed Bed* (2001).

PETER FALLON
A Refrain

Their name's a loveliness,
a darling
word, though each of them's
a splashy shitter, marling

the ground beneath their sudden roost,
each of them's one of a flock you'd count
that used to be uncountable, that dimmed
the sun, and now you watch mount

a sycamore and make of it
a vocal chord
until they wheel away, affrighted
or simply of their own accord,

a whim, a whoosh,
a whir.
The rowing wings of, say, a crow
stay solid. Theirs blur.

Then silence. Their one-part
chatter, two parts cackle,
betray the part they're mynah
bird or, if you like, southern grackle

working their way, wings
and grey mantle a fletch
of petrol stains,
till some of them fetch

up in the poisoned lands
of new estates, old farms,
their pesticides, while others stall
among the smoke alarms

of the oil fields on fire
along their flight
paths, through the flashpoints of the Tigris
and Euphrates, noon skies as black as night.

Iridescent scavengers,
they'd come and go
across your life,
like that apostle's shadow

healing all it brushed against.
They came and went for years,
a clockwork swipe across September,
and now one re-appears,

part of a warbling quarrel,
we say 'Where have you been, starling?
What tales you'd have!'
Our pleas and prayers for you are, *Sing.*

■ **Peter Fallon** (*b.* 1951) is an Irish poet and publisher. Born in Germany, he grew up on his uncle's farm near Kells in Co. Meath. At the age of 18 he founded the Gallery Press, now Ireland's premier poetry and drama publishing house, which he runs from his family farm in Loughcrew, Co. Meath. His own works include several poetry collections and a translation of Virgil's *Georgics*. Richard Wilbur has described how Fallon's poetry 'does not filter the world of the small farm for some urban reader; rather it takes him there. It does so without sentimentality, giving us for instance the brute weariness of farm work as well as the triumph of work well done.'

■ **Mark Doty** ➤ 56.

MARK DOTY
Migratory

Near evening, in Fairhaven, Massachusetts,
seventeen wild geese arrowed the ashen blue
over the Wal-Mart and the Blockbuster Video,

and I was up there, somewhere between the asphalt
and their clear dominion – not in the parking lot,
its tallowy circles just appearing,

the shopping carts shining, from above,
like little scraps of foil. Their eyes
held me there, the unfailing gaze

of those who know how to fly in formation,
wing-tip to wing-tip, safe, fearless.
And the convex glamour of their eyes carried

the parking lot, the wet field
troubled with muffler shops
and stoplights, the arc of highway

and its exits, one shattered farmhouse
with its failing barn... The wind
a few hundred feet above the grass

erases the mechanical noises, everything;
nothing but their breathing
and the perfect rowing of the pinions,

and then, out of that long, percussive pour
toward what they are most certain of,
comes their – question, is it?

Assertion, prayer, aria – as delivered
by something too compelled in its passage
to sing? A hoarse and unwieldy music

which plays nonetheless down the length
of me until I am involved in their flight,
the unyielding necessity of it, as they literally

rise above, ineluctable, heedless,
needing nothing...Only animals
make me believe in God now

– so little between spirit and skin,
any gesture so entirely themselves.
But I wasn't with them,

as they headed toward Acushnet
and New Bedford, of course I wasn't,
though I was not exactly in the parking lot

either, where the cars nudged in and out
of their slots, each taking the place another
had abandoned, so that no space, no desire

would remain unfilled. I wasn't there.
I was so filled with longing
– is that what that sound is for? –

I seemed to be nowhere at all.

MICHAEL LONGLEY
The Osprey

To whom certain water talents –
Webbed feet, oils – do not occur,
Regulates his liquid acre
From the sky, his proper element.

There, already, his eye removes
The trout each fathom magnifies.
He lives, without compromise,
His unamphibious two lives –

An inextinguishable bird whom
No lake's waters waterlog.
He shakes his feathers like a dog.
It's all of air that ferries him.

■ **Michael Longley** ➤ 60.

ROBERT ADAMSON
The stone curlew

I am writing this inside the head
of a bush stone curlew,
we have been travelling for days

moving over the earth
flying when necessary.
I am not the bird itself, only its passenger

looking through its eyes.
The world rocks slightly as we move
over the stubble grass of the dunes,

at night shooting stars draw lines
across the velvet dark
as I hang in a sling of light

between the bird's nocturnal eyes.
The heavens make sense, seeing this way
makes me want to believe

words have meanings,
that Australia is no longer a wound
in the side of the earth.

I think of the white settlers
who compared the curlew's song
to the cries of women being strangled,

and remember the poets who wrote
anthropomorphically as I sing softly
from the jelly of the stone curlew's brain.

The old windmill creaks in perfect time
to the wind shaking the miles of pasture grass,
and the last farmhouse light goes off.

Something moves nearby. Coyotes hunt
these hills and packs of feral dogs.
But standing here at night accepts all that.

You are your own pale shadow in the quarter moon,
moving more slowly than the crippled stars,
part of the moonlight as the moonlight falls,

Part of the grass that answers the wind,
part of the midnight's watchfulness that knows
there is no silence but when danger comes.

■ **Robert Adamson** ➤ 123.

DANA GIOIA
Becoming a Redwood

Stand in a field long enough, and the sounds
start up again. The crickets, the invisible
toad who claims that change is possible,

And all the other life too small to name.
First one, then another, until innumerable
they merge into the single voice of a summer hill.

Yes, it's hard to stand still, hour after hour,
fixed as a fencepost, hearing the steers
snort in the dark pasture, smelling the manure.

And paralysed by the mystery of how a stone
can bear to be a stone, the pain
the grass endures breaking through the earth's crust.

Unimaginable the redwoods on the far hill,
rooted for centuries, the living wood grown tall
and thickened with a hundred thousand days of light.

■ **Dana Gioia** (*b.* 1950) is an American writer of Italian and Mexican descent. A leading New Formalist poet, he is also a critic and outspoken literary commentator, with books including the controversial *Can Poetry Matter?* (1992), and Chairman of the National Endowment for the Arts. His highly musical poetry is quietly visionary, often showing human lives rooted in the natural world.

■ **Wendell Berry** (*b.* 1934) was born and raised on a farm in Kentucky. After teaching for several years in California and New York, he returned to Kentucky, where he has combined writing with farming for the past 40 years. Ploughing and tending his land, he has grown most of his family's food, cared for his lambs and sold them locally, and cut his own firewood. A conservationist, naturalist, social critic and defender of small-scale farming, he has written poems and essays protesting against war, industrialisation and the decline of traditional farming methods, as well as a large body of poetry affirming the holiness and wholeness of the natural world.

Every Sunday Berry has rested from weekday farm and literary labour, hiking into the hilly woods above his home to compose austere, meditative poems. From 1979 through 1997 he completed one to twelve poetic meditations per year. These **Sabbath Poems** are collected in his book-length sequence *A Timbered Choir* (1998).

Leonard M. Scigaj: 'Berry's Christian environmental vision developed gradually, in part as a direct response to the medieval historian Lynn White Jr's essay about the negative environmental effects of Christianity. Thirty years ago White startled environmentalists and traditionalists alike with his argument that the roots of our ecological crisis concern the assumptions of medieval Western Christianity about the dominance of humans over the natural world. According to White, Christianity fostered dualism and a linear technology, both of which eroded an individual's reliance on sensual participation in nature in the present moment. Moldboard plowing, which "attacked the land with such violence that cross-plowing was not needed", illustrations of human mastery over nature on medieval Frankish calendars, the Genesis account of Adam's domination over the creatures he named (1:26-28), the attribution of religious motives for the investigations of New Scientists such as Leibniz and Newton, and the extirpation of pagan animism by Christians – all of this evidence indicated to White that "Christianity made it possible to exploit nature in a mood of indifference to the feelings of natural objects."

'Christianity was not, of course, the only religion that resulted in the despoliation of nature, and the economics and power politics of individuals and nations throughout human history have certainly bent and in many cases subverted religious doctrine to underwrite environmentally suspect goals. Yet White's challenge remains; given that "no creature other than man has ever managed to foul its nest in such short order", it is certainly worthwhile to consider his point that "human ecology is deeply conditioned by beliefs about our nature and destiny – that is, by religion".

'Of the many direct responses to White's argument concerning the ecological effects of Christianity, Wendell Berry's in the title-essay of *The Gift of Good Land* is one of the most eloquent and most incisive. Berry argued that, although Adam *was* given dominion over other orders of nature, the Bible nowhere states that he was given power to destroy the land or any of the creatures living on it. Berry points us to Genesis 2:15, where Adam, newly exiled from Eden, is given the earth that he may "dress it and keep it" by the sweat of his brow. This for Berry implies a stewardship role for humans, and Berry reads the subsequent historical books of the Old Testament as the Israelites' slow growth to an understanding of how to acquire the Promised Land and keep it responsibly. [...]

'In the poems of *A Timbered Choir* Berry explores his belief that we must respond to the gift of good land with sustainable stewardship. [...] The poems of *A Timbered Choir* model a

way of revising our perceptions to comprehend the biocentric holiness of creation. The major premise of both [Matthew] Fox and Berry is unassailable: if we learn to perceive all creation as holy, in our everyday habits we would refrain as much as possible from polluting that holy creation. We would then live more harmoniously near choirs of forests far less subject to the logger's cry.'

WENDELL BERRY
from A Timbered Choir

1985 V

How long does it take to make the woods?
As long as it takes to make the world.
The woods is present as the world is, the presence
of all its past, and of all its time to come.
It is always finished, it is always being made, the act
of its making forever greater than the act of its destruction.
It is a part of eternity, for its end and beginning
belong to the end and beginning of all things,
the beginning lost in the end, the end in the beginning.

What is the way to the woods, how do you get there?
By climbing up through the six days' field,
kept in all the body's years, the body's
sorrow, weariness, and joy, by passing through
the narrow gate on the far side of that field
where the pasture grass of the body's life gives way
to the high, original standing of the trees.
By coming into the shadow, the shadow
of the grace of the straight way's ending,
the shadow of the mercy of light.

Why must the gate be narrow?
Because you cannot pass beyond it burdened.
To come in among these trees you must leave behind
the six days' world, all of it, all of its plans and hopes.
You must come without weapon or tool, alone,
expecting nothing, remembering nothing,
into the ease of sight, the brotherhood of eye and leaf.

1987   III

And now the lowland grove is down, the trees
Fallen that had unearthly power to please
The earthly eye, and gave unearthly solace
To minds grown quiet in that quiet place.
To see them standing was to know a prayer
Prayed to the Holy Spirit in the air
By that same Spirit dwelling in the ground.
The wind in their high branches gave the sound
Of air replying to that prayer. The rayed
Imperial light sang in the leaves it made.

To live as mourner of a human friend
Is but to understand the common end
Told by the steady counting in the wrist.
For though the absent friend is mourned and missed
At every pulse, it is a human loss
In human time made well; our grief will bless
At last the dear lost flesh and breath; it will
Grow quiet as the body in the hill.

To live to mourn an ancient woodland, known
Always, loved with an old love handed down,
That is a grief that will outlast the griever,
Grief as landmark, grief as a wearing river
That in its passing stays, biding in rhyme
Of year with year, time with returning time,
As though beyond the grave the soul will wait
In long unrest the shaping of the light
In branch and bole through centuries that prepare
This ground to pray again its finest prayer.

1988   II

It is the destruction of the world
in our own lives that drives us
half insane, and more than half.
To destroy that which we were given
in trust: how will we bear it?
It is our own bodies that we give
to be broken, our bodies

existing before and after us
in clod and cloud, worm and tree,
that we, driving or driven, despise
in our greed to live, our haste
to die. To have lost, wantonly,
the ancient forests, the vast grasslani
is our madness, the presence
in our very bodies of our grief.

1988   IV

The world of machines is running
Beyond the world of trees
Where only a leaf is turning
In a small high breeze.

1992   VIII

I have again come home
through miles of sky
from hours of abstract talk
in the way of modern times
when humans live in their minds
and the world, forgotten, dies
into explanations. Weary
with absence, I return to earth.
'Good to see you back down
on the creek!' Martin Rowanberry
would say if he were here
to say it, as he'll not be again.
I have departed and returned
too many times to forget
that after all returns
one departure will remain.
I bring the horses down
off the hillside, harness them,
and start the mornings work,
the team quick to the load
along the narrow road.
I am weary with days
of travel, with poor sleep,
with time and error,

with every summer's heat
and blood-drinking flies.
And yet I sink into
the ancient happiness
of slow work in unhastenable
days and years. Horse and cow,
plow and hoe, grass to graze
and hay to mow have brought me
here, and taught me where I am.
I work in absence not yet mine
that will be mine. In time
this place has come to signify
the absence of many, and always
more, who once were here.
Day by day their voices
come to me, as from the air.
I remember them in what I do.
So I am not a modern man.
In my work I would be known
by forebears of a thousand years
if they were here to see it.
So it has been. So be it.

1997 II

Even while I dreamed I prayed that what I saw was only
    fear and no foretelling,
for I saw the last known landscape destroyed for the sake
of the objective, the soil bulldozed, the rock blasted.
Those who had wanted to go home would never get
    there now.

I visited the offices where for the sake of the objective
    the planners planned
at blank desks set in rows. I visited the loud factories
where the machines were made that would drive ever
    forward
toward the objective. I saw the forest reduced to stumps
    and gullies; I saw
the poisoned river, the mountain cast into the valley;
I came to the city that nobody recognised because it
    looked like every other city.

I saw the passages worn by the unnumbered
footfalls of those whose eyes were fixed upon the
    objective.

Their passing had obliterated the graves and the
    monuments
of those who had died in pursuit of the objective
and who had long ago forever been forgotten, according
to the inevitable rule that those who have forgotten forget
that they have forgotten. Men, women, and children now
    pursued the objective
as if nobody ever had pursued it before.

The races and the sexes now intermingled perfectly in
    pursuit of the objective.
The once-enslaved, the once-oppressed were now free
to sell themselves to the highest bidder
and to enter the best-paying prisons
in pursuit of the objective, which was the destruction
    of all enemies,
which was the destruction of all obstacles, which was
    the destruction of all objects,
which was to clear the way to victory, which was to clear
    the way to promotion, to salvation, to progress,
to the completed sale, to the signature
on the contract, which was to clear the way
to self-realisation, to self-creation, from which nobody
    who ever wanted to go home
would ever get there now, for every remembered place
had been displaced; the signposts had been bent to the
    ground and covered over.

Every place had been displaced, every love
unloved, every vow unsworn, every word unmeant
to make way for the passage of the crowd
of the individuated, the autonomous, the self-actuated,
    the homeless
with their many eyes opened only toward the objective
which they did not yet perceive in the far distance,
having never known where they were going,
having never known where they came from.

WENDELL BERRY
The Wish To Be Generous

All that I serve will die, all my delights,
the flesh kindled from my flesh, garden and field,
the silent lilies standing in the woods,
the woods, the hill, the whole earth, all
will burn in man's evil, or dwindle
in its own age. Let the world bring on me
the sleep of darkness without stars, so I may know
my little light taken from me into the seed
of the beginning and the end, so I may bow
to mystery, and take my stand on the earth
like a tree in a field, passing without haste
or regret toward what will be, my life
a patient willing descent into the grass.

WENDELL BERRY
A Vision

If we will have the wisdom to survive,
to stand like slow-growing trees
on a ruined place, renewing, enriching it,
if we will make our seasons welcome here,
asking not too much of earth or heaven,
then a long time after we are dead
the lives our lives prepare will live
here, their houses strongly placed
upon the valley sides, fields and gardens
rich in the windows. The river will run
clear, as we will never know it,
and over it, birdsong like a canopy.
On the levels of the hills will be
green meadows, stock bells in noon shade.
On the steeps where greed and ignorance cut down
the old forest, an old forest will stand,
its rich leaf-fall drifting on its roots.
The veins of forgotten springs will have opened.
Families will be singing in the fields.

In their voices they will hear a music
risen out of the ground. They will take
nothing from the ground they will not return,
whatever the grief at parting. Memory,
native to this valley, will spread over it
like a grove, and memory will grow
into legend, legend into song, song
into sacrament. The abundance of this place,
the songs of its people and its birds,
will be health and wisdom and indwelling
light. This is no paradisal dream.
Its hardship is its possibility.

WENDELL BERRY
Dark with Power

Dark with power, we remain
the invaders of our land, leaving
deserts where forests were,
scars where there were hills.

On the mountains, on the rivers,
on the cities, on the farmlands
we lay weighted hands, our breath
potent with the death of all things.

Pray to us, farmers and villagers
of Vietnam. Pray to us, mothers
and children of helpless countries.
Ask for nothing.

We are carried in the belly
of what we have become
toward the shambles of our triumph,
far from the quiet houses.

Fed with dying, we gaze
on our might's monuments of fire.
The world dangles from us
while we gaze.

WENDELL BERRY
The Peace of Wild Things

When despair for the world grows in me
and I wake in the night at the least sound
in fear of what my life and my children's lives may be,
I go and lie down where the wood drake
rests in his beauty on the water, and the great heron feeds.
I come into the peace of wild things
who do not tax their lives with forethought
of grief. I come into the presence of still water.
And I feel above me the day-blind stars
waiting with their light. For a time
I rest in the grace of the world, and am free.

■ **Jim Harrison** (*b.* 1937) is an American poet, novelist, essay-ist and food writer. Much of his writing features sparsely populated parts of North America. He is a master of the novella, and his critically acclaimed trilogy *Legends of the Fall* reinvigorated the form in America (and was adapted into two films). His early influences include a childhood blinding in one eye, and hunting, fishing and hiking in the woods of north central Michigan. Recurrent themes in his writings include the sanctity of the natural world, hunting and fishing, Native American history, Zen Buddhism, love and death, sex and violence, human relationships and appetites, and the absolute importance of paying attention.

JIM HARRISON
from Geo-Bestiary

4

Some eco-ninny released
at least a hundred tame white doves
at our creek crossing. What a feast
he innocently offered, coyotes in the yard
for the first time, a pair of great horned
owls, male and then the female
ululating, two ferruginous hawks,
and then at dawn today all song-

birds vamoosed at a startling shadow,
a merlin perched in the willow,
ur-falcon, bird-god, sweetly vengeful,
the white feathers of its meal,
a clump, among others, of red-spotted snow.

9

I hedge when I say 'my farm'.
We don't ever own, we barely rent this earth.
I've even watched a boulder age,
changing the texture of its mosses
and cracking from cold back in 1983.
Squinting, it becomes a mountain fissure.
I've sat on this rock so long we celebrate
together our age, our mute geologic destiny.

PATTIANN ROGERS
A Common Sight

There is at least one eye
for everything here this afternoon.
The algae and the yeasts, invisible
to some, for instance, are seen
by the protozoa; and the black-tailed
seeds of tadpoles are recognised
on sight by the giant, egg-carrying
water beetle. Brook trout have eyes
for caddisfly larvae, pickerel
for dragonfly nymphs; redfin shiners
bear witness to the presence
of flocks of water fleas.

The grains of the goldenrod
are valued, sought out, found
by the red-legged grasshopper who is,
in turn, noticed immediately
by the short-tailed shrew whose least
flitter alarms and attracts
the rodent-scoped eye
of the white-winged hawk.

There is an eye for everything.
The two-lined salamander watches
for the horsehair worm, as the stilt spider
pays sharp attention to midge fly,
crane fly. The cricket frog
will not pass unnoticed, being spied
specifically by the ringed raccoon,
and, despite the night beneath
the field, the earthworm, the grub
and the leafhopper larva are perceived
by the star-nosed mole.

So odd, that nothing goes unnoticed.
Even time has its testimony,
each copepod in the colony possessing
a red eyespot sensitive to the hour,
the entire congregation rising
as one body at dusk to touch the dark
where it exists above the pond.

And I have an eye myself
for this particular vision, this continuous
validation-by-sight that's given
and taken over and over by clam shrimp,
marsh treader, bobcat, the clover-covering
honeybee, by diving teal, the thousand-eyed
bot fly the wild and vigilant,
shadow-seeking mollusk mya.

Watch now, for my sake, how I stalk. Watch
how I secure this vision. Watch how long
and lovingly, watch
how I feed.

PATTIANN ROGERS

The Laying On of Hands

There's a gentleness we haven't learned yet,
but we've seen it — the way an early morning haze
can settle in the wayside hedges of lilac and yew,
permeate the emptiness between every scaly

bud and leafstalk until it becomes bound,
fully contained, shaped by the spires,
the stiff pins and purple-white blossoms
of that tangled wall.

There's a subtlety we haven't mastered yet,
but we recognise it — the way moonlight passes
simultaneously upon, through, beyond
the open wing of the crane fly
without altering a single detail
of its smallest paper vein. We know
there is a perfect consideration
of touching possible. The merest snow
accomplishes that, assuming the exact
configuration of the bristled beggarweed
while the beggarweed remains
exclusively itself.

If I could discover that same tension
of muscle myself, if I could move, imagining
smoke finding the forest-lines of the sun
at dusk, if I could place my hand
with that motion, achieve the proper
stance of union and isolation
in fingers and palm, place my hand
with less pressure than a whaler strider
places by the seeds of its toes
on the surface of the pond, balance
that way, skin to bark, my hand
fully open on the trunk of this elm tree
right now, I know it would be possible
to feel immediately every tissue imposition
and ringed liturgy, every bloodvein
and vacuum of that tree's presence, perceive
immediately both the hard, jerking start
of the seedling in winter and the spore-filled
moss and liquid decay of the fallen trunk
to come, both the angle of tilt in the green sun
off every leaf above and the slow lightning
of hair roots in their buried dark below,
know even the reverse silhouette of my own hand
experienced from inner bark out,

even the moment of this very revelation
of *woman and tree* itself where it was locked
millennia before in those tight molecules
of suckers and sapwood.

Without harm or alteration or surrender
of any kind, I know my hand laid properly,
could discover this much.

PATTIANN ROGERS
The Singing Place

For the orange, saucer-eyed
lemurs indri of the family sifaka,
it is the perfect forest of the hot,
humid zones. There, at sunset and dawn,
they all pause arboreally and chorus,
howling, hooting, shaking the shadows
overhead, the fruits and burrowing
beetles inside the many-storied
jungle. They are the ushers,
the chaperones, the screaming
broadcast of darkness and light.

The house cricket, the field cricket,
the dead-leaf cricket make song places
of the warmest, darkest niches
they can find, at the bases of stones,
in grass stem funnels, the mossy
underbark of southside tree trunks.

For the sage grouse, male, the real
singing place is where he actually sings,
there inside the thimble-sized, flesh-
and-blood place of his voice, that air
sac burbling and popping, puffing
through the morning as he struts
and bows before his hens on the open
spring lek. Breath, I believe,
is place.

And maybe even the bulb and tuber
and root suck of the big black slug
of wet pastures could be called a long,
slow mud music and meter of sustenance,
by those lucky enough to be born
with a pasture sense for sound.

The whine and wind of heats
through ragged gorges make sandstone
and basalt a moving song. And place,
I think, is moments in motion.

As on the white-statue plains
of the moon's most weird winter
where no dusk scream or lingering suck
or floosing air sac of song has ever
existed, utter stillness is a singing
place too, moments where I first
must find a shape of silence,
where I then must begin?
to hum its structure.

■ **Pattiann Rogers** (*b*. 1940) is an American writer known for poetry that both embraces the natural world and unfolds the complexities of science. Her work echoes the ecological concerns of writers such as Whitman, Emerson, Annie Dillard and Mary Oliver, also embracing and connecting motherhood, art, science, spirituality with the tensions between humanity and wildness. In her essay 'This Nature', she writes: 'Nature is everything that is. We are not and cannot be "unnatural". Our choices and our actions are never for or against nature. They are always simply *of* nature. [...] This nature is not a single entity, not a consistent force that sanctions or condemns behavior, not a god-substitute that we can embrace or blame or escape. It composes the entire, complex myriad of ever-changing events and details, unpredictable, paradoxical, passing and eternal, known and mysterious. Nature is the vast expanse of abstractions and multiplicities; it is the void and the concrete presence, an unrestricted inclusiveness.'

JOHN CLARE
'All nature has a feeling'

All nature has a feeling: woods, fields, brooks
Are life eternal: and in silence they
Speak happiness beyond the reach of books;
There's nothing mortal in them; their decay
Is the green life of change; to pass away
And come again in blooms revivified.
Its birth was heaven, eternal is its stay,
And with the sun and moon shall still abide
Beneath their day and night and heaven wide.

THEODORE ROETHKE
Moss-gathering

To loosen with all ten fingers held wide and limber
And lift up a patch, dark-green, the kind for lining cemetery baskets,
Thick and cushiony, like an old-fashioned doormat,
The crumbling small hollow sticks on the underside mixed with roots,
And wintergreen berries and leaves still stuck to the top, –
That was moss-gathering,
But something always went out of me when I dug loose those carpets
Of green, or plunged to my elbows in the spongy yellowish moss of
     the marshes:
And afterwards I always felt mean, jogging back over the logging road,
As if I had broken the natural order of things in that swampland;
Disturbed some rhythm, old and of vast importance,
By pulling off flesh from the living planet;
As if I had committed, against the whole scheme of life, a desecration.

DINAH LIVINGSTONE
Sweetness
(Bagley Combe, August)

What is the smell of the earth
upthrusting in bracken and heather,
which add their own scent too?
I listen to water now dawdling down,
that sprang from deep inside it
further up the combe.

The earth's still damp
as, somewhat frazzled with aching feet,
I sink into soft turf,
sniff and almost taste,
listen again – are those stonechats? –
and with near-sight see
the ferny pattern above me,
over there glimpse ripening rowan,
hawthorn, curve of moorland
horizon meeting sky.

The buzzing flies recede.
I feel a whiteness
wiping behind my eyes,
let go, sleep a little
and wake less careworn,
still unable to say
what is the smell of the arth
except an indescribable
sense of belonging,
hard to tell from longing.

■ **Theodore Roethke** (1908-63) was an influential American poet of Prussian descent. He grew up in Saginaw, Michigan, where his father, uncle and grandfather all had greenhouses, the setting and central image of many of his poems. Educated at the University of Michigan, and briefly at Harvard, he had the first of a series of mental breakdowns in 1935. His breakthrough collection was *The Lost Son* (1948), whose poems – Roethke claimed – trace the spiritual and personal history of 'a protagonist (not "I" personally but of all haunted and harried men)'. The book featured his celebrated greenhouse sequence (including '**Moss Gathering**'), in which intense observation of the natural world yields insights into the violence, comedy, eroticism and regenerative potentiality inherent in all life. Roethke found spiritual correspondences in the physical world, an 'awareness of one's own self, *and*, even more mysteriously, in some instances, a feeling of the oneness of the universe'.

■ **John Clare** ➤ 45.

LOUISE BOGAN
Night

The cold remote islands
And the blue estuaries
Where what breathes, breathes
The restless wind of the inlets,
And what drinks, drinks
The incoming tide;

Where shell and weed
Wait upon the salt wash of the sea,
And the clear nights of the stars
Swing their lights westward
To set behind the land;

Where the pulse clinging to the rocks
Renews itself forever;
Where, again on cloudless nights,
The water reflects
The firmament's partial setting;

– O remember
In your narrowing dark hours
That more things move
Than blood in the heart.

FRANCES HOROVITZ
Rain – Birdoswald

I stand under a leafless tree
more still, in this mouse-pattering
   thrum of rain,
than cattle shifting in the field.
   It is more dark than light.
A Chinese painter's brush of deepening grey
   moves in a subtle tide.

The beasts are darker islands now.
Wet-stained and silvered by the rain
   they suffer night,
marooned as still as stone or tree.
   We sense each other's quiet.

Almost, death could come
inevitable, unstrange
   as is this dusk and rain,
and I should be no more
   myself, than raindrops
glimmering in last light
   on black ash buds

or night beasts in a winter field.

■ **Louise Bogan** (1897-1970) was an intensely private American poet who wrote most of her work in the earlier half of her life. Her poetry is notable for its strict adherence to lyrical forms while maintaining a high emotional pitch, and for its concern with love, grief, and the perpetual disparity of heart and mind.

■ **Dinah Livingstone** (*b.* 1940) is a poet, publisher and translator of Latin American poetry and prose. She had a rural childhood in in the West of England and has lived in London since 1966, where she runs the small press Katabasis and edits the magazine *Sofia*. Her many translations including two books of poetry by Ernesto Cardenal [➤ 166]. Her most recent prose book, *The Poetry of Earth* (2000), is an essay on poetry, language, theology, politics and ecology.

■ **Frances Horovitz** (1938-83) was an English poet, broadcaster and performer of poetry whose life was cut short (by cancer) at the age of 45. Her poetry is remarkable for the clarity, precision and attentiveness of her perceptions of the natural world and evocations of history and human relationships. Many of her poems were inspired by the remote Cotswold valley where she lived for ten years; others by the border country of Cumbria (including the poem here) and the Welsh Marches. Peter Levi admired her 'perfect rhythm, great delicacy and a rather Chinese yet very locally British sense of landscape'.

■ **Linda McCarriston** (*b.*1943) is an Irish American poet who has taught at the University of Alaska Anchorage since 1994. She survived a traumatic upbringing in Lynn, Massachusetts to reinvent herself as a writer of powerfully redemptive poetry.

Her work addresses difficult issues of family life and gender power but also presents loving portrayals of animals, children, friendships and landscapes. Her poetic vision combines an acute awareness of the anguish caused by the misuse of power with a deep love and tenderness for humanity and nature.

■ Denise Levertov ➤ 157.

DENISE LEVERTOV
The Life Around Us

Poplar and oak awake
all night. And through
all weathers of the days of the year.
There is a consciousness
undefined.
Yesterday's twilight, August
almost over, lasted, slowly changing,
until daybreak. Human sounds
were shut behind curtains.
No human saw the night in this garden,
sliding blue into morning.
Only the sightless trees,
without braincells, lived it
and wholly knew it.

LINDA McCARRISTON
Riding Out at Evening

At dusk, everything blurs and softens.
From here out over the long valley,
the fields and hills pull up
the first slight sheets of evening,
as, over the next hour,
heavier, darker ones will follow.

Quieted roads, predictable deer
browsing in a neighbor's field, another's
herd of heifers, the kitchen lights
starting in many windows. On horseback

I take it in, neither visitor
nor intruder, but kin passing, closer
and closer to night, its cold streams
rising in the sugarbush and hollow.

Half-aloud, I say to the horse,
or myself, or whoever: let fire not come
to this house, nor that barn,
nor lightning strike the cattle.
Let dogs not gain the gravid doe, let the lights
of the rooms convey what they seem to.

And who is to say it is useless
or foolish to ride out in the falling light
alone, wishing, or praying,
for particular good to particular beings
on one small road in a huge world?
The horse bears me along, like grace,
making me better than what I am,
and what I think or say or see
is whole in these moments, is neither
small nor broken. For up, out of
the inscrutable earth, have come my body
and the separate body of the mare:
flawed and aching and wronged. Who then
is better made to say *be well, be glad,*

or who to long that we, as one,
might course over the entire valley,
over all valleys, as a bird in a great embrace
of flight, who presses against her breast,
in grief and tenderness,
the whole weeping body of the world?

■ **Robert Wrigley** (*b.* 1951) is an American writer whose poetry tries to make sense of a chaotic world, and asks what it means to be human as well as part of the natural world. His work affirms that 'poetry can have a redemptive function [...] poetry is as close as I come to prayer' (Jeffrey Dodd interview). His books of poetry include *Reign of Snakes* (1999), *Lives of the Animals* (2003) and *Earthly Meditations: New and Selected Poems* (2006). He is director of the creative writing MFA at the University of Idaho, and lives on the Clearwater River.

ROBERT WRIGLEY
Kissing a Horse

Of the two spoiled, barn-sour geldings
we owned that year, it was Red –
skittish and prone to explode
even at fourteen years – who'd let me
hold to my face his own: the massive labyrinthine
caverns of the nostrils, the broad plain
up the head to the eyes. He'd let me stroke
his coarse chin whiskers and take
his soft meaty underlip
in my hands, press my man's carnivorous
kiss to his grass-nipping upper half of one, just
so that I could smell
the long way his breath had come from the rain
and the sun, the lungs and the heart,
from a world that meant no harm.

JAMES WRIGHT
A Blessing

Just off the highway to Rochester, Minnesota,
Twilight bounds softly forth on the grass.
And the eyes of those two Indian ponies
Darken with kindness.
They have come gladly out of the willows
To welcome my friend and me.
We step over the barbed wire into the pasture
Where they have been grazing all day, alone.
They ripple tensely, they can hardly contain their happiness
That we have come.
They bow shyly as wet swans. They love each other.
There is no loneliness like theirs.
At home once more,
They begin munching the young tufts of spring in the
    darkness.
I would like to hold the slenderer one in my arms,
For she has walked over to me

And nuzzled my left hand.
She is black and white,
Her mane falls wild on her forehead,
And the light breeze moves me to caress her long ear
That is delicate as the skin over a girl's wrist.
Suddenly I realise
That if I stepped out of my body I would break
Into blossom.

JAMES WRIGHT
Yes, But

Even if it were true,
Even if I were dead and buried in Verona,
I believe I would come out and wash my face
In the chill spring.
I believe I would appear
Between noon and four, when nearly
Everybody else is asleep or making love,
And all the Germans turned down, the motorcycles
Muffled, chained, still.

Then the plump lizards along the Adige by San Giorgio
Come out and gaze,
Unpestered by temptation, across the water.
I would sit among them and join them in leaving
The golden mosquitoes alone.
Why should we sit by the Adige and destroy
Anything, even our enemies, even the prey
God caused to glitter for us
Defenseless in the sun?
We are not exhausted. We are not angry, or lonely,
Or sick at heart.
We are in love lightly, lightly. We know we are shining,
Though we cannot see one another.
The wind doesn't scatter us,
Because our very lounges have fallen and drifted
Away like leaves down the Adige
Long ago.

We breathe light.

■ **James Wright** (1927-80) was one of the most influential American poets of the 20th century. Whether drawing on his native Ohio, the natural world, or the luminous resonant Italy of his later work, his powerful yet vulnerable voice embraces many facets of human experience through shifting tones and moods, both lyric and ironic, autobiographical and social.

■ **Mary Oliver** (*b.* 1935) is one of America's best-loved poets. Her luminous poetry celebrates nature and beauty, love and the spirit, silence and wonder, extending the visionary American tradition of Whitman, Emerson and Emily Dickinson. It is nourished by her intimate knowledge and minute daily observation of the New England coast around Cape Cod, its woods and ponds, its birds, animals, plants and trees.

Laird Christensen describes how Oliver's 'ecological pantheism' teaches us 'to embrace our participation in the community of all life': 'To Mary Oliver humans are no longer merely favoured by a divine power, as our Judeo-Christian heritage suggests; we are inextricable constituents of it. As she attempts to shift the basis of personal value from individual to collective identification, Oliver follows the lead of American romantics such as William Cullen Bryant and Walt Whitman in figuring physical mortality as redemptive regeneration.[…] As Jean Alford observes, Oliver redefines human immortality "as a self-denying mortal life in communion with the eternal processes of nature".'

In 'Winter Hours', Mary Oliver writes: 'I could not be a poet without the natural world. […] My work doesn't document any of the sane and learned arguments for saving, healing, and protecting the earth for our existence. What I write begins and ends with the act of noticing and cherishing, and it neither begins nor ends with the human world. […] The man who does not know nature, who does not walk under the leaves as under his own roof, is partial and wounded. I say this even as wilderness shrinks beneath our unkindnesses and our indifference. Nature there will always be, but it will not be what we have now, much less the deeper fields and woodlands many of us remember from our childhood. […] We can come to our senses yet, and rescue the world, but we will never return it to anything like its original form. […] I believe in the soul – in mine, and yours, and the bluejay's, and the pilot whale's. I believe each goldfinch flying away over the coarse ragweed has a soul, and the ragweed too, plant by plant, and the tiny stones in the earth below, and the grains of earth as well. Not romantically do I believe this, nor poetically, nor emotionally, nor metaphorically except as all reality is metaphor, but steadily, lumpishly, and absolutely.'

MARY OLIVER
Five A.M. in the Pinewoods

I'd seen
their hoofprints in the deep
needles and knew
they ended the long night

under the pines, walking
like two mute
and beautiful women toward
the deeper woods, so I

got up in the dark and
went there. They came
slowly down the hill
and looked at me sitting under

the blue trees, shyly
they stepped
closer and stared
from under their thick lashes and even

nibbled some damp
tassels of weeds. This
is not a poem about a dream,
though it could be.

This is a poem about the world
that is ours, or could be.
Finally
one of them – I swear it! –

would have come to my arms.
But the other
stamped sharp hoof in the
pine needles like

the tap of sanity,
and they went off together through
the trees. When I woke
I was alone,

I was thinking:
so this is how you swim inward,
so this is how you flow outward,
so this is how you pray.

MARY OLIVER
Morning Poem

Every morning
the world
is created.
Under the orange

sticks of the sun
the heaped
ashes of the night
turn into leaves again

and fasten themselves to the high branches —
and the ponds appear
like black cloth
on which are painted islands

of summer lilies.
If it is your nature
to be happy
you will swim away along the soft trails

for hours, your imagination
alighting everywhere.
And if your spirit
carries wthin it

the thorn
that is heavier than lead —
if it's all you can do
to keep on trudging —

there is still
somewhere deep within you
a beast shouting that the earth
is exactly what it wanted —

each pond with its blazing lilies
is a prayer heard and answered
lavishly
every morning

whether nor not
you have ever dared to be happy,
whether or not
you have ever dared to pray.

MARY OLIVER
Some Questions You Might Ask

Is the soul solid, like iron?
Or is it tender and breakable, like
the wings of a moth in the beak of the owl?
Who has it, and who doesn't?
I keep looking around me.
The face of the moose is as sad
as the face of Jesus.
The swan opens her white wings slowly.
In the fall, the black bear carries leaves into the darkness.
One question leads to another.
Does it have a shape? Like an iceberg?
Like the eye of a hummingbird?
Does it have one lung, like the snake and the scallop?
Why should I have it, and not the anteater
who loves her children?
Why should I have it, and not the camel?
Come to think of it, what about the maple trees?
What about the blue iris?
What about all the little stones, sitting alone in the moonlight?
What about roses, and lemons, and their shining leaves?
What about the grass?

KEN SMITH
Grass

Grass erupts slowly, locking the soil in frail roots.
Without these tenoned fingers earth would be as sea,
drifting, unsure. It is a sort of knowledge,
gripping together, confirming that hill's shape.

Do not forget the grass. That trodden softness
could only be an innocence that insists, comes back,
season by growing season. It cannot stop itself.
And though you kill it, grass does not seem to die.

Rocks morticed in themselves do not require it,
nor does its colour clutch the spaces of the desert.
Its absence is death's sign, brooding its own mystery.
Grass exists. All life revolves around its rooted blade.

And yet grass does not care. Accepting without flower,
it seeds on plains or in cracked rocks, indifferent
to a touch that sears the granite. Grass
moves on, impotent in will, a rooted apathy
exposed to hoof and fire. It cannot stop itself.
Grass waits the mower's knife, the ditcher's spade.

■ **Ken Smith** (1938-2003) was an English poet whose work
and example inspired a whole generation of younger poets.
His poetry shifted territory with time, from rural Yorkshire,
America and London to the war-ravaged Balkans and Eastern
Europe (before and after Communism). His early books span
a transition from a preoccupation with land and myth to his
later engagement with urban Britain and the politics of radical
disaffection.

■ **Pablo Neruda** (1904-73) was known in Chile as 'the people's
poet'. He was one of the greatest and most influential poets of
the 20th century, and received the Nobel Prize in Literature
in 1971. He served his country as a diplomat for many years
but also spent long periods in exile. His poetry embraces both
private and public concerns: he is known both for his love
and nature poetry and for works addressing Latin American
political history and social struggle. His early poetry was
fiercely surreal, reflecting ancient terrors, modern anxieties
and his near-religious desolation. The Spanish Civil War
changed his life and work as he moved to a personal voice
and to more politically involved and ideological positions.
The turning-point came with his epic volume *Canto general*
(1950), including 'The Heights of Macchu Picchu', which
marked 'a new stage in my style and a new direction in my
concerns'. Standing on the hallowed Inca ground, Neruda
vowed to make the stones speak on behalf of those who had
built and laboured on it. What had begun as a poem about
Chile turned into one that expressed the whole geological,
natural and political history of South America. His later work
was elemental in its concerns, including the three books of
Odes, which gave material things a life of their own. Nothing
was ordinary in Neruda's poetry: anything could be magical;
womanhood was linked to the regeneration of earth and the
cyclical processes of nature. [Other poem ➤ 108]

PABLO NERUDA
Oneness
translated from the Spanish by Stephen Kessler

There's something dense, united, sitting in the background,
repeating its number, its identical signal.
How clear it is that stones have handled time,
in their fine substance there's the smell of age,
and water the sea brings, salty and sleepy.

Just one thing surrounds me, a single motion:
the weight of rocks, the light of skin,
fasten themselves to the sound of the word night:
the tones of wheat, of ivory, of tears,
things made of leather, of wood, of wool,
aging, fading, blurring,
come together around me like a wall.

I toil deafly, circling above my self,
like a raven above death, grief's raven.
I'm thinking, isolated in the vastness of the seasons,
dead center, surrounded by silent geography:
a piece of weather falls from the sky,
an extreme empire of confused unities
converges, encircling me.

■ **Guillevic** (1907-97) was born in Carnac in Brittany, and although he never learned the Breton language, his personality was deeply marked by his feeling of oneness with his homeland.

His poetry has a remarkable unity, driven by his desire to use words to bridge a tragic gulf between man and a harsh and often apparently hostile natural environment. For Guillevic, the purpose of poetry is to arouse the sense of Being. In this poetry of description – where entire landscapes are built up from short, intense texts – language is reduced to its essentials, as words are placed on the page 'like a dam against time'. When reading these poems, it is as if time is being stopped for humanity to find itself again.

Carnac (1961) marked the beginning of Guillevic's mature life as a poet. A single poem in several parts, it evokes the rocky, sea-bound, unfinished landscape of Brittany with its sacred objects and its great silent sense of waiting. The texts are brief but have a grave, meditative serenity, as the poet seeks to effect balance and to help us 'to make friends with nature' and to live in a universe which is chaotic and often frightening.

Teo Savory: 'In his poetry the flower, the ant, the blackbird, the rocks – especially the rocks – are only themselves. He has extracted from the things of this world not their meaning to man, or the lessons they might teach, but, as it were, their philosophy of themselves in an alien world peopled by those strange beings, men. To grasp, not the philosophy of nature but a thing's philosophy of itself, the poet contemplates his subjects intensely and lets them communicate with him.'

GUILLEVIC
from Things
translated from the French by Teo Savory

Winter tree

Tree, here, now, standing,
nothing but wood,
like a bird, fixed, upright,
head hanging.

Tree surviving,
like wood,
like bird,
not moving.

Plum tree

What if you believed
that I'm nothing to you,

If you didn't know
that with you I've made
these fruits that ripened you,

If you didn't know
that I match you
as exactly as possible,

What if you wanted
to disown, to hide.

But we happen to be
no more incestuous
than many others.

Rock

I need to be hard
and durable with you,

Against all the enemies
halted by your surface,

I need us to be
accomplices in our vigil

Then night will pass
powerless to reduce us.

Whatever

Whatever's not in stone,
whatever's not in walls of stone and earth,
not even in trees,
whatever always trembles a little,

Well, that's in us.

GUILLEVIC
from Carnac
translated from the French by John Montague

The sea, a nothingness
Which longs to be sea

Which longs to give itself
Terrestrial attributes

And the drive that it
Derives from the wind.

[…]

A whole arithmetic
Lies dead in your waves.

[…]

If it is true that in you
Life began,

Is that any reason
You should keep us

As accomplices?

■ **Caitríona O'Reilly** (*b.* 1973) is an Irish poet and critic. Her poetry is remarkable for its precise observation of the natural world. Her themes include nature and history, childhood and adolescence, location and flight, and natural and cultural obsolescence. Capturing moments of imagistic stillness, her poems enact human dilemmas and anxieties amidst a rapidly changing environment.

Michael Longley: 'Though she might be, in her own words, "rational and unafraid", she keeps reminding us of the "the primitive darkness", its fearful disorderliness. Whether enthralled or appalled, she beholds and magnifies the world and its strange creatures (including ourselves) in poems that are formally versatile and linguistically copious). [Other poem ➤ 199]

CAITRÍONA O'REILLY
The River
FROM *Six Landscapes*

The coming night breathes an atmosphere
of childhood October in crisp light and wood-smoke,
    and the guy ropes
    sway in the harbour
while the black river pauses
    between two tides,
    shaping itself in shadow.

It is never changing, never the same –
the ancient trees of the rookery in silent commune
    with the river's
    different darkness
when we pass, and this time,
    an egg-speckled kestrel
    bullied by swallows.

A field that was mysteriously full of nothing
once but poisoned sparrows, a convulsive rain,
    is brown earth now,
    would not disturb
the bubble in a spirit level,
    with a manhole like
    a navel at its middle.

We wonder how will the river change, escape
development, or work its careless necromancy
    on the next ones
    to come here –
and who will watch its black dreams
    shatter into figments
    skulled and crossboned in light?

■ **Linda Gregerson** (*b.* 1950) is an American poet and critic who teaches Renaissance literature and creative writing at the University of Michigan. **'Waterborne'**, the title-poem of her third collection (2002), uses her trademark assymetrical tercet to register her dislocated sense of the river which runs beside her acre of woods, mapping the communal fate of people and wildlife: everything that lives or dies is its direct dependant. 'I've long felt that these tercets have saved my life,' she told Christine Marshall and Nadine Meyer. 'They actually generate the sentences they're up against. I turned to them, invented them after experimenting with other asymmetrical stanzas, when I desperately needed to let more light and air into my poems. [...] these tercets gave me a way to launch the syntax I experience as the mind-in-motion. The music I find most natural, most accommodating to cognitive discovery, is syncopation, and my homely little three-line stanza, especially the shortest, central "pivot" line, makes syncopation its foundation.'

LINDA GREGERSON
Waterborne

1

The river is largely implicit here, but part
        of what
           becomes it runs from east to west beside

our acre of buckthorn and elm.
        (And part
           of that, which rather weighs on Steven's mind,

appears to have found its way to the basement. Water
        will outwit
           a wall.) It spawns real toads, our little

creek, and widens to a wetland just
        across
           the road, where shelter the newborn

fawns in May. So west among the trafficked fields,
        then south, then
           east, to join the ample Huron on its

curve beneath a one-lane bridge. This bridge
        lacks every
           grace but one, and that a sort of throwback

space for courteous digression:
        your turn,
           mine, no matter how late we are, even

the county engineers were forced to take their road
        off plumb. It's heartening
           to think a river makes some difference.

2

Apart from all the difference in the world,
        that is.
           We found my uncle Gordon on the marsh

one day, surveying his new ditch and raining
        innovative
           curses on the DNR. That's Damn Near

Russia, since you ask. Apparently
        my uncle
           and the state had had a mild dispute, his

drainage scheme offending some considered
        larger
           view. His view was that the state could come

and plant the corn itself if it so loved
        spring mud. The river
           takes its own back, we can barely

reckon fast and slow. When Gordon was a boy
        they used to load
           the frozen river on a sledge here and

in August eat the heavenly reward – sweet
        cream –
           of winter's work. A piece of moonlight saved

against the day, he thought. And this is where
        the Muir boy
           drowned. And this is where I didn't.

3

Turning of the season, and the counter-
                turn
            from ever-longer darkness into light,

and look: the river lifts to its lover the sun
                in eddying
            layers of mist as though

we hadn't irreparably fouled the planet
                after all.
            My neighbor's favorite spot for bass is just

below the sign that makes his fishing
                rod illegal,
            you might almost say the sign is half

the point. The vapors draft their languorous
                excurses on
            a liquid page. Better than the moment is

the one it has in mind.

LORINE NIEDECKER
'Far reach'

Far reach
    of sand
        A man

bends to inspect
    a shell
        Himself

part coral
    and mud
        clam

LORINE NIEDECKER
Paean to Place

And the place
was water

Fish
    fowl
        flood
        Water lily mud
My life

in the leaves and on water
My mother and I
                born
in swale and swamp and sworn
to water

My father
thru marsh fog
    sculled down
        from high ground
saw her face

at the organ
bore the weight of lake water urn
    and the cold –
he seined for carp to be sold
that their daughter

might go high
on land
    to learn
Saw his wife turn
deaf

and away
She
    who knew boats
        and ropes
no longer played

She helped him string out nets
for tarring
        And she could shoot
                He was cool
to the man

who stole his minnows
by night and next day offered
        to sell them back
                He brought in a sack
of dandelion greens

if no flood
No oranges – none at hand
        No marsh marigolds
                where the water rose
He kept us afloat

I mourn her not hearing canvasbacks
their blast-off rise
        from the water
                Not hearing sora
rails's sweet

spoon-tapped waterglass-
descending scale-
        tear-drop-tittle
                Did she giggle
as a girl?

His skiff skimmed
the coiled celery now gone
        from these streams
                due to carp
He knew duckweed

fall-migrates
toward Mud Lake bottom
        Knew what lay
                under leaf decay
and on pickerel weeds

before summer hum
To be counted on:
        new leaves
                new dead
leaves

He could not
– like water bugs –
        stride surface tension
                He netted
loneliness

As to his bright new car
my mother – her house
        next his – averred:
                A hummingbird
can't haul

Anchored here
in the rise and sink
        of life –
                middle years' nights
he sat

beside his shoes
rocking his chair
        Roped not 'looped
                in the loop
other hair'

I grew in green
slide and slant
        of shore and shade
                Child-time – wade
thru weeds

Maples to swing from
Pewee-glissando
        sublime
                slime-
song

Grew riding the river
Books
    at home-pier
        Shelley could steer
as he read

I was the solitary plover
a pencil
    for a wing-bone
From the secret notes
I must tilt

upon the pressure
execute and adjust
    In us sea-air rhythm
'We live by the urgent wave
of the verse'

Seven year molt
for the solitary bird
    and so young
Seven years the one
dress

for town once a week
One for home
    faded blue-striped
as she piped
her cry

Dancing grounds
my people had none
woodcocks had –
backland-
air around

Solemnities
such as what flower
    to take
    to grandfather's grave
unless

water lilies –
he who'd bowed his head
    to grass as he mowed
    Iris now grows
on fill

for the two
and for him
    where they lie
    How much less am I
in the dark than they?

Effort lay in us
before religions
    at pond bottom
        All things move toward
the light

except those
that freely work down
    to oceans' black depths
        In us an impulse tests –
the unknown

River rising – flood
Now melt and leave home
    Return – broom wet
        naturally wet
Under

soak-heavy rug
water bugs hatched –
    no snake in the house
        Where were they? –
she

who knew how to clean up
after floods
    he who bailed boats, houses
    Water endows us
with buckled floors

You with sea water running
in your veins sit down in water
        Expect the long-stemmed blue
                speedwell to renew
itself

O my floating life
Do not save love
        for things
                Throw *things*
to the flood

ruined
by the flood
        Leave the new unbought –
                all one in the end –
water

I possessed
the high word:
        The boy my friend
                played his violin
in the great hall

On this stream
my moonnight memory
        washed of hardships
                maneuvers barges
thru the mouth

of the river
They fished in beauty
        It was not always so
                In Fishes
red Mars

rising
rides the sloughs and sluices
        of my mind
                with the persons
on the edge

■ **Lorine Niedecker** (1903-70) was an American modernist poet associated with the Objectivist movement. For most of her life she lived in a remote part of Wisconsin, on Black Hawk Island, 'a section of low land on the Rock River where it empties into Lake Koshkonong', where her father ran a carp-fishing business. **'Paean to Place'** is her extended reflection on life by water on Black Hawk Island ('and the place was water,' she told Kenneth Cox) .

Elizabeth Willis: 'Niedecker traced her poetic beginning to the discovery of the Objectivist issue of *Poetry* magazine, guest-edited by Louis Zukofsky and published in February 1931. She immediately wrote to Zukofsky, who had recently taught at the nearby University of Wisconsin, and so began their life-long friendship and correspondence. In 1933 Niedecker's poems appeared in *Poetry*, and she visited New York where she and Zukofsky became lovers for a time. The same year, Niedecker returned home to Black Hawk Island, devoting the rest of her creative life to her poetry and correspondence, often filling both with descriptions of local geography and overheard social commentary – much as Wordsworth, at about the same age, returned to his Lake District to find poetry in common speech. Having read Wordsworth and the Shelleys in her youth, she was conscious of the historical resonances between landscape and literature, the "traces of living things" imprinted on both. As a teenager, she took Wordsworth with her onto Lake Koshkonong, and in the magnificent late poem **'Paean to Place'** she notes with wonder that "Shelley could steer as he read".'

Jenny Penberthy: '"The Brontës had their moors, I have my marshes," Lorine Niedecker wrote of watery, flood-prone Black Hawk Island near the town of Fort Atkinson, Wisconsin, where she lived most of her life. Although few people endured for long the seasonal hardships of life on Black Hawk Island, Niedecker's attachments to the place ran deep. Her life by water could not have been further removed from the avant-garde poetry scene where she also made herself a home. [...]

'Lorine recalled, "I spent my childhood outdoors – red-winged blackbirds, willows, maples, boats, fishing (the smell of tarred nets), twittering and squawking noises from the marsh." Her work is distinguished by its attentive use of sound, a consequence perhaps of her poor eyesight and her experience of her mother's deafness, but also of her immersion in the rich soundscape of Black Hawk Island.'

Basil Bunting: 'Her work was austere, free of all ornament, relying on the fundamental rhythms of concise statement, so that to many readers it must have seemed strange and bare.'

BASIL BUNTING
from **Briggflatts**

from I

Brag, sweet tenor bull,
descant on Rawthey's madrigal,
each pebble its part
for the fells' late spring.
Dance tiptoe, bull,
black against may.
Ridiculous and lovely
chase hurdling shadows
morning into noon.
May on the bull's hide
and through the dale
furrows fill with may,
paving the slowworm's way.

A mason times his mallet
to a lark's twitter,
listening while the marble rests,
lays his rule
at a letter's edge,
fingertips checking,
till the stone spells a name
naming none,
a man abolished.
Painful lark, labouring to rise!
The solemn mallet says:
In the grave's slot
he lies. We rot.

Decay thrusts the blade,
wheat stands in excrement
trembling. Rawthey trembles.
Tongue stumbles, ears err
for fear of spring.
Rub the stone with sand,
wet sandstone rending
roughness away. Fingers
ache on the rubbing stone.

The mason says: Rocks
happen by chance.
No one here bolts the door,
love is so sore.

from V

Shepherds follow the links,
sweet turf studded with thrift;
fell-born men of precise instep
leading demure dogs
from Tweed and Till and Teviotdale,
with hair combed back from the muzzle,
dogs from Redesdale and Coquetdale
taught by Wilson or Telfer.
Their teeth are white as birch,
slow under black fringe
of silent, accurate lips.
The ewes are heavy with lamb.
Snow lies bright on Hedgehope
and tacky mud about Till
where the fells have stepped aside
and the river praises itself,
silence by silence sits
and Then is diffused in Now.

Basil Bunting (1900-85) grew up in Newcastle, spending many summers near Sedbergh. Acknowledged since the 1930s as a major figure in Modernist poetry, first by Pound and Zukofsky and later by younger writers, the Northumbrian master poet had to wait over 30 years before his genius was finally recognised in Britain – in 1966, with the publication of *Briggflatts*, which Cyril Connolly called 'the finest long poem to have been published in England since T.S. Eliot's *Four Quartets*'.

In *The Song of the Earth*, Jonathan Bate writes that it is 'because Bunting at his best was a bioregional poet that we need to reclaim him now', and calls *Briggflatts* 'a deeply Wordsworthian autobiographical meditation on loss and recovery in which identity is forged in place'. In his study of Bunting's poetry, Peter Makin describes how *Briggflatts* traces a complex web of relations in 'an ecology of fox, slow-worm, rat, blowfly, and weed; sheepdogs and pregnant sheep; light on water and foam on rock: things seen.'

DENISE LEVERTOV
Living

The fire in leaf and grass
so green it seems
each summer the last summer.

The wind blowing, the leaves
shivering in the sun,
each day the last day.

A red salamander
so cold and so
easy to catch, dreamily

moves his delicate feet
and long tail. I hold
my hand open for him to go.

Each minute the last minute.

R.S. THOMAS
Autumn on the Land

A man, a field, silence – what is there to say?
He lives, he moves, and the October day
Burns slowly down.
             History is made
Elsewhere; the hours forfeit to time's blade
Don't matter here. The leaves large and small,
Shed by the branches, unlamented fall
About his shoulders. You may look in vain
Through the eyes' window; on his meagre hearth
The thin, shy soul has not begun its reign
Over the darkness. Beauty, love and mirth
And joy are strangers there.
                  You must revise
Your bland philosophy of nature, earth
Has of itself no power to make men wise.

JOHN KEATS
To Autumn

Season of mists and mellow fruitfulness,
   Close bosom-friend of the maturing sun;
Conspiring with him how to load and bless
   With fruit the vines that round the thatch-eaves run;
To bend with apples the mossed cottage-trees,
   And fill all fruit with ripeness to the core;
      To swell the gourd, and plump the hazel shells
With a sweet kernel; to set budding more,
   And still more, later flowers for the bees,
   Until they think warm days will never cease;
      For Summer has o'erbrimmed their clammy cells.

Who hath not seen thee oft amid thy store?
   Sometimes whoever seeks abroad may find
Thee sitting careless on a granary floor,
   Thy hair soft-lifted by the winnowing wind;
Or on a half-reaped furrow sound asleep,
   Drowsed with the fume of poppies, while thy hook
      Spares the next swath and all its twinèd flowers:
And sometimes like a gleaner thou dost keep
   Steady thy laden head across a brook;
   Or by a cyder-press, with patient look,
      Thou watchest the last oozings, hours by hours.

Where are the songs of Spring? Ay, where are they?
   Think not of them, thou hast thy music too, –
While barrèd clouds bloom the soft-dying day
   And touch the stubble-plains with rosy hue;
Then in a wailful choir the small gnats mourn
   Among the river-shallows, borne aloft
      Or sinking as the light wind lives or dies;
And full-grown lambs loud bleat from hilly bourn;
   Hedge-crickets sing; and now with treble soft
   The redbreast whistles from a garden-croft;
      And gathering swallows twitter in the skies.

■ **Denise Levertov** ➤ 157.

W.S. MERWIN
Chord

While Keats wrote they were cutting down the sandal-
    wood forests
while he listened to the nightingale they heard their
    own axes echoing through the forests
while he sat in the walled garden on the hill outside
    the city they thought of their gardens dying far
    away on the mountain
while the sound of the words clawed at him they
    thought of their wives
while the tip of his pen travelled the iron they had
    coveted was hateful to them
while he thought of the Grecian woods they bled
    under red flowers
while he dreamed of wine the trees were falling from
    the trees
while he felt his heart they were hungry and their faith
    was sick
while the song broke over him they were in a secret
    place and they were cutting it forever
while he coughed they carried the trunks to the hole in
    the forest the size of a foreign ship
while he groaned on the voyage to Italy they fell on
    the trails and were broken
when he lay with the odes behind him the wood was
    sold for cannons
when he lay watching the window they came home
    and lay down
and an age arrived when everything was explained in
    another language

■ **W.S. Merwin** ➤ 78.

■ **R.S. Thomas** (1913-2000) was one of the major poets of
our time as well as one of the finest religious poets in the
English language and Wales's greatest poet. He was an Anglican
priest, an isolated figure who worked in only three parishes
over a lifetime. Most of his poetry covers ground he treads
repeatedly: man and God, science and nature, time and his-
tory, the land and people of Wales.

■ **John Keats** (1795-1821) is now regarded as one of the prin-
cipal figures of the English Romantic movement, but in his
tragically short lifetime he only published three books, none
well received. The most productive period of his life was the
spring and summer of 1819, when he wrote most of his best-
known Odes, including '**To Autumn**'. [Other poem ➤ 79]

Kim Taplin: 'The "Ode to Autumn" shows his awareness
of the real processes of nature, as it bends with apples "the
mossed cottage-trees". It is a leafy world in which his imagin-
ation can work and in which his good life is prefigured. The
age he lived in was beginning to set him apart from the true
source of his poetic nourishment, but he was instinctively
searching for it. Part of the sadness in his poetry is the pain
of modern man in his separation from the earth.'

In *The Song of the Earth*, Jonathan Bate offers an ecological
reading of Keats's famous ode, which he describes as 'a medit-
ation on how human culture can only function through links
and reciprocal relations with nature. For Keats, there is a dir-
ect correlation between the self's bonds with its environment
and the bonds between people which make up society. [...]
Life depends upon sociability and warmth: in order to survive,
our species needs both social and environ-mental networks,
both human bonds and good weather. "To Autumn" is a poem
about these networks. [...] The ecosystem of "To Autumn"
is something larger than an image of agribusiness. Agribusiness
sprays the cornfields with pesticides, impatient of poppies and
gnats. Agribusiness removes hedgerows, regarding them as
wasteful; "To Autumn", in contrast, listens to hedge-crickets.
The poem is concerned with a larger economy than the human
one: its bees are there to pollinate flowers, not to produce
honey for humans to consume [...]

'Keats wrote of his ideal of interassimilation between men;
in the poem he is interassimilated with the environment. Indeed,
environment is probably the wrong word, because it presupposes
an image of man at the centre, *surrounded* by things; ecosystem
is the better word exactly because an ecosystem does not have
a centre, it is a network of relations. [...] Where the poem has
begun is with an intensely managed but highly fertile domestic
economy in a cottage-garden [...] the movement through the
poem, with its intricate syntactical, metrical and aural inter-
linkings, is not one which divides the culture from the nature.
There is no sense of river, hill and sky as the opposite of
house and garden. Rather, what Keats seems to be saying is
that to achieve being-at-homeness-in-the-world you have to
begin from your own dwelling-place. Think globally, the
poem might be saying – act locally.'

DAVID SCOTT
A Long Way from Bread

1

We have come so far from bread.
Rarely do we hear the clatter of the mill wheel;
see the flour in every cranny,
the shaking down of the sack, the chalk on the door,
the rats, the race, the pool,
baking day, and the old loaves:
cob, cottage, plaited, brick.

We have come so far from bread.
Once the crock said 'BREAD'
and the bread was what was there,
and the family's arm went deeper down each day
to find it, and the crust was favoured.

We have come so far from bread.
Terrifying is the breach between wheat and table,
wheat and bread, bread and what goes for bread.
Loaves come now in regiments, so that loaf
is not the word. *Hlaf*
is one of the oldest words we have.

2

I go on about bread
because it was to bread
that Jesus trusted
the meaning he had of himself.
It was an honour for bread
to be the knot in the Lord's handkerchief
reminding him about himself. So,
O bread, breakable;
O bread, given;
O bread, a blessing;
count yourself lucky, bread.

3

Not that I am against wafers,
especially the ones produced under steam
from some hidden nunnery

with our Lord crucified into them.
They are at least unleavened, and fit the hand,
without remainder, but it is still
a long way from bread.
Better for each household to have its own bread,
daily, enough and to spare,
dough the size of a rolled towel,
for feeding angels unawares.
Then if the bread is holy,
all that has to do with bread is holy:
board, knife, cupboard,
so that the gap between all things is closed
in our attention to the bread of the day.

4

I know that
'man cannot live on bread alone'.
I say, let us get the bread right.

■ **David Scott** (*b.* 1947) is an English Anglican priest whose compassionate poetry achieves resonance through careful observation and quiet understatement. Springing from ordinary events or an aspect of the priestly life, his poems work up a detail into a moment of significance. Much of his poetry evokes the delicate, intense qualities of rural England – its people and places, its wildlife, history and traditions.

SEAMUS HEANEY
Churning Day

A thick crust, coarse-grained as limestone rough-cast,
hardened gradually on top of the four crocks
that stood, large pottery bombs, in the small pantry.
After the hot brewery of gland, cud and udder,
cool porous earthenware fermented the buttermilk
for churning day, when the hooped churn was scoured
with plumping kettles and the busy scrubber
echoed daintily on the seasoned wood.
It stood then, purified, on the flagged kitchen floor.

Out came the four crocks, spilled their heavy lip
of cream, their white insides, into the sterile churn.
The staff, like a great whiskey-muddler fashioned
in deal wood, was plunged in, the lid fitted.
My mother took first turn, set up rhythms
that slugged and thumped for hours. Arms ached.
Hands blistered. Cheeks and clothes were spattered
with flabby milk.

            Where finally gold flecks
began to dance. They poured hot water then,
sterilised a birchwood bowl
and little corrugated butter-spades.
Their short stroke quickened, suddenly
a yellow curd was weighting the churned-up white,
heavy and rich, coagulated sunlight
that they fished, dripping, in a wide tin strainer,
heaped up like gilded gravel in the bowl.

The house would stink long after churning day,
acrid as a sulphur mine. The empty crocks
were ranged along the wall again, the butter
in soft printed slabs was piled on pantry shelves.
And in the house we moved with gravid ease,
our brains turned crystals full of clean deal churns,
the plash and gurgle of the sour-breathed milk,
the pat and slap of small spades on wet lumps.

DENNIS O'DRISCOLL
Life Cycle
(in memory of George Mackay Brown)

January. Wind bellows. Stars hiss like smithy sparks.
The moon a snowball frozen in mid-flight.
George is rocking on his fireside chair.

February. The sea loud at the end of the street.
Ferries cancelled. Snowdrops seep through dampness.
George is sitting down to mutton broth.

March. Oystercatcher piping. Early tattie planting.
Gull-protected fishing boats wary of the equinoctial gales.
George is tired by now of his captivity.

April. Cloud boulders roll back from the Easter sun.
The tinker horse, a cuckoo, in the farmer's field.
George is taking the spring air on Brinkie's Brae.

May. Scissors-tailed swallows cut the tape, declare summer open,
A stray daddy-long-legs, unsteady on its feet as a new foal.
George is sampling home-brew from his vat.

June. Butterfly wings like ornamental shutters. Day scorches
down to diamonds, rubies before being lost at sea.
George is picnicking with friends on Rackwick beach.

July. Another wide-eyed sun. Its gold slick pours like oil
on the untroubled waves. Shoppers dab brows as they gossip.
George is drafting poems in a bottle-green shade.

August. Pudgy bees in romper suits suckled by flowers.
Well water rationed. Trout gills barely splashed.
George is hiding from the tourists' knock.

September. A brace of wrapped haddocks on the doorstep.
Mushrooms, snapped off under grass tufts, melt in the pan.
George is stocking up his shed with coal and peat.

October. Porridge and clapshot weather. Swan arrivals, divers.
Sun hangs, a smoking ham, suspended in the misty air.
George is ordering a hot dram at the pub.

November. Rain shaken out slantwise like salt. Hail pebbles
flung against the window to announce winter's return.
George is adding a wool layer to his clothes.

December. Three strangers, bearing gifts, enquire the way
to byre and bairn. A brightness absent from the map of stars.
George's craft is grounded among kirkyard rocks.

GEORGE MACKAY BROWN
Christmas Poem

We are folded all
In a green fable
And we fare
From early
Plough-and-daffodil sun
Through a revel
Of wind-tossed oats and barley
Past sickle and flail
To harvest home,
The circles of bread and ale
At the long table.
It is told, the story –
We and earth and sun and corn are one.

Now kings and shepherds have come.
A wintered hovel
Hides a glory
Whiter than snowflake or silver or star

GEORGE MACKAY BROWN
Horse

The horse at the shore
Casks of red apples, skull, a barrel of rum

The horse in the field
Plough, ploughman, gulls, a furrow, a cornstalk

The horse in the peatbog
Twelve baskets of dark fire

The horse at the pier
Letters, bread, paraffin, one passenger, papers

The horse at the Show
Ribbons, raffia, high bright hooves

The horse in the meadow
A stallion, a russet gale, between two hills

The horse at the burn
Quenching a long flame in the throat

■ **Dennis O'Driscoll** (*b.* 1954) is an Irish poet, critic and anthologist who has worked as a civil servant since the age of 16. He is a poet of humanity whose wittily observant poetry is attuned to the tragedies and comedies of contemporary life. His books include *Troubled Thoughts, Majestic Dreams: Selected Prose Writings* (2001), *New & Selected Poems* (2004), *The Bloodaxe Book of Poetry Quotations* (2006) and *Reality Check* (2007).

■ **George Mackay Brown** (1921-96) was an Orkney writer who celebrated island life and its ancient rhythms in poetry, novels, short stories and plays. Apart from two periods of education in mainland Scotland in the 1950s, he never left Orkney, and all his work celebrates the history of the islands (from the distant mythical past to the present), their landscape, seascape and people. Many of Mackay Brown's works are concerned with protecting Orkney's cultural heritage from the relentless march of progress and the loss of myth and archaic ritual in the modern world, an anxiety further influenced by his conversion in 1961 to Catholicism. In his novel *Greenvoe* (1972), the permanence of island life is threatened by 'Black Star', a mysterious nuclear development.

Terry Gifford (1995) notes that **'Christmas Poem'** shows 'how the constants in nature for Mackay Brown are to be found in the seasons and the elements. The cycles of bread and ale at harvest home symbolise the cycle of the seasons and the unity of people with the elements of growth in nature.'

■ Influenced by the work of Ted Hughes and Patrick Kavanagh, **Seamus Heaney**'s early poetry is notable for its sensory lyrical evocations of rural childhood, nature and rural life. **'Churning Day'** celebrates daily human unity with the seasonal processes of nature. Full note ➤ 213.

■ **Patrick Kavanagh** (1904-67) was the foremost Irish poet in the generation after Yeats. Brought up in Co. Monaghan, he left school at 13 to work on the family farm, heading to Dublin in 1939 to take up the literary life, a move he later described as 'the worst mistake of my life'.

Edna Longley: 'He met Dublin writers who, in the aftermath of the Irish revival, were "trying to be peasants". Hence the anger that drives his long poem *The Great Hunger* (1942), which centres on the restricted life actually lived by small farmers. [...] Kavanagh criticised the effects of Irish nationalism on poetry, and learned from the concreteness of English pastoral. He was also able integrate visionary Romanticism (Wordsworth) with his Catholic sense of the material world as manifesting God (immanence). '**A Christmas Childhood**' traces an almost medieval cosmic harmony. Like the father's melodion, the poem orchestrates the townland.'

PATRICK KAVANAGH

A Christmas Childhood

I

One side of the potato-pits was white with frost –
How wonderful that was, how wonderful!
And when we put our ears to the paling-post
The music that came out was magical.

The light between the ricks of hay and straw
Was a hole in Heaven's gable. An apple tree
With its December-glinting fruit we saw –
O you, Eve, were the world that tempted me

To eat the knowledge that grew in clay
And death the germ within it! Now and then
I can remember something of the gay
Garden that was childhood's. Again

The tracks of cattle to a drinking-place,
A green stone lying sideways in a ditch
Or any common sight the transfigured face
Of a beauty that the world did not touch.

II

My father played the melodion
Outside at our gate;
There were stars in the morning east
And they danced to his music.

Across the wild bogs his melodion called
To Lennons and Callans.
As I pulled on my trousers in a hurry
I knew some strange thing had happened.

Outside in the cow-house my mother
Made the music of milking;
The light of her stable-lamp was a star
And the frost of Bethlehem made it twinkle.

A water-hen screeched in the bog,
Mass-going feet
Crunched the wafer-ice on the pot-holes,
Somebody wistfully twisted the bellows wheel.

My child poet picked out the letters
On the grey stone,
In silver the wonder of a Christmas townland,
The winking glitter of a frosty dawn.

Cassiopeia was over
Cassidy's hanging hill,
I looked and three whin bushes rode across
The horizon – the Three Wise Kings.

An old man passing said:
'Can't he make it talk' –
The melodion. I hid in the doorway
And tightened the belt of my box-pleated coat.

I nicked six nicks on the door-post
With my penknife's big blade –
There was a little one for cutting tobacco.
And I was six Christmases of age.

My father played the melodion,
My mother milked the cows,
And I had a prayer like a white rose pinned
On the Virgin Mary's blouse.

PATRICK KAVANAGH
Canal Bank Walk

Leafy-with-love banks and the green waters of the canal
Pouring redemption for me, that I do
The will of God, wallow in the habitual, the banal,
Grow with nature again as before I grew.
The bright stick trapped, the breeze adding a third
Party to the couple kissing on an old seat,
And a bird gathering materials for the nest for the Word
Eloquently new and abandoned to its delirious beat.
O unworn world enrapture me, encapture me in a web
Of fabulous grass and eternal voices by a beech,
Feed the gaping need of my senses, give me ad lib
To pray unselfconsciously with overflowing speech
For this soul needs to be honoured with a new dress woven
From green and blue things and arguments that cannot
     be proven.

DENISE LEVERTOV
Web

    Intricate and untraceable
    weaving and interweaving,
    dark strand with light:

    designed, beyond
    all spiderly contrivance,
    to link, not to entrap:

elation, grief, joy, contrition, entwined;
shaking, changing,
        forever
            forming,
                transforming:

all praise,
    all praise to the
        great web.

■ **Denise Levertov** (1923-97), one of the 20th century's foremost American poets, was born in England, the daughter of a Russian Jewish scholar turned Anglican priest and a Welsh Congregationalist mother, both parents descended from mystics. She emigrated to the US in 1948, where she became involved with the Objectivist and Black Mountain schools of poetry, and was much influenced by the work of William Carlos Williams, a lifelong friend and correspondent. Her poetry is noted for its visionary approach to the natural world and to the dynamics of being human. 'Meditative and evocative, Levertov's poetry concerns itself with the search for meaning. She sees the poet's role as a priestly one; the poet is the mediator between ordinary people and the divine mysteries' (Susan J. Zeuenbergen).

In the preface to her selection of her poems on nature *The Life Around Us* (1997), Levertov wrote: 'In these last few decades of the 20th century it has become ever clearer to all thinking people that although we humans are a part of nature ourselves, we have become, in multifarious ways, an increasingly destructive element within it, shaking and breaking "the great web" – perhaps irremediably. So a poet, though impelled, as always, to write poems of pure celebration, is driven inevitably to lament, to anger, and to the expression of dread […] celebration and the fear of loss are necessarily conjoined. I believe this flux and reflux echo what readers also feel in their response to "the green world".' [Other poems ➢ 71, 93, 108, 138, 151, 194]

■ **Peter Redgrove** ➢ 200.

PETER REDGROVE
My Father's Spider

The spider creaking in its rain-coloured harness
Sparking like a firework. In the cold wind
Round the sharp corner of the house,

In the cold snap of that wind,
Many turned to ice:
Circular icicles.

My father lifted one off
Very carefully over the flat of his glove.
When I see these hedgerow webs

It is always with the sighing of the sea
In my heart's ear; it was at the seaside
In the smell of sand and tar that I first

Understood the universal perfection
Of these carnivorous little crystals
Coiling from their centres like the shells.

They were cruel and beautiful
At the same time; abominable
And delightful; why else did the silly

Flies dart into them to be drunk
Up like horny flasks, as if
The pints of beer had veiny wings –

If I could see those dartboard webs
Surely they could. They are doorways
To death and the mandala-sign

Of renewed and centred life. And this one,
Here, look, with its array of full lenses
(For the thread is fine enough for minutest

Beads to catch and roll the light in strings)
Is like a Washington of the astronomers,
Planned, powerful, radial city, excited by flying things,

At every intersection and along each boulevard
Crowded with lenses gazing upwards, pointing light.

■ **Jane Hirshfield** (b. 1953) is an American poet, critic and anthologist who trained as a Zen Buddhist. She has lived in northern California since 1974, for the past 20 years in a small white cottage looking out on fruit trees, old roses and Mt Tamalpais. Her poems are both sensual meditations and passionate investigations which reveal complex truths in language luminous and precise. Rooted in the living world, they celebrate and elucidate a hard-won affirmation of our human fate. [Other poem ➤ 215]

■ **A.R. Ammons** ➤ 98.

A.R. AMMONS
Identity

        1) An individual spider web
            identifies a species:

an order of instinct prevails
        through all accidents of circumstance,
            though possibility is
high along the peripheries of
spider
                        webs:
                you can go all
            around the fringing attachments

            and find
disorder ripe,
entropy rich, high levels of random,
        numerous occasions of accident:

        2) the possible settings
            of a web are infinite:

    how does
the spider keep
        identity
    while creating the web
    in a particular place?

    how and to what extent
        and by what modes of chemistry
        and control?

it is
wonderful
        how things work: I will tell you
                about it
                because

it is interesting
and because whatever is
moves in weeds
        and stars and spider webs

158

and known
        is loved:
  in that love,
  each of us knowing it,
  I love you,

for it moves within and beyond us,
    sizzles in
to winter grasses, darts and hangs with bumblebees
by summer windowsills:

      I will show you
the underlying that takes no image to itself,
    cannot be shown or said,
but weaves in and out of moons and bladderweeds,
    is all and
    beyond destruction
    because created fully in no
particular form:

      if the web were perfectly pre-set,
      the spider could
  never find
  a perfect place to set it in: and

      if the web were
perfectly adaptable,
if freedom and possibility were without limit,
      the web would
lose its special identity:

    the row-strung garden web
keeps order at the center
where space is freest (intersecting that the freest
      "medium" should
      accept the firmest order)

and that
order
      diminishes toward the
periphery
    allowing at the points of contact
      entropy equal to entropy.

JANE HIRSHFIELD

Happiness

I think it was from the animals
that St Francis learned
it is possible to cast yourself
on the earth's good mercy and live.
From the wolf who cast off
the deep fierceness of her first heart
and crept into the circle of sunlight
in full wariness and wolf-hunger,
and was fed, and lived; from the birds
who came fearless to him until he
had no choice but return that courage.
Even the least amoeba touched on all sides
by the opulent Other, even the baleened
plankton fully immersed in their fate –
for what else might happiness be
than to be porous, opened, rinsed through
by the beings and things?
Nor could he forget those other companions,
the shifting, ethereal, shapeless:
Hopelessness, Desperateness, Loneliness,
even the fire-tongued Anger –
for they too waited with the patient Lion,
the glossy Rooster, the drowsy Mule, to step
out of the trees' protection and come in.

GALWAY KINNELL

Saint Francis and the Sow

The bud
stands for all things,
even for those things that don't flower,
for everything flowers, from within, of self-blessing;
though sometimes it is necessary
to reteach a thing its loveliness,
to put a hand on its brow
of the flower

and retell it in words and in touch
it is lovely
until it flowers again from within, of self-blessing;
as Saint Francis
put his hand on the creased forehead
of the sow, and told her in words and in touch
blessings of earth on the sow, and the sow
began remembering all down her thick length,
from the earthen snout all the way
through the fodder and slops to the spiritual curl of
    the tail,
from the hard spininess spiked out from the spine
down through the great broken heart
to the sheer blue milken dreaminess spurting and
    shuddering
from the fourteen teats into the fourteen mouths
    sucking and blowing beneath them:
the long, perfect loveliness of sow.

GALWAY KINNELL
The Bear

1

In late winter
I sometimes glimpse bits of steam
coming up from
some fault in the old snow
and bend close and see it is lung-colored
and put down my nose
and know
the chilly, enduring odor of bear.

2

I take a wolf's rib and whittle
it sharp at both ends
and coil it up
and freeze it in blubber and place it out
on the fairway of the bears.

And when it has vanished
I move out on the bear tracks,
roaming in circles
until I come to the first, tentative, dark
splash on the earth.

And I set out
running, following the splashes
of blood wandering over the world.
At the cut, gashed resting places
I stop and rest,
at the crawl-marks
where he lay out on his belly
to overpass some stretch of bauchy ice
I lie out
dragging myself forward with bear-knives in my fists.

3

On the third day I begin to starve,
at nightfall I bend down as I knew I would
at a turd sopped in blood,
and hesitate, and pick it up,
and thrust it in my mouth, and gnash it down,
and rise
and go on running.

4

On the seventh day,
living by now on bear blood alone,
I can see his upturned carcass far out ahead, a scraggled,
steamy hulk,
the heavy fur riffling in the wind.

I come up to him
and stare at the narrow-spaced, petty eyes,
the dismayed
face laid back on the shoulder, the nostrils
flared, catching
perhaps the first taint of me as he
died.

I hack
a ravine in his thigh, and eat and drink,
and tear him down his whole length
and open him and climb in
and close him up after me, against the wind,
and sleep.

      5

And dream
of lumbering flatfooted
over the tundra,
stabbed twice from within,
splattering a trail behind me,
splattering it out no matter which way I lurch,
no matter which parabola of bear-transcendence,
which dance of solitude I attempt,
which gravity-clutched leap,
which trudge, which groan.

      6

Until one day I totter and fall –
fall on this
stomach that has tried so hard to keep up,
to digest the blood as it leaked in,
to break up
and digest the bone itself: and now the breeze
blows over me, blows off
the hideous belches of ill-digested bear blood
and rotted stomach
and the ordinary, wretched odor of bear,

blows across
my sore, lolled tongue a song
or screech, until I think I must rise up
and dance. And I lie still.

      7

I awaken I think. Marshlights
reappear, geese
come trailing again up the flyway.
In her ravine under old snow the dam-bear

lies, licking
lumps of smeared fur
and drizzly eyes into shapes
with her tongue. And one
hairy-soled trudge stuck out before me,
the next groaned out,
the next,
the next,
the rest of my days I spend
wandering: wondering
what, anyway,
was that sticky infusion, that rank flavor of blood, that
      poetry, by which I lived?

■ **Galway Kinnell** (*b.* 1927) is an American poet whose diverse work ranges from odes of kinship with nature to realistic evocations of urban life, from religious quest to political statement, from brief imagistic lyrics to extended, complex meditations. Like the hunter in his celebrated poem **'The Bear'**, he seeks out the primitive bases of existence obscured by the overlay of modern civilisation. His poems examine the effects of personal confrontation with violence and inevitable death, attempts to hold death at bay, the plight of the urban dispossessed, and the regenerative powers of love and nature.

Richard Gray has described how the traditional Christian sensibility of Kinnell's early work gave way to the sacramental, transfiguring dimension of the later poetry, which 'burrows fiercely into the self away from traditional sources of religious authority or even conventional notions of personality. [...] Short, chanting lines, a simple, declarative syntax, emphatic rhythms, bleak imagery, and insistent repetition: all are used here to generate the sense of the poet as shaman who throws off the "sticky infusions" of speech and becomes one with the natural world, sharing in the primal experiences of birth and death'. [Other poems ➤ 124, 159]

7. EXPLOITATION

This section brings together poems concerned with the destruction of both the natural world and indigenous peoples, with postcolonial and ecofeminist perspectives represented by writers such as Derek Walcott, Ernesto Cardenal, Oodgeroo and Susan Griffin. They demonstrate the impact on nature and people of colonialism, patriarchy and other insidious brands of tyranny (political, economic, technological, self-interest). The section ends with *Dispossessing America*, a series of poems by contemporary Native American writers (followed by a redemptive "action" by Joseph Beuys). Their work shows how indigenous people have lived for centuries in tune with the natural environment; how those connecting beliefs are still cherished by the poets and their alienated communities; and how the balance and wholeness of their lives has been devastated along with the land and wildlife of North America.

MARGARET ATWOOD
The Moment

The moment when, after many years
of hard work and a long voyage
you stand in the centre of your room,
house, half-acre, square mile, island, country,
knowing at last how you got there,
and say, *I own this,*

is the same moment the trees unloose
their soft arms from around you,
the birds take back their language,
the cliffs fissure and collapse,
the air moves back from you like a wave
and you can't breathe.

No, they whisper. *You own nothing.*
You were a visitor, time after time
climbing the hill, planting the flag, proclaiming.
We never belonged to you.
You never found us.
It was always the other way round.

KATHLEEN McPHILEMY
Blackthorn

Who has seen the blackthorn
gift of the lengthening evenings?
Pledging another spring
it mantles the edge of the wood
and white as the ghost of March
flowers by the edge of the road.

Whose is the blackthorn blossom?
Does it belong to the name at Lloyds
who owns these woods and fields?
Where among the shivering walls
that have built the cardboard city
could the blackthorn blossom flower?

The flower itself is a wall
hiding that shameful city;
its fires of invisible anguish
are a white and burning bush.

PASCALE PETIT
Landowners

What does it mean to own a half-hectare?
I stood on the bank of the stream

and asked the stones and the pools:
how deep do my boundaries extend,

through how many seams of mantle?
How high? Up to where the indigo sky

is feathered with black?
For a full hour the cork oaks were silent

while I questioned each leaf.
Then a voice came from the branch

and I saw two kingfishers.
Tchi chee, they said, *kwee kwee*,

and I knew they were speaking
the lost language of the land,

that this estate I'd inherited
was theirs.

Their costumes confirmed it –
wings of the intensest sun blue

shimmering like atmospheres
over the bronze earths of their bodies.

PETER READING
Corporate

In polystyrene, snug sarcophagi,
corporate burgers (each in uniform
coat of congealed bright ketchup) are served up
by a drum-majorette with *Hi! I'm Sharon*
emblazoned on a badge close to her heart.

*

Flunkeys and bell-hops (pawns of Corporate
Imagery con-men) slyly multiply.
Handcuffs and truncheons burgeon, wielded by
bullethead bullnecks, quondam night-club bouncers,
ex-SAS with homicidal skills,
lager-louts, dandy privatised militia.

*

Garbage-men clad in incandescent pink
testify to our Nation's Corporate
Success – seldom has shit been shunted round
with such decorum, pageantry and pomp.

*

Furled brolly, dandruffed pinstripe, slimline briefcase,
on Friday nights give way to leisure mufti –
trainers and Levi's, golfing garb and Barbour,
green wellies...
          All too soon Monday's commuter
resumes the swindling, sartorial City.

*

Quite probably the last things we shall see
are the starched yashmak of the Trust Fund surgeon
and dapper paramedics dressed to kill.

■ **Margaret Atwood** ➤ 52.

■ **Kathleen McPhilemy** (*b.* 1947) writes a poetry of witness in which the personal and domestic are set against the wider world of violence and conflict, from Northern Ireland to Iraq. Born in Belfast, she wrote a doctoral study at Edinburgh of open form poetics, and now lives in Oxford, where she works in further education. Her books include three collections, *Witness to Magic* (1989), *A Tented Peace* (1995) and *The Lion in the Forest* (2004), and *Home: An Anthology* (1999).

■ **Pascale Petit** (*b.* 1953) is a French/Welsh poet who lives in London. She co-founded The Poetry School and the magazine *Poetry London*. Trained as a sculptor, Petit has worked as an environmental artist in schools. She has travelled extensively and her poetry reflects this, not least her explorations of the Amazon rainforest. Her most recent work examines fraught family relationships, with her estranged father in *The Zoo Father* (2001), and a mentally ill mother in *The Huntress* (2005). 'My poetry is a poetry of extremes, I've never been one for lukewarmth,' she told Livia Vianu. 'Tension too – nothing relaxed about the homes I describe. I hope tension creates drama, that I create dramatic tension, that I somehow transform uncomfortable tension into highly charged art.'

■ **Peter Reading** ➤ 104.

■ **Elizabeth Bishop** (1911-79) was an American poet who has come to be regarded as one of the greatest writers in English of the 20th century. Her sharply observant poetry avoids explicit personal references, focusing instead with great subtlety on her impressions of the physical world. She lived in Brazil for over 20 years, from 1951 to 1974, and in '**Brazil, January 1, 1502**' she pictures the timeless beauty of the once virgin rainforest, on a precise date whose significance Jonathan Bate explains in his study *The Song of the Earth*: 'On 1 January 1502, the Portuguese sailed into a bay on the eastern coast of South America, thought it was a river and named it from the date: River of January, Río de Janeiro. From that moment on, Brazil was sucked into European history. Furthermore, the Westerner's perception of the place cannot but be influenced by Western aesthetics. Bishop's poem carries an epigraph from Kenneth Clark's book *Landscape into Art*, a study of how the artistic representation of nature is always just that – a representation, part of the meaning of which is prior representations and symbolic formations.'

Bate relates the end of the poem to Bishop's early fascination with the tropics, fed by books such as W.H. Hudson's *Green Mansions: A Romance of the Tropical Forest* (1904), in which the Indian bird-girl Rima represents 'the symbolic spirit of being-in-the-state of nature […] In the stanza's final image, the rape of the native women and the rape of the virgin forest are brought together by means of a direct allusion to Rima.' Bishop's biographer Lorrie Goldensohn tells how she wrote, at 17, of her longing to search for South America's 'forgotten bird-people […] I felt sure that if I could only find the right spot, the right sun-lighted arches of the trees, and wait patiently, I would see a bright-haired figure slipping away among the moving shadows, and hear the sweet, light music of Rima's voice.'

'Just so the Christians,' writes Bishop, knowing, says Bate, that 'as a visitor to Brazil, not a native inhabitant of the forest, she is in the position of the coloniser, not of Rima. Elizabeth Bishop shared Friedrich Schiller's knowledge that Nature is calling to us in a voice like that of our primal mother. But together with that Romantic knowledge she carried a wry, ironic, modern recognition that in the very act of answering the call we penetrate the veil of Nature's purity. In so doing, we force Rima to retreat, always to retreat further and further into an ever-diminishing unknown. When there is no more unknown, when the last of the tropical rainforest has been cleared, it may then be only in art – in poetry – that we will be able to hear the cry of Rima.'

ELIZABETH BISHOP
Brazil, January 1, 1502

…embroidered nature…tapestried landscape.
SIR KENNETH CLARK: *Landscape into Art*

Januaries, Nature greets our eyes
exactly as she must have greeted theirs:
every square inch filling in with foliage –
big leaves, little leaves, and giant leaves,
blue, blue-green, and olive,
with occasional lighter veins and edges,
or a satin underleaf turned over;
monster ferns
in silver-gray relief,
and flowers, too, like giant water lilies
up in the air – up, rather, in the leaves –
purple, yellow, two yellows, pink,
rust red and greenish white;
solid but airy; fresh as if just finished
and taken off the frame.

A blue-white sky, a simple web,
backing for feathery detail:
brief arcs, a pale-green broken wheel,
a few palms, swarthy, squat, but delicate;
and perching there in profile, beaks agape,
the big symbolic birds keep quiet,
each showing only half his puffed and padded,
pure-colored or spotted breast.
Still in the foreground there is Sin:
five sooty dragons near some massy rocks.
The rocks are worked with lichens, gray moonbursts
splattered and overlapping,
threatened from underneath by moss
in lovely hell-green flames,
attacked above
by scaling-ladder vines, oblique and neat,
'one leaf yes and one leaf no' (in Portuguese).

The lizards scarcely breathe; all eyes
are on the smaller, female one, back-to,
her wicked tail straight up and over,
red as a red-hot wire.

Just so the Christians, hard as nails,
tiny as nails, and glinting,
in creaking armor, came and found it all,
not unfamiliar:
no lovers' walks, no bowers,
no cherries to be picked, no lute music,
but corresponding, nevertheless,
to an old dream of wealth and luxury
already out of style when they left home –
wealth, plus a brand-new pleasure.
Directly after Mass, humming perhaps
L'Homme armé or some such tune,
they ripped away into the hanging fabric,
each out to catch an Indian for himself –
those maddening little women who kept calling,
calling to each other (or had the birds waked up?)
and retreating, always retreating, behind it.

DEREK WALCOTT
from The Schooner *Flight*

FROM 1 *Adios, Carenage*

I know these islands from Monos to Nassau,
a rusty head sailor with sea-green eyes
that they nickname Shabine, the patois for
any red nigger, and I, Shabine, saw
when these slums of empire was paradise.
I'm just a red nigger who love the sea,
I had a sound colonial education,
I have Dutch, nigger, and English in me,
and either I'm nobody, or I'm a nation.
[…]

FROM 3 *Shabine Leaves the Republic*

I had no nation now but the imagination.
After the white man, the niggers didn't want me
when the power swing to their side.

The first chain my hands and apologise, 'History';
the next said I wasn't black enough for their pride.
Tell me, what power, on these unknown rocks –
a spray-plane Air Force, the Fire Brigade,
the Red Cross, the Regiment, two, three police dogs
that pass before you finish bawling 'Parade!'?
I met History once, but he ain't recognise me,
a parchment Creole, with warts
like an old sea-bottle, crawling like a crab
through the holes of shadow cast by the net
of a grille balcony; cream linen, cream hat.
I confront him and shout, 'Sir, is Shabine!
They say I'se your grandson. You remember Grandma
your black cook, at all?' The bitch hawk and spat.
A spit like that worth any number of words.
But that's all them bastards have left us: words.
[…]

6 *The Sailor Sings Back to the Casuarinas*

You see them on the low hills of Barbados
bracing like windbreaks, needles for hurricanes,
trailing, like masts, the cirrus of torn sails;
when I was green like them, I used to think
those cypresses, leaning against the sea,
that take the sea-noise up into their branches,
are not real cypresses but casuarinas.
Now captain just call them Canadian cedars.
But cedars, cypresses, or casuarinas,
whoever called them so had a good cause,
watching their bending bodies wail like women
after a storm, when some schooner came home
with news of one more sailor drowned again.
Once the sound 'cypress' used to make more sense
than the green 'casuarinas', though, to the wind
whatever grief bent them was all the same,
since they were trees with nothing else in mind
but heavenly leaping or to guard a grave;
but we live like our names and you would have
to be colonial to know the difference,
to know the pain of history words contain,
to love those trees with an inferior love,

and to believe: 'Those casuarinas bend
like cypresses, their hair hangs down in rain
like sailors' wives. They're classic trees and we,
if we live like the names our masters please,
by careful mimicry might become men.'

■ **Derek Walcott** (*b.* 1930) was born in St Lucia. He is not
only the foremost Caribbean poet of modern times (as well as
a dramatist and painter) but a major figure in world literature,
recognised with the award of the Nobel Prize in Literature in
1992 'for a poetic *œuvre* of great luminosity, sustained by a
historical vision, the outcome of a multicultural commitment'.
Most of his work explores the Caribbean cultural experience,
the history, landscape and lives of its multiracial people, fusing
folk culture and oral tales with the classical, avant-garde and
English literary tradition.

Roy Osamu Kamada: 'Walcott, like [Barry] Lopez or Words-
worth, shares concerns and themes that the ecocritic might
consider ecologically oriented; however, Walcott is not just
writing about the human encounter with the natural world to
which he may or may not completely belong. His concerns
are also historical. Walcott, also writing about a sublime land-
scape, is unable to detach that landscape from its history of
colonialism and all the attendant consequences of that history.
[...] The landscape he writes about is necessarily politicised;
his own subjectivity is intimately implicated in both the nat-
ural beauty and the traumatic history of the place; he must
directly acknowledge the history of St Lucia and the Carib-
bean, the history of diaspora, of slavery, of the capitalist com-
modification of the landscape, and the devastating consequen-
ces this history has on the individual. [...]

'Walcott, in his poem '**The Schooner** *Flight*', explores
landscape even as he explores the problematics of a postcolonial
subjectivity. In this poem, which prefigures his obsession
with *The Odyssey*, Walcott yokes together the identity of his
poet/speaker, Shabine, with descriptions of the landscape to
create a notion of self that, like the landscape he describes, is
capable of containing multiple and conflicting terms. [...]
Walcott creates a character whose very nature is a dynamic
model of postcolonial identity, a model that finds its mirror in
Walcott's presentation of the problematic relationship between
a sublime landscape and a history of dispossession and trauma.'

■ **W.S. Merwin** ➤ 78.

W.S. MERWIN
The Asians Dying

When the forests have been destroyed their darkness
    remains
The ash the great walker follows the possessors
Forever
Nothing they will come to is real
Nor for long
Over the watercourses
Like ducks in the time of the ducks
The ghosts of the villages trail in the sky
Making a new twilight

Rain falls into the open eyes of the dead
Again again with its pointless sound
When the moon finds them they are the color of
    everything

The nights disappear like bruises but nothing is healed
The dead go away like bruises
The blood vanishes into the poisoned farmlands
Pain the horizon
Remains
Overhead the seasons rock
They are paper bells
Calling to nothing living

The possessors move everywhere under Death their star
Like columns of smoke they advance into the shadows
Like thin flames with no light
They with no past
And fire their only future

■ **Ernesto Cardenal Martínez** (*b.* 1925) is a poet generally
considered second only to Rubén Darío in Nicaraguan liter-
ature. A Christian-Marxist Catholic priest, he was one of the
most celebrated liberation theologians of the Sandinistas, and
was Minister of Culture from the overthrow of the Somoza
dictatorship in 1979 until 1987. He was also the founder of
the primitivist art community in the Solentiname islands
based on Christian liberation theology and principles of social

justice and community sharing. Cardenal's influences as a poet and thinker include Walt Whitman, Ezra Pound and Pablo Neruda as well as his former mentor Thomas Merton who helped him to broaden his spiritual awareness. Robert Bly wrote that 'Cardenal continues the tradition of Pablo Neruda, who said, "all the pure poets will fall on their face in the snow". Cardenal's poetry is impure, defiantly, in that it unites political ugliness and the beauty of imaginative vision.'

ERNESTO CARDENAL
New Ecology
translated from the Spanish by Dinah Livingstone

In September more coyotes were seen
        round San Ubaldo.
More alligators shortly after the triumph,
        in the rivers near San Ubaldo.
           More rabbits in the road and grisons…

       The bird population has tripled, they say,
          especially the tree duck.
The noisy ducks fly down to swim
        where they see the water shining.

Somoza's men also destroyed
        lakes, rivers and mountains.
        They diverted rivers for their estates.
The Ochomogo dried up last summer.
The Sinecapa dried
       because of the great landowners' tree-felling.

The Matagalpa Rio Grande ran dry during the war,
         over the plains of Sebaco.
They built two dams on the Ochomogo
        and capitalist chemical waste
crashed into the river
        whose fish staggered like drunks.

       The River Boaco has filthy water
The Moyuá lagoon dried up. A Somoza colonel
stole the lands from the peasants and built a dam.

The Moyuá lagoon for centuries so lovely where it lay.
       (But now the little fishes will come back.)
       They felled and dammed.

         Few iguanas in the sun, few armadillos.
Somoza sold the green Caribbean turtle.
They exported sea turtle and iguana eggs in lorries.
        The caguama turtle is becoming extinct.

José Somoza has been putting an end
        to the sawfish in the Great Lake.
Extinction threatens the ocelot
       with its soft wood-coloured pelt,
and the puma and the tapir in the mountains
        (like the peasants in the mountains).

And poor River Chiquito! Its disgrace
shames the whole country.
       Somoza's ways befouling its waters.
The River Chiquito of Léon, choked with sewage,
and effluent from soap and tanning factories,
its bed bestrewn with plastic junk,
        chamber pots and rusty iron.
That was Somoza's legacy.
We must see it running clear and sweet again
        singing its way to the sea.)

All Managua's filthy water in Lake Managua
and chemical waste.
       And over in Solentiname
on the isle of La Zanate a big white heap
       of stinking sawfish bones.

But now the sawfish and the freshwater shark
can breathe again.
Once more Tisma's waters mirror many herons.
It has lots of little grackles,
       garganeys, tree ducks, kisakadees.

    And flowers are flourishing.
Armadillos are very happy with this government.
   We are recovering forests, streams, lagoons.

We are going to decontaminate Lake Managua.

Not only humans longed for liberation.
All ecology groaned. The revolution
is also for animals, rivers, lakes and trees.

ERNESTO CARDENAL
The Parrots
translated from the Spanish by Dinah Livingstone

My friend Michel is an army officer
in Somoto up near the Honduran border,
and he told me he had found some contraband parrots
waiting to be smuggled to the United States
to learn to speak English there.

There were 186 parrots
with 47 already dead in their cages.
He drove them back where they'd been taken from
and as the lorry approached a place known as The Plains
near the mountains which were these parrots' home
(behind those plains the mountains stand up huge)
the parrots got excited, started beating their wings
and shoving against their cage-sides.

When the cages were let open
they all shot out like an arrow shower
straight for their mountains.

The Revolution did the same for us I think:
It freed us from the cages
where they trapped us to talk English,
it gave us back the country
from which we were uprooted,
their green mountains restored to the parrots
by parrot-green comrades.

But there were 47 that died.

OODGEROO
Time Is Running Out

The miner rapes
The heart of earth
With his violent spade.
Stealing, bottling her black blood
For the sake of greedy trade.
On his metal throne of destruction,
He labours away with a will,
Piling the mountainous minerals high
With giant tool and iron drill.

In his greedy lust for power,
He destroys old nature's will.
For the sake of the filthy dollar,
He dirties the nest he builds.
Well he knows that violence
Of his destructive kind
Will be violently written
Upon the sands of time.

But time is running out
And time is close at hand,
For the Dreamtime folk are massing
To defend their timeless land.
Come gentle black man
Show your strength;
Time to take a stand.
Make the violent miner feel
Your violent
Love of land.

■ **Oodgeroo** (1920-93) was the first Aboriginal Australian to publish a book of poetry. As well as *We Are Going* (1964), her collections included *The Dawn Is at Hand* (1966) and *My People* (1970). She grew up on the traditional lands of the Noonuccal people at Minjerribah (Stradbroke Island), spending much of her childhood exploring the sea shore and bushland. The unity between nature and the indigenous people of Australia is one of her main themes. Known for most of her life as the writer, painter and political activist, Kath Walker, Oodgeroo Noonuccal reclaimed her traditional name in 1988 and returned her MBE in protest at the condition of her people in the year of Australia's Bicentenary celebrations. She said of her work and role: 'I felt that poetry would be the breakthrough for the Aboriginal people because they were story-tellers and song-makers, and I thought poetry would appeal to them more than anything else. It was more a book of their voices I was trying to bring out.'

■ **Ken Saro-Wiwa** (1941-95) was a Nigerian writer and activist who fought for ecological and social justice for the Ogoni people of the Niger Delta, accusing the oil companies and the Nigerian government of waging an ecological war against the Ogoni which threatened their survival. Working for the Movement for the Survival of the Ogoni People (MOSOP), Saro-Wiwa led a non-violent campaign against the multinationals, especially Shell. In June 1994 he was falsely charged with murder and arrested by the Nigerian authorities; his poem **'Ogoni! Ogoni'** was smuggled out of prison.

In November 1995 Saro-Wiwa was executed with eight other MOSOP activists, their deaths provoking international outrage. Nigeria was suspended from the Commonwealth and condemned by the United Nations. In 1996, Cameron Duodu in the *Observer* reported that Shell had 'admitted importing weapons into Nigeria to help arm the police. The company revealed to the *Observer* that the weapons are to help protect its oil installations. However, activists accuse Shell of arming the death squads who have been brutally suppressing the Ogoni people.' (*The Observer*, 28 January 1996)

KEN SARO-WIWA
Ogoni! Ogoni!

Ogoni is the land
The people, Ogoni
The agony of trees dying
In ancestral farmlands
Streams polluted weeping
Filth into murky rivers
It is the poisoned air
Coursing the luckless lungs
Of dying children
Ogoni is the dream
Breaking the looping chain
Around the drooping neck of a shell-shocked land.

JAYNE CORTEZ
What Do They Care

What do they care about ecological devastation
    & survival of the Ogoni people
They're just into
  smiling, eating, making money,
  & fucking up the planet
They are not concerned about the future
  because killers have no future
It's about the oil,
   the pipeline
   & the road to the docks
It's about selling off resources
   receiving revenues
   having a place in the global glut
   & moving greed, mediocrity & stupidity
   to a new plateau of power
What do they care about customs or traditions or
  cultural invasion
  living conditions
  & the Ogoni homeland

They don't speak Ogoni
They speak financial profits
        that's their language
        that's their ideology
& you cannot change the mind & spirit of those who
distort themselves like Sani Abacha & his friends who
      all wear the same uniform
      buy the same weapons
      have the same name of general
      & are a part of the same
      corporate committee of shit heads
          responsible for
          the escalation of poverty
          & the organisation of death squads

What do they care about
        melting ice caps
        carbon dioxide
        land erosion
        atmospheric pollution
        & industrial waste
They like to instill fear, show dominance
They don't care about the ocean or space
or co-operating with people interested in developing
      their community
             Ken Saro Wiwa and the other Ogoni 8.
             That's why the struggle continues

■ **Jayne Cortez** (*b.* 1936) is an African American poet who grew up in the Watts ghetto of Los Angeles, but has spent most of her adult life in the New York City area. Her poetry is celebrated for its political, surrealistic, dynamic innovations in lyricism and visceral sound, and her performances – many with her band The Firespitters – for her almost mesmerising chanting style. Interviewed in 1982 about her poetry's roots in jazz and blues, she said: 'I started writing poetry about my relationship to Black music, talking about the rhythms or what I liked about it, and of course, talking about the musicians who play the music. It's like praise poetry, the old African praise poetry.'

IAN HAMILTON FINLAY
Estuary

RUSH	SEDGE	COUCH	MARRAM	BENT
CURLEW	WHIMBREL	GULL	LAPWING	TERN
ESSO	MOBIL	BP	EXXON	SHELL

■ **Ian Hamilton Finlay** (1925-2006) was a landscape artist, sculptor, painter and poet, born in the Bahamas, whose family returned to Scotland when he was a child. 'Finlay's work as poet, artist and creator of a famous garden – "Little Sparta" – is all of a piece, and challenges the way in which we categorise art-forms. The garden contains poems and texts carved in stone, ceramic and wood. This is one way of making "concrete poetry" or making poetry concrete.' (Edna Longley)

■ **Aharon Shabtai** (*b.* 1939) is a prolific Israeli poet and the foremost Hebrew translator of Greek drama. His sharp views, powerful modes of expression and critical approach to political and social matters have made him a controversial figure in Israel. Much of his poetry is direct and uncompromising, and unsparingly open in relation to his personal experiences of depression, sex and marriage. '**The Trees Are Waiting**' is from his provocative sequence *J'accuse*, many poems from which first appeared in Israel's daily newspaper *Ha'aretz*. Playing on Zola's famous letter denouncing the anti-Semitism of the French government in the Dreyfus affair, Shabtai's title charges his government and people with crimes against the humanity of their Arab neighbours.

AHARON SHABTAI
The Trees Are Weeping
for Tu biShevat

translated from the Hebrew by Peter Cole

The trees are weeping
in the Land of Israel.
Rome's soldiers are razing
acre after acre;
there is no compassion
for the land's raiment –
its seven species.
The trees will all
be sold to a broker;
they won't be made
into crosses
for Jesus and Barabbas.
And on these parcels of land
concessions will be granted
to Burger King
and Kentucky Fried Chicken.

TRANSLATOR'S NOTE:

Tu biShevat: A Jewish holiday, also known as the New Year
of Trees. Literally, the fifteenth of Shevat, the fifth month
in the Hebrew calendar. The festival evolved in part from a
kabbalistic rite that in turn derived from an esoteric inter-
pretation of the biblical verse, 'For man is like the tree of
the field' (Deuteronomy 20:19). It is now celebrated as Arbor
Day and marked by the ceremonial planting of trees.

'Seven species': Seven foods characteristic of the Land of
Israel in Deuteronomy 8:8: 'For the Lord thy God bringeth
thee into a good land [...] a land of wheat and barley, and
vines and fig trees and pomegranates; a land of olive trees
and honey', with honey there indicating dates.

ROBERT HASS
Ezra Pound's Proposition

Beauty is sexual, and sexuality
is the fertility of the earth and the fertility
of the earth is economics. Though he is no
    recommendation
for poets on the subject of finance,
I thought of him in the thick heat
of the Bangkok night. Not more than fourteen, she
    saunters up to you
outside the Shangri-la Hotel
and says, in plausible English,
'How about a party, big guy?'

Here is more or less how it works:
The World Bank arranges the credit and the dam
floods three hundred villages, and the villagers find
    their way
to the city where their daughters melt into the teeming
    streets,
and the dam's great turbines, beautifully tooled
in Lund or Dresden or Detroit, financed
by Lazares Frères in Paris or the Morgan Bank in
    New York,
enabled by judicious gifts from Bechtel of San Francisco
or Halliburton of Houston to the local political elite,
spun by the force of rushing water,
have become hives of shimmering silver
and, down river, throw that bluish throb of light
across her cheekbones and her lovely skin.

■ Robert Hass ➤ 212.

■ **William Heyen** (*b.* 1940) is an American poet, editor and
critic. He grew up in Long Island and taught American lit-
erature and creative writing the State University of New York
in Brockport for over 30 years. The themes of his many books
have ranged from Crazy Horse (Tasunke Witko) to the Holo-
caust to the Gulf War, from the Alice in Wonderland world

of Princess Diana to the trauma humans inflict on the natural world. All the poems here are taken from his 1991 collection *Pterodactyl Rose: poems of ecology*.

Interviewed by Philip Brady, Heyen refers to an essay in his book *Pig Notes & Other Dumb Music: Prose on Poetry* (1998) which seems now 'to be spoken by someone filled with dread' who was asking too much: 'I complain that Seamus Heaney's assumptions about the political dispensations of poetry will no longer serve, as they always have, because now our entire planet is on the verge of ecological catastrophe. I argue that we need a new poetry, one somehow still evocative and interesting but one direct and filled with Truth in ways it has not been before, or else it will be less than marginal and trivial. [...] I called for a poem that could obliterate a tank and slap a tyrant upside the head and make us all saints, and in so doing save the world.'

Bernard W. Quetchenbach: 'William Heyen combines a regional Long Island sensibility he traces to Walt Whitman with the apocalyptic sense he brings to the other major social subject in his work, the Holocaust. Heyen's poems of extinction and despair are especially aimed at placing the individual experience, even when it seems innocent, in the larger sphere of the world economy, where the trivial expands powerfully into nightmare...'

[Other poem ➤ 70]

WILLIAM HEYEN
The Global Economy

You've got a dollar. You deposit it in your savings account. Now you've got a dollar and the bank's got a dollar.

The bank loans a dollar to Joe's Construction. Now you've got a dollar, the bank's got a dollar, and Joe's got a dollar.

Joe buys a board from Hirohito Lumber. Now Hirohito's got a dollar, too.

Where did you get your dollar?
How much money is there in the world?
Who's got it?
Where is it?
What happened to all the trees?

WILLIAM HEYEN
Fast Food

I sit at McDonald's eating my fragment of forest.
The snail and slug taste good, the leaves,
the hint of termite and bat, the butterfly trans-

substantiated by steer karma, and mine.
Another pleasure: to breathe distillate of foam
scented with coffee and chemical cream.

Another virtue: groups of us all trained
the same way, millions across America
where we flourish, at present, under the golden arches.

WILLIAM HEYEN
Emancipation Proclamation

Whereas it minds its own business
& lives in its one place so faithfully
& its trunk supports us when we lean against it
& its branches remind us of how we think

Whereas it keeps no bank account but hoards carbon
& does not discriminate between starlings & robins
& provides free housing for insects & squirrels
& lifts its heartwood grave into the air

Whereas it holds our firmament in place
& writes underground gospel with its roots
& whispers us oxygen with its leaves
& may not survive its new climate of ultraviolet

We the people for ourselves & our children
necessarily proclaim this tree
free from commerce & belonging to itself
as long as it & we shall live.

SUSAN GRIFFIN
from Woman and Nature:
The Roaring Inside Her

FROM *Prologue*

He says that woman speaks with nature. That she hears voices from under the earth. That wind blows in her ears and trees whisper to her. That the dead sing through her mouth and the cries of infants are clear to her. But for him this dialogue is over. He says he is not part of this world, that he was set on this world as a stranger. He sets himself apart from woman and nature.

And so it is Goldilocks who goes to the home of the three bears. Little Red Riding Hood who converses with the wolf, Dorothy who befriends a lion, Snow White who talks to the birds, Cinderella with mice as her allies, the Mermaid who is half fish, Thumbelina courted by a mole. (*And when we hear in the Navaho chant of the mountain that a grown man sits and smokes with bears and follows directions given to him by squirrels, we are surprised. We had thought only little girls spoke with animals.*)

We are the bird's eggs. Bird's eggs, flowers, butterflies, rabbits, cows, sheep; we are caterpillars; we are leaves of ivy and sprigs of wallflower. We are women. We rise from the wave. We are gazelle and doe, elephant and whale, lilies and roses and peach, we are air, we are flame, we are oyster and pearl, we are girls. We are woman and nature. And he says he cannot hear us speak.

But we hear. [...]

Consequences (What Always Returns)

And I pray one prayer – I repeat it till my tongue stiffens – Catherine Earnshaw, may you not rest as long as I am living! You said I killed you – haunt me, then!... Be with me always – take any form – drive me mad! Only *do* not leave me in this abyss, where I cannot find you! Oh God! It is unutterable! I cannot live without my life! I *cannot* live without my soul.

EMILY BRONTË: *Wuthering Heights*

To have risked so much in our efforts to mould nature to our satisfaction and yet to have failed in achieving our goal would indeed be the final irony. Yet this, it seems, is our situation.

RACHEL CARSON: *Silent Spring*

We say you cannot divert the river from the riverbed. We say that everything is moving, and we are a part of this motion. That the soil is moving. That the water is moving. We say that the earth draws water to her from the clouds. We say the rainfall parts on each side of the mountain, like the parting of our hair, and that the shape of the mountain tells where the water has passed. We say this water washes the soil from the hillsides, that the rivers carry sediment, that rain when it splashes carries small particles, that the soil itself flows with water in streams underground. We say that water is taken up into roots of plants, into stems, that it washes down hills into rivers, that these rivers flow to the sea, that from the sea, in the sunlight, this water rises to the sky, that this water is carried in clouds, and comes back as rain, comes back as fog, back as dew, as wetness in the air.

We say everything comes back. And you cannot divert the river from the riverbed. We say every act has its consequences. That this place has been shaped by the river, and that the shape of this place tells the river where to go.

We say he should have known his action would have consequences. We say our judgment was that when she raised that rifle, looking through the sight at him, and fired, she was acting out of what had gone on before. We say every act comes back on itself. There are consequences. You cannot cut the trees from the mountainside without a flood. We say there is no way to see his dying as separate from her living, or what he had done to her, or what part of her he had used. We say if you change the course of this river you change the shape of the whole place. And we say that what she did then could not be separated from what she held sacred in herself, what she had felt when he did that to her, what we hold sacred to ourselves, what we feel we could not go on without, and we say if this river leaves this place, nothing will grow and the mountain will crumble away, and we say what he did to her could not be separated from the way that he looked at her, and what he felt was

173

right to do to her, and what they do to us, we say, shapes how they see us. That once the trees are cut down, the water will wash the mountain away and the river be heavy with mud, and there will be a flood. And we say that what he did to her he did to all of us. And that one act cannot be separated from another. And had he seen more clearly, we say, he might have predicted his own death. How if the trees grew on that hillside there would be no flood. And you cannot divert this river. We say look how the water flows from this place and returns as rainfall, everything returns, we say, and one thing follows another, there are limits, we say, on what can be done and everything moves. We are all a part of this motion, we say, and the way of the river is sacred, and this grove of trees is sacred, and we ourselves, we tell you, are sacred. [...]

Forest: The Way We Stand

> The poor little working-girl who had found strength to gather up the fragments of her life and build herself a shelter with them seemed to Lily to have reached the central truth of existence.
>
> EDITH WHARTON: *The House of Mirth*

> The bank was dense with magnolia and loblolly bay, sweet gum and gravy-barked ash.... He went down to the spring in the cool darkness of the shadows. A sharp pleasure came over him. This was a secret, lovely place.
>
> MARJORIE KINNAN RAWLINGS: *The Yearling*

The way we stand, you can see we have grown up this way together, out of the same soil, with the same rains, leaning in the same way toward the sun. See how we lean together in the same direction. How the dead limbs of one of us rest in the branches of another. How those branches have grown around the limbs. How the two are inseparable. And if you look you can see the different ways we have taken this place into us. Magnolia, loblolly bay, sweet gum, Southern bayberry, Pacific bayberry; wherever we grow there are many of us; Monterey pine, sugar pine, white-bark pine, four-leaf pine, single-leaf pine, bristle-cone pine, foxtail pine, Torrey pine, Western red pine, Jeffry pine, bishop pine. And we are various, and amazing in our variety, and our differences multiply, so that edge after

edge of the endlessness of possibility is exposed. You know we have grown this way for years. And to no purpose you can understand. Yet what you fail to know we know, and the knowing is in us, how we have grown this way, why these years were not one of them heedless, why we are shaped the way we are, not all straight to your purpose, but to ours. And how we are each purpose, how each cell, how light and soil are in us, how we are in the soil, how we are in the air, how we are both infinitesimal and great and how we are infinitely without any purpose you can see, in the way we stand, each alone, yet none of us separable, none of us beautiful when separate but all exquisite as we stand, each moment heeded in this cycle, no detail unlovely.

■ **Susan Griffin** (*b.* 1943) is a feminist philosopher, poet, essayist, playwright and filmmaker from California. Her book *Woman and Nature: The Roaring Inside Her* (1978) is a key text in ecofeminist literature. 'It exists in a realm between essay and poems, between reality and myth,' she later wrote in *Made from this Earth*: 'Though the book contains analytic ideas, it moves by the force of echoes and choruses, counterpoints and harmonies. In one way the book is an extended dialogue between two voices (each set in a different typeface), one the chorus of women and nature, an emotional, animal, embodied voice [*italic type*], and the other a solo part, cool, professorial, pretending to objectivity, carrying the weight of cultural authority [*roman type*]. Yet, though the book is shaped by the conflict between these two voices, it sings more than it argues.' Three separate extracts from *Woman and Nature* are printed above with Griffin's typography (with epigraphs in smaller type counterpointing her two voices).

Like Joy Harjo, Linda Hogan, Pattiann Rogers, Leslie Marmon Silko and others – Susan Griffin makes explicit the 'connection between oppressed human populations and nonhuman nature' which Bernard W. Quetchenbach sees as 'the core of ecofeminist writing': 'Because feminism is fundamentally a liberation movement, ecofeminists have provided environmentalists with a clear sense of the essential and reciprocal relationship between environmental concerns and social justice.' In her essay 'A Collaborative Intelligence', Griffin argues that if 'one would create an egalitarian society, nature must be restored as the common ground of existence. Yet this common ground cannot be reclaimed without the transformation of an unjust social order.'

PAULA GUNN ALLEN
Molly Brant, Iroquois Matron, Speaks

I was, Sir, born of Indian parents, and lived while a child among
those whom you are pleased to call savages; I was afterwards
sent to live among the white people, and educated at one of
your schools; ...and after every exertion to divest myself of
prejudice, I am obliged to give my opinion in favor of my own
people.... In the government you call civilised, the happiness of
the people is constantly sacrificed to the splendor of empire...
        JOSEPH BRANT

We knew it was the end
long after it ended, my brother Joseph
and I. We were so simple in those days
taking a holiday to see the war,
the one they would later call
the Revolution. It was that,
at that. Something turned,
something was revolting.
And when I learned that I was
no longer honored matron
but only heathen squaw,
when I learned my daughters
were less than dirt,
then I knew that it was changed,
and our lives were ended.
I wonder why I did not see it coming
all along.

It's a funny thing about revolutions.
Wheels turn. So do planets.
Stars turn. So do galaxies.
What's odd is that when a human
system turns, so many believe
it will turn their way.
So many think any turn is for the better.
I suppose we thought so,
my brother Joseph and myself.
I suppose we thought that if the whites
were fighting we Iroquois couldn't help

but come out ahead. We had held power
for so long. We played the international
political game to our advantage
for two hundred years –
seemed like we had always had
our way in things. Seemed like
we always would. The Matrons had held
power for so long – for as long as anyone
could remember – how could we know
the turn events would take, the turn
that would plow us under
like last year's crop?

And now another turn is up.
They plan to blow it up.
Or poison it to death rather than change.
Fire and poison, their own tools
of conquest will conquer them, it seems.
They want revolution,
but not that kind, I guess,
any more than we hoped for
the kind of revolution that we got.
So they are planning to blow it up,
obliterate it. And good riddance
is what I say. What do I have to lose,
having lost all that mattered, all I loved
so long ago? And what is there more to lose?
Great cities, piling drifting clouds
of chemical poisons that have long since
killed the air? Rivers and lakes long since
dead beneath the burden of filth dumped into
them for years? Earth so sick of attempts
to cure it of its life that it is nearly dead?
Places now called Oregon, California, New York,
filled with those who replaced the people
long since murdered in the revolution
that turned the red lands white?
If death is in the wind
it will only blow our enemies away.
When a wheel turns
what is on the underside
comes up.

175

■ **Paula Gunn Allen** (*b.* 1939) is a Native American poet, fiction writer, critic and activist. Born in Albuquerque, of mixed Laguna, Sioux, Scottish and Lebanese-American descent, she grew up in Cubero, New Mexico, a Spanish-Mexican land grant village bordering the Laguna Pueblo reservation. Her poetry addresses Native American, feminist and environmental issues and finds common threads in all three. Like fellow Laguna writer Leslie Marmon Silko, she draws on Pueblo tales of Grandmother Spider and the Corn Maiden in much of her writing. Her many books include the seminal and controversial study *The Sacred Hoop: Recovering the Feminine in American Indian Traditions* (1986).

JOY HARJO
Remember

Remember the sky you were born under,
know each of the star's stories.
Remember the moon, know who she is.
Remember the sun's birth at dawn, that is the
strongest point of time. Remember sundown
and the giving away to night.
Remember your birth, how your mother struggled
to give you form and breath. You are evidence of
her life, and her mother's, and hers.
Remember your father. He is your life, also.
Remember the earth whose skin you are:
red earth, black earth, yellow earth, white earth
brown earth, we are earth.
Remember the plants, trees, animal life who all have their
tribes, their families, their histories, too. Talk to them,
listen to them. They are alive poems.
Remember the wind. Remember her voice. She knows the
origin of this universe.
Remember you are all people and all people
are you.
Remember you are this universe and this
universe is you.
Remember all is in motion, is growing, is you.
Remember language comes from this.
Remember the dance language is, that life is.
Remember.

JOY HARJO
For Alva Benson, and for Those Who Have Learned to Speak

And the ground spoke when she was born.
Her mother heard it. In Navajo she answered
as she squatted down against the earth
to give birth. It was now when it happened,
now giving birth to itself again and again
between the legs of women.

Or maybe it was the Indian Hospital
in Gallup. The ground still spoke beneath
mortar and concrete. She strained against the
metal stirrups, and they tied her hands down
because she still spoke with them when they
muffled her screams. But her body went on
talking and the child was born into their
hands, and the child learned to speak
both voices.

She grew up talking in Navajo, in English
and watched the earth around her shift and change
with the people in the towns and in the cities
learning not to hear the ground as it spun around
beneath them. She learned to speak for the ground,
the voice coming through her like roots that
have long hungered for water. Her own daughter
was born, like she had been, in either place
or all places, so she could leave, leap
into the sound she had always heard,
a voice like water, like the gods weaving
against sundown in a scarlet light.

The child now hears names in her sleep.
They change into other names, and into others.
It is the ground murmuring, and Mount Saint Helens
erupts as the harmonic motion of a child turning
inside her mother's belly waiting to be born
to begin another time.

And we go on, keep giving birth and watch
ourselves die, over and over.
And the ground spinning beneath us
goes on talking.

JOY HARJO
What Music

      I would have loved you then, in
the hot, moist tropics of your young womanhood.
Then
      the stars were out and fat every night.
They remembered your name
                and called to you
as you bent down in the doorways of the whiteman's houses.
You savored each story they told you,
and remembered
        the way the stars entered your blood
                      at birth.
Maybe it was the Christians' language
              that captured you,
or the bones that cracked in your heart each time
you missed the aboriginal music that you were.
But then,
      you were the survivor of the births
of your two sons. The oldest one envies you, and the other
wants to marry you. Now they live in another language
in Los Angeles
        with their wives.
And you,
      the stars return every night to call you back.
They have followed your escape
       from the southern hemisphere
               into the north.
Their voices echo out from your blood and you drink
the Christians' brandy and fall back into
   doorways in an odd moonlight.
            You sweat in the winter in the north,
and you are afraid,
      sweetheart.

■ **Joy Harjo** (*b.* 1951) is a Native American poet and storyteller. She is also a multi-talented performer and saxophonist, combining poetry and chanting with tribal music, jazz, funk and rock. Influenced not only by her own Mvskoke (Creek) traditions but also by the Navajo Beauty Way and by Pueblo stories, her poetry is grounded in her relationship with the earth on a physical, spiritual and mythopoetic level. Her work achieves its universal vision by focusing on the individual plight of Native Americans struggling to survive in the alienating urban landscape of modern America as well as in the harsh mesa, mountain and sagebrush flat landscapes of New Mexico and Arizona where both people and wildlife were decimated by the colonisers who took over their land.

Harjo sees herself as part of a larger process: 'I am driven to explore the depths of creation and the depths of meaning. Being native, female, a global citizen in these times is the root, even the palette. I mean, look at the context: human spirit versus the spirits of the earth, sky, and universe. We are part of a much larger force of sense and knowledge. Western society is human-centric. We're paying the price of foolish arrogance, of forgetfulness.' (*Terrain* interview) [Other poem ➤ 243]

LINDA HOGAN
To Light

At the spring
we hear the great seas traveling
underground,
giving themselves up
with tongues of water
that sing the earth open.

They have journeyed through the graveyards
of our loved ones,
turning in their graves
to carry the stories of life to air.

Even the trees with their rings
have kept track
of the crimes that live within
and against us.

We remember it all.
We remember, though we are just skeletons
whose organs and flesh
hold us in.
We have stories
as old as the great seas
breaking through the chest,
flying out the mouth,
noisy tongues that once were silenced,
all the oceans we contain
coming to light.

LINDA HOGAN
Bees in Transit: Osage County

Like a hundred white bedroom chests
being driven to the county dump,
clean drawers of honey
pass through autumn and stop
by the highway.
Noisy bees in transport
work their way through white sheets
draped over hives.

The air is filled with workers
on strike
and drones the truck deserted.
In its absence
cold leaves drop away from trees,
brush smoke rises,
and green Osage oranges are free
one moment before hitting earth
where dark women, murdered for oil
under the ground
still walk in numbers
through smoky dusk.

The air is full.
Bewildered bees are a lost constellation.

Through compound eyes
they see me again and again.
Multiplied
divided
in the confusion of a hundred earths
and rising moons.

Desertion's sorrow has not yet touched them
but it is growing death cold
and there is no place to go at dark
when the air fills up with sirens and suicides,
gray women wavering above tthe ambert heat
of brushfires
and a thousand porchlights.
I would like to tell the noisy bees
there is a way back home.
I would like to tell them
there is nothing more than air between us all.

LINDA HOGAN
Mountain Lion

She lives on the dangerous side
of the clearing
in the yellow-eyed shadow of a darker fear.
We have seen each other
inside mortal dusk,
and what passed between us
was the road
ghosts travel
when they cannot rest
in the land of the terrible other.
Red spirits of hunters
walked between us
from the place where blood
goes back to its wound
before fire
before weapons.
Nothing was hidden
in our eyes.

I was the wild thing
she had learned to fear.
Her power lived
in a dream of my leaving.
It was the same way
I have looked so many times at others
in clear light
before lowering my eyes
and turning away
from what lives inside those
who have found
two worlds cannot live
inside a single vision.

LINDA HOGAN
The Fallen

It was the night
a comet with its silver tail
fell through darkness
to earth's eroded field,
the night I found
the wolf,
starved in metal trap,
teeth broken
from pain's hard bite,
its belly swollen with unborn young.

In our astronomy
the Great Wolf
lived in sky.
It was the mother of all women
and howled her daughter's names
into the winds of night.

But the new people,
whatever stepped inside their shadow,
they would kill,
whatever crossed their path,
they came to fear.

In their science,
Wolf was not the mother.
Wolf was not wind.
They did not learn healing
from her song.

In their stories
Wolf was the devil, falling
down an empty,
shrinking universe,
God's Lucifer
with yellow eyes
that had seen their tailings
and knew that they could kill the earth,
that they would kill each other.

That night
I threw the fallen stone back to sky
and falling stars
and watched it all come down
to ruined earth again.

Sky would not take back
what it had done.

That night, sky was a wilderness so close
the eerie light of heaven
and storming hands of sun
reached down the swollen belly
and dried up nipples of a hungry world.

That night,
I saw the trapper's shadow
and it had four legs.

■ **Linda Hogan** (*b.* 1947) is a Native American poet, story-teller, academic, playwright, fiction writer and environmentalist. Her ancestry is Chickasaw, but her family's military background meant that she grew up in different parts of Colorado and Oklahoma without a sense of belonging to a particular Native community. All her work shows a holistic understanding of the world, often related to environmental, anti-nuclear and feminist themes, and she has been involved in wildlife rehabilitation as a volunteer. Her historical novels focus on historical wrongs done to both Native Americans and the American landscape during the colonisation of North America.

The main focus and movement of her work concerns the traditional indigenous view of and relationship to the land, animals and plants, and her many books include *Dwellings: A Spiritual History of the Living World* (1995) and (co-edited with Brenda Peterson and Deena Metzger) *Intimate Nature: The Bond Between Women and Animals* (1998). In her preface to *Dwellings*, she writes: 'As an Indian woman I question our responsibilities to the caretaking of the future and to the other species who share our journeys. These writings have grown out of those questions, out of wondering what makes us human, out of a lifelong love for the living world and all its inhabitants. They have grown, too, out of my native understanding that there is a terrestrial intelligence that lies beyond our human knowing and grasping.'

Interviewed by Camille Colatosti (2002), she said: 'When I think about the relationship between people and animals, the thing that I have always understood is that we are not only in relationship in an ecosystem but are as humble as the animals in our own rightful place. This is the difference between other religions and indigenous tradition. For Indians, if you are a seal hunter, you pray while you make your tools; you sing to the seal and you pray to the seal. You tell it why you are taking its life. If you are going to kill it, you respect it. [...] My mother is of Germanic background and my father was Chickasaw. He was always good to animals but he was not traditional. My grandmother was kind and had a special relationship with animals. I remember that a large land tortoise was heading out and my grandmother stopped it and told the turtle not to go the way it was traveling because there were dogs there. The turtle turned around. I have always had an empathic relationship with animals that can't be explained. [...] The Western mind has the idea that there is dominion over animals. If you see animals in a zoo, you do not see an animal, you see a creature of loss that has been created by humans, a marginal creature. All its significance has been taken away. The animal is without his environment. It has no den, no place where it catches food; it has nothing. Animals lose their very selves. Animals live very complex lives and have their own significant intelligence in their true environment. The Western mind does not see that.'

Emily Hegarty: 'Hogan connects the Native American experience of genocide with the contemporary threat of extinction posed by the destruction of the global environment. [...] She believes that "language contains the potential to restore us to a unity with earth and the rest of the universe". [...] Hogan presents the holistic Native American view of language as affecting the world. [...] Some of Hogan's most environmental work unites the voices of past generations with voices of the earth. [...] The speaking earth is a quintessentially environmental and Native American gesture. One example beside Hogan is Harjo's poem **'For Alva Benson, and for Those Who Have Learned to Speak'** [➤ 176], in which generations of women hear and "speak for the ground" when they give birth. [...] Outside of Native American traditional knowledge, the speaking earth has been promoted by Gary Snyder as the ecopoetic concept of biomass. Biomass is an ecological concept that refers to biological information stored at the cellular level in both human and nonhuman nature. [...]

'In **'Bees in Transit: Osage County'** [➤ 178] Hogan compares Osage women murdered for their oil-rich land to doomed bees that have escaped from hives being transported by truck. [...] Another complex human/animal connection is found in **'Mountain Lion'** [➤ 179], wherein the speaker recognises in the endangered mountain lion's fear of humans her own fear of those who do not share her holistic worldview. Hogan interrogates the definitions of *wild* and, by implication, *civilised*. [...] The analogy between Native Americans and endangered animals is repeated in **'The Fallen'** [➤ 179], in which the speaker watches an asteroid fall and finds a pregnant wolf dead of starvation in a steel trap in an "eroded field". She contrasts the Native American and Western views of the wolf as symbol. [...] the pregnancy of the dead wolf suggests not only the deaths of future generations but also the destruction of the Native American world and cosmology. The poem is a likely allusion to an incident in South Dakota in which starving Nakota people were reduced to eating the poisoned animal carcasses used to bait wolf traps and died of strychnine poisoning [see Hogan, *Dwellings*]. Hogan's critique has obvious commonalities with the environmental critique of Judeo-Christian traditions about the earth. [...] Her writing is an effort to counteract the effects of physical and cultural genocide and an attempt to reproduce for future generations Native American culture and the viable environment with which it is entwined.'

PETER BLUE CLOUD
Sweet Corn

the edge of autumn touches leaves
     and sharpens
       the morning air
white breath the river speaks
in tumbling, slowly tumbling
              rising
     mists of steam
a biting axe
       is a dog bark
a cracking rifle
       antlers
hollow ringing woods

a crow graws us welcome
     (imagined)
as we harvest sweet corn
the field her summer warmth
     still holds
     in deep, rich earth
          we bend to,
as a running breeze begins
the shushing corn dance
     of our tall sisters
and the sweet grace of their motion
     is the sacred ritual
     of our people.

now, kneeling here upon a blanket
as rain taps lightly the windows,
braiding the sister corn into circlets
to be dried for the season of cold,

     at winter's table
     may we all
think upon
     the first green shoots
     those gone
        and those to come.

PETER BLUE CLOUD
We sit balanced

     between
end and beginning
upon the back
     of turtle
and the pools
       of light
     we see in water
is sky deepness roots
     moist earth womb
seedling hawk
       born
screaming joy

     life precious
praise earth
     sky
     water
     sun fire
life spark praise
       forever,
and once
and only once
     until
each is absorbed
through reflected waters
     backward
     into tomorrow
sideways
     sometimes
our dance
     yes.
(ah,
  to dance
       lightly as
finger weavings
lightly

            as breast down
        floating)
    and it is corn
            placed in earth
            a short while
                        ago
    and now
            the shoots
    give life to eyes
    which see
                again
            the people.

■ **Peter Blue Cloud (Aroniawenrate)** (*b.* 1935) belongs to the Turtle Clan of the Mohawk tribe on the Caughnawaga Reserve in Kahnawake, Quebec, Canada. He worked as ironworker, logger, carpenter and woodcutter, and began publishing his poems in the late 60s. His poems and stories are noted for their combining of Native American myths with contemporary issues, and in particular for his use of the Coyote figure. Blue Cloud emphasised and introduced traditional ways of thinking into contemporary American literature in relation to humankind, nature and history, and humankind and nature as one.

LESLIE MARMON SILKO
from **Storyteller**

He was walking along the pavement when she found him. He did not stop or turn around when he heard her behind him. She walked beside him and she noticed how slowly he moved now. He smelled strong of woodsmoke and urine. Lately he had been forgetting. Sometimes he called her by his sister's name and she had been gone for a long time. Once she had found him wandering on the road to the white man's ranch, and she asked him why he was going that way; he laughed at her and said, 'You know they can't run that ranch without me,' and he walked on determined, limping on the leg that had been crushed many years before. Now he looked at her curiously, as if for the first time, but he kept shuf-

fling along, moving slowly along the side of the highway. His gray hair had grown long and spread out on the shoulders of the long overcoat. He wore the old felt hat pulled down over his ears. His boots were worn out at the toes and he had stuffed pieces of an old red shirt in the holes. The rags made his feet look like little animals up to their ears in snow. She laughed at his feet; the snow muffled the sound of her laugh. He stopped and looked at her again. The wind had quit blowing and the snow was falling straight down; the southeast sky was beginning to clear and Ayah could see a star.

'Let's rest awhile,' she said to him. They walked away from the road and up the slope to the giant boulders that had tumbled down from the red sandrock mesa throughout the centuries of rainstorms and earth tremors. In a place where the boulders shut out the wind, they sat down with with their backs against the rock. She offered half of the blanket to him and they sat wrapped together.

The storm passed swiftly. The clouds moved east. They were massive and lull, crowding together across the sky. She watched them with the feeling of horses – steely blue-gray horses startled across the sky. The powerful haunches pushed into the distances and the tail hairs streamed white mist behind them. The sky cleared. Ayah saw that there was nothing between her and the stars. The light was crystalline. There was no shimmer, no distortion through earth haze. She breathed the clarity of the night sky; she smelled the purity of the half moon and the stars. He was lying on his side with his knees pulled up near his belly for warmth. His eyes were closed now, and as in the light from the stars and the moon, he looked young again.

She could see it descend out of the night sky: an icy stillness from the edge of the thin moon. She recognised the freezing. It came gradually, sinking snowflake by snowflake until the crust was heavy and deep. It had the strength of the stars in Orion, and its journey was endless. Ayah knew that with the wine he would sleep. He would not feel it. She tucked the blanket around him, remembering how it was when Ella had been with her; and she felt the rush so big inside her heart for the babies. And she sang the only song she knew to sing for babies. She could not remember if she had ever sung it to her children, but she knew that her grandmother had sung it and her mother had sung it:

> *The earth is your mother,*
> *she holds you.*
> *The sky is your father,*
> *he protects you.*
> *Sleep,*
> *sleep.*
> *Rainbow is your sister,*
> *she loves you.*
> *The winds are your brothers,*
> *they sing to you.*
> *Sleep,*
> *sleep.*
> *We are together always*
> *We are together always*
> *There never was a time*
> *when this*
> *was not so.*

LESLIE MARMON SILKO
from Storyteller

Long time ago
in the beginning
there were no white people in this world
there was nothing European.
And this world might have gone on like that
except for one thing:
witchery.
This world was already complete
even without white people.
There was everything
including witchery.

Then it happened.
These witch people got together.

Some came from far far away
across oceans
across mountains.
Some had slanty eyes
others had black skin.
They all got together for a contest
the way people have baseball tournaments nowadays
except this was a contest
in dark things.

[…]

Finally there was only one
who hadn't shown off charms or powers.
The witch stood in the shadows beyond the fire
and no one ever knew where this witch came
which tribe
or if it was a woman or a man.
But the important thing was
this witch didn't show off any dark thunder charcoals
or red ant-hill beads.
This one just told them to listen:
'What I have is a story.'

At first they all laughed
but this witch said
Okay
go ahead
laugh if you want to
but as I tell the story
it will begin to happen.

Set in motion now
set in motion by our witchery
to work for us.

Caves across the ocean
in caves of dark hills
white skin people
like the belly of a fish
covered with hair.

Then they grow away from the earth
then they grow away from the sun
then they grow away from the plants and animals.
They see no life.
When they look
they see only objects.
The world is a dead thing for them
the trees and rivers are not alive
the mountains and stones are not alive.
The deer and bear are objects
They see no life.

They fear
They fear the world.
They destroy what they fear.
They fear themselves.

The wind will blow them across the ocean
thousands of them in giant boats
swarming like larvae
out of a crushed ant hill.

They will carry objects
which can shoot death
faster than the eye can see.

They will kill the things they fear
all the animals
the people will starve.

They will poison the water
they will spin the water away
and there will be drought
the people will starve.

They will fear what they find
They will fear the people
They kill what they fear.

Entire villages will he wiped out
They will slaughter whole tribes.

Corpses for us
Blood for us

Killing killing killing killing.

And those they do not kill
will die anyway
at the destruction they see
at the loss
at the loss of the children
the loss will destroy the rest.

Stolen rivers and mountains
the stolen land will eat their hearts
and jerk their mouths from the Mother.
The people will starve.

They will bring terrible diseases
the people have never known.
Entire tribes will die out
covered with festered sores
shitting blood
vomiting blood.
Corpses for our work

Set in motion now
set in motion by our witchery
set in motion
to work for us.

They will take this world from ocean to ocean
they will turn on each other
they will destroy each other
Up here
in these hills
they will find the rocks,
rocks with veins of green and yellow and black.
They will lay the final pattern with these rocks
they will lay it across the world
and explode everything.

Set in motion now
set in motion
To destroy
To kill

Objects to work for us
objects to act for us
Performing the witchery
for suffering
for torment
for the stillborn
the deformed
the sterile
the dead.

Whirling
Whirling
Whirling

Whirling
set into motion now
set into motion.

So the other witches said
'Okay you win; you take the prize,
but what you said just now –
it isn't so funny.
It doesn't sound so good.
We are doing okay without it
we can get along without that kind of thing.
Take it back.
Call that story back.'

But the witch just shook its head
at the others in their stinking animal skins, fur
and feathers.
It's already turned loose.
It's already coming.
It can't be called back.

■ **Leslie Marmon Silko** (*b*. 1948) is a novelist, poet, essayist and activist, and the 'first acclaimed Native American woman author'. Born in Albuquerque, New Mexico, of mixed ancestry (Laguna, Pueblo, Mexican and white), she grew up on the Laguna Pueblo reservation, where members of her family had lived for generations, learning traditional stories and legends from her grandmother and aunt.

Her novel *Ceremony* (1977), the first published novel by a Native American woman writer, tells the story of a mixed blood veteran who returns to his Laguna reservation after fighting against Japan in the Second World War. The book shows how vital storytelling is to the Pueblo culture and how White culture has made many attempts to destroy these stories as well as their ceremonies. *Storyteller* (1981) draws on Native American stories to recreate narratives of her own family, using a mixture of poetry, prose, family history and photographs. Her best-known novel, *Almanac of the Dead* (1991), is a darker work dealing with issues related to Native American history, in particular the white European conquest of the people and land. *Yellow Woman* (1993) and *Yellow Woman and a Beauty of the Spirit* (1996) are both works on Laguna society before the arrival of the Christian missionaries as well as political statements against racist policies. Silko's Laguna 500-year-old culture and natural environment have suffered further traumas since the coming of the white man, including the development of the atom bomb and the first atomic explosion 150 miles away, followed by open-cast uranium mining on Pueblo land; nuclear destruction is one of Silko's concerns in *Ceremony*.

The late James Wright's early praise of Silko's *Ceremony* led to a friendship between two writers from very different backgrounds. After his death, his widow Anne Wright edited their correspondence in *With the Delicacy and Strength of Lace: Letters Between Leslie Marmon Silko and James Wright* (1986), winner of the Boston Globe prize for non-fiction.

Silko has been a controversial figure in American letters. Criticised by Paula Gunn Allen for divulging tribal secrets in *Ceremony*, she herself has made famous attacks on other writers, claiming that Anishinaabe writer Louise Erdrich had abandoned the Native American struggle in writing postmodern fiction, and accusing Gary Snyder of profiting from Native American culture, particularly in his collection *Turtle Island* [➤ 102-03], which took its name and theme from Pueblo mythology.

'Silko emphasises the need to return to rituals and oral traditions of the past in order to rediscover the basis for one's cultural identity' (LaVonne Ruoff in Melody Graulich's introduction to *Yellow Woman*).

JOSEPH BEUYS
Coyote:
I Like America and America Likes Me
Description and photograph by Caroline Tisdall

'The spirit of the coyote is so mighty that the human being cannot understand what it is, or what it can do for human-kind in the future.'

The Coyote action began on the journey from Europe to America. After the ice fields of Labrador, the uninhabited no-man's-land of the mind, the man covered his eyes, and that was the last he saw of America.

At Kennedy Airport he was wrapped from head to foot in felt, the material which for him is both insulator and warmth preserver. He was loaded into an ambulance, mobile reminder of scientific therapy, and driven straight to the place which he was to share with the coyote. The action ended a week later when, once more insulated in felt, he was carried back to the ambulance on the first stage of his journey back to Europe. Red Cross for the man. Blue Cross for the animal.

In between there was the day-in day-out public dialogue: long, calm, concentrated, almost silent days of dialogue between representatives of two species together in the same space for the first time. It was a long, light space, three windows casting the changing light and shade of passing days. The late spring sun cast a glow that was somehow rural, blond, brown and grey, certainly nothing to do with the urban scene beyond the windows. A heavy chain-link barrier separated the man and the coyote from the people who came and went all day. It came to mark an area of freedom for the protagonists, while ambiguously caging the spectators. In the far corner of this space was the straw that had been brought with the coyote.

The man had brought objects and elements from his world to place in this space, silent representatives of his ideas and beliefs. He introduced them to the coyote. The coyote responded coyote-style by claiming them with his gesture of possession. One by one as they were presented he pissed on them slowly and deliberately: felt, walking-stick, gloves, flashlight and *Wall Street Journal*. The elements were arranged in the space. The two long lengths of felt were placed in the middle, one drawn into a heap with the flashlight shining out of it. And at the front of the space, by the barrier, were two neat piles of the *Wall Street Journal*, fifty a day, and the edition of each changing day.

The man had also brought a repertoire of movements with him, and a notion of time. These too were then subject to the coyote's responses, and were modulated and conditioned by them. The man never took his eyes off the animal. The line of sight between them became like the hands of a spiritual clockface measuring the timing of movements, a choreography directed towards the coyote, the timing and the mood regulated by the animal. Generally the sequence lasted about an hour and a quarter, sometimes much longer. In all it was repeated well over thirty times, but the mood and the tone were never the same.

The man walked towards one length of the felt with a brown walking-stick over his arm, and pulled on the brown gloves. Then he swathed himself in the felt, easing it up over his hat until nothing but the raised stick, its curving end stretched upward, emerged above the grey tent. The image was a hieratic one, upright and distant, the clear outline of a tall shepherd figure glimpsed across the distance of the steppes.

The gaunt outline of felt and stick was a sculptural image too, and like a sculpture it was taken through successive forms and stages: vertical, crook directed upwards; bent at a right angle, crook to the ground; crouching upright as if for a long wait, then crouching again with the stick inclined to the floor. All the time the figure shifted slightly on its axis, following the direction and movements of the coyote. Then the calm silence and the slow passage of time were abruptly broken. The figure fell sideways to the ground, transformed into a prone body wrapped in felt, a reminder of another event in the life of the man, the vulnerable object. The general structure of the movements was always the same, but those of the coyote varied with every sequence. Sometimes he behaved as if this kind of thing was run of the mill to him. Sometimes he kept a certain distance, or seemed quite detached from what was going on, and the atmosphere was dignified and calm. At other times he hovered, waiting and watchful, circling cautiously round the felt figure, nervous of the slightest movement. And occasionally he went quite mad with excitement, mischief and malice mixed, playful to the point of aggression, leaping at the stick, mauling the felt, tearing it apart until it was reduced to tiny shreds that resembled the moulting tufts of his own pelt. He reacted particularly strongly when the felt-figure was lying prone and motionless, nosing at it apprehensively, poking it solicitously, pawing at it with wary suspicion.

Occasionally he lay down with the figure, or tried to creep beneath the felt.

But the coyote's usual dozing place was the other pile of felt. He would stretch out on it or curl up, eyes half-closed, relaxed or wary, and the strange blond fire of those eyes always shone in the same direction as the glowing flashlight. His back was never turned on the people watching from behind the barrier. Maybe he sensed that more danger could come from them than from the man in there with him, or maybe it was simply because he was a splendid showman. His routine and timing were never dull. Sometimes he took over the show completely, ranging up and down the space, stopping now and then to stare back at the staring visitors, suddenly turning on the mean look his audience might have been expecting. Now and then he would remember the windows and the world outside, and stare out in amazement at New York and the bustle of the street below. Then he would go to town on *Wall Street Journals*, clawing at them, chewing them, dragging them across the space, pissing and shitting on them. And every so often, with uncanny wolf rhythm, he would circle back to his mute felt-swathed companion.

Suddenly the inert figure stretched out on the ground would spring up, casting off the felt as he did so, and striking three clear resounding notes on the triangle at his waist, the high sharp sound shattered the silence. Then the silence built up again over the next ten seconds to be blotted out again, this time by the reverberation of a 20-second-long blast of noise: the roar of turbine engines projected from a tape-recorder beyond the barrier. The chaotic sound ended as abruptly as it had begun, and as it did so the man relaxed, took off his brown gloves, and threw them to the coyote to toss around. Then he walked across to rearrange the mauled and scattered *Wall Street Journals* into two neat piles again, and came up front to chat with a friend through the barrier and to down a glass of shocking-pink five-fruits flavour Hawaiian Punch.

Then back to the far corner for a quiet smoke in the coyote's straw. Oddly enough, or surely enough, this was the only time the coyote took any notice of the straw. Usually he preferred the felt. But when the man was in the corner he joined him, and that interlude always had the atmosphere of a farmyard: long moments of far-away filtered sunlight. By and by the man got up, sorted out the piles of felt, drew the long grey length up over his head, and the sequence started again.

And so the days and the sequences went slowly by. The damp sweaty heat of the felt took its toll on the man's familiar hat, transforming him into a bedraggled clodhopper. Man and animal grew closer together: it was as if they had always been there. And then it was time to go. The man took the animal's straw and scattered it slowly over the space. He took his leave of Little John, hugging him close without concealing the pain of separation.

Then once more insulated in felt the man was carried out to the ambulance, the airport, and the world in which he is Joseph Beuys. He was not there to see the coyote's reaction. Suddenly finding himself alone without man's presence, Little John behaved for the first time like a caged and live animal, padding up and down with the true wolf's swinging gait, back and forth, sniffing, searching, whining and scenting the air with fear.

The energies and the traumas of a continent are deeply connected and move along together, affecting each other reciprocally in the fabric of history. The crossing point of energy and trauma in Europe and Eurasia has been a constant theme in Beuys's work. With *Coyote* he concentrated on an American equivalent which he feels has affected the course of the history of the United States: 'I believe I made contact with the psychological trauma point of the United States' energy constellation: the whole American trauma with the Indian, the Red Man.'

This is where the figure of the coyote appears, respected and venerated by the Red Man, despised and persecuted by the White Man: a polarity and a gulf. Somehow the trauma has to be reversed and amends made: 'You could say that a reckoning has to be made with the coyote, and only then can this trauma be lifted.'

For the Indians, the coyote was one of the most mighty of a whole range of deities. He was an image of transformation, and like the hare and the stag in Eurasian myths, he could change his state from the physical to the spiritual and vice versa at will. His sexual prowess was redoubtable, and he could even turn inside out through his anus…. Then came the White Man, and the transition in the coyote's status. He was reduced from being an admirably subversive power on a cosmic scale to what Jung in his preface to Pueblo Indian legends called 'the Archetype of the Trickster'. His ingenuity and adaptability were now interpreted as low and common cunning: he became the mean coyote. And having classed him as an antisocial menace, white society could take its legalised revenge on him and hound him like a Dillinger.

For Beuys, the persecution of the coyote is an example of man's tendency to offload his own sense of inferiority on to an object of hatred or a minority. It is this hatred and sense of inferiority that constantly drives him to exterminate the object of his hatred – the scapegoat and underdog in every society, as Europe of the pogroms and concentration camps well knows, or chooses to forget. America has many minorities, but the Indians as original inhabitants are a special case in the history of persecution, and the coyote complex continues as 'an unworked-out trauma towards the Indians themselves'.

That is why Beuys insulated himself from the rest of America: 'The manner of the meeting was important. I wanted to concentrate only on the coyote. I wanted to isolate myself, insulate myself, see nothing of America other than the coyote.'

There were other reasons too for singling out the coyote. Beuys thinks ('or at least that is what I believe I have seen') that the coyote was among the animals that came over to America with the Indians, that they were both originally natives of Eurasia and crossed the polar cap with the wanderings of prehistory. As such they would both be an adapted extension to the life of Eurasia, the vast expanse of continent crossed by East-West/West-East currents which Beuys represents with the curved energy conductor of the Eurasian Staff, a

MAINSTREAM running through his drawings, sculpture, environments and actions to link up now with Coyote in America. In this way the coyote became part of this organic cycle, joining the animals of the steppes, his close relation the Siberian wolf, and the hare, creatures which like the white horse in Beuys's 1969 action *Iphigenie/Titus Andronicus*, have the attributes of spiritual transformation.

■ The German sculptor and performance artist **Joseph Beuys** (1921-86) was one of the most influential figures in modern and contemporary art. His charismatic presence, extraordinary life and unconventional artistic style (incorporating ritualised movement and sound, and materials such as fat, felt, earth, honey, blood, and even dead animals) gained him international fame and notoriety. Beuys's innovative influence is particularly felt in the field of sculpture, whose definition he expanded to encompass performance art, vitrine cases and site-specific environments. In *Joseph Beuys: Actions, Vitrines, Environments* (2004), Mark Rosenthal argues that Beuys's self-generated persona needs to be viewed in the context of Western society in the early to mid-1960s: 'This era of peace marches, idealism, and collaborative societies was led by charismatic figures…he preached a brand of peace and love, individual responsibility and creativity, and advanced political development, with environmental concerns thrown in.'

In keeping with Beuys's redefinition of sculpture, I've included this account of one of his "actions" in this book of eco-poems, to serve as a redemptive "endpiece" to the *Dispossessing America* sequence of poems by Native American writers.

For three days in May 1974, Beuys lived with a coyote in a room of the René Block Gallery in New York. As Caroline Tisdall observed, the action began when Beuys arrived at Kennedy Airport, was packed into felt and driven by ambulance to the gallery. He did not once touch American soil. In the gallery, in a room divided by a grating, a coyote called Little John was waiting for him.

Alain Borer has described Beuys as a shepherd or psychopomp: 'If Beuys managed to cohabit with a coyote from Texas for several days in a New York gallery during what was one of his finest actions, *I Like America and America Likes Me*, wielding only his shepherd's staff and protect by a felt cloak, it was undoubtedly to mobilise deep-seated energies, to bridge the gap between vast modern cities and the natural state, to bring into opposition the knowledge of the decimated Indian population (for whom the coyote was a divine symbol of harmony) and the settlers' present-day America; but it was above all a demonstration of control. Beuys's meeting with the coyote – their territorial exchange, sharing straw and felt – opened the way: like a scout (or leading light similar to certain of his favoured materials), Beuys says at one and the same time "I'll go first" and "Follow me".' (*The Essential Joseph Beuys*, ed. Lothar Schirmer, Thames and Hudson, 1996)

Beuys's working partnership with **Caroline Tisdall** (*b.* 1945) was one of the most productive relationships between artist and amanuensis of recent times. Her books documented their wide-ranging travels for Beuys's actions, installations and lectures over two decades with both photographs and text. These included her seminal book *Joseph Beuys* (1979), which accompanied the exhibition she curated for the Guggenheim Museum in New York, and *We Go This Way* (1998), whose title refers to a phrase used by Beuys in his travels with Tisdall, suggesting a way forward through the often daunting complexity of his philosophy and art. Her observations on Beuys's art reach a poetic simplicity rarely achieved in art writing – all the more remarkable given the multi-layered nature of his work. In recent years Tisdall has been involved in the conservation of wild places, tree planting, rare breeds and the preservation of the countryside.

8. FORCE OF NATURE

These poems all capture some sense of the force of nature, beginning with a series looking at the whole planet. Other poems showing the effects of global warming and climate change on nature and on people's lives. The warnings given in these poems presage disaster in the book's final section.

ROBERT PACK
Watchers

Photographed from the moon, [the Earth] seems to be a kind of organism. It's plainly in the process of developing, like an enormous embryo. It is, for all its stupendous size and the numberless units of its life forms, coherent. Every tissue is linked for its viability to every other tissue.
        LEWIS THOMAS, The Medusa and the Snail

And so I'm linked to you
like cells within a growing embryo,
    and you are linked to me,
and we, together, linked to everyone
    as watchers from the moon can see.

The patient watchers from the moon can tell
    what currents pushing through the tide
direct vast spawnings from the swaying deep,
    and what ancestral pathways
through the buoyant air wedged wild geese keep

    inscribed within their brains
that safely store stupendous images –
    range after range of mountain snow,
    and shadowed woodland green
blue sky reflected in blue sea below.

    Although they see all parts as one,
wholly dependent and yet numberless,
    the watchers from the moon
surmise some flaw may be developing,
    some rampant cells may soon

outgrow the rest, presuming that their lives
    were all life meant. And yet
    for now, the watchers still are full
    of admiration, awe;
each tissue seems connected, viable –

    like you and me, together,
linked as one with our increasing kind,
    taking dominion everywhere,
now cultivating forests, now the seas,
    now blasting even through the air.

    The membrane of the sky
holds in accumulated oxygen,
    welcomes the visible, good light,
protects from lethal ultraviolet,
    and guards against the flight

    of random meteors that burn out,
harmless at the edge of our home space, as if
    by miracle, although
just friction from our atmosphere is what
    the watchers from the moon must know

    keeps us alive and linked
each to the other, each to the sunlit cycles
    of exhaling plants and trees.
For pollination, fruits and flowers have
    warm winds and their obliging bees;

forests renew themselves from their decay,
    aided by intermittent rain;
and plankton, drifting in the sun to breed,
    provide the herring and the whale
    with all the food they need

    to keep revolving life alive
    in this appointed place –
to which we're linked and which replenishes
    ambrosia of the air
    and animates the sea that says

> *Coherence is the law*
> *we must obey*, although the watchers see
> certain relentless cells below,
> dividing, and divided from the rest,
> forming a monster embryo.

■ **Robert Pack** (*b.* 1929) is an American poet, critic and editor. His poetry celebrates humanity's organic relationship with nature. Many of his poems are responses to his reading in physics and astronomy, exploring the mysteries of the physical universe, the human cosmos, and the archaeological, biological and mythic hints of our collective past. His many books include a compilation of his later work, *Fathering the Map* (1993), which gathers together poems of intimate experience and philosophical wonder, scientific meditations, poems that breathe the knowledge of man and woman, young and old, artist and human animal. The biologist Stephen Jay Gould said that 'precious contacts of science and poetry are now sadly rare, but Bob Pack revitalises the ancient union with incisive poems that sing with lyricism or bite with insight – but always seem to add wisdom to the scientist's epigram'. The Bread Loaf anthology *Poems for a Small Planet: Contemporary Nature Poetry* (1993), which he co-edited with Jay Parini, includes his essay 'Taking Dominion Over the Wilderness' [➤ 14].

John Elder: 'Hunting and gathering are the words with which I have described Gary Snyder's relation, as a poet, with nature, just as cultivation described the plowman-poet Berry's responses to the land. For Robert Pack, pruning is the corresponding verb of interaction with the physical world. Pack's more stationary form of groundedness may be contrasted with Snyder's wandering encounters and with Berry's active, engendering life in the soul; but his quiet shaping vision may also be connected with their art, as another attempt to participate in an order larger than the merely human.'

■ **William Stafford** (1914-93) was a much loved American poet. His contemplative poetry celebrates human virtues and universal mysteries, with nature, war, technology and Native American people as his abiding themes. In a typical Stafford poem he seeks an almost sacred place in the wilderness untouched by man, finding meaning in the quest itself and its implications. Stafford once said: 'I don't want to write good poems. I want to write *inevitable* poems – to write the things I will write, given who I am.'

WILLIAM STAFFORD

In Response to a Question

The earth says have a place, be what that place
requires; hear the sound the birds imply
and see as deep as ridges go behind
each other. (Some people call their scenery flat,
their only picture framed by what they know:
I think around them rise a riches and a loss
too equal for their chart – but absolutely tall.)

The earth says every summer have a ranch
that's minimum: one tree, one well, a landscape
that proclaims a universe – sermon
of the hills, hallelujah mountain,
highway guided by the way the world is tilted,
reduplication of mirage, flat evening:
a kind of ritual for the wavering.

The earth says where you live wear the kind
of color that your life is (gray shirt for me)
and by listening with the same bowed head that sings
draw all into one song, join
the sparrow on the lawn, and row that easy
way, the rage without met by the wings
within that guide you anywhere the wind blows.

Listening, I think that's what the earth says.

WILLIAM STAFFORD

Gaea

Our earth, the whole of it, is alive, they say,
like a plant or animal, each part in touch
and reaching so that the whole survives.
In such a life, in even a selfish act,
you contribute, and the world says, 'Thanks, goodbye.'
So, often, while the barn braces itself
to hear the wind I stand quietly
all alone and read the hay.

Or, sometimes, not to know, but to spend
the time learning, I make the guitar say
a certain tone again and again
till it all adds up and becomes
what God intended from my part
of the world today. Then I pause,
and what follows that sound I make is music.

Such times, I almost know what the world
keeps telling me. It's the birds and a certain
other hum just beyond. It's the sound
the sun makes when it finds gold.
Everyone, stop whatever you're doing
and listen.

ARTHUR SZE
from Archipelago

1

I walk along the length of a stone-and-gravel garden
and feel without looking how the fifteen stones
appear and disappear. I had not expected the space
to be defined by a wall made of clay boiled in oil
nor to see above a series of green cryptomeria
pungent in spring. I stop and feel an April snow
begin to fall on the stones and raked gravel and see
how distance turns into abstraction desire and ordinary
things: from the air, corn and soybean fields are
a series of horizontal and vertical stripes of pure color:
viridian, yellow ocher, raw sienna, sap green. I
remember in Istanbul at the entrance to the Blue Mosque
two parallel, extended lines of shoes humming at
the threshold of paradise. Up close, it's hard to know
if the rattle of milk bottles will become a topaz,
or a moment of throttled anger tripe that is
chewed and chewed. In the distance, I feel drumming
and chanting and see a line of Pueblo women dancing
with black-on-black jars on their heads; they lift
the jars high then start to throw them to the ground.

ARTHUR SZE
from **The Leaves of a Dream Are
the Leaves of an Onion**

2

A Galápagos turtle has nothing to do
with the world of the neutrino.
The ecology of the Galápagos Islands
has nothing to do with a pair of scissors.
The cactus by the window has nothing to do
with the invention of the wheel.
The invention of the telescope
has nothing to do with a red jaguar.
No. The invention of the scissors
has everything to do with the invention of the telescope.
A map of the world has everything to do
with the cactus by the window.
The world of the quark has everything to do
with a jaguar circling in the night.
The man who sacrifices himself and throws a Molotov
cocktail at a tank has everything to do
with a sunflower that bends to the light.

6

Crush an apple, crush a possibility.
No single method can describe the world;
therein is the pleasure
of chaos, of leaps in the mind.
A man slumped over a desk in an attorney's office
is a parrot fish caught in a seaweed mass.
A man who turns to the conversation in a bar
is a bluefish hooked on a cigarette.
Is the desire and collapse of desire in an unemployed carpenter
the instinct of salmon to leap upstream?
The smell of eucalyptus can be incorporated
into a theory of aggression.
The pattern of interference in a hologram
replicates the apple, knife, horsetails on the table,
but misses the sense of chaos, distorts
in its singular view. Then
touch, shine, dance, sing, be, becoming, be.

■ **Arthur Sze** (*b.* 1950) is a second generation Chinese American poet, born in New York, who lives in New Mexico. Through a startling juxtaposition of images and ideas, Sze reveals the interconnectedness of our world. Familiar images of nature are mingled in his poems with those of metaphysics and quantum physics.

Zhou Xiaojing: 'By titling his sixth volume of poetry *The Redshifting Web*, Sze articulates a worldview that underlies his poetics. The term *redshift* describes the astronomical phenomenon that occurs when stars are moving away from us and the light emitted from them shifts toward the red end of the spectrum. In fact scientists have discovered that most galaxies appear to be "redshifted"; that is, nearly all galaxies are moving away from us and from one another. This indicates that the universe is not static; it is expanding. The distance among galaxies are increasing all the time [see Stephen Hawking, *A Brief History of Time*]. Sze uses the term *redshift* to suggest his sense of the constant motion, change, and transformation of all things in the universe and in our everyday experience. At the same time, all things in the universe and their constant changes, including those in the human world, are intricately connected, interacting with one another and mutually influencing each other's transformation. This concept of the world, based on the quantum principle, parallels the basic philosophy of Daoism and the Native American view of the universe. Sze is familiar with all three frames of reference – natural sciences, Chinese culture, and Native American culture, and he absorbs them in his poetics, which might be called "ecopoetics".'

■ **P.K. Page** (*b.* 1916) is a Canadian poet, fiction writer and visual artist as well as a campaigner for peace and ecological responsibility. Born in Swanage, Dorset, she moved with her family to Canada in 1919 and grew up on the prairies. She lived in Brazil, Mexico and Australia at various times with her diplomat husband, Arthur Irwin. Over six decades she has made a major contribution to Canadian modernism with her many books, including, most recently, *Planet Earth: Poems Selected and New* (2002). Her poetry has been admired for its brilliant imagery, technical virtuosity, metaphysical questioning and intuition of an unseen order beyond the senses, and for being 'startling, authoritative, and anti-sentimental, able to bear cool as well as passionate gazing at our own species' (Griffin Prize citation).

Eric Ormsby: 'She is the shrewdest of observers but at the same time she celebrates life, low and high, in all its manifestations.'

P.K. PAGE

Planet Earth

It has to be spread out, the skin of this planet,
has to be ironed, the sea in its whiteness;
and the hands keep on moving,
smoothing the holy surfaces.
PABLO NERUDA
'In Praise of Ironing'

It has to be loved the way a laundress loves her linens,
the way she moves her hands caressing the fine muslins
knowing their warp and woof,
like a lover coaxing, or a mother praising.
It has to be loved as it it were embroidered
with flowers and birds and two joined hearts upon it.
It has to be stretched and stroked.
It has to be celebrated.
O this great beloved world and all the creatures in it.
It has to be spread out, the skin of this planet.

The trees must be washed, and the grasses and mosses.
They have to be polished as if made of green brass.
The rivers and little streams with their hidden cresses
and pale-coloured pebbles
and their fool's gold
must be washed and starched or shined into brightness,
the sheets of lake water
smoothed with the hand
and the foam of the oceans pressed into neatness.
It has to be ironed, the sea in its whiteness

and pleated and goffered, the flower-blue sea
the protean, wine-dark, grey, green, sea
with its metres of satin and bolts of brocade.
And sky – such an O! overhead – night and day
must be burnished and rubbed
by hands that are loving
so the blue blazons forth
and the stars keep on shining
within and above
and the hands keep on moving.

It has to be made bright, the skin of this planet
till it shines in the sun like gold leaf.
Archangels then will attend to its metals
and polish the rods of its rain.
Seraphim will stop singing hosannas
to shower it with blessings and blisses and praises
and, newly in love,
we must draw it and paint it
our pencils and brushes and loving caresses
smoothing the holy surfaces.

DENISE LEVERTOV
It Should Be Visible

If from Space not only sapphire continents,
swirling oceans, were visible, but the wars –
like bonfires, wildfires, forest conflagrations,
flame and smoky smoulder – the Earth would seem
a bitter pomander ball bristling with poison cloves.
And each war fuelled with weapons: it should be visible
that great sums of money have been exchanged,
great profits made, workers gainfully employed
to construct destruction, national economies distorted
so that these fires, these wars, may burn
and consume the joy of this one planet
which, seen from outside its transparent tender shell,
is so serene, so fortunate, with its water, air
and myriad forms of 'life that wants to live'.
It should be visible that this bluegreen globe
suffers a canker which is devouring it.

DENISE LEVERTOV
Urgent Whisper

It could be the râle of Earth's slight chest,
her lungs scarred from old fevers, and she asleep –

but there's no news from the seismographs,
the crystal pendant
hangs plumb from its hook;

and yet at times (and I whisper because
it's a fearful thing I tell you)
a subtle shudder has passed
from outside me into my bones,

up from the ground beneath me,
beneath this house, beneath
the road and the trees:

a silent delicate trembling no one has spoken of
as if a beaten child or a captive animal
lay waiting the next blow.

It comes from the Earth herself, I tell you
Earth herself. I whisper
because I'm ashamed. Isn't the earth our mother?
Isn't it we who've brought
this terror upon her?

MAURICE RIORDAN
The Check-up – June 1992

God, coming back from his tour of the galaxies,
decides to drop in on Earth. At first
he cannot pinpoint its whereabouts. Then he remembers
the exquisite colouring. So much smaller, it looks,
now he's no longer involved with the details.
Still it's a beaut, and in its prime – good,
he reckons, for a few more billion years.
He turns it round, to admire the elegance
of design. And once again, now justly proud
of the balance, patience, sense of humour,
the fluidity and tact of the execution.

He gives it the routine check-up. Temperature?
A little high, though nothing to worry over.
Some evidence of polar wobble but self-correcting.
He graphs the trajectories of the 70-odd asteroids
that will, from time to time, cut across its path.
Briskly, he redoes those ticker-tape sums,
while popping questions about geological ache,
species count, toxin distribution, who's President.
He does a comprehensive, in-depth brain scan –
but not the Veep's, ha-ha. Finds all is in order,
nothing untoward or original. Normal development.

He folds his instruments, decides on a friendly chat.
He loves to catch up on the gossip: the current craze
in particle theory or installation sculpture,
what Ms Bordes is up to these days, the latest in
bar-slang, cyberpunk, Kerry jokes. That sort of stuff.
It is then he happens on a detail, something slight
– but unprecedented, unforeseen – that wipes the smile
clean from his face. He flushes with impotent rage,
for there is nothing, nothing at all that he can do.
Sweet Jesus, he seems to mutter, as he hurries
away, looking suddenly old and frail.

MICHAEL SYMMONS ROBERTS
Pelt

I found the world's pelt
nailed to the picture-rail
of a box-room in a cheap hotel.

So that's why rivers dry to scabs,
that's why the grass weeps every dawn,
that's why the wind feels raw:

the earth's an open wound,
and here, its skin hangs
like a trophy, atrophied beyond all

taxidermy, shrunk into a hearth rug.
Who fleeced it?
No record in the guest-book.

No one paid, just pocketed the blade
and walked, leaving the bed
untouched, TV pleasing itself.

Maybe there was no knife.
Maybe the world shrugs off a hide
each year to grow a fresh one.

That pelt was thick as reindeer,
so black it flashed with blue.
I tried it on, of course, but no.

■ **Denise Levertov** ➤ 157.

■ **Maurice Riordan** (*b.* 1953) is an Irish poet, editor and lecturer who lives in London. His books include three collections, and two anthologies, *A Quark for Mister Mark: 101 Poems about Science* (with science journalist Jon Turney, 2000) and *Wild Reckoning* (with John Burnside, 2004) [➤ 18], a selection of ecological poems marking the 40th anniversary of the publication of Rachel Carson's *Silent Spring*, the book that helped launch the environmental movement. Often concerned with instability and flux, his poems are closely observed narratives seemingly grounded in the familiar which take unexpected turns. Old and new coexist in his poetry, which mixes childhood tales of rural Ireland and the ancient wisdom of signs and wonders with the questioning science of the quantum age.

■ **Michael Symmons Roberts** (*b.* 1963) is an English poet, dramatist, broadcaster, novelist and librettist. He is a lyric and dramatic poet with philosophical and metaphysical concerns whose writing roots out the miraculous in the everyday. In his adolescent years his daily experience was living a mile from the missile base and peace camp at Greenham Common in Berkshire, the subject of his third collection, *Burning Babylon* (2001). Science, medicine and the human body – its organs, its urges, its existence now and after death – are recurrent themes in his work, notably in *Corpus* (2004).

SIMON RAE
One World Down the Drain

*One World Week focused on global warming, with a UN
report promising the direst consequences from the greenhouse
effect. However, in the clash between long-term and short-
term interests, the future looks likely to be the loser.*
[26 May 1990]

It's goodbye half of Egypt,
   The Maldives take a dive,
And not much more of Bangladesh
   Looks likely to survive.

Europe too will alter,
   Book flights to Venice now.
It won't be there in fifty years –
   Great City. Pity. Ciao.

     But we don't care,
     We won't be there,
       Our acid greenhouse party
     Will carry on
     Until we're gone,
       So bad luck Kiribati

– And all the other atolls
   That sink beneath the seas,
The millions who will suffer from
   Drought, famine and disease.

The weather map is changing
   But what are we to do?
Let's have another conference on
   The ills of CO_2.

     Oh global warming
     's habit-forming,
       But do not rock the boat;
     We're doing our best,
     Although we're pressed
       (The future has no vote).

BENJAMIN ZEPHANIAH
Me green poem

Everybody talking bout protecting de planet
As if we jus cum on it
It hard fe understan it.
Everybody talking bout de green revolution
Protecting de children an fighting pollution
But check – capitalism an greed as caused us to need
Clean air to breathe, Yes
When yu get hot under de collar
Yu suddenly discover dat yu going Green all over.
Fe years
Yu hav been fighting wars an destroying de scene
An now dat yu dying
Yu start turn Green

A few years ago if yu wanted peace yu would hav fe mek
      a demonstration.
Yu were called a traitor, a Russian infiltrator,
De scourge of de nation
A few years ago if yu said yu were Green
Yu were really seen as Red.
Yes a few years ago yu were seen as a weirdo
If yu were to eat brown bread.
Now yu don't hav to be clever fe know bout salmonella
An dere are many reasons fe diet like a vegan.
Now it is official, don't eat too artificial
When yu told yu hav no future, try some acupuncture.
Fe live long, get wise an try some exercise.
Feget de Harp, stay sharp
An tek care of yu heart
To go jogging is belonging
Walk instead of driving
Now dat yu are dying, start tinking of surviving.
Yu start tinking of surviving now dat yu are dying
Remember old time saying: Beware of what yu spraying
Now is de time fe panic
So let's go eat organic
Yu fridge will burn creation
Dis is so-called progression

Fe years
Yu hav been fighting wars an destroying de scene
An now dat yu dying
Yu start turn Green

Many singer-songwriters hav it as a topic
De rainforests, dose hungry people
'Daddy we must stop it.'
De ozone layer's fading
I mus make an LP
I'll get de credit an I'll give de cash to charity
I mus be really honest,
An I speak personally,
I don't hav dat much money fe give to charity,
My people were rich but robbed
An we were healthy
So I don't know bout yu, but me, I plead Not Guilty.
So now yu hav a house
World music gets yu high
An now yu exercising hard cause yu don't want to die
An yu got loadsamoney but yu don't need nu cash
Cause yu got loadsa credit cards an yu so proud a dat
De greenhouse effect meks de world hotta
If yu hav loadsamoney really it nu matta.
Nobody knows what's happening to de weather
An all of a sudden we're told to pull together
Pull together?
Pull together
An recycle ya paper.
De government said if yu don't yu will regret it later.
Dem used to sey dat Green was soft
Don't worry bout de atmosphere
An now a scientist has said,
'Oh damn, we're going to disappear.'
Fe years
Yu hav been fighting wars an destroying de scene
An now dat yu dying
Yu start turn Green

Now when it come to wars, governments are funny
Lives are secondary, first is bloody money
Troops out if it costs too much, troops in if it pays

An in de English dictionary what is war anyway?
Angola ....dat's war
Afghanistan...........................dat's war
Tibet.....................................dat's war
Far-off people hav dem,
Ethiopia ....dat's war
El Salvador ....dat's war
Bolivia..................................dat's war
Feel sorry fe de children,
Lebanon...............................dat's war
Gaza......................................dat's war
Mozambique ....dat's war
An someone's got to stop dem,
Korea ....dat's war
Haiti ....dat's war
Northern Ireland...........................dat's something else
Now dat is just a problem.
Still we don't hav nu constitution
An so-called progress breeds pollution
Yu can buy a share in de illusion
Or yu can gu to school an study de Green solution,
Fe years Green tings hav been pushed aside
Now we're going fast on a downward slide
Who's going Green on de sly?
Is dat kinda business upset I
Fe years
Yu hav been fighting wars an destroying de scene
An now dat yu dying
Yu start turn Green

Everybody talking bout protecting de planet
As if we just cum on it
It hard fe understan it.
Everybody talking bout de Green revolution
Protecting de children an fighting pollution.
But check
Humans hav been taking an not giving
An now de boat is sinking yu stop an start tinking,
Now we see dere is a change of tone
De problem's cumming home
De world's a danger zone

Fe years
Yu hav been fighting wars an destroying de scene
An now dat yu dying
Yu start turn Green
Fe years yu hav been getting technological
But ignoring de facts
An now yu so technical
But yu cannot relax,

Blue	will	turn	Green
When	votes	are	seen

An yu will get   lead-free   gasoline

■ **Benjamin Zephaniah** (*b.* 1958) is an oral poet, novelist, playwright, children's writer and reggae artist. Born in Birmingham, he grew up in Jamaica and in Handsworth, where he was sent to an approved school for being uncontrollable, rebellious and 'a born failure', ending up in jail for burglary. After prison he turned from crime to music and poetry. In 1989 he was nominated for Oxford Professor of Poetry. Best known for his performance poetry with a political edge for adults and his poetry with attitude for children, he has his own rap/reggae band. He has produced many recordings, and his numerous books include the collections *City Psalms* (1992), *Propa Propaganda* (1996) and *Too Black Too Strong* (2001); his poetry books for children, *Talking Turkeys* (1994), *Funky Chickens* (1996) and *Wicked World* (2000); and his novels for teenagers, *Face* (1999), *Refugee Boy* (2001) and *Gangsta Rap* (2004).

■ **Simon Rae** (*b.* 1952) is an English poet, broadcaster, biographer, playwright, cricketer and cricket writer. For several years during the 1990s he wrote a topical satirical poem every week for the *Guardian* newspaper, which yielded two collections, *Soft Targets* (1991) and *Rapid Response* (1997). His collection *Gift Horses* (2006) explores the dark side of human nature. He also has edited several anthologies, including *The Orange Dove of Fiji: Poems for the Worldwide Fund for Nature* (1989) and *News That Stays News: The 20th Century in Poems* (1999).

JOHN POWELL WARD
Hurry Up Please, It's Time

They saved the rain in butts; took pulp and jars
To the new recycling plant; they halved
Their electricity and bore the single bulb
Of a furtive lamp; they adapted the car
To clean-fuel specification. They grew carrots
And turned the Sunday papers into compost.
They walked or bicycled instead of drove;
They put on heavy sweaters and thick
Socks, and thus cut down their central heating.
They considered the lilies, how they grow,
And read their secondhand books, still wondering
If even Solomon's wisdom could suffice
To save the human venture that began
In Eden; its art, its building and its law.

But I can't tell you how this is all worked out;
Its hour had not yet come; only
The unaborted children who survive
Will know of that, staring at their hands
Like monkeys, asking what to do next.

FLEUR ADCOCK
The Greenhouse Effect

As if the week had begun anew –
and certainly something has:
this fizzing light on the harbour, these
radiant bars and beams and planes
slashed through flaps and swags of sunny vapour.
Aerial water, submarine light:
Wellington's gone Wordsworthian again.
He'd have admired it –
admired but not approved, if he'd heard
about fossil fuels, and aerosols,
and what we've done to the ozone layer,
or read in last night's *Evening Post*

that 'November ended the warmest spring
since meteorological records began'.
Not that it wasn't wet:
moisture's a part of it.

As for this morning (Friday),
men in shorts raking the beach
have constructed little cairns of evidence:
driftwood, paper, plastic cups.
A seagull's gutting a bin.
The rain was more recent than I thought:
I'm sitting on a wet bench.
Just for now, I can live with it.

CAITRÍONA O'REILLY
Bempton Cliffs

The blank-faced gun emplacements
    stare out to sea.
Nothing's changed since the war.
    It is land for the grasshopper
and lark, then suddenly air
    and the sea's sharp glance.
The first time we almost missed them,
    the wind carried
away their voices, that football-roar
    from the terraces.
Then an updraft like a wave's explosion
    brought guano-stink,
and with it rumours of a high-rise civilisation:
    so garrulous, so peeping-busy.
Down where the sea heaves
    like the quilt of a restless sleeper,
the feeders are. Industry will not cease
    for questioning – the heating seas,
the sand-eels' migration –
    but fewer each year
from their chalky sockets
    those swart eyes stare.

■ **John Powell Ward** (*b.* 1937) is an Anglo-Welsh poet and critic. His poetry covers themes ranging from faith and history to the human peril to the natural world. He taught at the University of Wales, Swansea, where he is now an Honorary Research Fellow. As well as critical books on Wordsworth, Hardy and R.S. Thomas, he has written three studies of poetry in relation to sociology, Englishness, and the alphabet. He edited *Poetry Wales* from 1975 to 1980 and has published seven books of poetry, including *Selected and New Poems* (2004).

■ **Fleur Adcock** ➤ 52.

■ **Caitríona O'Reilly** ➤ 144.

■ **Peter Redgrove** (1932-2003) was a prolific English poet, novelist and dramatist. A Jungian psychologist, he drew upon his scientific training to present, in all his varied work, an all-encompassing theory of nature and creation. Redgrove called himself 'the scientist of the strange', and believed his relations to the natural world and to his own unconscious were transformed by the instruction and revelations of the 'Black Goddess'. He argued that humanity had repressed its animal awareness of invisible natural forces, and that 'our approach to reality, our sense of reality, cannot assume that the text of nature, the book of life, is a cryptogram concealing just a single meaning. Rather it is an expanding riddle of a multiplicity of resonating images.' His kaleidoscopic vision of nature is evident in the all-embracing range of his work: he wrote ecstatically about clouds, storms, rain, bees, oceans, witches, Cornwall, clothes, magic and sex. His numerous books include two psycho-socio-sexual studies, his collaboration with Penelope Shuttle, *The Wise Wound* (1978), and *The Black Goddess and the Sixth Sense* (1987). [Other poem ➤ 157]

■ **Patience Agbabi** (*b.* 1965) is a poet, performer and workshop facilitator. Born in London to Nigerian parents, she studied at Pembroke College, Oxford. Her collections include *R.A.W.* (1995) and *Transformatrix* (2000). Often drawing on the myths and realities of contemporary life, she writes in the voices of many different women and from locations around the globe. She has described herself as 'bi-cultural' and issues of racial, sexual and gender identity are important in her work. Her sequence *Indian Summer* [➤ 200-02] was commissioned by *Poet in the City* and Lloyd's as part of the *Trees in the City* collaboration, designed to raise awareness of the need for action on climate change, and is reproduced by kind permission of *Poet in the City* and Lloyd's.

PETER REDGROVE
On the Patio

A wineglass overflowing with thunderwater
Stands out on the drumming steel table

Among the outcries of the downpour
Feathering chairs and rethundering on the awnings.

How the pellets of water shooting miles
Flying into the glass of swirl, and slop

Over the table's scales of rust
Shining like chained sores,

Because the rain eats everything except the glass
Of spinning water that is clear down here

But purple with rumbling depths above, and this cloud
Is transferring its might into a glass

In which thunder and lightning come to rest,
The cloud crushed into a glass.

Suddenly I dart out into the patio,
Snatch the bright glass up and drain it,

Bang it back down on the thundery steel table for a refill.

TED HUGHES
October Dawn

October is marigold, and yet
A glass half full of wine left out

To the dark heaven all night, by dawn
Has dreamed a premonition

Of ice across its eye as if
The ice-age had begun its heave.

The lawn overtrodden and strewn
From the night before, and the whistling green

Shrubbery are doomed. Ice
Has got its spearhead into place.

First a skin, delicately here
Restraining a ripple from the air;

Soon plate and rivet on pond and brook;
Then tons of chain and massive lock

To hold rivers. Then, sound by sight
Will Mammoth and Sabre-tooth celebrate

Reunion while a fist of cold
Squeezes the fire at the core of the world,

Squeezes the fire at the core of the heart,
And now it is about to start.

PATIENCE AGBABI
Indian Summer

Prologue

Ninety days hath September
since October and November
were deleted one by one
excepting one fine day alone
when the sky is cold and clear
enough to deconstruct the year.

October Dawn Revisited
(after Ted Hughes)

That glass half full of wine left out
all night – a fine chilled muscadet

with a long finish – and the print
of a lipstick longing, has of late

become half empty; and that hint
of stalagmite and stalactite,

that ice-age vision with the scent
of marigold and summer fruit,

though freeze-framed as a work of art,
melted to drizzle. A glass of light

rain not wine, grey not white,
filling to meniscus height,

is mercury rising thick as hate
by Centigrade, by Fahrenheit,

till overflowing. Now forked and sheet
battle the air this day, this date

and the wine glass melting like a cut
glass tulip drowning in the heat

with twisted stem, and yellow tint
has scorched the lips that worshipped it.

Tsunami

Chennai, India

We do not have a word
for it in Tamil, she said.

When we saw the horizon rise like a god
from the sea bed

we never believed.
The beach, the trees, the beach huts, drowned.

Nobody died
here but south of here whole villages buried,
the beach a burial ground.

The children they found
were not full of water but of sand.

I'm afraid

of the two kinds of disaster in this world:
the natural ones we can't avoid,
the acts of God

and the man-made.

$ECO_2nomics$

*The average Briton produces 126 times more carbon
dioxide than someone living in Nepal.*
GUARDIAN, 2 December 2006

I read about freak floods in Nepal
as my London-Delhi long-haul

airbus cuts a tunnel through the air.
0°C. *It was like a wall of water.*

-1… -3, up here it's Winter;
down there, December, Printemps

is early on the banks of the Seine.
It means that crop yields are going down.

The plane – it sounded like 10,000 lorries –
makes a constant burr, a snowdrop buries

its name, beats its estimated time of arrival.
Then all the land started moving like a river.

10,000 metres above sea level
the plane heaves like a tidal wave.

37°C

We made him out of love
and like our love he grew

inside me where I loved
and fed and watered him
until he grew too big
for love to keep him in
and so I let him out
and loved him skin to skin

and yet I was afraid
each breath would injure him,
that air was full of taint,
that he would sink not swim,
afraid each peekaboo
of sun would burn his skin,
that it was not enough
to give the earth to him.

Lullaby for a Worker Bee

Creature of black and luminous yellow,
of starless night and sunsoaked day,
why do you wish to be the belle
of the ball when skies are wintery grey?

Your song is a lullaby of buzzing
a busy buzzy bass so deep
when I hear your constant mellow zzzzzz
it sounds to me like the sound of sleep.

The lavender that fed you nectar,
scented my silk from the clothes moth's bite
has faded now from Summer's neglect
and waits for Spring to set it alight.

Sunflower, wild thyme, lavender honey
that glosses the lips and sweetens the tongue
is food for sweet sweet dreams to sun
your slumber when my song is sung.

Creature of sun, all soft and furry,
of gossamer wing and Midas touch,
may Nature, your sweet manager,
grant you the night you desire so much.

I cannot sleep for the air is too balmy
Autumn is Summer and Winter is Spring.
I can only sleep if I do you harm,
I can only sleep if I lose my sting.

OLIVER BERNARD
West Harling

Under the lime trees' yellow leaves and damp
October sunlight, out of the wind and warm,
Nature's unnaturally kind this autumn.
But four young people take me for a walk
To a deserted church in good repair,
And one says weather will be like this now:
Warm and not as it used to be, with storms
And droughts that last for months, and the landscape
    changing.
And life being rarer and perhaps confined
To unlikely regions, soon not possible.

We visit the churchyard and stare in through glass
Panes at the silence of the lectern, pews
Gathering fine dust. Possibly even bats
Don't find a toehold in this shut up place
Restored and then used once a year since then.
Norfolk's a dream of how things might have been,
A different proposition from the life
We all return to, Monday. Something narrow
About the present moment if we ever
Managed to live in it and nowhere else.

■ **Oliver Bernard** (*b.* 1925) is an English poet and translator of French poetry who has lived in Norfolk for 30 years. He has worked as an advisory teacher of drama, and has been a director of the Speak a Poem Competition since its inception. His books include translations of Rimbaud and Apollinaire, an autobiography, *Getting Over It* (1992), and a selection of poems from the past twenty years, *Verse &c* (2001).

JEAN 'BINTA' BREEZE
earth cries

she doesn't cry for water
she runs rivers deep
she doesn't cry for food
she has suckled trees
she doesn't cry for clothing
she weaves all that she wears
she doesn't cry for shelter
she grows thatch everywhere
she doesn't cry for children
she's got more than she can bear
she doesn't cry for heaven
she knows it's always there
you don't know why she's crying
when she's got everything
how could you know she's crying
for just one humane being

TED HUGHES
A Wind Flashes the Grass

Leaves pour blackly across.
We cling to the earth, with glistening eyes, pierced
    afresh by the tree's cry.

And the incomprehensible cry
From the boughs, in the wind
Sets us listening for below words,
Meanings that will not part from the rock.

The trees thunder in unison, on a gloomy afternoon,
And the ploughman grows anxious, his tractor
    becomes terrible,
As his memory litters downwind
And the shadow of his bones tosses darkly on the air.

The trees suddenly storm to a stop, in a hush
Against the sky, where the field ends.
They crowed there shuddering
And wary, like horses bewildered by lightning.

The stirring of their twigs against the dark, travelling sky
Is the oracle of the earth.

They too are afraid they too are momentary
Streams rivers of shadow.

■ **Ted Hughes** ➤ 66.

■ **Jean 'Binta' Breeze** (*b.* 1956) is a popular Jamaican poet, actress and storyteller who writes and performs both in standard English and Jamaican patois. She grew up in a small village with her peasant farmer grandparents, moved to Kingston to study at the Jamaica School of Drama in 1978, and since 1985 has divided her time between Britain and Jamaica. She first achieved international recognition as a dub poet writing in a poetic style that fuses reggae music with the spoken word. Much of her poetry explores personal, social and political relationships as well as grappling with the everyday experiences of ordinary Jamaican women.

■ **John Burnside** (*b.* 1955) is a Scottish writer of radiant, meditative poetry and dark, brooding fiction. His books include several collections of poetry and one of short stories, several novels, and a memoir, *A Lie About My Father* (2006). He co-edited with Maurice Riordan the anthology *Wild Reckoning* (2004) [➤ 18], a selection of ecological poems marking the 40th anniversary of the publication of Rachel Carson's *Silent Spring*, the book that helped launch the environmental movement. In his essay in *Strong Words* (2000), Burnside wrote: 'Our response to the world is essentially one of wonder, confronting the mysterious with a sense, not of being small, or insignificant, but of being part of a rich and complex narrative.'
    His sequence *Certain Weather* [➤ 204-07] was commissioned by *Poet in the City* and Lloyd's as part of the *Trees in the City* collaboration, designed to raise awareness of the need for action on climate change, and is reproduced by kind permission of *Poet in the City* and Lloyd's. [Other poem ➤ 224]

JOHN BURNSIDE
Certain Weather

The wind bloweth where it listeth, and thou hearest the sound thereof, but canst not tell whence it cometh, and whither it goeth.
JOHN 3:8

Climate is what we expect, weather is what we get.
MARK TWAIN

I *Livestock*

A weather we cannot describe,
the terminology disused, the beauty of it

alien, crossbills and pine woods
forgotten
        and the softness underfoot

deepening, year after year,
while the maps are redrawn:

a household of wind
and water, the marsh-gods

walking in their sleep, the chapels
decked out in rot;

when the age of the nameable
ends
        and the future begins,

our beasts will no longer
answer to us, when summoned,

standing in huddles, unbending
and dumb as the stones,

remembering themselves
in light and warmth,

the sway of a summer, the plum orchard
tidal with bees.

II *The Little Crake*

Encountered, though rarely seen,
a voice in the shadows, a rumour, delectable
phantom,

  one, caught alive near Beeding chalkpit, 1845

noisy, 'with a yapping *ku-a* call',
yet secretive, they wade into the mud,
the blue-grey face thrust forward:
                          a fistful of pulse
and feathers, the blood-warmed bones
precise as forgetting

  hunted out of a brick pit at Pevensey by a dog
  and caught alive in a hat hurled at it haphazardly on
  14 April, 1869

but these will be first to go
in the changing weather

  killed near Hastings on or about 16 April, 1876

the reed-beds flooded or burned; the flight-lines gone

  one, killed near Worthing on 22 October, 1894

and always so close to an absence that no one will know,
a gap in the world bleeding through, when the song is
    gone,
that sense of something missed, that nameless space,

  caught by a dog at Whatlington, near Battle on 30 June,
  1895

then records; pictures; folk-tales; memories:

  one female, at the Fisherman's Institute on Eastbourne
    front:
  mistaken for a mouse, was hit by a thrown boot 3 March,
  1913

spectres and emblems, a cry in the blackness of noon

an extremely confiding female present in the lower
  Cuckmere Valley,
in a ditch just south of Exceat, from at least 6 to 16
  March, 1985

the pull of an absence, intact, under brickwork and ashes

III *Power cut*

After a week of storms, when the house turns to water,
we fall back on what we know best: the childhood spells,

street-names and rivers; rare objects fashioned from glass
and copper:
        hand tools;
              borrowed fountain pens;

or, crossing the lines of a dream,
on a cold afternoon,

the animals from field guides, fed and bright,
as if they had wandered home

from a world without shadows.
This morning, we wake in the dark:

no power yet; only a candle guttering out
and the last of the coal in the fireplace, haw-red and damp

as it dwindles and fails.
                  A new year, and everything blurs,
as if we were crossing the fields in a fall of snow

that never ends
          and never quite arrives:
the present, the here and now, the kingdom of heaven

provisional, still;
        still
offered up to change:

mist on the windows, fog in a basket of laundry,
traces of damp on the knives in the kitchen drawer,

molecular, mineral,
one thing becoming another,

ash in the grate, spent beeswax, the dreams we forget
but carry all day in our hands

and the signs we recover,
the colours of rainfall, the blood-red and ash-pink I hear

in the sound of your voice, or taste
in the blur of my mouth

when I go out into the wind
for a bucket of kindling

and stand in the eye of it, wiped out, then finding a shape
that works, for the moment, unfinished and bleeding away

through fence-posts and ditches
              and out, along hedgerows and phone lines,
to streetlamps, dormers, foyers, office blocks.

IV *Drought*

Sooner or later it comes,
the impossible world:
a memory of snowfall in the trees,
rock pools and harp seals
lost in a glass of water,

and, sometimes,
on the way from *A* to *B*,
a house like the house
we abandoned, catching the last
of the daylight, as the town prepares itself

for evening:
street trees doused and put away,
the light turning gold
in bookshops
and fishmongers' windows.

Nobody here
is prepared to discuss the weather,
but sometimes an elderly man
will stop what he's doing
to talk about birds, or moths,

or how the snow
wavered between the houses
all day long,
before the power-cuts
and long-term shortages,

his body haunted, still,
by the sound of the wind
on the night he remembered himself
and came to a stop
at the near edge of ruin,

turning away, not forgetting, but clearing his head
to listen to the gap, far in the sky
– the tiniest gap in an index of movement and stars –
where something we cannot imagine
runs on through the silence.

V *The Afterlife of Animals*

Buried in silt, or concrete; washed away;
incinerated; drowned; or dead from thirst;

they will also decay
in the mind, till they come to resemble

those captive beasts
in medieval paintings, wolfhound and monkey

gracing the chambered decline
of merchants and popes;

and, far in the life to come,
through quicklime, or ice,

we'll either forget,
or remember without knowing why,

the songs of all the birds that ever
nested in these walls: the shifting

dialects of mistle-thrush and wren,
the sparrows in the hedge, the herring gulls,

and out along the fence, the bright ascent
of skylarks, faded now

to static, in a tuft
of scalded grass

– and this is the story we'll tell,
of our childhood journeys:

rain on the windscreen, turning to sleet
at evening;

the one birch set in its own
cold flame, by the road to the quarry;

then, out on the road,
a flicker across the headlights,

some animal from childhood stealing out
to where the snow began, in light and stillness;

how, all the way home,
they kept coming, within and about us,

bodies and movement
hurrying out from the dark

to draw us in, becoming
then losing the way

from one shape to another: nuzzles
and murmurs

folded in the drift
from dust to skin;

from knowledge to hearsay;
from language to mother tongue.

VI *The Arctic Poppy*

– sun watcher, tracking the light
in perpetual motion,

the stem engineered
for infinitesimal movements

repeated, day after day,
in unceasing light,

nourished, observant,
drinking its fill of sky

till the seed breaks
and darkness returns.

We scarcely begin to know
what remains to be known

– not the mechanics,
but how this could all come about

by happenstance;
                    though
happenstance it is,

or grace,
we might have said,

in its other guise:
how everything turns

to the sun,
how we sometimes mistake

the wind
for a god, that *bloweth where it listeth*,

and how, when it falls,
no matter when or why,

the rain is always
other than it seems,

mercy, perhaps,
or something akin

to redemption
                    and redemption
nothing more

than a form we have yet to learn
or the secret law

that unifies us all: godless,
divine,

keeping our place
in the story, repairing the fabric's

perpetual motion:
water and light and the mind

that turns with the poppy,
unnameable
                    selfless
observer.

HELEN DUNMORE
Ice coming
(after Doris Lessing)

First, the retreat of bees
lifting, heavy with the final
pollen of gorse and garden,
lugging the weight of it, like coal sacks
heaped on lorry-backs
in the ice-cream clamour of August.

The retreat of bees, lifting
all at once from city gardens –
suddenly the roses are scentless
as cold probes like a tongue,
crawling through the warm crevices

of Kew and Stepney. The ice comes
slowly, slowly, not to frighten anyone.

Not to frighten anyone. But the Snowdon
valleys are muffled with avalanche,
the Thames freezes, the Promenade des Anglais
clinks with a thousand icicles, where palms
died in a night, and the sea
of Greece stares back like stone
at the ice-Gorgon, white as a sheet.

Ice squeaks and whines. Snow slams
like a door miles off, exploding a forest
to shards and matchsticks. The glacier
is strangest, grey as an elephant,
too big to be heard. Big-foot, Gorgon –
a little mythology
rustles before it is stilled.

So it goes. Ivy, mahonia, viburnum
lift their fossilised flowers
under six feet of ice, for the bees
that are gone. As for being human
it worked once, but for now
and the foreseeable future
the conditions are wrong.

G.F. DUTTON
Bulletin

The glaciers have come down
dead white
at the end of the street. All over town

cold mist of their breath,
and along gutters
water runs

freezing beneath. But
the machines are out, lined up,
beautiful, their great lights

tossing back darkness. And the engineers
have promised to save us,
they have left their seats

for a last meal, when they return
all will be well, under control,
it is their skill, listen –

already upstairs
they are teaching their children
to sing like the ice.

PHILIP GROSS
What This Hand Did

This is the one. This is the hand
that made a castle in the sand.
    When the tide turned present to past
    this hand tried to hold it fast.
When drops trickled through its grip
this hand let the moment slip.
    When the hour was getting late
    this hand reached out for its mate.
When that touch was no relief
two hands tangled in their grief.
    When grief was too much to bear
    two hands wrung themselves in prayer.
When the prayer had been ignored
one hand fastened on a sword.
    When its knuckles went bone white
    this hand carved up wrong and right.
When the laws began to twist
this hand made an iron fist.

When the laws began to break
this hand grabbed what it could take.
When the whole world's banks went bust
this hand scratched the moon for dust.
When the seasons came undone
this hand tried to forge the sun.
When that sun began to rise
this hand tried to shield its eyes.

This hand. This one.
What has it done? What has it done?

CAROL SNYDER HALBERSTADT
The Road Is Not a Metaphor

There are no symbols. Only
the hesitant, the shy slight wonder
and bewildered glance
of an animal
crossing the road.

The road is not a metaphor: it cuts
through trees,
the rocks fall away,
even the sea parts, helpless at its coming.
These are signs – intent on passage
through borrowed air
and water, oiled and torn.

The earth bleeds and the cut trees –
these are not metaphors,
they happen inside
the tense and fragile skin
at the very edge.

■ **Helen Dunmore** ➤ 209.

■ **G.F. Dutton** (*b.* 1924) is a Scottish poet and scientist who has published books on wildwater swimming, mountaineering and mountain gardening, as well as numerous scientific publications on biomolecular research. His austerely passionate poems search and illuminate the world about us, and are as much explorations as his notable scientific work: both draw on one continuous spectrum of experience. His poetry is collected in *The Bare Abundance: Selected Poems 1975-2001* (2002). His 44-year 'ecological dialogue' with a few rocky windblasted East Highland acres led to various articles, radio and TV features, and two acclaimed books, *Harvesting the Edge* (1995) and *Some Branch Against the Sky* (1997). [Other poem ➤ 101]

■ **Philip Gross** (*b.* 1952) is an English poet and children's writer of Cornish and Estonian refugee parentage who has described himself an east-west hybrid.

John Greening: 'He should be recognised as one of England's very best poets, not only for the exuberance of his imagination, but because of what he is writing about. An urban poet, who knows the rural mythologies and lost Romantic instincts, he has fixed many transient details of modern life for his readers; but he also speaks, often playfully, and always with a consummate formal control, of a sense of nothingness [...] he has important things to say and the storyteller's instinct for clarity. If he looks at the world with the hungry eye of a child, he is never merely looking; a troubled fabulist always stands in the background, weighing what has been seen.'

■ **Carol Snyder Halberstadt** (*b.* 1938) is an American poet as well as an editor, artist and activist who lives near Boston, Massachusetts. She is cofounder and president of the Black Mesa Weavers for Life and Land (www.blackmesaweavers.org), a non-profit, fair trade organisation of the Diné (Navajo) in Arizona, whose mission is grounded in the knowledge that human and environmental justice are unseparable. '**The Road Is Not a Metaphor**' was written in the 1980s in response to news of the devastation being wrought in the Amazon Basin where logging companies, mining corporations and spreading pressures of cattle ranching and population growth were opening up land which had been roadless to roads.

ROBERT HASS
State of the Planet

(On the occasion of the 50th anniversary
of the Lamont-Doherty Earth Observatory

1

October on the planet at the century's end.
Rain lashing the windshield. Through blurred glass
Gusts of a Pacific storm rocking a huge, shank-needled
Himalayan cedar. Under it a Japanese plum
Throws off a vertical cascade of leaves the color
Of skinned copper, if copper could be skinned.
And under it, her gait as elegant and supple
As the young of any of earth's species, a schoolgirl
Negotiates a crosswalk in the wind, her hair flying,
The red satchel on her quite straight back darkening
Splotch by smoky crimson splotch as the rain pelts it.
One of the six billion of her hungry and curious kind.
Inside the backpack, dog-eared, full of illustrations,
A book with a title like *Getting to Know Your Planet.*

The book will tell her that the earth this month
Has yawed a little distance from the sun,
And that the air, cooling, has begun to move,
As sensitive to temperature as skin is
To a lover's touch. It will also tell her that the air –
It's likely to say 'the troposphere' – has trapped
Emissions from millions of cars, idling like mine
As she crosses, and is making a greenhouse
Of the atmosphere. The book will say that climate
Is complicated, that we may be doing this,
And if we are, it may explain that this
Was something we've done quite accidentally,
Which she can understand, not having meant
That morning to have spilled the milk. She's
One of those who's only hungry metaphorically.

2

Poetry should be able to comprehend the earth,
To set aside from time to time its natural idioms
Of ardor and revulsion, and say, in a style as sober

As the Latin of Lucretius, who reported to Venus
On the state of things two thousand years ago –
'It's your doing that under the wheeling constellations
Of the sky,' he wrote, 'all nature teems with life.'
Something of the earth beyond our human dramas.

Topsoil: going fast. Rivers: dammed and fouled.
Cod: about fished out. Haddock: about fished out.
Pacific salmon nosing against dams from Yokohama
To Kamchatka to Seattle and Portland, flailing
Up fish-ladders, against turbines, in a rage to breed
Much older than human beings and interdicted
By the clever means that humans have devised
To grow more corn and commandeer more lights.
Most of the ancient groves are gone, sacred to Kuan Yin
And Artemis, sacred to the gods and goddesses
In every picture book the child is apt to read.

3

Lucretius, we have grown so clever that mechanics
In our art of natural philosophy can take the property
Of luminescence from a jellyfish and put it in mice.
In the dark the creatures give off greenish light.
Their bodies must be very strange to them.
An artist in Chicago – think of a great trading city
In Dacia or Thracia – has asked to learn the method
So he can sell people dogs that glow in the dark.

4

The book will try to give the child the wonder
Of how, in our time, we understand life came to be:
Stuff flung off from the sun, the molten core
Still pouring sometimes rivers of black basalt
Across the earth from the old fountains of its origin.
A hundred million years of clouds, sulfurous rain.
The long cooling. There is no silence in the world
Like the silence of rock from before life was.
You come across it in a Mexican desert,

A palo verde tree nearby, moss-green. Some
Insect-eating bird with wing feathers the color
Of a morning sky perched on a limb of the tree.

That blue, that green, the completely fierce
Alertness of the bird that can't know the amazement
Of its being there, a human mind that somewhat does,
Regarding a black outcrop of rock in the desert
Near a sea, charcoal-black and dense, wave-worn,
And all one thing: there's no life in it at all.

It must be a gift of evolution that humans
Can't sustain wonder. We'd never have gotten up
From our knees if we could. But soon enough
We'd fashioned sexy little earrings from the feathers,
Highlighted our cheekbones by rubbings from the rock,
And made a spear from the sinewy wood of the tree.

5

If she lived in Michigan or the Ukraine,
She'd find, washed up on the beach in a storm like this
Limestone fossils of Devonian coral. She could study
The faint white markings: she might have to lick the
    stone
To see them if the wind was drying the pale surface
Even as she held it, to bring back the picture of what
    life
Looked like forty millions years ago: a honeycomb
    with mouths.

6

Cells that divided and reproduced. From where? Why?
(In our century it was the fashion in philosophy
Not to ask unanswerable questions. That was left
To priests and poets, an attitude you'd probably
Approve.) Then a bacterium grew green pigment.
This was the essential miracle. It somehow unmated
Carbon dioxide to eat the carbon and turn it
Into sugar and spit out, hiss out the molecules
Of oxygen the child on her way to school
Is breathing, and so bred life. Something then
Of DNA, the curled musical ladder of sugars, acids.
From there to eyes, ears, wings, hands, tongues.
Armadillos, piano-tuners, gnats, sonnets,
Military interrogation, the Coho salmon, the Margaret
    Truman rose.

7

The people who live in Tena, on the Napo River,
Say that the black, viscid stuff the pools in the selva
Is the blood of the rainbow boa curled in the earth's core.
The great trees in that forest house ten thousands of
    kinds
Of beetle, reptiles no human eyes has ever seen changing
Color on the hot, green, hardly changing leaves
Whenever a faint breeze stirs them. In the understory
Bromeliads and orchids whose flecked petals and womb-
Or mouth-like flowers are the shapes of desire
In human dreams. And butterflies, larger than her palm
Held up to catch a ball or ward off fear. Along the river
Wide-leaved banyans where flocks of raucous parrots,
Fruit-eaters and seed-eaters, rise in startled flares
Of red and yellow and bright green. It will seem to be
    poetry
Forgetting its promise of sobriety to say the rosy shinings
In the thick brown current are small dolphins rising
To the surface where gouts of the oil that burns inside
The engine of the car I'm driving oozes from the banks.

8

The book will tell her that the gleaming appliance
That kept her milk cold in the night required
Chlorofluorocarbons – Lucretius, your master
Epictetus was right about atoms in a general way.
It turns out they are electricity having sex
In an infinite variety of permutations, Plato's
Yearning halves of a severed being multiplied
In all the ways that all the shapes on earth
Are multiple, complex; the philosopher
Who said that the world was fire was also right –
Chlorofluorocarbons react with ozone, the gas
That makes air tingle on a sparkling day.
Nor were you wrong to describe them as assemblies,
As if evolution were a town meeting or a plebiscite.
(Your theory of wind, and of gases, was also right
And there are more of them than you supposed.)
Ozone, high in the air, makes a kind of filter
Keeping out parts of sunlight damaging to skin.
The device we use to keep our food as cool

As if it sat in snow required this substance,
And it reacts with ozone. Where oxygen breeds it
From ultra-violet light, it burns a hole in the air.

9

They drained the marshes around Rome. Your people,
You know, were the ones who taught the world to love
Vast fields of grain, the power and the order of the green,
Then golden rows of it, spooled out almost endlessly.
Your poets, those in the generation after you,
Were the ones who praised the packed seedheads
And the vineyards and the olive groves and called them
'Smiling' fields. In the years since we've gotten
Even better at relentless simplification, but it's taken
Until our time for it to crowd out, savagely, the rest
Of life. No use to rail against our curiosity and greed.
They keep us awake. And are, for all their fury
And their urgency, compatible With intelligent restraint.
In the old paintings of the Italian renaissance,
– In the fresco painters who came after you
(It was the time in which your poems were rediscovered –
There was a period when you, and Venus, were lost;
How could she be lost? You may well ask.) Anyway
In those years the painters made of our desire
An allegory and a dance in the figure of three graces.
The first, the woman coming toward you, is the appetite
For life; the one who seems to turn away is chaste restraint,
And the one whom you've just glimpsed, her back to you,
Is beauty. The dance resembles wheeling constellations.
They made of it a figure for something elegant or lovely
Forethought gives our species. One would like to think
It makes a dance, that the black-and-white flash
Of a flock of buntings in October wind, headed south
Toward winter habitat, would find that the December
    fields
Their kind has known and mated in for thirty centuries
Or more, were still intact, that they will not go
The way of the long-billed arctic curlews who flew
From Newfoundland to Patagonia in every weather
And are gone now from the kinds on earth. The last of
    them
Seen by any human alit in a Texas marsh in 1964.

10

What is to be done with our species? Because
We know we're going to die, to be submitted
To that tingling dance of atoms once again,
It's easy for us to feel that our lives are a dream –
As this is, in a way, a dream: the flailing rain,
The birds, the soaked red backpack of the child,
Her tendrils of wet hair, the windshield wipers,
This voice trying to speak across the centuries
Between us, even the long story of the earth,
Boreal forests, mangrove swamps, Tiberian wheatfields
In the summer heat on hillsides south of Rome – all of it
A dream, and we alive somewhere, somehow outside it,
Watching. People have been arguing for centuries
About whether or not you thought of Venus as a
    metaphor.
Because of the rational man they take you for.
Also about why ended the poem with a plague,
The bodies heaped in the temples of the gods.
To disappear. first one, then a few, then hundreds,
Just stopping over here, to vanish in the marsh at dusk.
So easy, in imagination, to tell the story backwards,
Because the earth needs a dream of restoration –
She dances and the birds just keep arriving,
Thousands of them, immense arctic flocks, her teeming
    life.

■ **Robert Hass** (*b.* 1941) is an American poet, critic, environ-
mentalist and translator (notably of Czesław Miłosz). As US
Poet Laureate in 1995-97, he worked not only to improve
the wider public's perception of poetry (including through
his nationally syndicated *Poet's Choice* newspaper column),
but also to create a greater awareness of both environmental
issues and illiteracy (with the mantra, 'imagination makes
communities'), bringing together noted novelists, poets and
storytellers to talk about writing, nature and community. For
Hass, everything is connected: natural beauty must be tended
to; caring for a place means knowing it intimately; and poets,
especially, need to pay constant attention to the interaction
of mind and environment.
Rooted in the landscapes of his native Northern California,
Hass's musical, descriptive, meditative poetry is noted for its

eloquence, clarity and force. His first collection *Field Guide* (1973) was selected for the Yale Younger Poets Series by Stanley Kunitz, who wrote: 'Reading a poem by Robert Hass is like stepping into the ocean when the temperature of the water is not much different from that of the air. You scarcely know, until you feel the undertow tug at you, that you have entered into another element.' His later collections are *Praise* (1979), *Human Wishes* (1989), *Sun Under Wood* (1996) and *Time and Materials* (2007). His other books include *Twentieth Century Pleasures: Prose on Poetry* (1984), *Poet's Choice: Poems for Everyday Life* (1998) and *Now and Then: The Poet's Choice Columns, 1997-2000* (2007).

Hass founded River of Words (ROW), an organisation that promotes environmental and arts education with the Library of Congress Center for the Book, and is a board member of International Rivers Network. He is a professor of English at the University of California, Berkeley. [Other poem ➤ 171]

SEAMUS HEANEY
Anything Can Happen
(after Horace, Odes, *I, 34)*

Anything can happen. You know how Jupiter
Will mostly wait for clouds to gather head
Before he hurls the lightning? Well, just now
He galloped his thunder cart and his horses

Across a clear blue sky. It shook the earth
And the clogged underearth, the River Styx,
The winding streams, the Atlantic shore itself,
Anything can happen, the tallest towers

Be overturned, those in high places daunted,
Those overlooked regarded. Stropped-beak Fortune
Swoops, making the air gasp, tearing the crest off one,
Setting it down bleeding on the next.

Ground gives. The heaven's weight
Lifts up off Atlas like a kettle-lid.
Capstones shift, nothing resettles right.
Telluric ash and fire-spores boil away.

SEAMUS HEANEY
Höfn

The three-tongued glacier has begun to melt.
What will we do, they ask, when boulder-milt
Comes wallowing across the delta flats

And the miles-deep shag-ice makes its move?
I saw it, ridged and rock-set, from above,
Undead grey-gristed earth-pelt, aeon-scruff,

And feared its coldness that still seemed enough,
To iceblock the plane window dimmed with breath,
Deepfreeze the seep of adamantine tilth

And every warm, mouthwatering word of mouth.

■ **Seamus Heaney** (*b.* 1939) is a world-renowned Irish poet and critic, the winner of the Nobel Prize in Literature in 1995. Born into a Catholic farming family in Mossbawm, Co. Derry, he left Northern Ireland in 1972 and has since lived in America, Wicklow and Dublin. His concerns for the land, language and troubled history of Ireland run through all of his work. His early poetry is notable for its sensory lyrical evocations of childhood, nature and rural life. **'Churning Day'** [➤ 153], from *Death of a Naturalist* (1966), celebrates daily human unity with the seasonal processes of nature, while in the later poem [➤ 116] from his sequence **'Squarings'** (from *Seeing Things*), the awareness of change heightens the present generation's appreciation of the natural cycle.

When the Northern Irish "Troubles" began in 1969, he looked for 'images and symbols adequate to our predicament' and found a powerful metaphor for the violence of the time in the archaeological discoveries made in peat bogs in Ireland and northern Europe, expressed in the 'bog people' poems of *Wintering Out* (1972) and *North* (1975). For Heaney, the peat bog is a memory bank just as the land itself is a repository for history and continuity across time. In his lecture 'The Sense of Place' (1977), he said: 'We are no longer innocent, we are no longer just parishioners of the local. [...] Yet those primary laws of our nature are still operative. We are dwellers, we are namers, we are lovers, we make homes and search for our histories. And when we look for the history of our sensibilities I am convinced, as Professor J.C. Beckett was convinced about the history of Ireland generally, that it is to what he called the stable element, the land itself, that we must look for continuity.'

In her essay 'Pastoral Theologies' in *Poetry & Posterity* (2000), Edna Longley wrote: 'If Heaney is a Green or environmental poet, it is usually not in the sense that he subordinates human consciousness or human rights to ecosystems, but in the sense that the fabric of his poems heals modern splits between/within self and world. He "assumes" what Wordsworth aspires to reassert. [...] Heaney is not a "post-pastoral" poet (Gifford) who has digested Wordsworth and Thomas and moved on. Rather, some aspects of his sensibility hark back to a pre-Reformation, pre-Cartesian order. His animism is rooted in Catholicism as well as in Romantic Nature [...] When the proponents of an emergent Celto-Catholic ecology "claim a moral perspective for environmental awareness, grounding it in our responsibility to appreciate the natural world as God's first revelation", they continue the theological tradition of "immanence" whereby Nature encodes messages from the creator to mankind. Heaney's most recent collections, *Seeing Things* (1991) and *The Spirit Level* (1996), explicitly read the poet's surroundings for immanence, for signs of "where the spirit lives".'

Heaney has published two further collections since Edna Longley made that assessment, *Electric Light* (2001) and *District and Circle* (2006). In the latter book, scenes from a rural childhood spent far from the horrors of the Second World War are coloured by a strongly contemporary sense that (in Heaney's version of Horace) 'Anything Can Happen' [➤ 213], and other images from a dangerous present (a melting glacer in 'Höfn', ➤ 213) are fraught with this same anxiety. In several of these recent poems which 'do the rounds of the district', threats to the planet are intuited in the local place, as Heaney turns full circle to where he began: 'the land itself', once 'the stable element', now holds the measure of global discontinuity. In 'A Shiver', as Heaney describes the power of wielding a sledge-hammer, asking...

> does it do you good
> To have known it in your bones, directable,
> Withholdable at will,
> A first blow that could make air of a wall,
> A last one so unanswerably landed
> The staked earth quailed and shivered in the handle?

...it feels as though he has found – in this stirring late work – fresh 'images and symbols adequate to our predicament'.

■ **Matthew Hollis** (*b.* 1971) is an English poet, editor and anthologist who grew up in East Anglia. Much of his poetry connects people to land and water, immersing us in the undercurrents of our own lives. Rainwater, floodwater, flux – the liquid landscapes shifting relentlessly in his poems – threaten and comfort by turns. Reviewing his collection *Ground Water* (2004), D.J. Taylor wrote: 'Matthew Hollis is fixated on water, and the idea of environments defined and symbolised by the liquid that flows through them or descends from on high [...] the metaphorical language is finely judged, touching both the landscapes and the people crawling its surface with a shrewd but never less than sympathetic gaze.' (*Guardian*, 10 April 2004)

His poem 'The Diomedes' was commissioned by *Poet in the City* and Lloyd's as part of the *Trees in the City* collaboration, designed to raise awareness of the need for action on climate change, and is reproduced by kind permission of *Poet in the City* and Lloyd's.

■ **Micheal O'Siadhail** (*b.* 1947) [pronounced *Mee-hall Oh Sheel*] is a prolific Irish poet and linguist whose work sets the intensities of a life against the background of worlds shaken by change. He has published eleven books of poetry, including *Our Double Time* (1998), *Poems 1975-1995* (1999), *The Gossamer Wall: poems in witness to the Holocaust* (2002) and *Love Life* (2005). In his most recent collection, *Globe* (2007), from which '**Sifting**' is taken, he explores how a world is shaped; how the past and memories bear on the present; how to face the open wounds of tragedies and loss.

■ Jane Hirshfield ➤ 158.

MATTHEW HOLLIS

The Diomedes

Summers he would leave for Alaska,
working the crabbers as deckhand or galley;
autumns returning with cold-weather stories of
clam catchers, fur trappers, and the twin isles
of Diomede: two miles and a continent between them;
and how, in winter, when the straits froze over,
the islanders could walk from one to the other,
crossing the ice-sheet to see family, swap

scrimshaw, the season's stories, or marry,
passing the Date Line that ran through the channel,
and so stepping between days as they went.

As far as I know he never went back;
if he had he'd have learned that
only the bravest now track on foot,
the winter ice no longer reliable,
for walrus, ski-plane or the human step,
leaving the skin boats alone to wait for the summer,
to edge themselves into the melt-water.

Even now, there's something to his story
I find difficult to fathom. At home, in London,
listening to my neighbours' raised voices,
I wonder, what it is we will do to be neighbourly,
how part of us longs for it to matter that much,
to be willing to nudge our small boat into the waves,
or set foot on the winter ice,
to be half-way from home, in no safety,
unsure if we're headed for tomorrow or yesterday.

MICHEAL O'SIADHAIL
Sifting

In all these leap years of change
How easily from heights of now
We view what was as obsolete
Forgetting how
So many things loop and repeat
As gain and loss rearrange,

How in this upping of our pace
What's knitted over centuries
Could unravel half-unnoticed.
Behind our ease
A velvet glove and greedy fist,
Soft tyranny of the market-place,

Bytes of facts and hardnosed
Figures, our problems best
Scanned by instruments. Screening
Out the rest,
We quickly lose a thread of memory,
The poetry in us so readily prosed.

Given a globe of sudden upheaval,
We thrill at change but fear chaos.
In dizzy worlds that begin
To criss-cross
And fuse, we can only trust in
Loops and circuits of retrieval

As trade winds shift and sweep
Over older boundaries
And faithful to our past's debt
We sift memories
For what to recall, what to forget
To steady us now before we leap.

JANE HIRSHFIELD
Global Warming

When his ship first came to Australia,
Cook wrote, the natives
continued fishing, without looking up.
Unable, it seems, to fear what was too large to be
    comprehended.

9. NATURAL DISASTERS

After poems covering both man-made environmental disasters and so-called "acts of God" or "natural disasters", this section ends with planetary catastrophe and Eco-Armageddon. Scientists are not yet crediting climate change or global warming as a direct cause of extremely powerful hurricanes such as Katrina, but there are increasingly clear links between human-caused global warming of the oceans and increased storm strength. Articles in *Nature* and *Science Magazine* in 2005 argued that global warming has significantly affected hurricane destructiveness. The number of Category 4 and 5 hurricanes has almost doubled in the last 30 years. The research published in *Nature* showed a strong correlation between sea temperature and annual hurricane power in three different hurricane basins, the North Atlantic and two in the Pacific.

Hurricane Katrina was the most destructive hurricane in the history of the United States. It was the sixth-strongest Atlantic hurricane ever recorded and the third-strongest hurricane to make landfall. Katrina caused massive devastation along much of the north-central Gulf Coast in August 2005. The most severe loss of life and property damage occurred in New Orleans, which flooded as the levees broke, in many cases hours after the storm had moved inland. Nearly 2000 people are said to have died in the Katrina disaster.

Katrina also had a profound impact on the environment. The storm surge caused substantial beach erosion, completely devastating some coastal areas, notably Dauphin Island, obliterating the Chandeleur Islands and permanently destroying large areas of coastal marshland. The lands lost included the breeding grounds of marine mammals, brown pelicans, turtles and fish, as well as migratory species such as redhead ducks. Sixteen National Wildlife Refuges had to be closed. The habitats of sea turtles, Mississippi sandhill cranes, red-cockaded woodpeckers and Alabama beach mice were all affected. As part of the clean-up operation, the flood waters from New Orleans were pumped into Lake Pontchartrain, along with a mixture of raw sewage, bacteria, heavy metals, pesticides, toxic chemicals and millions of gallons of oil; the effect of this on the fish is unimaginable.

Diane Darby Beattie's personal account was published as the prelude to *Hurricane Blues: Poems about Katrina and Rita* (2006), edited by Philip C. Kolin and Susan Swartwout The poems by Louisiana writers **Catharine Savage Brosman** and **Elizabeth Foos** are from the same anthology.

DARBY DIANE BEATTIE
Memories of Katrina

I am 62 years old, life has been good to me, and I am so glad to be alive.

I rode out the storm; no money or transportation to leave New Orleans. Katrina made landfall August 29, 2005. The winds' fury took my kitchen walls and blew out the roof from my Napoleon Avenue apartment uptown. The winds howled nonstop in the total darkness. Rain poured like a broken water main, pulled the drains off the roof. It was humid and 100 degrees as I lay on the floor under a boxspring all night long – no sleep, no food, no water. Morning was no relief; the winds and rain stayed on until 3 P.M.

Outside, the apartment was covered with uprooted trees. The balcony hung off the building. The street looked like a science fiction war zone. People were desperate for water. No one had any utilities. A nearby swimming pool was blocked by fallen walls and pump equipment, but I climbed a wall to salvage water in a plastic bucket. No sign of help until two days after the storm, when streams of helicopters from the Coast Guard headed for the drowning pools of the City. There was no help from the local police. Local politicians and civic leaders were nonexistent.

I struggled through the front gates to see if I could help anyone. People were milling in the heat, looking for food and water. Children were scared and cried for water. There was no food until the fifth day.

On the fifth day, the first evacuations to the Superdome occurred. The National Guard gave us military rations and patrolled the streets with weapons. Desperation led to looting. The evacuation caused panic in the masses of people. I tried to walk there, but there was too much water still and dangerous heat for that distance. I went back to the apartment.

The military meals were edible and provided nutrition. I ate one each day, waiting for rescue. I felt like a refugee from a far country, not an American. Desperate people, senior citizens, were dying from dehydration.

The stench of death was overwhelming and inescapable. I didn't want to die there. On the eighth day, the National Guard units came door to door. They used trucks to move us to the Convention Center, then helicopters to get us on an airflight out of New Orleans. The pilot wouldn't tell us where we were going until we were en route. Then he announced to some eighty homeless survivors that the U.S. Government was sending us to sunny Tucson, Arizona. I thought, *At least there is no levee there.*

Writing keeps me sane; I write every day. I thank God for the good people of Tucson and their welcome to me. I am 62 years old. A Katrina survivor.

so the whole city can't see or eat and the heat swells
and somewhere down one of those roads you know
the levees kick out and the water starts rising
and there are people everywhere – on couches,
churches, floors, and there's no room at the inns
or the Marriott and there is no bread or milk
or meat and the heat keeps rising
and the streets wrap up and sirens squall all day
into the blackest nights a city's ever seen
and nothing moves until the helicopters
thwup thwup thwup thwup thwup thwup
thwup thwup thwup the silent sky to pieces
so you start raking and thinking of all the other
places you've ever been and how to get there again.

ELIZABETH FOOS

How to lose your hometown in seven days

Hometowns aren't good for much, except
knowing them longer than anywhere else,
you know they will take you back
when nowhere else will, and knowing them
longer you know the great dive for cornbread
off 22nd and who used to live in the corner
house and when that road didn't go through,
and you can always find a job or a cheap place
to sleep or an old friend with a back slap
with your name on it or news of nobody
you've thought of in years, and knowing how
to get home from all directions and the numbers
of highways and interstates out to everywhere,
and knowing always knowing it will wait there
like first love and never give up on you, unless –

unless the globe gets hot enough to make monsters
from thin air, twisted and one-eyed and send them
tearing through the streets, cracking power
poles, grabbing trees by the boughs and pushing
them down on anything dumb enough to live
under a water oak or live oak or gone pecan tree

CATHARINE SAVAGE BROSMAN

Three Modes of Katrina

I *Katrina's Darkness*

One might say unnatural; but night, like day, shapes
round our lives and orders them – while reassuring stars,
or sparkling imitations we devise, trace out
designs for us. No stars tonight. Uneasy, then,
for the Big Easy – as, flailed by the hurricane,
it hunches down in utter darkness, with no street lamps

on the Avenue, no glow around the Dome, no rooms
lit brightly for the ones who cannot sleep,
or did not wish to, who had rather read, or brood
in bars, or stake their fates on card games or with women.
And here I am awake with them, though not by choice –
treading in soggy slippers on the tile along the windows,

mopping up water that I feel but cannot see,
wringing out rags to use again, adding old newspapers,
waiting for dawn, when I can see how deep it is,
how far it's soaked the carpet, whether books
along the wall are wet. We'll eat cold food tonight,
heat coffee water by a candle, watch the waves that prance

up Second Street, and wonder when the power
will return. But Paul says, 'This is nothing, really.'
He is right; it's just a blast of noise as from a boom-box –
drum-rolls, tedious blare, and constant whining – and a bit
of inconvenience. Or so we think; we can't yet know
it's not a rap song, but the overture to *Götterdämmerung*.

II *Katrina's War*

So she was not bluffing, though by Monday afternoon
our streets were nearly clear. True, the trees were tattered,
skeletal, all stripped of limbs and leaves, and water
had collected in the kitchen of an absent friend,
where I went after it with mop and pail. The air
was steamy, but we lasted, innocent, till Tuesday morning.

Meanwhile, storm surge in the lakes has breached,
or topped, the levees; yet the radio (a single station
working in a bunker on the West Bank) tells us
nothing. All we know about is crowds of ill and helpless
gathered in the Superdome – discomfort, thirst
and hunger, crying children, sleeplessness, and fear. Then

the news: the dykes have broken; Poydras and Canal Street
are awash, the water rising, close. We're the lucky
ones: my Jeep's not flooded, we've got gasoline
(enough to cross the river, get to New Iberia) and friends
in Texas. *Still*, we do not get it – like a war,
when just a skirmish that should soon be over turns

quite nasty, and the battle lines are drawn, and next,
it's full-scale conflict in the trenches, while the locals,
caught in the cross-fire, barely know what's happening.
We saw the war on television, with another –
young men dying in the desert; old men, women,
dogs and children drowned or on an overpass, abandoned.

III *Katrina's Gifts*

I cannot think like Nagin, who announced *
the storm was sent to punish us for war
abroad and selfishness at home – and thus

I do not purpose to explain such ways
of God to man. But Milton saw things well:
all history is *Sturm und Drang*, the winds

and seas of human action in the world
contending, force and counter-force, the tides
now wildly drowning everything, now drawn
by other moons and falling – whether men
alone contest and struggle, or enroll
the wiles of nature, or invoke divine

intentions. Coming back, we saw the wrath
of Rita first: beheaded pine trees, roofs
wrenched off, debris. And then Katrina's deeds –
swamps stripped, shacks gone, the city's spectral face
reflected in the water. One gives thanks,
however, for such gifts as whirlwinds leave –

not like the Pharisee, self-gratified,
but knowing how precarious is life –
a fragile causeway over turbulence –
as risk and chance conspire in destiny;
so that we grieve, but live in greater love –
good friends, dry bed, a spirit fired white.

* *Ray Nagin: the New Orleans mayor, comment in a Martin
Luther King, Jr. Day speech, January 2006.*

NEIL ASTLEY

Darwin Cyclone

We weren't afraid. There wasn't time. We'd lost
the radio, and all the lights had gone.
We weren't aware of what was going on,
but watched an apparition: trees possessed

and shaking, frenzied, thrashing in the night;
watched water seeping in, creeping across
the carpet like a shadow; were shocked as
something hit the house, somewhere out of sight.

I felt the window strain and heave behind
my hand, stepped back the moment when it groaned
its shrillest note, and burst before I'd turned
the corner, running to my room to find

the wind already in the corridor.
Some flying curtains slashed me in the face.
We grabbed a mattress, shook off all the glass
and wedging it against the bathroom door

dived under it, just as a rafter broke
through, showering bricks and plasterboard on top.
Our bodies ached with crouching, water slopped
around us in the dark. We didn't speak.

The house was being torn apart with us
inside, each wall the wind was breaking down
felt like the final blow, each rending sound
the firing squad which faced us for six hours.

We didn't crack. The darkness screamed and roared.
They wouldn't shoot. I knew if we survived
I'd not want anything. Being alive
was all I thought about, until they fired…

A crack of light at dawn. The noise died down,
replaced by belting rain. Who looked out first
I don't remember, only that I raised
my head up warily. And saw. As when

someone emerges after an air raid
not knowing whether neighbours have been spared,
so I climbed up all innocent, and stared
at what I never thought I'd see outside:

a silent film of houses smashed to bits –
and streets away, in flickering rain, someone
staggering from the ruins in slow motion
(an insect crawling from its chrysalis).

The rows of trees beyond had been stripped bare.
I saw my room had gone. I had no clothes
except the things I wore, I'd lost my shoes,
and spiked my foot before I found a pair.

I hopped about, and should have been in pain
but felt more like a dopey fool. Instead
of crying, grinned. *Hey look at me, I've cut
my bloody foot*, I shouted at the rain.

■ The city of Darwin in Australia's Northern Territory was destroyed by Cyclone Tracy on Christmas Day, 1974. Three days earlier I was working the late shift on the *Northern Territory News* when I took a call from the weather bureau: a tropical storm just over a hundred miles away had intensified and was now officially a cyclone. I remember writing down the name it had just been given, *Tracy*. I typed out a paragraph for the stop press of the next morning's paper, feeling like a herald of doom. Tracy turned into the most compact and destructive tropical cyclone on record (around the same strength as Hurricane Katrina, or possibly even more powerful). Its eye passed directly over the city's largest residential area. The storm lasted from midnight on Christmas Eve until dawn, with the strongest gusts probably reaching 185 MPH (all the gauges were broken). Darwin had not been hit by a cyclone for nearly 40 years (the previous ones were in 1937 and 1897), and had expanded rapidly after the War without appropriate building controls. Many houses were built on stilts, but even the brick-built ones like my brother's house couldn't withstand the force of a cyclone's direct hit. We were trapped under the wreckage in total howling darkness for six hours, unable to imagine what devastation was being wreaked outside. The destruction of Darwin by Cyclone Tracy was the worst "natural" disaster in Australian history. When I saw the pictures of New Orleans in 2005, I felt like I was back there.

MICHAEL HAMBURGER
A Massacre
(17th October 1987)

It came like judgement, came like the blast
Of power that, turned against itself, brings home
Presumption to the unpresuming also,
To those who suffered power and those unborn.

In the small hours
We woke to it, a howling, lashing
That rocked the house; then, muffled
By the closed, curtained windows, crashes, cracks,
Far off or near. We did not rise
And did not peer, but listened
Into the darkness even when overhead
Things hurtled, burst or boomed,
But in the havoc coupled, as though to pit
One wholeness, though the last we had, against
So general a fission, and lay unmoved
Till daybreak roused us from our drowsing,
While still the hurricane rushed,
Half-light allowed a hesitant half-looking.

She saw what, before action, my sight refused,
Fearful because she loved it best,
Went straight to it in mind, the mulberry tree,
Straight to the space its bunched and knotted mass
Down to the lawn had filled, the low boughs propped
On rests made for them by a gardener dead,
Not for our tenure, lest their own weight break them.
These only upright now; the sound, live growth
Of centuries undone
By the roots' wrenching, the full foliage withered,
Curled round no fruit that had been lately sweet
Within the woody roughness of its fibre.

And while the gale swept on,
Beyond the dawn's, no light marked farm or village,
She met another absence, at the lawn's far edge,
Pyramid of the larch that leaned, not sprawled
From rootwork, a mere decade's, partly ripped
Out of the soil a rainy year had softened;
Yet grown too tall and wide for us to raise,
Lever from sure starvation, though its drooping
Girdled a rarer sapling, purple maple
Endangered by more subsidence, when the fall
Had neither bent nor rent it.

This was for later finding, later care
Among the lack and wreckage that she sensed

Before the morning brightened
And we went out.
Already, too, her care had found its way
To larger emptiness, left by the Lombardy poplar
Gone from the eastern sky,
Live column, fluttering spire so tall
That miles away on walks they'd shown us home;

Only the longest, though, of the tree corpses
Lying across the marsh
With ramparts now of great root clusters
And loam, their matrix, raised on the dyke's bank;
New pools inside it, scooped from its bed;
New wilderness along it, tangle of trunks and limb –
Ash, linden, birches, plane, and the white poplar
Less set on rising than the Lombardy,
Its greater bulk and girth stopped in their fall
By a slim cable pole, therefore to be dismembered,
Cut to the stump, mocking memorial
No one will need where a whole skyline gapes,
Beyond our ravaged acre and worldwide
A slow or sudden killing
Comes to the trees like judgement, not on them.

Until the mended house
Is hit again by worse than any weather
Its beams of oak withstood,
Dead wood still older than the mulberry,
Though sheltered by whichever trees remain
Of those we tended, planted or let be,
The beech not toppled, or self-seeded hawthorn,
Sycamore, elder, scrub of the blighted elm,
Our work is clearance, unremembering
And unforeknowing, too,
For what resurgence, change or progeny
The labour will make room,
What of the lumber burned and what removed,
What, by discarding, we give back to roots
As food for leafage, food for whose need of leaves.

More emptiness, then. Now to be filled
Less by our choosing, less by one grain, one savour,

One shape accepted only or loved best
Among those made by air, earth, water, fire
In multiple mutation, fusion, fission,
Than by their bare subsistence that's our own;
And light above all, as long as light will shine.

■ **Michael Hamburger** (1924-2007) was a leading English poet, critic and translator of literature from his native German, known especially for his translations of Friedrich Hölderlin, Paul Celan and Gottfried Benn, and latterly of W.G. Sebald, who described a visit to his house in *The Rings of Saturn* (1998). Influenced in his early years by Yeats and Eliot, Hamburger discovered his appetite for what he called 'the roughage of lived experience', and started to write poems in which loyalty to the primacy of experience could admit the intense exchange of dream, memory and observation. Moving to Suffolk in 1976, he found respite from his literary labours as well as sustenance from his garden and orchard, became a passionate breeder of rare apples, and produced some of his finest work, 'memorably disquieting' poetry (one reviewer's description) profoundly engaged with both the natural and human world.

ALLISON FUNK
Living at the Epicenter

Eliza Bryan, of New Madrid, Missouri, wrote one of the few surviving accounts of the series of earthquakes that shook the region in late 1811 and early 1812.

2 A.M. she wakes to a babel of trees,
    wind and wildfowl, stones
and a hollow thunder confounded.
    Hoarse. Vibrations.
        Family and neighbors

reeling in the darkness of sinking acres.
    Shock after shock
until morning –
    an uncontrollable passion
        seizes everything:

the Mississippi
    like an animal in heat,
oaks thrusting at one another,
    the houses come unfastened.
        Heaved from their nests,

birds land
    on her shoulders and head.
Wings in her face.
    Odor of sulfur.
        Shower of dust.

                    *

Later, she wondered who cared
    for her grief, what point
remembering the night
    the Mississippi flowed backwards,
        erupting like artillery.

Boats torn from their moorings,
    New Madrid's women and men
spilling in every direction.
    But the wrecked boats covering the river
        would not vanish from memory.

In one, a lady and six children,
    all lost.
Flatboat, raft, all the tenuous breaths,
    the young cottonwoods
        broken with such regularity

from a distance
    they might look like a work of art.
Not this faithlessness
    of hundreds of acres,
        a river's bad blood.

If only the intervals
    between the aftershocks
were longer,
    if she didn't see
        as if underwater –

                    *

Then, again
   dead animals and household belongings
litter the fields,
    the furious river
      murders its banks,

and she is stumbling miles
   waist deep in blood-warm water –
where is there dry land?
    When she holds out her arms
      to the children

silt runs through her fingers,
   Borderless,
nothing's familiar.
    Yard, road.
      Others, self.

         *

Stop moving.
   The leafless branches outside
keep shifting,
    she cannot focus,
      present capsizing into past.

Sometimes it's as muddy to her
   as the river she lives on,
but there must have been signs.
    Maybe the passenger pigeons
      arriving suddenly

like the Pharoah's locusts, swarming,
   in the fields, hundreds in a single tree.
And earlier (was it June?)
    grey squirrels in thousands
      drowned trying to cross the river.

Her memory returns like a fever,
   the hailstones
that beat the blighted crops.
    Summer? Spring?
      The seasons all unmoored.

How was it she didn't see it coming,
   she asks herself,
remembering the eclipse
   of the moon, autumns comet
     and the monster born between its legs.

         *

A great blue heron
   starts up out of the wetlands slowly,
looking broken at first,
    long legs trailing
      before, heavy winged, it flies.

Another sign, she thinks,
   dreaming the bird
in the balmy dark, the river
    she drifts in.
      Some mornings

it takes the earth's tremors
   to rouse her in her new home
on the higher ground of the bluff.
    After a year, nothing steady,
      nothing to be trusted.

What does she think will change
   if she puts it all down?
Still, bending over the page,
    she tries to tell
      what she's learned:

how in the middle of one night
   the world we've known
can open up without warning,
    all of nature
      begin speaking in tongues.

■ **Allison Funk** (*b.* 1951) is an American poet, editor and translator of Catalan poetry. She has published three books of poetry, *Forms of Conversion* (1986), *Living at the Epicenter* (1995) and *The Knot Garden* (2002). She is Professor of English and Creative Writing at Southern Illinois University Edwardsville, where she also co-edits the journal *Sou'wester*.

Sonia Sanchez on *Living at the Epicenter*: 'There is a distinct desire in the work for reunification of earthly forces and human forces. Several poems affirm a level of dialogue, relationship, and connectedness between the two. Through earthquake, flood, or even the slow kiss of erosion, power and meaning are traded back and forth between men and women on one hand, rock and water on the other.' [Other poem ➤ 110]

■ **Kofi Awoonor** (*b.* 1935) is a Ghanaian poet, novelist and critic whose work combines the poetic traditions of his native Ewe people and contemporary and religious symbolism to depict Africa during decolonisation. Born George Awoonor-Williams, he spent many years as a political exile in the States, and was later imprisoned (1975-76) for harbouring a political fugitive. Awoonor is a respected analyst on issues relating to African and global politics, and from 1990 to 1994 was Ghana's Ambassador to the United Nations, heading the committee against apartheid. His earliest poetic influences came from his grandmother, who was a dirge-singer, and one of his recurrent themes is the alienation of the Western-educated African.

■ **Tishani Doshi** (*b.* 1975) is an Indian poet, writer and dancer. Born in Madras, where she now lives, she studied in India and the USA. Her first book of poems, *Countries of the Body*, won the 2006 Forward Prize for Best First Collection. 'The Day We Went To The Sea' was written in Madras after the tsunami of 2004.

KOFI AWOONOR
The Sea Eats the Land at Home

At home the sea is in the town,
Running in and out of the cooking places,
Collecting the firewood from the hearths
And sending it back at night;
The sea eats the land at home.
It came one day at the dead of night,
Destroying the cement walls,
And carried away the fowls,
The cooking-pots and the ladles,
The sea eats the land at home;
It is a sad thing to hear the wails,
And the mourning shouts of the women,

Calling on all the gods they worship,
To protect them from the angry sea.
Aku stood outside where her cooking-pot stood,
With her two children shivering from the cold,
Her hands on her breast,
Weeping mournfully.
Her ancestors have neglected her,
Her gods have deserted her,
It was a cold Sunday morning,
The storm was raging,
Goats and fowls were struggling in the water,
The angry water of the cruel sea;
The lap-lapping of the bark water at the shore,
And above the sobs and the deep and low moans,
Was the eternal hum of the living sea.
It has taken away their belongings
Adena has lost the trinkets which
Were her dowry and her joy,
In the sea that eats the land at home,
Eats the whole land at home.

TISHANI DOSHI
The Day We Went to the Sea

The day we went to the sea
Mothers in Madras were mining
The Marina for missing children.
Thatch flew in the sky, prisoners
Ran free, houses danced like danger
In the wind. I saw a woman hold
The tattered edge of the world
In her hand, look past the temple
Which was still standing, as she was –
Miraculously whole in the debris of gaudy
South Indian sun. When she moved
Her other hand across her brow,
In a single arcing sweep of grace,
It was as if she alone could alter things,
Bring us to the worldless safety of our beds.

JOHN BURNSIDE
Swimming in the Flood

Later he must have watched
the newsreel,

his village erased by water: farmsteads and churches
breaking and floating away

as if by design;
bloated cattle, lumber, bales of straw,

turning in local whirlpools; the camera
panning across the surface, finding the odd

rooftop or skeletal tree,
or homing in to focus on a child's

shock-headed doll.
Under it all, his house would be standing intact,

the roses and lime trees, the windows,
the baby grand.

He saw it through the water when he dreamed
and, waking at night, he remembered the rescue boat,

the chickens at the prow, his neighbour's pig,
the woman beside him, clutching a silver frame,

her face dislodged, reduced to a puzzle of bone
and atmosphere, the tremors on her skin

wayward and dark, like shadows crossing a field
of clouded grain.

Later, he would see her on the screen,
trying to smile, as they lifted her on to the dock,

and he'd notice the frame again, baroque and absurd,
and empty, like the faces of the drowned.

GEORGE SZIRTES
Death by Deluge

I have seen roads come to a full stop in mid-
sentence as if their meaning had fallen off
the world. And this is what happened, what meaning did

that day in August. The North Sea had been rough
and rising and the bells of Dunwich rang
through all of Suffolk. One wipe of its cuff

down cliffs and in they went, leaving birds to hang
puzzled in the air, their nests gone. Enormous
tides ran from Southend to Cromer. They swung

north and south at once, as if with a clear purpose,
thrusting through Lincolnshire, and at a rush
drowning Sleaford, Newark, leaving no house

uncovered. Nothing remained of The Wash
but water. Peterborough, Ely, March, and Cambridge
were followed by Royston, Stevenage, the lush

grass of Shaw's Corner. Not a single ridge
remained. The Thames Valley filled to the brim
and London Clay swallowed Wapping and Greenwich.

Then west, roaring and boiling. A rapid skim
of Hampshire and Dorset, then the peninsula:
Paignton, Plymouth, Lyme, Land's End. A slim

line of high hills held out but all was water-colour,
the pure English medium, intended for sky, cloud,
and sea. Less earth than you could shift with a spatula.

■ **George Szirtes** (b. 1948) came to England from Budapest
after the 1956 Hungarian uprising. He was educated in Eng-
land, trained as a painter, and has always written in English;
in recent years he has worked a translator of Hungarian lit-
erature. Haunted his family's knowledge and experience of
war, occupation and the Holocaust as well as by loss, danger
and exile, all of his poetry covers universal themes: love, desire
and illusion; loyalty and betrayal; history, art and memory;

humanity and truth. **'Death by Deluge'** is from his sequence *An English Apocalypse* (2001), which imagines England's destruction in five apocalypses.

■ **John Burnside** ➤ 203.

■ **Annemarie Austin** (*b.* 1943) is an English poet. Her richly imaginative, unsettling poems are like paintings in which what is seen is held as it is about to happen, or as it has just happened. They evoke thresholds or border states. Anne Stevenson has described her as 'a fable maker', and her poems often draw from history, myth and dream, but the story behind **'Very'** is all too real: the European heat wave of August 2003 which killed 35,000 people. **C.K. Williams** lives in France, and his poem **'Rats'** is a personal response to the same national disaster. [Other poem and author note ➤ 228-29]

ANNEMARIE AUSTIN
Very

It was very hot. In France old people
died, and their desiccated dark bodies
with transparent paper wings were piled
too high in morgues that were very cold.

Among those days was the one when I
turned officially old myself, but today
a little bubble of milk settled precisely
on my nipple when I made white coffee –

which discomfited me. I am not so young
yet. There's interpenetration of extremes
along my arm: the bluish white inside
the elbow, speckled criss-crossing at the wrist –

neither exactly has an edge, but each
slides into other. And that heat abated
into overcast will-it-won't-it stasis
for a while – in France as well as here.

The tide was very low. It seemed maybe
they could walk to Cardiff on the skin
of estuary mud, like flies treading cream.
So they set off, and sank to their armpits

where there was no bottom of the mix of silt
and sea, where overnight sandbanks
shifted to discomfit mapmakers...
Then the tide turned to very high again.

C.K. WILLIAMS
Rats
August 2005

1

From beneath the bank
of the brook, in the first
searing days
of the drought, water

rats appeared,
two of them,
we'd never known
even were there.

Unlike city
rats skulking
in cellars or sliding
up from a sewer-

mouth – I saw this,
it wasn't dusk –
these, as blithe
as toy tanks,

sallied into the garden
to snitch the crusts
we'd set
out for the birds.

But still, who
knows what filth
and fetor and rot
down in their dark

world they were
before? I shouted
and sent them
hurtling back.

2

Now the brute
crucible of heat
has been upon us
for weeks,

just breathing is work,
and we're frightened.
The planet all
but afire, glaciers

dissolving, deserts
on the march,
hurricanes without end,
and the president

and his energy-company
cronies still insist
global warming
isn't real. The rats

rove where they will
now, shining and fat,
they've appropriated
the whole lawn.

From this close,
they look just
like their cousins
anywhere else,

devious, ruthless,
rapacious, and every
day I loathe
them more.

MARK JARMAN
Skin Cancer

Balmy overcast nights of late September;
Palms standing out in street light, house light;
Full moon penetrating the cloud-film
With an explosive halo, a ring almost half the sky;
Air like a towel draped over shoulders;
Lightness or gravity deferred like a moral question;
The incense in the house lit; the young people
Moving from the front door into the half-dark
And back, or up the stairs to glimpse the lovers' shoes
Outside the master bedroom; the youngest speculating;
The taste of beer, familiar as salt water;
Each window holding a sea view, charcoal
With shifting bars of white; the fog filling in
Like the haze of distance itself, pushing close, blurring.

As if the passage into life were through such houses,
Surrounded by some version of ocean weather,
Lit beads of fog or wind so stripped it burns the throat;
Mildew-spreading, spray-laden breezes and the beach sun
Making each grain of stucco cast a shadow;
An ideal landscape sheared of its nostalgia;
S. with his black hair, buck teeth, unsunned skin,
Joking and disappearing; F. doing exactly the same
But dying, a corkscrew motion through green water;
And C. not looking back from the car door,
Reappearing beside the East River, rich, owned, smiling at last.

Swains and nymphs. And news that came with the sea damp,
Of steady pipe-corrosions, black corners,
Moisture working through sand lots, through slab floors,
Slowly, with chemical, with molecular intricacy,
Then, bursting alive: the shrieked confessions
Of the wild parents; the cliff collapse; the kidnap;
The cache of photos; the letter; the weapon; the haunted dream;
The sudden close-up of the loved one's degradation.

Weather a part of it all, permeating and sanctifying,
Infiltrating and destroying; the sun disc,
Cool behind the veil of afternoon cloud,

With sun spots like flies crawling across it;
The slow empurpling of skin all summer;
The glorious learned flesh and the rich pallor
Of the untouched places in the first nakedness;
The working of the lesion now in late life,
Soon to be known by the body, even the one
Enduring the bareness of the inland plains,
The cold fronts out of Canada, a sickness
For home that feels no different from health.

MAUREEN DUFFY
Song of the Stand-pipe

Look the trees are dying in the drought
beech and birch keel over
shallow roots clutch at crumbling earth
copper and silver become uncurrent
beaten too soon into autumn
yet the leaden plane
sheds again
its patched hide
with seventeenth-century resilience
whatever civil war
the elements embark on
sun against rain
it stands
making its rough balls to propagate
citizen not recorded in the wild state
hybrid
tough cockney
that will uproot the paving stones
if we should ever
decamp
and lace its branches beautifully
over the crumpled streets.
When elm and oak
are bugged and broken
like love it will be here
nave and aisles

when the next first men
come wondering back
into the tumbled city
to begin again.

■ **Maureen Duffy** (*b.* 1933) is a British writer, novelist, poet and activist for writers' and animal rights causes who has published over 30 books, including five volumes of poetry. Much of her work draws on Freudian ideas and Greek myth. Her non-fiction books include *Men And Beasts: An Animal Rights Handbook* (1984), in which she argues for a more enlightened attitude towards animals, based on equality and respect for their rights. Her concern with animal rights is reflected also in her fiction, including her novels *I Want to Go to Moscow* (1973), which dramatises the moral problems posed for society by its own outlaws and by its relations to animals, and *Gor Saga* (1981), a futuristic tale with a laboratory-created half-human half-gorilla protagonist who is reared as a human child.

■ **Mark Jarman** (*b.* 1952) is a key poet in the "schools" of New Narrative and New Formalism in American poetry. His seminal book-length narrative poem *Iris* (1992) adapted Robinson Jeffers's double pentameter line, and was described by R.S. Gwynn as possibly 'the best example of the long pastoral poem in English since Wordsworth's "Michael".'

Robert McDowell: 'Mark Jarman's poems, more than those of any other poet of his generation, effectively combine the difficult Audensque virtues of versatility, precision, and lyric resonance. The key word behind Jarman's poetry is "recovery", reclaiming the past in a society intent on erasing the past as soon as its currency fades and in healing the wounds of painful experience. [...] Jarman, long a believer in the poet's responsibility to root poems in the landscape of a particular region, often returns to Scottish and southern California settings, his personal landscapes of childhood and adolescence, and to Kentucky and Tennessee, where he has lived and taught for a number of years. [...] A minister's son, he forever pushes against inherited faith, testing both its truthfulness and his own capacity to believe.'

NORMAN NICHOLSON
Windscale

The toadstool towers infest the shore:
Stink-horns that propagate and spore
    Wherever the wind blows.
Scafell looks down from the bracken band,
And sees hell in a grain of sand,
    And feels the canker itch between his toes.

This is a land where dirt is clean,
And poison pasture, quick and green,
    And storm sky, bright and bare;
Where sewers flow with milk, and meat
Is carved up for the fire to eat,
    And children suffocate in God's fresh air.

COLIN SIMMS
West Cumberland 10/11 October 1957

"burning" churns spurned
'pour all the milk down the drains and the burns'
leaching each reach, wreaking what wreck in the becks
effects not reflected, any reports, not reckoned in any checks

'No cause for concern'
No mention of Polonium, not much of Caesium or
    Plutonium
Americium or even Iodine isotopes, and there'd been a
    minimum
of 240 curies of Polonium 210 alone

'The Cumbrian cattle murrain'
is still mourned; they were burned; how many children
came down with leukaemia, how many more will burn
with the pain to come within, with us now, and borne on.

for the scientist Urquhart without whom even this finding
(made public 1983) would not yet be known

■ 'According to the excellent *Greenpeace Book of the Nuclear Age*, the near-catastrophic 1957 fire at Windscale (now Sellafield) in Cumbria released more than 40 isotopes, including the particularly lethal one that did for Alexander Litvinenko. John Urquhart, a statistician at Newcastle University, reckons the resulting cloud of radioactive fallout contained enough polonium to kill 1,000 people, and even the regulatory body that advised the government on nuclear safety and radiation limits conceded in the 1980s that there would be at least 32 deaths from the Windscale disaster – half of them directly attributable to polonium 210. Who needs the KGB?' (Jon Henley, *The Guardian*, 30 November 2006).
    Colin Simms: ➤ 60.

■ **Norman Nicholson** (1914-87) was an English poet closely associated with his home town of Millom in Cumbria, whose vernacular speech he voiced in his work. Many of his poems were concerned the effects of industry on the local landscape and people, including mining, quarrying and ironworks, as well as, in this poem, the presence of the nearby Windscale nuclear power plant. After the incident in 1957 when the graphite core of the reactor caught fire, releasing substantial amounts of radioactive contamination into the atmosphere, part of the plant was renamed Sellafield. The Windscale fire was considered the world's worst nuclear accident until the Three Mile Island accident in 1979; both were dwarfed by the Chernobyl disaster in 1986.

C.K. WILLIAMS
Tar

The first morning of Three Mile Island: those first dis-
    quieting, uncertain, mystifying hours.
All morning a crew of workmen have been tearing the
    old decrepit roof off our building,
and all morning, trying to distract myself, I've been
    wandering out to watch them
as they hack away the leaden layers of asbestos paper and
    disassemble the disintegrating drains.
After half a night of listening to the news, wondering
    how to know a hundred miles downwind
if and when to make a run for it and where, then a
    coming bolt awake at seven

when the roofers we've been waiting for since winter
    sent their ladders shrieking up our wall,
we still know less than nothing: the utility company
    continues making little of the accident,
the slick federal spokesmen still have their evasions in
    some semblance of order.
Surely we suspect now we're being lied to, but in the
    meantime, there are the roofers,
setting winch-frames, sledging rounds of tar apart, and
    there I am, on the curb across, gawking.

I never realised what brutal work it is, how matter-of-
    factly and harrowingly dangerous.
The ladders flex and quiver, things skid from the edge,
    the materials are bulky and recalcitrant.
When the rusty, antique nails are levered out, their heads
    pull off; the underroofing crumbles.
Even the battered little furnace, roaring along as patient
    as a donkey, chokes and clogs,
a dense, malignant smoke shoots up, and someone has
    to fiddle with a cock, then hammer it,
before the gush and stench will deintensify, the dark,
    Dantean broth wearily subside.
In its crucible, the stuff looks bland, like licorice, spill
    it, though, on your boots or coveralls,
it sears, and everything is permeated with it, the furnace
    gunked with burst and half-burst bubbles,
the men themselves so completely slashed and mucked
    they seem almost from another realm, like trolls.
When they take their break, they leave their brooms
    standing at attention in the asphalt pails,
work gloves clinging like Br'er Rabbit to the bitten shafts,
    and they slouch along the precipitous lip,
the enormous sky behind them, the heavy noontime air
    alive with shimmers and mirages.

Sometime in the afternoon I had to go inside: the advent
    of our vigil was upon us.
However much we didn't want to, however little we would
    do about it, we'd understood:
we were going to perish of all this, if not now, then soon,
    if not soon, then someday.

Someday, some final generation, hysterically aswarm
    beneath an atmosphere as unrelenting as rock,
would rue us all, anathematise our earthly comforts, curse
    our surfeits and submissions.
I think I know, though I might rather not, why my
    roofers stay so clear to me and why the rest,
the terror of that time, the reflexive disbelief and dis-
    tancing, all we should hold on to, dims so.
I remember the president in his absurd protective booties,
    looking absolutely unafraid, the fool.
I remember a woman on the front page glaring across
    the misty Susquehanna at those looming stacks.
But, more vividly, the men, silvered with glitter from the
    shingles, clinging like starlings beneath the eaves.
Even the leftover carats of tar in the gutter, so black they
    seemed to suck the light out of the air.
By nightfall kids had come across them: every sidewalk on
    the block was scribbled with obscenities and hearts.

■ **C.K. Williams** (*b.* 1936) is an American poet and critic noted for his discursive poems of psychological insight, most of which use his characteristic long line to tease meaning from the chaos of everyday life. They are startlingly intensive narratives on love, death, secrets and wayward thought which examine the inner life with unflinching candour. He lives for part of the year in France, latterly in Normandy, and part in Princeton, New Jersey. [Other poem ➤ 225]

The Three Mile Island accident began on 28 March 1979 following a partial core meltdown in the nuclear power plant at Three Mile Island on the Susquehanna River in Dauphin County, Pennsylvania near Harrisburg. For several days various authorities tried to deal with the problem as rumours spread about a possible evacuation affecting not just the immediate local community (25,000 people lived within eight miles). The official line is that the amount of radiation released into the atmosphere was minimal. Some studies suggested a link between local cases of lung cancer and offsite exposures, but no conclusive link was proved. However, a later study carried out at the University of North Carolina at Chapel Hill (published in *Environmental Health Perspectives* in 1997) showed that incidences of lung cancer and leukaemia after the accident were two to ten times higher downwind of the plant than upwind. Epidemiologist Dr Steven Wing reported: 'The cancer findings, along with studies of animals, plants and chromosomal damage in Three Mile Island area residents, all point to much higher radiation levels than were previously reported. If you say that there was no high radiation, then you are left with higher cancer rates downwind of the plume that are otherwise unexplainable.' The only study documenting contamination to the wild food chain was one published in 1983 which examined levels of radioactive Iodine-131 in the thyroids of meadow voles in the vicinity of the plant. The accident had serious economic and public relations consequences for the US nuclear industry, and the clean-up process was only completed in 1993 at a cost of $975 million. Until Chernobyl seven years later it was considered the world's worst civilian nuclear accident.

■ **Mario Petrucci** (*b.* 1958) is an English poet of Italian parentage as well as an ecologist and physicist, and has been resident poet at the Imperial War Museum. His book-length poem *Heavy Water: a poem for Chernobyl* (2004) was inspired by *Voices from Chernobyl*, a book of first-hand accounts of the disaster drawn from hundreds of interviews by journalist Svetlana Alexievich, who was irradiated as a result of her work. Petrucci won the Arvon International Poetry Competition in 2002 with a series of excerpts from the book, which has been adapted into an award-winning film by Seventh Art, *Half Life: a Journey to Chernobyl*. His other books include *Flowers of Sulphur* (2007), which pungently conveys 'the wonders and exactitudes of science' (Moniza Alvi).

Heavy Water is written in the voices of the ordinary people who dealt with the Chernobyl disaster at ground-level: the fire-fighters, the soldiers, the "liquidators" and their families. On 26 April 1986, reactor four at the Chernobyl nuclear power station exploded, sending an enormous radioactive cloud over northern Ukraine and neighbouring Belarus. At first the danger was kept secret by the Soviet authorities from the rest of the world as well as from the nearby population, who went their business as usual. May Day celebrations began, children played and the residents of Pripyat marvelled at the spectacular fire raging at the reactor. After three days, an area the size of England had become contaminated with radioactive dust, creating a massive "zone" of poisoned land. *Heavy Water* tells the inside human story at local level of what turned into an ecological disaster of global magnitude.

[Other poem ➤ 234]

MARIO PETRUCCI
from Heavy Water: a poem for Chernobyl

Soldier

They gave us underwear. Socks, real leather boots.
Shoulder boards, trousers, two belts, shirts, a pack and cap.

This week I have to work on top. They call me *stork*.
The farmers say – *Where are the crickets? The slugs?*

but still something glistens in their gardens. Cherry
with each leaf perforated. Green lacework trees.

The old women scrub our clothes. Bend till their palms
blister, dissolve. They tell us – *It is not the soap.*

On concrete steps, in the shade of lintels – a fine
shimmer. Like finest snow. A ginger kitten

stretched in a kitchen window, its head a dried
apricot. One old man was weeding, the very

day he had to leave. *Why do you do that?* I asked.
Because he said, *that is the work you do*

in the summer. That's how it is as a soldier.
Those peasants. Painting door-planks and fences with

parting notes: *'10 May. Dawn. By donkey and cart.'*
'May 24. There is pilaf in the blue pan.'

'Don't kill our Zhuchok. He's a good dog – 4th June.'
'June 1st. Forgive us, house.' On the walls their photos

tilt – as though the rooms were trying to recall them.
One village had spilled out a wedding, the bride's

red lips barely kissed, and we were removing
topsoil. Spraying foam. Now the looters have started –

pink candy crushed on asphalt. Their currency
of bottles. What can we do? Chernobyl has left,

gone from the map. To flea markets, second-hand stores,
dachas. One man, they say, bought a pillbox hat –

you know, black market. Had to watch his wife's head
grow the black brim. No joke. Our captain. Sleeps with his

Geiger under the bed. A woman came past
playing the accordion. *Where did you get that?*

he barks. Prods his Tube at her keys as though It
could smell music. *Bury it. Now.* Her mouth – just like

my mother's when she saw the letter's red stripe
and knew what it meant. That's fine – I wanted to stop

bullets with my chest. But these bullets are as strange
as needles. And this, a strange war. You get killed

when you get back. Most nights I hear my mother's voice,
my grandmother's. Doctor says – *It's the heat. Just*

wash your hands before eating. Today I get
my commendation. Some hero! Always nodding.

The boys lift me onto their shoulders. Take slugs
of vodka. Twelve each. Today at the reactor

I will have my picture taken.

'My parents kissed – and I was born.'

Then black clouds. Black rain.
Our garden all white. Not a white
like snow – but glass. We lived
in the cellar. Grandma told me to
count my sins – in case the devil
burst through the bricks with all
his heat behind him. I saw that frog
me and Vadik burst with a stick. How

its insides came out red like the jam I
dropped that made mama swear.

Dad came home black. Not his
clothes. His face. He said he got
too close. We visited him in a white
room. A man chased Kitty with a Geiger.
Tried to put the clicks on Kitty's tail
like salt. He had a big plastic bag. Got
angry when I giggled – when I shouted
Run Kitty! When we saw Dad I told
the story. Then he got angry too.

Some old women met the train
when we stopped. They threw
brown stones at us. Then we saw
it was bread. One had a face like
Grandma. But when I asked for water
she made the sign of the cross. Took
one step back. A woman in a white
apron brought us ice cream. She let us
keep the glass. Then soldiers came –
kept washing our train. I looked for
the old woman. The one who looked
like Grandma. But she was gone.

A man in a white spacesuit and mask
met us at the hospital. He said – *Put
all your clothes in this bag.* I thought
about Kitty. I didn't laugh. He said
he was a doctor but I didn't believe him.
He didn't look like the doctors you see
in the films. Mama tried to keep her ring.
He shook his head. Told her something
about half a life. I was crying but happy
I would see the city. From the window
the city was grey. Now if a bee stings
you die. At night I look out the window
to see if there is a fox with three tails.
I will so to sleep. Like Dad. Dad
said we will all sleep forever.
And become science.

I dreamed I was dead – but
mama was crying in the dream,
She cried so loud it woke me up.
She woke me up so I wouldn't die.
But when I looked around for her
she wasn't there. They take me to her
on Tuesday. *Remember – she can't
talk.* That's what he says. The man
who thinks he is a doctor. But he's
wrong. Mama speaks to me. She
does. With her eyes. Mama told me –
We all come back as someone else.
Vadik told me my parents kissed
and I was born. I will find a boy
in the ward. A boy like Vadik.
And kiss him.

They put me in a white room.
To paint. No one hugs me.
Under the window is a nest.
I wait to see if there are babies.
To see if the daisies will open –
if they are black. A woman with
red hair looks at what I paint.
She sits with her hands folded.
Says her name is not important.
I make a painting and she holds it
up to the window. Like X-rays.
She says – *Are all your people
black?* I don't answer. I twist
my brush in the paint. The way
Dad would do with his fork
with noodles. I pick up as much
of the dark as I can. I ask him
for more – the man who pretends
to be a doctor. I tell him. *There
is never enough black.*

'Every day I found a new man' – LUDMILA IGNATENKO

Do not kiss him they said, starting back, as though
he were an animal in its cot cocking its head to listen

but understanding nothing. *Do you understand? Are you
pregnant? No? And find him milk. Three litres a day.*

I poured that whiteness into him. Felt I was feeding
a goose its own feathers. He retched and cursed –

the thin dribble each side of his mouth worse than a child.
Each time you hold his hand is a year off your life. Can you

*hear us? His bones are more active than the Core.
Understand? That is no longer your husband.* I boiled

chickens until the bones sagged, fresh, handfuls of parsley
chopped so fine it melted between finger and thumb,

pot barley, apples (from Michurinsk they told me) pared
and pulped, everything minced and sieved, every trace

of rind or pip removed, no husk or shell or pod, and all of it
spewed back down his chest as though he could not take

a single particle more. The black of his forearms and thighs
cracked like pastry. His eyelids swelled so tight with water

he could not see for skin. The lightest sheet peeled away
fat as flypaper, the slightest edge of thumbnail was to him

more vicious than any cut-throat – if I moved his head it
streaked hair down the pillow as though he were a used match,

if I pressed a knuckle in – our wedding flesh – the indent
remained like hot grey putty, he coughed bile, acid

froth and lung, shreds of stomach and liver and still he
stayed – refused that first, that last, step onto the Jacob Ladder.

Those reptile eggs of his eyelids, turned always towards me.
Until I said *Go, I love you. But Go.* Until that moment

I still believed I would save him. Milk, soup, kisses. As if
he could digest the touch of my lips, feel my making of broth

in his dissolving heart-chambers. When his breath shut,
when he began to cool – then – I called for family. It was

almost a miracle, the Doctors said. Four times the fatal dose
and he nearly turned round. I felt myself the wrong side

of a door – a partition thin as plywood, thinner, as though
you could hear everything that was going on inside.

His mother hugged me. The brothers kissed me. *Now we
are your brothers*. Have you ever been the wrong side

of that door, knowing all you needed was the key and you
could walk straight in? That's how it was. We were that close.

Envoy

Take our words. Enrich them.
They are already active – but enrich them.

This is dangerous. May even be impossible.
They are dispersed through a great mass

and you may need to quarry this vastness
to elicit one bald grain. You may have

to detach yourself. Use robots and machines.
But at the end – after immense effort – you

will forge from our cries a single silver rod.
You will put it on display behind a screen.

Your scientists will marvel. Your politicians
quake. You will have to control and subdue it –

contain it with great care. Many will not wish
to have it near them. Or their children. You will

protect yourselves with suits. Put your ear to it
and hear it hum. It will make you shudder.

One night – in early darkness. When you are
thinking of something else. It will escape.

SARAH MAGUIRE
May Day, 1987
(for Tadeusz Sławek)

Yesterday, the weather in Warsaw
was the same as London's: *Sunny, 18°*
(sixty-four Fahrenheit). I am sitting
in a walled garden drinking gin,
the fading sky as blue as this tonic water
loosening its bubbles against the flat ice.

What is the the air? The first midges;
a television three doors down, its hum
like this lone bat avoiding the walnut tree.
A dog barks. In other houses lights come on –
the street an Advent Calendar opening
its doors. This house is in darkness,

its seven windows admitting the night.
I'm trying to read *Mansfield Park*, to learn
how Fanny finds love and a mansion
through keeping silence. All week
the weather report has plotted the wind
leaving Chernobyl with its freight

of fall-out: cancer settling on Poland –
the radioactivity an inaudible fizz
in the cells, rupturing thorax or liver.
The intimacy of the bowel. They say it won't
reach here. I stare at the sky till all
I can see are the dead cells of my eyes,

jumping and falling. It's too dark to read –
only the flare of a late *Kerria japonica*,
trained to the wall. I think of your letter
in my drawer with the handkerchiefs,
one page torn by an earlier reader. Socrates
distrusted writing, its distance from

the grain of the voice. I come indoors
to write you all the things I couldn't say
a year ago. Later, on the news, they will show

gallons of contaminated Polish milk
swilled into sewage, a boy crying
at the sting of iodine he must swallow

against the uncertain air.

MATTHEW SWEENEY
Zero Hour

Tomorrow all the trains will stop
and we will be stranded. Cars
have already been immobilised
by the petrol wars, and sit
abandoned, along the roadsides.
The airports, for two days now,
are closed-off zones where dogs
congregate loudly on the runways.

To be in possession of a bicycle
is to risk your life. My neighbour,
a doctor, has somehow acquired a horse
and rides to his practice, a rifle
clearly visible beneath the reins,
I sit in front of the television
for each successive news bulletin
then reach for the whisky bottle.

How long before the shelves are empty
in the supermarkets? The first riots
are raging as I write, and who
out there could have predicted
this sudden countdown to zero hour,
all the paraphernalia of our comfort
stamped obsolete, our memories
fighting to keep us sane and upright?

■ **Sarah Maguire** (*b.* 1957) is an English poet who trained
as a gardener and has always lived in west London. She is
known especially for her symbolically resonant poems about
flowers and gardens; like all of her richly lyrical poetry, these
open out into densely textured explorations of themes such
as loss and desire, death and oppression, grounding precise,
sensual detail within the wider context of world events. She
is the founder and director of the Poetry Translation Centre
at SOAS, and has co-translated the work of several Arab poets
as well as Afghan writer Atiq Rahimi's *A Thousand Rooms of
Dream and Fear* (2006). Her books include the collections
Spilt Milk (1991), *The Invisible Mender* (1997), *The Florist's at
Midnight* (2001) and *The Pomegranates of Kandahar* (2007),
and *Flora Poetica: The Chatto Book of Botanical Verse* (2001).

■ **Matthew Sweeney** (*b.* 1952) is an Irish poet and children's
writer who left Donegal to live in England, Germany and
Romania. He studied in London and Freiburg, and his blackly
humorous yet acutely serious poetry shows the influence of
both the Irish and German literary traditions. He described
his poetry as 'imagistic narrative' in an interview with Lidia
Vianu: 'I consider poetry – or at least this kind of poetry – to
have a lot in common with film. [...] Some of it strays beyond
realism into the territory I call alternative realism (which is not
to be confused with surrealism, although many people do this).'

■ **Mario Petrucci** ➤ 230.

MARIO PETRUCCI
Repossession

Down the long leg of the catwalker fishnets melt

to mesh-work tobacco spittle. A black liquid garter.
Asphalt picks itself up – each scaly skin spread
between kerbstones is pulling free with a bass

pop. Every city suddenly a kicked nest of adders
coiling together into a spitting rope of pitch.
All along their spines household molecules un-

crack – hydrocarbon vertebrae whose Lego atoms
snap back into place in a chiropracty of electron-volts.
Cars at last cough up. Judder to a stop. Dig ignition-

deep to sputter swart apologies across the crisp white
shirts of their hosts. And every sump on its scrap-heap
bumps and boils its box-black kettle – rejoices openly

as through the stratosphere water-vapour and dioxide
recombine: weave fine mists of oil to drop charred
tapeworms of cirrus. Videos slime in the hand like

jumbo choc-ices. CDs in the rack pucker and shrink
to mushy black peas. Dentures gum up the works
in toothless gaga. Those precise blocks

and avenues of electronics crinkle dark and
medieval. In the fast lane of the bowling alley
a caviar cannonball splashes ten full bottles of

devil's milk – while those of the mobile who gas
this world down to its last nook into Porlock hell
shriek as they peel hot tar from lobes – Yes every

biro   mothball   racquet   sags   bleeds   gutters
till the black string vest of tributaries resolves –
untangles towards tonsured ozone. Finally

we notice. On satellite-replays Presidents track
their sloed candyfloss economies writhing round
earth's spindle – are caught on camera in black lip-

stick salve leaning to kiss the screen goodbye – and for
that moment the globe has a single gathering purpose
as a girl glances up from her fractions to witness

the filaments merge in that mother of all twisters –
merge and rise and take her place. She watches
the whole black mass lift up and out into daytime

where it balls itself – steadies a wobbling edge
against blue to sling there its low fat circle. Crude
and glossy. She sees the birth of the full black moon

that lights our ways with dark.

DAVID CONSTANTINE
Mappa Mundi

1

This was a pleasant place.
This was a green hill outside the city.
Who would believe it now? Unthink
The blood if you can, the pocks and scabs,
The tendrils of wire. Imagine an apple tree
Where that thing stands embedded.

2

There is nowhere on earth now but
Some spoke will find us out
Some feeler from the impaled hill. On sunny days
That broken thing at the dead centre
Its freezing shadow comes round. At nights
Turning and turning like
The poor shepherd Cyclops for his bearings
It colours moonlight with a hurt eye.

3

Blood then, in a downpour.
For weather continued, the sun
Still drank what sea was available.
The indifferent wind herded his sagging clouds
That wept when they could not bear any more.

4

Our nearest sea lies at the mercy of certain rivers.
The rivers themselves cannot avert themselves.
They begin blindly where, so we believe,
There is clean ice, snow and rare blue flowers.
They come on headlong and before they know it
We have them in our cities.

If they could die that would be better.
If they were lambs and we their abattoirs.
But they emerge like many of our children
Suddenly old, big-eyed,
Inclining to apathy. What was before

What they saw in our cities
They cannot at all remember. Day after day
They sink their trauma in the helpless sea.

5

The flat earth is felloed with death.
At every world's end, in some visited city,
Diminished steps go down into the river of death.
The salt river fills the throats of severed bridges.
Mors, the serpent, encircles the world.
His tail is in his mouth. He lives for ever.

6

Paradise lay in the river of death.
Before we slept we listened to the lapping water.
Our sands went steeply down, we bathed,
Rolling for joy like dolphins. Smiling,
We felt the dry salt on our faces;
Salt on our lips. She could halve
The mouth-watering apples exactly with her fingers.

We had four cardinal springs, they rose at the centre.
They rose from a love-knot continually undoing.

One day Charon arrived in a black boat,
One morning early, we were still sleeping.
Naked we were taken away from home.

7

The rivers of Paradise swam under the sea,
Unmixed with salt, death had no hold on them.
They surfaced miles apart, like fugitives
They calmed their breathing, they assumed
A local pace and appearance. Inland somewhere
Ordinary people
Receive driftwood from their broadcasting arms.

8

All rivers, even this, remain persuasive.
We have a house whose open windows listen.
At nights, my hand on your cold hand that rests
Upon your belly where our child curls,

We listen anxiously. Suppose we left,
Suppose we left this place and leaving below us
City, town, village and the interference
Of fence and throttling wire, suppose we found
The crack in the ice where one of the four emerges
Thrown, gasping, lying in the thin air
Like lambs that wait for strength from the sun to stand,
What could we do, holding that dangling thread?
Where could we go, knowing our need for breath?

Frightened at nights, hearing our city river,
We feel through our divining hands the pulse
Of the first four springs, we feel the kick
Of their departure diving, sweet through salt,
Their shouldering like smooth seals,
Their wriggling through the earth's rock like white hot
    quartz
Passing the creatures pressed
With starting eyes in carapaces
Whom fire and weight put out from the shape they had.

9

We shall not harm them now, they seem to pity us.
They have come out of a few last hiding-places.
They are solemn and curious, they have formed a ring.
Little by little they are coming forward, shy as birds.
We might have fed them. Or perhaps they are drawn
Against good manners, thinking it rude to stare, but as
Our children used to be drawn to pavement corpses
When deaths were singular. They are all true, all those
That we imagined; but many we never imagined.
They stare particularly at our little ones
Who cannot be frightened by anything we imagine,
Who are not alarmed by Blemyae and Sciapods,
By Dogheads, Cyclops, Elephant Men,
By some mouthless, feeding through a reed, others in a
    caul,
Some with the stumps of wings, some webbed, some
    joined, some swagged
With dewlaps, some diaphanous, some thin, with eyes.
Our children smile at them all. They are glad perhaps,
Our children, not to be unprecedented.

ANNA AKHMATOVA
'Distance collapsed in rubble...'
translated from the Russian by Richard McKane

Distance collapsed in rubble and time was shaken,
the devil of speed stamped on the brows
of great mountains and reversed the river's flow,
the seed lay poisoned in the earth,
the sap flowed poisoned in the stem.
A mighty generation of people died out
but everyone knew that the time was very near.

PETER READING
Thucydidean

Continents then were affected by violent
   earthquakes, eclipses,
withering droughts and subsequent famines,
   pestilent outbreaks...
Faced with the Plague, the ignorant Faculty
   shewed itself impotent;
equally useless were all of our sciences,
   oracles, arts, prayers...
Burning sensations occurred in our heads, our
   eyes became bloodshot,
inside our mouths there was bleeding from throat and
   tongue, we grew breathless,
coughing and retching ensued, producing
   bile of all species,
genitals, fingers and toes became festered,
   diarrhoea burgeoned...

Terrible was the despair into which all
   fell when they realised
fully the weight and the magnitude of their
   diresome affliction...
Not enough living to bury the dead or
   cover the corpses...
Seeing how swift and abrupt were the changes
   Fortune allotted

(money and life alike being transient
   under the Pestilence),
profligate wretched citizens turned to
   lawless dishonour,
heedless of gods and of law for they thought themselves
   already sentenced –
then was there bloody and slaughterous civil
   mass insurrection.

■ Many of Peter Reading's poems of disaster and foreboding rework old texts relating to earlier periods of upheaval: above, the Greek historian Thucydides chronicling the fall of Athens; in **'Fragmentary'** [➤ 238], the Anglo-Saxon poem 'The Ruin', probably describing the ruins of Bath three centuries after the departure of the Romans. Author note ➤ 104.

■ **Anna Akhmatova** (1889-1966) was Russia's greatest modern poet. She was persecuted for her work along with fellow poets Mandelstam, who died in a camp, and Tsvetaeva, who committed suicide. As she fought for her son's release from prison, she was writing her greatest poetry: the cycle *Requiem*, which commemorated all of Stalin's victims, and *Poem without a hero*, which she began in 1940 and worked on for over 20 years. All she wrote she committed to memory. Writing nothing down, she survived, the people's conscience, the one who kept 'the great Russian word' alive. Much of her work is haunted by death and disaster, including this poem from the 1950s.

■ **David Constantine** (*b.* 1944) is an English poet known also for his translations of poets such as Enzensberger, Goethe, Hölderlin and Jaccottet. Like the work of the European and English poets who have nourished him, his poetry is informed by a profoundly humane vision of the world as by the beauty and harshness of nature. His early influences included Graves, Lawrence and Edward Thomas, poets he admired 'for their passion and attention to the real and the mythic world' (*Write Words* interview, 22 June 2005); other poets important for him and his work would include Keats, Wordsworth, Clare and Hardy. His poems often place people in relation to particular landscapes, in particular, the Pennines, North Wales, Cornwall, Scilly and the Greek islands. In **'Mappa Mundi'**, he fills the 13th-century map in Hereford Cathedral with apocalyptic images reminiscent of the battlefields of the Somme, post-nuclear disaster and the panoramas of Hieronymus Bosch. [Other poems ➤ 23, 241]

PETER READING
Fragmentary

felled by Fate,   this fine-wrought wall.
…castle is crumbled,   constructed by giants.
Rooftrees are wrecked,   ruined towers
fester and fall.   Fate fells all.
What of the craftsmen?   Clasped in earth.
In the grave's grasp   great men perish.
Grey lichen grows   on the gore-stained stone,
the gate is mouldered,   masons of genius
bound with iron   the base of the wall…
buildings abounded,   bath-houses, dwellings,
mead-halls were many   where men would boast,
but all was felled   by Fate's onslaught.
Pestilence came,   killing abundantly.
Those men who might   have re-made it lay dead.
What was once fought for   is wasteland now.
These courts have become   coldly bereft;
ripped from the rooftrees,   wrecked tiles lie.
…once, many men   in moods of confidence,
girt in gold,   the gear of warriors,
flushed with wine,   wealthy in silver,
counted their prized   possessions jealously…
Stonework stood here,   a spa of water
gushed forth hotly…

        [Hiatus, lacuna…
as the city is sunken   so is the word-hoard,
faded the fragile   fragment of manuscript,
parchment eroded   round the sad utterance.]

CHARLES BUKOWSKI
Dinosauria, we

born like this
into this
as the chalk faces smile
as Mrs Death laughs

as the elevators break
as political lands apes dissolve
as the supermarket bag boy holds a college degree
as the oily fish spit out their oily prey
as the sun is masked

we are
born like this
into this
into these carefully mad wars
into the sight of broken factory windows of emptiness
into bars where people no longer speak to each other
into fist fights that end as shootings and knifings

born into this
into hospitals which are so expensive that it's cheaper to die
into lawyers who charge so much it's cheaper to plead guilty
into a country where the jails are full and the madhouses closed
into a place where the masses elevate fools into rich heroes

born into this
walking and living through this
dying because of this
muted because of this
castrated
debauched
disinherited
because of this
fooled by this
used by this
pissed on by this
made crazy and sick by this
made violent
made inhuman
by this

the heart is blackened
the fingers reach for the throat
the gun
the knife
the bomb
the fingers reach toward an unresponsive god
the fingers reach for the bottle

the pill
the powder

we are born into this sorrowful deadliness
we are born into a government 60 years in debt
that soon will be unable even to pay the interest on that debt
and the banks will burn
money will be useless
there will be open and unpunished murder on the streets
it will be guns and roving mobs
land will be useless
food will become a diminishing return
nuclear power will be taken over by the many
explosions will continually shake the earth
radiated robot men will stalk each other
the rich and the chosen will watch from space platforms
Dante's *Inferno* will be made to look like a children's play-
    ground

the sun will not be seen and it will always be night
trees will die
all vegetation will die
radiated men will eat the flesh of radiated men
the sea will be poisoned
the lakes and rivers will vanish
rain will be the new gold

the rotting bodies of men and animals will stink in the dark
    wind

the last few survivors will be overtaken by new and hideous
    diseases
and the space platforms will be destroyed by attrition
the petering out of supplies
the natural effect of general decay

and there will be the most beautiful silence never heard

born out of that,

the sun still hidden there

awaiting the next chapter

■ **Charles Bukowski** (1920-94) was a prolific American novelist, short story writer and poet who published over 50 books after quitting his post office job at the age of 49. Strongly influenced by the geography and atmosphere of Los Angeles, much of his writing chronicles everyday life in vividly vernacular language, dealing with desperate, dreadful events in his own and others' downtrodden lives with a distanced stance, hard-won wisdom and black wit. In both his work and his life, Bukowski created a loathsome legend of himself as an angry drunk, cheating lover and vulnerable egotist, an outsider trapped in a gutter world of comic pathos and glimpsed beauty. 'Foul-mouthed and potbellied, ravaged by self-neglect and alcohol, with a huge misshapen head, matted hair and lump, pitted, porridge-coloured skin, he looked in his prime like something risen from the dead.' (Hilary Spurling, *Daily Telegraph*).

LORD BYRON
Darkness

I had a dream, which was not all a dream.
The bright sun was extinguished, and the stars
Did wander darkling in the eternal space,
Rayless, and pathless, and the icy Earth
Swung blind and blackening in the moonless air;
Morn came and went – and came, and brought no day,
And men forgot their passions in the dread
Of this their desolation; and all hearts
Were chilled into a selfish prayer for light:
And they did live by watchfires – and the thrones,
The palaces of crowned kings – the huts,
The habitations of all things which dwell,
Were burnt for beacons; cities were consumed,
And men were gathered round their blazing homes
To look once more into each other's face;
Happy were those who dwelt within the eye
Of the volcanos, and their mountain-torch:
A fearful hope was all the World contained;
Forests were set on fire – but hour by hour
They fell and faded – and the crackling trunks
Extinguished with a crash – and all was black.
The brows of men by the despairing light

Wore an unearthly aspect, as by fits
The flashes fell upon them; some lay down
And hid their eyes and wept; and some did rest
Their chins upon their clenched hands, and smiled;
And others hurried to and fro, and fed
Their funeral piles with fuel, and looked up
With mad disquietude on the dull sky,
The pall of a past World; and then again
With curses cast them down upon the dust,
And gnashed their teeth and howled: the wild birds
    shrieked,
And, terrified, did flutter on the ground,
And flap their useless wings; the wildest brutes
Came tame and tremulous; and vipers crawled
And twined themselves among the multitude,
Hissing, but stingless – they were slain for food.
And War, which for a moment was no more,
Did glut himself again: – a meal was bought
With blood, and each sate sullenly apart
Gorging himself in gloom: no Love was left;
All earth was but one thought – and that was Death,
Immediate and inglorious; and the pang
Of famine fed upon all entrails – men
Died, and their bones were tombless as their flesh;
The meagre by the meagre were devoured,
Even dogs assailed their masters, all save one,
And he was faithful to a corse, and kept
The birds and beasts and famished men at bay,
Till hunger clung them, or the dropping dead
Lured their lank jaws; himself sought out no food,
But with a piteous and perpetual moan,
And a quick desolate cry, licking the hand
Which answered not with a caress – he died.
The crowd was famished by degrees; but two
Of an enormous city did survive,
And they were enemies: they met beside
The dying embers of an altar place
Where had been heaped a mass of holy things
For an unholy usage; they raked up,
And shivering scraped with their cold skeleton hands
The feeble ashes, and their feeble breath
Blew for a little life, and made a flame

Which was a mockery; then they lifted up
Their eyes as it grew lighter, and beheld
Each other's aspects – saw, and shrieked, and died –
Even of their mutual hideousness they died,
Unknowing who he was upon whose brow
Famine had written Fiend. The World was void,
The populous and the powerful – was a lump,
Seasonless, herbless, treeless, manless, lifeless –
A lump of death – a chaos of hard clay.
The rivers, lakes, and ocean all stood still,
And nothing stirred within their silent depths;
Ships sailorless lay rotting on the sea,
And their masts fell down piecemeal: as they dropped
They slept on the abyss without a surge –
The waves were dead; the tides were in their grave,
The moon their mistress had expired before;
The winds were withered in the stagnant air,
And the clouds perished; Darkness had no need
Of aid from them – She was the Universe.

■ **George Gordon, Lord Byron** (1788-1824) was an Anglo-Scottish poet who was a highly influential figure in Romanticism as well as a controversial satirist whose poetry and personality cult captured the imagination of Europe. Famously described by Lady Caroline Lamb as 'mad, bad, and dangerous to know', he died of fever while engaged in the Greek struggle for independence from the Turks.

Byron wrote **'Darkness'** in Switzerland in the cold, rainy summer of 1816, 'the year without a summer' as it became known, when his storytelling challenge to guests at Lake Geneva inspired two seminal Gothic novels, Mary Shelley's *Frankenstein* (1818) and John Polidori's *The Vampyre* (1819). In his persuasive account of 'Darkness' in *The Song of the Earth*, Jonathan Bate 'unlocks the impulse behind the poem': Byron's experience of the worst summer on record, which was followed by poor harvests, 'a hemispheric subsistence crisis, basic food shortage and concordant public disorder'. Bate quotes contemporary reports of 'a consistently dense haze permanently on the horizon', 'smoking vapour' and the darkening of the sun which 'led to fears of apocalypse – the exact situation of Byron's poem'.

He locates the cause in the eruption of Tamboro volcano in Indonesia in 1815, 'which killed some 80,000 people on the islands of Sumbawa and Lombok. It was the greatest eruption since 1500. The dust blasted into the stratosphere reduced the transparency of the atmosphere, filtered out the sun and consequently lowered surface temperatures. The effect lasted for three years, straining the growth-capacity of life across the planet. Beginning in 1816, crop failure led to food riots in nearly every country in Europe. [...]

'Byron does not set culture apart from nature. [...] The poem darkly narrates a history in which war temporarily ceases as humankind pulls together in the face of inclement weather but is then renewed on a global scale as a result of the famine consequent on the absence of sunlight. The global struggle for subsistence leads ultimately to the extinction of mankind. In 1815, Byron and his public witnessed the cessation of a European, indeed worldwide, war which had lasted for more than twenty years; in 1816, they endured a year without a summer. The poem is as contemporary as it is apocalyptic. [...] But contemporary as it was, the poem remains powerfully prophetic [...] the vision of a world seasonless, herbless, treeless, the rivers, lakes and oceans silent. [...] When we read "Darkness" now, Byron may be reclaimed as a prophet of – to adopt Bruno Latour's word – ecocide.'

■ David Constantine ➤ 237.

DAVID CONSTANTINE
'There used to be forests'

There used to be forests beyond the peripherals.
We knew whenever one burned: it quietened our wheels
With skins and beheaded beasts would appear
Upended on the market and into the centre

There was a fall-out of the bipeds it evicted,
You saw them in the queues; or in the precinct, stupid;
Or getting the shittiest deals under the bridges;
And I used to think of Pan, naked, uprooted,

Limping on his goat-feet, come into town
After Daphnis died, and I tried hard to imagine
This town on a grief like that. Midsummer again.
Last night I woke from a dream crying my heart out.

Lovers forget the news. They will ask for places
Heard of near the perimeter and put
A pretty shock through the network but
Where will they run to when you catch their faces

Like souls in your blaring lamps, their clothes
Already fallen away and root and stem
Already they are being translated and from their mouths
The need for a forest babbles, bewildering them

Like antlers, the need for glades and pools, and as
Beasts they arrive where a whistling forest was
And clothing again is impossible and the moon beams
Back at the ash its last programme of screams?

HANS MAGNUS ENZENSBERGER
The End of the Owls
translated from the German by Jerome Rothenberg

I speak for none of your kind,
I speak for the end of the owls.
I speak for the flounder and whale
in their unlighted house,
for the seven cornered sea,
for the glaciers
they will have calved too soon,
raven and dove, feathery witnesses,
for all those that dwell in the sky
and the woods, and the lichen in gravel,
for those without paths, for the colourless bog
and the desolate mountains.

Glaring on radar screens,
interpreted one final time
around the briefing table, fingered
to death by antennas, Florida's swamps
and the Siberian ice, beast
and bush and basalt strangled
by early bird, ringed
by the latest manoeuvres, helpless

under the hovering fireballs,
in the ticking of crises.

We're as good as forgotten.
Don't fuss with the orphans,
just empty your mind
of its longing for nest eggs,
glory or psalms that won't rust.
I speak for none of you now,
all you plotters of perfect crimes,
not for me, not for anyone.

I speak for those who can't speak,
for the deaf and dumb witnesses.
for otters and seals,
for the ancient owls of the earth.

■ **Hans Magnus Enzensberger** (*b.* 1929) is Germany's most important poet, as well as a provocative cultural essayist, a highly influential editor and one of Europe's leading political thinkers. His poetry's social and moral criticism of the post-war world owes much to Marxism, yet insists on the freedoms which have often been denied by Communist governments; like Orwell he maintains that satire and criticism should not be party-political. Enzensberger's many books include several on culture and politics which have been translated into English, among these *Europe, Europe* (1989), *Mediocrity and Delusion* (1992) and *Civil War* (1994), as well as two bestselling works for young people, *The Number Devil* (1998), an entertaining look at maths, and *Where Were You, Robert?* (2000), about history.

■ **Primo Levi** (1919-87) was an Italian-Jewish writer and chemist, and one of the major literary voices of the 20th century. His restrained account of his experiences of Auschwitz, and of his survival and homecoming in *If This Is a Man* (1958) and *The Truce* (1963) are without parallel in any literature. In his extraordinary memoir *The Periodic Table* (1975) he scrutinises significant events in his own life and examines the nature of the human condition and civilised values. Reviewing his *Collected Poems* (1988), translated into English by Ruth Feldman and Brian Swann, Carol Ann Duffy wrote: 'The courage and steadiness of his gaze lift his poetry to the level of great music and give it a universality that translations cannot restrict.' (*Guardian*)

LAVINIA GREENLAW
The Recital of Lost Cities

It started with the polar ice caps.
A slight increase in temperature and the quiet
was shattered. The Australian Antarctic
wandered all over the Norwegian Dependency
as mountainous fragments lurched free
with a groan like ships mahogany.

And then there was the continental shift:
everywhere you went, America was coming closer.
Hot weather brought plague and revolution.
Nations disappeared or renamed themselves
as borders moved, in, out, in, out,
with tidal persistence and threat.

Cartographers dealt in picture postcards.
The printing plates tor the last atlas
were archived unused. Their irrelevant contours
gathered dust, locked in a vault
to save the public from the past
and the danger of wrong directions.

The sea rose by inches, unravelled the coastline,
eased across the lowlands and licked at the hills
where people gathered to remember names:
Calcutta, Tokyo, San Francisco,
Venice, Amsterdam, Baku,
Alexandria, Santo Domingo…

■ **Lavinia Greenlaw** (*b.* 1962) is an English poet and freelance writer. Born into a family of scientists, she is noted for drawing on scientific subject-matter in her work, but art, music, history and travel are just as significant sources of inspiration, and displacement, loss and belonging are recurrent themes in both her poetry and her fiction. Her publications include three poetry collections, *Night Photograph* (1993), *A World Where News Travelled Slowly* (1997) and *Minsk* (2003), two novels, *Mary George of Allnorthover* (2001) and *An Irresponsible Age* (2006), and a work of non-fiction, *The Importance of Music to Girls* (2007).

JOY HARJO
Perhaps the World Ends Here

The world begins at a kitchen table. No matter what, we must eat to live.

The gifts of earth are brought and prepared, set on the table. So it has been since creation, and it will go on.

We chase chickens or dogs away from it. Babies teethe at the corners. They scrape their knees under it.

It is here that children are given instructions on what it means to be human. We make men at it, we make women.

At this table we gossip, recall enemies and the ghosts of lovers.

Our dreams drink coffee with us as they put their arms around our children. They laugh with us at our poor falling-down selves and as we put ourselves back together once again at the table.

This table has been a house in the rain, an umbrella in the sun.

Wars have begun and ended at this table. It is a place to hide in the shadow of terror. A place to celebrate the terrible victory.

We have given birth on this table, and have prepared our parents for burial here.

At this table we sing with joy, with sorrow. We pray of suffering and remorse. We give thanks.

Perhaps the world will end at the kitchen table, while we are laughing and crying, eating of the last sweet bite.

PRIMO LEVI
Almanac
translated from the Italian by Ruth Feldman & Brian Swann

The indifferent rivers
Will keep on flowing to the sea
Or ruinously overflowing dikes,
Ancient handiwork of determined men.
The glaciers will continue to grate,
Smoothing what lies beneath them,
Or suddenly fall headlong,
Cutting short fir trees' lives.
The sea, captive between
Two continents, will go on struggling,
Always miserly with its riches.
Sun, stars, planets and comets
Will continue on their course.
Earth too will fear the immutable
Laws of the universe.
Not us. We, rebellious offspring
With great brainpower, little sense,
Will destroy, defile,
Always more feverishly.
Very soon we will extend the desert
Into the Amazon forests,
Into the living heart of our cities,
Into our very hearts.

■ Joy Harjo ➤ 177.

BIBLIOGRAPHY

This bibliography covers works referred to in the notes and introductory material. Where an author's name is cited but has more than one title listed below, the reference will be to the first title. Sources for poems included in this anthology are given in the Acknowledgements.

*Asterisked titles are key texts.

* Peter Abbs: *Earth Songs: A Resurgence anthology of contemporary eco-poetry* (Foxhole, Dartington: Green Books & Hartland, Bideford: *Resurgence* magazine, 2002).

Peter Abbs: contribution to 'Nature Poetry: What is it? Do we need it? Do we write it', *Acumen*, 57 (January 2007).

Jean Alford: 'The Poetry of Mary Oliver: Modern Renewal through Mortal Acceptance', *Pembroke Magazine*, 20 (1988).

Jody AllenRandolph, interview with Michael Longley, *Colby Quarterly*, XXXIX/3 (September 2003).

A.R. Ammons: interview with William Warsh, in *Set in Motion: Essays, Interviews, and Dialogues*, ed. Zofia Burr (Ann Arbor: U. of Michigan Press, 1996).

Margaret Atwood: *Conversations*, ed. Earl G. Ingersoll (Princeton: Ontario Review Press, 1990).

* Jonathan Bate: *The Song of the Earth* (London: Picador, 2000).

Jonathan Bate: *Romantic Ecology: Wordsworth and the Environmental Tradition* (New York & London: Routledge, 1991).

Wendell Berry: *A Continuous Harmony* (New York: Harcourt Brace Jovanovich, 1975).

Paul Brooks: *The House of Life: Rachel Carson at Work* (Boston: Houghton Mifflin, 1972).

* John Burnside & Maurice Riordan (eds.): *Wild Reckoning: an anthology provoked by Rachel Carson's* Silent Spring (Calouste Gulbenkian Foundation, 2004).

Peter Blue Cloud: 'For Rattlesnake: A Dialogue of Creatures', in *The Remembered Earth: An Anthology of Contemporary Native American Literature*, ed. Geary Hobson (Albuquerque: U. of New Mexico Press, 1980).

Daniel Bourne: extracts from 'A Conversation with W.S. Merwin', *Artful Dodge*, 3 no. 3 (Fall 1982), reprinted in *Bloodaxe Poetry Introductions: 3*, ed. Neil Astley (Tarset: Bloodaxe Books, 2007).

Philip Brady: 'A Conversation with with William Heyen', *Artful Dodge*, 40/41 (2002).

Alan Brownjohn: contribution to 'Nature Poetry: What is it? Do we need it? Do we write it', *Acumen*, 57 (January 2007).

* J. Scott Bryson: *Ecopoetry: A Critical Introduction* (Salt Lake City: U. of Utah Press, 2002).

J. Scott Bryson: '"Between the Earth and Silence": Place and Space in the Poetry of W.S. Merwin', in Bryson (101-16).

Basil Bunting: letter paying tribute to Lorine Niedecker, *Wisconsin Star-Journal*, 5 January 1971.

Rachel Carson: *Silent Spring* (Boston: Houghton Mifflin, 1962).

Caroline Carver: contribution to 'Nature Poetry: What is it? Do we need it? Do we write it', *Acumen*, 57 (January 2007).

Laird Christensen: 'The Pragmatic Mysticism of Mary Oliver', in Bryson (135-52).

Camille Colatosti: 'Holding a world in balance: An interview with Linda Hogan', *The Witness* (September 2002), see www.thewitness.org/archive/sept2002/colatostiinterview.html

Laurence Coupe (ed.): *The Green Studies Reader: From Romanticism to Ecocriticism* (Abingdon: Routledge, 2000).

Margaret Drabble (ed.): *The Oxford Companion to English Literature*, 5th edition (Oxford: Oxford University Press, 1985)

Jeffrey Dodd, Zachary Vineyard & Jeremiah Webster: 'A Conversation with Robert Wrigley, April 21, 2006': *Willow Springs*, 60 (Spring 2007).

* John Elder: *Imagining the Earth: Poetry and the Vision of Nature* (Urbana & Chicago: U. of Illinois Press, 1985; Athens, Georgia: U. of Georgia Press, 1996).

Deborah Fleming: 'Landscape and the Self in W.B. Yeats and Robinson Jeffers', in Bryson (39-57).

Matthew Fox: *The Coming of the Cosmic Christ* (San Francisco: HarperCollins, 1988).

* Terry Gifford: *Green Voices: Understanding contemporary nature poetry* (Manchester: Manchester U.P.; New York: St Martin's Press, 1995).

Terry Gifford: 'Gary Snyder and the Post-Pastoral', in Bryson, 2002 (77-87).

Lorrie Goldensohn: *Elizabeth Bishop: The Biography of a Poet* (New York: Columbia University Press, 1992).

Al Gore: *An Inconvenient Truth: The Planetary Emergency of Global Warming and What We Can Do About It* (London: Bloomsbury, 2006).

John Greening: 'Mining the air' (review of *Changes of Address* by Philip Gross), *Times Literary Supplement*, 15 March 2002.

Susan Griffin: 'A Collaborative Intelligence', in *The Eros of Everyday Life: Essays on Ecology, Gender, and Society* (New York: Anchor/Doubleday, 1995).

Susan Griffin: *Made from this Earth: Selections from her writing, 1967-1982* (London: The Women's Press, 1982).

Susan Griffin: *Woman and Nature: The Roaring Inside Her* (New York: Harper & Row, 1978; San Francisco: Sierra Club Books, 2000).

Claire Harman: entry in *The Oxford Companion to Twentieth-century Poetry in English*, ed. Ian Hamilton (Oxford: Oxford University Press, 1994).

Joy Harjo: 'The Roots of Poetry Lead to Music', interview, *Terrain.org: A Journal of the Built & Natural Environments*, 19 (Fall/Winter 2006).

Seamus Heaney: 'The Sense of Place', lecture given in the Ulster Museum (January 1977), in *Preoccupations: Selected Prose 1968-1978* (London: Faber, 1980).

Emily Hegerty: 'Genocide and Extinction in Linda Hogan's Ecopoetry', in Bryson (162-75).

Linda Hogan: *Dwellings: A Spiritual History of the Living World* (New York: Norton, 1995).

Ted Hughes: 'The Environmental Revolution', in *Winter Pollen: Occasional Prose*, ed. William Scammell (London: Faber & Faber, 1994), 128-35.

Richard Hunt: 'How to Love This World: The Transpersonal Wild in Margaret Atwood's Ecological Poetry', in Bryson (232-44).

Dan Jacobson: entry in *The Oxford Companion to Twentieth-century Poetry in English*, ed. Ian Hamilton (Oxford: Oxford University Press, 1994).

Roy Osamu Kamada: 'Postcolonial Romanticisms: Derek Walcott and the Melancholic Narrative of Landscape', in Bryson (207-20).

X.J. Kennedy & Dana Gioia (eds): *Literature: An Introduction to Fiction, Poetry, Drama, and Writing* (New York: Pearson Longman, tenth edition, 2007).

John Kinsella (ed.): *Landbridge: Contemporary Australian Poetry* (Fremantle, Australia: FACP; Todmorden, UK: Arc, 1999).

Stanley Kunitz (with Genine Lentine): *The Wild Braid: A Poet Reflects on a Century in the Garden*, with photographs by Marnie Crawford Samuelson (New York: Norton, 2005).

David Lehman (ed.): *A.R. Ammons: Selected Poems* (New York: The Library of America, 2006).

Hilary Llewellyn-Williams: review in *Poetry Wales*, 'Special Green Issue', 26 no.1 (1990).

Edna Longley (ed.): *The Bloodaxe Book of 20th Century Poetry* (Tarset: Bloodaxe Books, 2000).

Edna Longley: *Poetry & Posterity* (Tarset: Bloodaxe Books, 2000).

James Lovelock: *Gaia: A New Look at Life on Earth*, new edition (Oxford: Oxford U.P., 2000).

James Lovelock: *The Ages of Gaia: A Biography of Our Living Earth*, new edition (Oxford: Oxford U.P., 2000).

James Lovelock: *The Revenge of Gaia: Why the Earth Is Fighting Back and How We Can Still Save Humanity* (London: Allen Lane, 2006).

Robert McDowell: entry in *Contemporary Poets*, 7th edition, ed. Thomas Riggs (New York: St James Press, 2001).

Peter Makin: *Basil Bunting: The Making of His Verse* (Oxford: Oxford University Press, 1992).

Derek Mahon: introduction to *Words in the Air: A selection of poems by Philippe Jaccottet*, tr. & intr. Derek Mahon (Oldcastle: Gallery Press, 1998).

Christine Marshall & Nadine Meyer: 'A Conversation with Linda Gregerson, *Center: A Journal of the Literary Arts*, 4 (2005), 44-54.

Carolyn Merchant: *The Death of Nature: Women, Ecology, and the Scientific Revolution* (New York: Harper & Row, 1982).

Robert Nye: Introduction to *William Barnes: Selected Poems* (Manchester: Carcanet, 1972, 1988).

Eugene P. Odum: *Fundamentals of Ecology*, 3rd edition (Philadelphia: W.B. Saunders Co., 1971).

Mary Oliver: 'Winter Hours', in *Winter Hours: prose, prose poems, and poems* (Boston & New York: Houghton Mifflin, 1999).

* Alice Oswald: *The Thunder Mutters: 101 Poems for the Planet* (London: Faber & Faber, 2005).

Robert Pack: 'Afterword: Taking Dominion over the Wilderness', *Poems for a Small Planet: Contemporary American Nature Poetry*, A Bread Loaf Anthology (Hanover, NH: Middlebury College Press / U.P. of New England, 1993).

Jenny Penberthy: introduction to Lorine Niedecker: *Collected Works*, ed. Jenny Penberthy (Berkeley & Los Angeles: U. of California Press, 2002).

Neil Powell, obituary of John Heath-Stubbs, *The Independent*, 27 December 2006.

Peter Redgrove: *The Black Goddess and the Sixth Sense* (London: Bloomsbury, 1987).

Bernard W. Quetchenbach: 'Primary Concerns: The Development of Current Environmental Identity Poetry', in Bryson (245-62).

Teo Savory: Introduction to *Guillevic: Selected Poems* (Harmondsworth: Penguin, 1974).

Michael Schmidt: *The Lives of the Poets* (London: Weidenfeld & Nicolson, 1998).

C.H. Sisson: *Art and Action* (London: Methuen, 1965).

Jules Smith: article on www.contemporarywriters.com (2003).

Gary Snyder: 'The Wilderness', in *Turtle Island* (New York: New Directions, 1974).

Leonard M. Scigaj: 'Panentheistic Epistemology: The Style of Wendell Berry's *A Timbered Choir*', in Bryson (117-34).

William Stafford: remark recorded by Kim Stafford in his memoir *Early Morning: Remembering My Father* (Graywolf Press, USA, 2002)

Kim Taplin: *Tongues in Trees: Studies in Literature and Ecology* (Hartland, Bideford: Green Books, 1989).

Harriet Tarlo: 'Radical Landscapes: experiment and environment in contemporary poetry', *Jacket*, 32 (April 2007), http://jacketmagazine.com/32/p-tarlo.shtml#fn20

Gyorgyi Voros: 'Earth's Echo: Answering Nature in Ammons's Poetry', in Bryson (88-100).

Lynn White Jr: 'The Historical Roots of Our Ecologic Crisis', *Science*, 155 (10 March 1967), 1203-07.

Elizabeth Willis: 'Who Was Lorine Niedecker?', *American Poet* (2006), www.poets.org.

David Wojahn: review of *Search Party: Collected Poems* by William Matthews, *Blackbird*, 3 no.2 (Fall 2004).

Pamela Woof: 'The Wordsworths and the Cult of Nature', *BBC History* (2002), http://www.bbc.co.uk/history/british/empire_seapower/wordsworths_01.shtml

Lidia Vianu: *Desperado Essay-Interviews* (Bucharest: Editura Universitatii din Bucuresti, 2006)

Zhou Xiaojing: '"The Redshifting Web": Arthur Sze's Ecopoetics', in Bryson (179-94).

Susan J. Zeuenbergen: entry in *The Oxford Companion to Women's Writing in the United States*, ed. Cathy N. Davidson et al (New York: Oxford University Press, 1995).

ACKNOWLEDGEMENTS

The poetry and prose in this anthology is reprinted from the following books or sources, all with the permission of the publishers listed unless stated otherwise. Thanks are due to all the copyright holders cited below for their permission.

The Wilderness Poetry of Ancient China [➤ 21-24]: Tu Fu: 'Spring Prospect', tr. Burton Watson, from *The Selected Poems of Du Fu*, tr. Burton Watson, copyright © 2002 Columbia University Press. All other poems from *Mountain Home: The Wilderness Poetry of Ancient China*, tr. David Hinton (New Directions, 2005), by permission of Pollinger Ltd and New Directions Publishing Corporation.

Natural Disasters: Hurricane Katrina [➤ 216-18]: Work by Darby Diane Beattie, Elizabeth Foos and Catharine Savage Brosnan from *Hurricane Blues: Poems about Katrina and Rita*, ed. Philip C. Kolin & Susan Swartout (Southeast Missouri State University Press, 2006).

Poet in the City [➤ 199-202, 203-07, 214-15]: The sequences *Indian Summer* by **Patience Agbabi** and *Certain Weather* by **John Burnside**, and the poem 'The Diomedes' by **Matthew Hollis**, were all commissioned by *Poet in the City* and Lloyd's as part of the *Trees in the City* collaboration, designed to raise awareness of the need for action on climate change, and is reproduced by kind permission of *Poet in the City* and Lloyd's. Trees in the City is also supported by Arts & Business.

Poet in the City is a registered charity committed to attracting new audiences to poetry, making new connections for poetry, and raising money for poetry education, in particular the placing of poets in schools. Charity Commission number 1117354, company limited by guarantee. You can find out more about *Poet in the City* at http://www.poetinthecity.co.uk

poet in the city

Robert Adamson: *Reading the River: Selected Poems* (Bloodaxe Books, 2004). Fleur Adcock: *Poems 1960-2000* (Bloodaxe Books, 2000). Patience Agbabi: see *Poet in the City*. Anna Akhmatova: *Selected Poems*, tr. Richard McKane (Bloodaxe Books, 1989). Paula Gunn Allen: *Life Is a Fatal Disease: Collected Poems 1962-1995* (West End Press, Albuquerque, 1997). A.R. Ammons: 'The City Limits' and 'Gravelly Run', copyright © 1960 by A.R. Ammons by permission of W.W. Norton & Company, Inc.; 'Identity' from *Collected Poems 1951-1971*, copyright © 1972 by A.R. Ammons, by permission of W.W. Norton & Company, Inc. Neil Astley: 'Darwin Cyclone' from *Darwin Survivor* (Peterloo Poets, 1988); 'The Green Knight's Lament' from *The End of My Tether* (Flambard Press, 2002; Scribners, 2003), by permission of A.P. Watt Ltd. Margaret Atwood: 'Elegy for the Giant Tortoises' from *Poems 1965-1975* (Virago, 1991), by permisson of the Little, Brown Book Group Ltd; 'Frogless' and 'The Moment' from Morning in the Burned House (Virago, 1995), copyright © 1995 Margaret Atwood by permission of Curtis Brown Group Ltd, London. Annemarie Austin: *Very: New & Selected Poems* (Bloodaxe Books, 2008); Kofi Awoonor: *Rediscovery and Other Poems* by George Awoonor-Williams (Mbari, Ibadan, Nigeria, 1964), by permission of Kofi Awoonor.

Oliver Bernard: *Verses &c.* (Anvil Press Poetry, 2001). Wendell Berry: 'Dark with Power', 'The Peace of Wild Things', 'The Wish To Be Generous' and 'A Vision' from *The Selected Poems of Wendell Berry* (Counterpoint, 1998); sections 1985 V, 1987 III , 1988 II, 1988 IV, 1992 VIII, 1997 II from *A Timbered Choir: The Sabbath Poems 1979-1997* (Counterpoint, 1998), all by by permission of Counterpoint Press, a member of Perseus Book Group. John Betjeman: *Collected Poems* (John Murray, 2003), copyright © Estate of John Betjeman, by permission of John Murray (Publishers); Joseph Beuys: 'Coyote: I Like America and America Likes Me' from Caroline Tisdall: *Joseph Beuys: We Go This Way* (Violette Editions, 1998), by permission of Caroline Tisdall. Elizabeth Bishop: 'Brazil, January 1, 1502' from *The Complete Poems 1927-1979* (Farrar, Straus and Giroux, 1983), copyright © 1979, 1983 by Alice Helen Methfessel, by permission of Farrar, Straus and Giroux, LLC. Peter Blue Cloud: *Clans of Many Nations: Selected Poems 1969-94* (White Pine Press, USA, 1995). Louise Bogan: *The Blue Estuaries* (Ecco Press, 1968), copyright © 1968 by Louise Bogan, copyright renewed 1996 by Ruth Limmer,

reproduced by permission of Farrar, Straus and Giroux, LLC. Jean 'Binta' Breeze: *The Arrival of Brighteye and other poems* (Bloodaxe Books, 2000). Edwin Brock: *Five Ways to Kill a Man: New and Selected Poems* (Enitharmon Press, 1990). Charles Bukowski: *The Last Night of the Earth Poems* (Black Sparrow Press, 1992), copyright © 1992 by Charles Bukowski, by permission of HarperCollins Publishers. Basil Bunting: *Complete Poems* (Bloodaxe Books, 2000). John Burnside: 'Swimming in the Flood' from *Swimming in the Flood* (Jonathan Cape, 1995) by permission of The Random House Group Ltd; *Certain Weather*: see *Poet in the City*.

Ernesto Cardenal: *Nicaraguan New Time: Poems by Ernesto Cardenal*, tr. & intr. Dinah Livingstone (Journeyman Press, 1988), by permission of Dinah Livingstone. David Constantine: *Collected Poems* (Bloodaxe Books, 2004). Jayne Cortez: 'What Do They Care?' first published in *Dance the Guns to Silence: 100 Poems for Ken Saro-Wiwa*, ed. Nii Ayikwei Parkes & Kadija Sesay (Flipped Eye, 2005), now published in *The Beautiful Book* (Flipped Eye, 2007), copyright © 2007 Jayne Cortez. David Craig: *Against Looting* (Giant Steps, 1987), by permission of the author.

James Dickey: *The Whole Motion: Collected Poems 1945-1992* (Wesleyan University Press, USA, 1992). Tishani Doshi: *Countries of the Body* (Aark Arts, 2006), copyright © 2006 Tishani Doshi, by permission of the author. Mark Doty: 'Migratory' from *Atlantis* (Jonathan Cape, 1996); 'Visitation' from *Sweet Machine* (Jonathan Cape, 1998), by permission of The Random House Group Ltd. Maureen Duffy: *Collected Poems 1949-84* (Hamish Hamilton, 1985), by permission of Jonathan Clowes Ltd. Helen Dunmore: 'Ice coming' and 'Ploughing the roughlands' from *Out of the Blue: Poems 1975-2001* (Bloodaxe Books, 2001); 'Dolphins whistling' from *Glad of These Times* (Bloodaxe Books, 2007). G.F. Dutton: *The Bare Abundance: Selected Poems 1970-2001* (Bloodaxe Books, 2002).

Hans Magnus Enzensberger: 'The End of the Owls', tr. Jerome Rothenberg, by permission of the author.

Peter Fallon: *The Company of Horses* (Gallery Press, 2007), by permission of the author and The Gallery Press, Loughcrew, Oldcastle, County Meath, Ireland. Ian Hamilton Finlay: 'Estuary', by permission of Wild Hawthorn Press, Stonypath, Little Sparta, Dunsyre, Lanarkshire, ML11 8NG, Scotland. Allison Funk: 'The Whooping Cranes' from *The Knot Garden* (Sheep Meadow Press, 2002), by permission of the author; 'Living at the

Epicenter' from *Living at the Epicenter* (Northeastern University Press, Boston, 1995), copyright © 1995 Allison Funk, by permission of University Press, New England, Hanover, NH. **Max Garland**: *Hunger Wide as Heaven* (Cleveland State University Poetry Center, 2006), by permission of the author. **Dana Gioia**: *The Gods of Winter* (Graywolf Press, 1991). **Cynthia Gomez**: 'San José: a poem' from *From Totems to Hip-Hop: A Multicultural Anthology of Poetry Across the Americas 1900-2002*, ed. Ishmael Reed (Thunder's Mouth Press, 2003), by permission of Ishmael Reed. **Lavinia Greenlaw**: *Night Photograph* (Faber & Faber, 1993). **Linda Gregerson**: *Waterborne* (Houghton Mifflin, 2002). **Susan Griffin**: extracts from *Women and Nature: The Roaring Inside Her* (Sierra Club Books, San Francisco, 1978). Philip Gross: *Changes of Address: Poems 1980-1998* (Bloodaxe Books, 2001). **Guillevic**: extracts from *Carnac*, tr. John Montague *Carnac* (Bloodaxe Books, 1999); extracts from 'Things', from: *Guillevic: Selected Poems*, tr. Teo Savory (Penguin Books, 1974), translation copyright © 1974 Teo Savory, by permission of Penguin Books Ltd.

Carol Snyder Halberstadt: 'The Road Is Not a Metaphor' from *Wild Song: Poems of the Natural World*, ed. John Daniel (University of Georgia Press, 1998), copyright © 1990, 1998 Carol Snyder Halberstadt, by permission of the University of Georgia Press, Athens, Georgia, and the author. **Michael Hamburger**: *Roots in the Air* (Anvil Press Poetry, 1991). **Joy Harjo**: 'What Music': *She Had Some Horses* (Thunder's Mouth Press, 1982); 'Perhaps the World Ends Here', 'Remember' and 'For Alva Benson, and for Those Who Have Learned to Speak' from *How We Became Human: New and Selected Poems 1975-2001* (W.W. Norton & Company, 2002), copyright © 2002 Joy Harjo, by permission of W.W. Norton & Company, Inc. by permission of the author and publishers. **Jim Harrison**: *The Shape of the Journey: New and Collected Poems* (Copper Canyon Press, 1988), copyright © 1998 Jim Harrison, by permission of Copper Canyon Press, www.coppercanyonpress.org. **Tony Harrison**: *Collected Poems* (Viking Penguin, 2007), by permission of Gordon Dickerson and the author. **Robert Hass**: *Time and Materials* (HarperCollins, USA, 2007), by permission of the author. **Paal-Helge Haugen**: '(He comes into view)' from *Brother Pig*, English translation from *Wintering the Light*, tr. Roger Greenwald (Sun & Moon Press, 1997), copyright © 1997 by Roger Greenwald; copyright © 1985 by det Norske Samlaget, by permission of the author and translator. **Robert Hayden**: *Collected Poems*, ed. Frederick Glaysher (Liveright, 1985; reissue 1995), copyright © 1972 by Robert Hayden, by permission of Liveright Publishing Corporation. **Dermot Healy**: *The Reed Bed* (Gallery Press, 2001), by permission of the author and The Gallery Press, Loughcrew, Oldcastle, County Meath, Ireland. **Seamus Heaney**: 'Augury' from *Wintering Out* (Faber & Faber, 1972); 'Churning Day' and 'Squarings', XLII from *Opened Ground: Poems 1966-1996* (Faber & Faber, 1998); 'Höfn' and 'Anything Can Happen' from *District and Circle* (Faber & Faber, 2006), by permission of Faber & Faber Ltd. **John Heath-Stubbs**: 'The Green Man's Last Will and Testament' from *Selected Poems* (Carcanet Press, 1990), by permission of David Higham Associates. **William Heyen**: Pterodactyl Rose: Poems of Ecology (Time Being Books, 1991), copyright © 2001 Time Being Books, by permission of Time Being Press. **Jane Hirshfield**: 'Happiness' from *Each Happiness Ringed by Lions: Selected Poems* (Bloodaxe Books, 2005); 'Global Warming' from *After* (Bloodaxe Books, 2006). **Linda Hogan**: 'Mountain Lion' from *The Book of Medicines* (Coffee House Press, 1993) and 'The Fallen' from *The Book of Medicines* (Coffee House Press, 1993), by permission of Coffee House Press, Minneapolis; 'To Light' and 'Bees in Transit: Osage County' from *Seeing through the Sun* (University of Massachusetts Press, 1985), copyright © 1995 Linda Hogan, by permission of the University of Massachusetts Press. **Matthew Hollis**: 'The Diomedes': see *Poet in the City*. **Frances Horovitz**: *Collected Poems* (Bloodaxe Books, 1985). **Andrew Hudgins**: *Saints and Strangers* (Houghton Mifflin, 1985). **Ted Hughes**: *Collected Poems*, ed. Paul Keegan (Faber & Faber, 2003), by permission of Faber & Faber Ltd and the Estate of Ted Hughes. **Richard Hugo**: *Making Certain It Goes On: The Collected Poems of Richard Hugo* (W.W. Norton, 1984), copyright © 1984 Estate of Richard Hugo, by permission of W.W. Norton & Company, Inc.

Esther Iverem: *The Time: Portrait of a Journey Home, Poems and Photographs* (Africa World Press, Inc, 1993), by permission of the author.

Philippe Jaccottet: *Words in the Air*, tr. Derek Mahon (Gallery Press, 1998), by permission of the translator and The Gallery Press, Loughcrew, Oldcastle, County Meath, Ireland. **Kathleen Jamie**: *The Tree House* (Picador, 2004), by permission of Macmillan Publishers Ltd. **Mark Jarman**: *Questions for Ecclesiastes* (Storyline Press, 1997), copyright © 1997 by Mark Jarman, by permission of the author.

Robert Pack: *Fathering the Map: New and Selected Later Poems* (University of Chicago Press, 1993). **P.K. Page:** *The Hidden Room: Collected Poems*, volume two (The Porcupine's Quill, Canada, 1997). **Don Paterson:** from *Orpheus: A Version of Rilke's Die Sonette an Orpheus* (Faber & Faber, 2006). **Pascal Petit:** *The Zoo Father* (Seren, 2001). **Mario Petrucci:** *Heavy Water: a poem for Chernobyl* (Enitharmon Press, 2004); **Mario Petrucci:** 'Repossession' from *Dance the Guns to Silence: 100 Poems for Ken Saro-Wiwa*, ed. Nii Ayikwei Parkes & Kadija Sesay (Flipped Eye, 2005), by permission of the author. **Sylvia Plath:** *Collected Poems* (Faber & Faber, 1991).

Simon Rae: 'One World Down the Drain' from Simon Rae & Willie Rushton: *Soft Targets: poems from the Weekend Guardian* (Bloodaxe Books, 1991), by permission of the author. **Peter Reading:** 'Thucydidean', 'Fragmentary' and 'Corporate' from *Collected Poems: 2: Poems 1985-1996* (Bloodaxe Books, 1996); 'Endangered' from *Faunal* (2002), from *Collected Poems: 3: Poems 1997-2003* (Bloodaxe Books, 2003); extract from *-273.15* (Bloodaxe Books, 2005). **Peter Redgrove:** *The Apple Broadcast* (1981), reprinted from *Selected Poems* (Jonathan Cape, 1999), by permission of David Higham Associates. **Fred Reed:** *The Northumborman: The dialect poetry of Fred Reed* (Iron Press, 1999), by permission of Raymond Reed. **Rainer Maria Rilke:** 'The Eighth Elegy' and 'The Panther', tr. Stephen Mitchell, copyright © 1995 by Stephen Mitchell, from *Ahead of All Parting: The Selected Poetry and Prose of Rainer Maria Rilke*, ed. & tr. Stephen Mitchell (The Modern Library, New York, 1995), by permission of Random House, Inc. **Maurice Riordan:** *A Word from the Loki* (Faber & Faber, 1995). **Michael Symmons Roberts:** *Corpus* (Jonathan Cape, 2004), by permission of the Random House Group Ltd. **Theodore Roethke:** *Collected Poems* (Faber & Faber, 1968). **Pattiann Rogers:** *Firekeeper: Selected Poems* (Milkweed Editions, 2005), copyright © 2005 Pattiann Rogers, by permission of Milkweed Editions, www.milkweed.org

Ken Saro-Wiwa: 'Ogoni! Ogoni!' by permission of the Estate of Ken Saro-Wiwa. **David Scott:** *Selected Poems* (Bloodaxe Books, 1998). **Aharon Shabtai:** *J'Accuse*, tr. Peter Cole (New Directions, 2003). **Leslie Marmon Silko:** two extracts from *Storyteller* (Seaver Books, New York, 1981; Arcade Publishing), by permission of the author. **Colin Simms:** 'Three Years in Glen Garry' and ''Now that the rivers are bringing down some loam' from *Otters and Martens* (Shearsman Books, 2004); 'Apart from a hundred peacocks: a menu...' and 'West Cumberland 10/11 October 1957', all four poems by permission of the author. **Ken Smith:** *The Poet Reclining: Selected Poems 1962-1980* (Bloodaxe Books, 1982). **Gary Snyder:** 'Front Lines', 'Mother Earth: Her Whales', 'By Frazier Creek Falls' and 'For the Children' from *Turtle Island* (New Directions, 1974), copyright © 1974 Gary Snyder, by permission of Pollinger Ltd and New Directions Publishing Corporation; 'For All' from *Axe Handles* (North Point Press, 1983; Shoemaker & Hoard, 2005). **William Stafford:** 'Gaea' from *Poems for a Small Planet: Contemporary American Nature Poetry, A Breadloaf Anthology*, ed. Robert Pack & Jay Parini (Middlebury College Press, 1993); 'In Response to a Question' from *The Way It Is: New & Selected Poems* (Graywolf Press, USA, 1998), by permission of Graywolf Press, Saint Paul, Minnesota, copyright © 1962, 1998 the Estate of William Stafford. **Anne Stevenson:** (Bloodaxe Books, 2005). **Susan Stewart:** 'The Forest' from *The Forest* (University of Chicago Press, 1995), reprinted by permission of the author. **Matthew Sweeney:** 'Zero Hour' *Sanctuary* (Jonathan Cape, 2004), by permission of The Random House Group Ltd. **Arthur Sze:** extracts *from* 'Archipelago' (1) and 'The Leaves of a Dream Are the Leaves of an Onion' (2 & 6), from *The Redshifting Web: Poems 1970-1998* (Copper Canyon Press, 1998), copyright © 1994 Arthur Sze, by permission of Copper Canyon Press, www.coppercanyonpress.org. **Wisława Szymborska:** *Poems New & Collected 1957-1997*, tr. Stanisław Baranczak & Clare Cavanagh (Faber & Faber, 1999). **George Szirtes:** 'Death by Deluge' from *An English Apocalypse* (Bloodaxe Books, 2001), reprinted in *Collected Poems* (Bloodaxe Books, 2008).

Edward Thomas: *The Annotated Collected Poems*, ed. Edna Longley (Bloodaxe Books, 2008). **R.S. Thomas:** 'Autumn on the Land' from *Song at the Year's Turning* (Rupert Hart-Davis, 1955), by permission of Gwydion Thomas. **Caroline Tisdall:** *see* Joseph Beuys. **Tomas Tranströmer:** *New Collected Poems* (Bloodaxe Books, 1997). **Chase Twichell:** The Ghosts of Eden (Faber & Faber, 1995).

David Wagoner: *Traveling Light: Collected and New Poems* (University of Illinois Press, 1999), copyright © David Wagoner 1999, by permission of the author and the University of Illinois Press. **Derek Walcott:** extracts from 'The Schooner *Flight*' from *Collected Poems 1948-1984* (Faber & Faber, 1986), by permission of the author and Faber & Faber Ltd. **John Powell Ward:** *Selected & New Poems* (Seren, 2004). **C.K. Williams:** *Collected Poems*

(Bloodaxe Books, 2006). **Heathcote Williams:** extract from *Whale Nation* (Jonathan Cape, 1988) by permission of Curtis Brown Group Ltd, London. **James Wright:** *Above the River: Complete Poems* (Farrar, Straus & Giroux, Inc., USA, 1990; Bloodaxe Books, 1992), by permission of Wesleyan University Press. **Robert Wrigley:** *Earthly Meditations: New & Selected Poems* (Penguin Books, New York, 2006), copyright © Robert Wrigley, by permission of the author.

    Benjamin Zephaniah: *City Psalms* (Bloodaxe Books, 1992).

Every effort has been made to trace copyright holders of the poems published in this book. We apologise if any material has been included without permission or without the appropriate acknowledgement, and would be glad to be told of anyone who has not been consulted.

    I regret that we were unable to include poems in this book by several writers published in Britain by Carcanet Press, which imposes unacceptable conditions in granting permission for poems to be reprinted in other publishers' anthologies. Had that not been the case, readers of this anthology would have been able to discover some excellent ecopoetry by Gillian Clarke, Alistair Elliot, Louise Glück, Brigit Pegeen Kelly, Hugh MacDiarmid, Robert Minhinnick, Edwin Morgan, Les Murray, William Carlos Williams, Judith Wright and Andrew Young. We are grateful to all the other publishers, authors, agents and rights holders for their kindness and cooperation, and to Catherine Taylor for her work and commitment to this project.

INDEX

Boldface figures indicate writings by the author concerned.
The letter **n** denotes a note on the author or their work.

FSC

Like all Bloodaxe titles, *Earth Shattering* is printed on acid-free paper sourced from mills with FSC & PEFC chain of custody certification – an assurance that wood comes from a certified, properly managed forest. The Forest Stewardship Council (FSC) is an international, non-governmental organisation dedicated to promoting responsible management of the world's forests. It was founded in 1993 in response to public concern over deforestation, and demand for a trustworthy labelling scheme showing that materials have been derived from sustainable sources. The scheme goes further than good management of timber, also considering the impact of forestry on the environment. This includes the people who live in and benefit from the woods; the water courses that flow through forested areas; and the wild-life affected. It also considers the types of timber re-planted and whether they are appropriate for the area.

The paper used for this book is James McNaughton's Festival Offset supplied by Stora Enso's Nymolla mill in southern Sweden. Nymolla's own pulp is produced on site, and its paper stock benefits from high opacity from precipitated calcium carbonate used as a filler. Festival Offset is aged resistant to ISO 9706 standard, and achieves its whiteness using a totally chlorine-free process. The papermill is 85% self-sufficient in power production, and waste water from pulp production supplements the hot water circulation system for nearby communities.

For its binding Bloodaxe uses a chemically-based glue not derived from any animal product which only contains waxes and polymers. This is pliable and non-brittle, allowing the book to be opened repeatedly without the spine being split; because the signatures are sewn as well as glued, the pages will not drop out. As with the choice of paper, Bloodaxe is concerned to maintain durability and quality as well as sensitivity to environmental considerations in making book production decisions.